© 2021 by University Press of Colorado

Published by University Press of Colorado
245 Century Circle, Suite 202
Louisville, Colorado 80027

 The University Press of Colorado is a proud member of
the Association of University Presses.

The University Press of Colorado is a cooperative publishing enterprise supported, in part,
by Adams State University, Colorado State University, Fort Lewis College, Metropolitan
State University of Denver, Regis University, University of Colorado, University of Northern
Colorado, University of Wyoming, Utah State University, and Western Colorado University.

∞ This paper meets the requirements of the ANSI/NISO Z39.48–1992 (Permanence of Paper)

ISBN: 978-1-64642-100-8 (hardcover)
ISBN: 978-1-64642-187-9 (ebook)
https://doi.org/10.5876/9781646421879

Library of Congress Cataloging-in-Publication Data

Names: Gonlin, Nancy, editor. | Reed, David M., editor.
Title: Night and darkness in ancient Mesoamerica / edited by Nancy Gonlin and David M.
Reed.
Description: Louisville : University Press of Colorado, [2021] | Includes bibliographical refer-
ences and index.
Identifiers: LCCN 2021034814 (print) | LCCN 2021034815 (ebook) | ISBN 9781646421008
(hardcover) | ISBN 9781646421879 (ebook)
Subjects: LCSH: Night—Social aspects. | Night—Religious aspects. | Indians of Central
America—Antiquities. | Indians of Mexico—Antiquities. | Antiquities, Prehistoric—Central
America. | Antiquities, Prehistoric—Mexico.
Classification: LCC GT3408 .N54 2021 (print) | LCC GT3408 (ebook) | DDC 306.4—dc23
LC record available at https://lccn.loc.gov/2021034814
LC ebook record available at https://lccn.loc.gov/2021034815

Cover photograph, Classic Maya ceramic cylinder vessel no. K1278, © Justin Kerr.

To our friend and colleague—W. Scott Zeleznik

Scott was our friend, peer, and fellow archaeologist whose contributions resonate in this volume. During his too short life, Scott had many admirable qualities. He was an inquisitive and empirical anthropological archaeologist, an explorer and world traveler, the finest of friends, and a devoted father. He is genuinely missed by his family, friends, and colleagues.

Contents

Tables

Preface

Nancy Gonlin
and David M. Reed

> For all the reasons that we need to see Earth during
> the day, we also need to see Earth at night.
> —Miller 2012

The cycle of time from night into day is one of the most fundamental changes experienced on earth. The darkness that rises with night is as natural as the light brought by day. This natural cycling has been given profound meanings the world over, with the prehistoric and historic peoples of Mexico and Central America being no exception. This phenomenon has figured prominently in the worldviews and mythologies of all peoples living in this region. Here, we embark on a new archaeological emphasis by presenting this volume about night and darkness in the past of Mexican and Central American peoples. This publication follows a previous one (Gonlin and Nowell 2018) wherein the archaeology of the night was introduced. By incorporating the element of darkness, metaphors abound and the richness of the iconographic, epigraphic, and archaeological record expands.

Our acknowledgments are many for a project of this range and depth. When organizing a symposium for the 2017 Society for American Archaeology annual meetings from which this volume emanated (figure P.1), the task was to convince participants that we archaeologists and art historians already have the data at hand to address deep questions about living in darkness, living in the night. We sincerely thank our authors and

DOI: 10.5876/9781646421879.c000a

FIGURE P.1. *Participants in the 2017 SAA Symposium on Pre-Columbian Nights in Mexico and Central America. Front row (left to right): Julia Hendon, Nancy Gonlin, Payson Sheets, Jan Marie Olson, Linda Brown, Rachel Egan, and Cecelia Klein. Second row (left to right): Jeanne Lopiparo, Randolph Widmer, Venicia Slotten, and David Reed.*

discussant for sticking out their necks to join us in this novel approach. We were grateful that Linda Brown participated in the symposium, but she was unable to contribute a chapter for this volume.

It is a pleasure to work with the University Press of Colorado (UPC). Acquisitions Editor Charlotte Steinhardt provided guidance, support, and the occasional nudge when needed. We were fortunate to have an excellent copyeditor, Cheryl Carnahan, who skillfully clarified and corrected our work. Dan Pratt at UPC creatively designed the artistic and apropos cover, Laura Furney ensured a smooth production process, and Beth Svinarich effectively publicized this book. Darrin Pratt coordinated efforts to ensure timely publication. At Bellevue College Library, Benayah Israel has been indispensable to Nan through the years in tracking down obscure references and extending their availability. K. Viswanathan has served as a sounding board and general support for this project.

One of our dearest friends, W. Scott Zeleznik, faced more than a decade of darkness in his fight with a rare, spontaneous cancer. Year after year since his diagnosis, Scott's treatments slowed but never stopped the disease's progression. Throughout the hardship, his constitution—built from running marathons during graduate school and beyond—allowed him to remain physically active, travel, and raise two boys, Sef and Tate. Scott was a kind, smart, generous, and funny human being who never failed to help, lend his ear, and provide expertise or camaraderie. His death in late 2017 left us with an emptiness, as we miss him dearly. We dedicate this volume to Scott, who we know would enjoy the exploration of night and darkness.

REFERENCES

Gonlin, Nancy, and April Nowell. 2018. *Archaeology of the Night: Life after Dark in the Ancient World*. Boulder: University Press of Colorado.

Miller, Steve. 2012. https://www.nasa.gov/mission_pages/NPP/news/earth-at-night .html.

Night and Darkness in Ancient Mesoamerica

All lies placid and silent in the darkness, in the night.
—POPOL VUH (CHRISTENSON 2007, 58)

DAVID M. REED
AND NANCY GONLIN

Not so long ago, nighttime was an essentially dark experience throughout the world. The nocturnal light that emanated from natural sources[1] did not entirely drown out the darkness, making the night inherently linked with the dark. Our restless planet does not sleep at night but carries on with many phenomena, which we have imbued with cultural significance. Had the Earth been seen from above at night even a hundred years ago, much of it would have remained in shadowy darkness, as the archaeological consideration of the night has for so long, too. Nights of the past were far darker than those of today. There was no glitter or glare pouring forth from incandescent, fluorescent, or LED bulbs that overpowered the nocturnal habits of our planet (Edensor 2015a). Perhaps our twenty-first-century experiences with bright nights have left us with little imagination on how humanity prospered for eons under dark skies and how integral this darkness was to their existence. Throughout the past, interior and outdoor lighting was partial, limited, costly, and often dangerous. Only in modern times, with ubiquitous illumination, have humans' encounters of night and its darkness become rarer and disengaged from their activities. One author put our reliance on nocturnal lighting in this fashion: "We treat light like a drug whose price is spiraling toward zero" (Hanson 2014, 4).

DOI: 10.5876/9781646421879.c000b

It may be because of our modern experience with the night that we have not fully considered how ancient peoples navigated the night, the significance of having dark nights (Bogard 2013), the meaning of darkness and night throughout the ancient world (Mothrè and Becquelin 2016; Nagao 2020), and the role of luminosity in the past (Bille and Sørensen 2007). How does one establish an "Archaeology of Darkness," and what benefits might be derived from such a field of inquiry? Also, what constituted darkness in the past? How and why were dark places illuminated, and what was the role of such lighting? In some instances, ancients purposely sought out darkness, sought out the night. A couple of broad inquiries we believe are worth pondering include: (1) whether the study of human behavior is of interest when it occurs only during the day, and (2) whether existing anthropological concepts and theories hold equal applicability to daytime, nighttime, and levels of darkness. Research on nights and the symbolism of darkness adds an essential component to our understanding of human lifeways in the past and present, regardless of whether we explore ancient, historical, or contemporary times (Becquelin and Galinier 2016; Dowd and Hensey 2016b; Edensor 2017; Ekirch 2005; Galinier et al. 2010; Gonlin and Nowell 2018a; Koslofsky 2011; Palmer 2000; Schnepel and Ben-Ari 2005).

The authors in this volume address the topics of night and darkness for some of the peoples who lived in Mexico and Central America before the advent of electricity and mass lighting. Anthropological archaeology is well suited to undertake such studies and contribute to an archaeology of the night (Gonlin and Nowell 2018a) and darkness (Dowd and Hensey 2016b). The initial foray into these concepts has fostered a fuller appreciation of the past. Such work has underscored the cultural diversity and similarities across the globe. Understanding the influences of light and darkness across the totality of day and night or in other contexts is as vital as the recognition of the influences of gender (Conkey 2018), ideology, ecology, economics, or materiality to culture and human behavior. Nightscapes and darkscapes possess qualities divergent from day-lit ones. Our anthropological archaeological frameworks, such as cultural ecology, cultural materialism, economics, power, gender, agency, or practice theory, fail to explicitly incorporate, recognize, or take for granted the dimensions of nighttime and darkness as part of human lifeways. We need to build a framework for how ancient Mesoamericans interacted with night and darkness (Nagao 2020). One way in which we can do so is to examine how ancient Mesoamericans themselves viewed these concepts: "While scholars have critiqued many of the details of Levi-Strauss's analyses, structural oppositions have consistently been shown to be of great import to Mesoamerican myth and cosmology as expressions of dualistic religious and cultural concepts (Graulich 1983: 575)" (Looper 2019, 12; see Chinchilla Mazariegos 2017). An example of the utility of this dualism is the concept of *tz'ak*, as expressed in Classic Mayan glyphs. It represents an abstraction that connotes a single whole, as in day and night completing a diurnal cycle (Stuart 2003). Night comes before the day, but only when the two are joined is order achieved, completeness reached, and the world is whole.

To address the paucity of studies in these realms, we reconsider the relationship among humans, night, and darkness by gathering scholars to explore aspects of these concepts in ancient Mesoamerica while showing the value of integrating humanistic issues into the scientific practice of archaeology. The authors explore diverse topics from sweat baths (*temazcales*) to dark, wild untamed forests to blindfolds to glyphs to remains of plants, ceramics, lighting, and other realia.

The value of inquiring into the dichotomy of night and day is a rewarding theoretical experience (Fogelin 2019, 63–66), but we are not suggesting a simplistic, reductionist approach. Darkness itself is an obvious component of nighttime, but without requiring the temporal aspect. Darkened spaces can exist outside the boundaries of the time of day, such as within the interiors of structures, whether they are houses, sweat baths, or temples; in portals to the underworld, such as caves and cenotes; and in the deep dark depths of forests. Darkness is created by eclipses (Aveni 2018), a natural phenomenon that ancient Mesoamericans were adept at tracking and imbuing with cultural significance. Dark skies can be created by volcanic eruptions (Egan, this volume), many of which continue to plague contemporary peoples in Mexico and Central America and others living along the Pacific Ring of Fire. Darkness exists in certain conditions, such as being in the womb, being blindfolded (Klein, this volume), or being blind.

Darkness is intricately linked to liminality, indicating a sensory threshold. In darkness, our identities are masked. Many rites of passage have a "dark" component that corresponds to liminality; such life-changing events have been well studied. For example, Victor Turner (1969, 95) writes, "Thus, liminality is frequently likened to death, to being in the womb, to invisibility, to darkness, to bisexuality, to the wilderness, and to an eclipse of the sun or moon." Darkness does indeed have a psychological component. Cecelia Klein (this volume) investigates the temporary blindness induced by the wearing of a blindfold in Aztec society (also referred to as the Mexica), harkening back to the beginning of time when all was obscured in darkness. Liminality among the Classic Maya was symbolized by deer, a creature whose prominence at dusk and dawn was well-known (Looper 2019). The sun during the dry season and during its daily setting was perceived to be weakened (Looper 2019, 167), especially as it made its way to the underworld.

In scientific terms, shades of darkness range from the phases before and after nightfall (e.g., golden hour, blue hour, and civil, nautical, and astronomical twilight at dawn and dusk [Geoscience Australia 2018; Spitschan et al. 2016, 2017; Time and Date AS 2018]), to ill-lit or low artificial illumination, to moonlit and starlit, to lightless pitch-dark and the absence of light, as well as visual deprivation with blindfolds or blindness.

Location, in terms of latitude and season, notably impacts experiences and durations of night and darkness. Hence, in addition to differences in cultural interpretations of night, regional perspectives of the night influenced perceptions. The remains of ancient lifeways of Mexico and Central America provide productive candidates for researching nightways due to the massive amount of excavations that have been conducted (Evans 2013), interpretations of iconography and epigraphy, the abundance of ethnohistoric sources, and insightful ethnographic research. In terms of modern national boundaries, the culture area of Mesoamerica includes central and southern Mexico, Belize, Guatemala, western Honduras, and western El Salvador. These areas and areas just outside of Mesoamerica are the focus of this volume. Located between the Tropic of Cancer and the equator, this region has relatively consistent hours of darkness throughout the year. For reference, figure 0.1 is a map of the main locations mentioned in this volume, and table 0.1 provides a comparative overview of the time periods our authors discuss.

DEFINITIONS PERTAINING TO THE DARK AND NIGHT

Several terms are useful for studying the night and darkness. Darkness has been removed from the archaeological record, often intentionally by us archaeologists (Hensey 2016, 3), a situation that dramatically alters the relationship among place, object, and experience in the modern world. Artifacts are excavated from the dark depths of the Earth, and monuments are lit up to better view them (2016, 3). By envisioning darkscapes, "the sensory experience of physically and spiritually navigating dark . . . spaces" (Dowd and Hensey 2016a, xi), we can more accurately duplicate the experience of past lives. Shadows and darkness were essential elements of numerous past practices. The nightscape is part of the darkscape, but the reverse is not necessarily true. The nightscape is composed of all the material objects, non-material culture, activities, and sensations associated with or used during the time of day when the sun has set

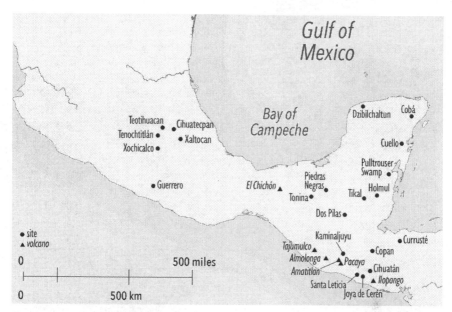

FIGURE O.I. *Map locating the main sites mentioned in the volume.*

and before it rises (or in the most northern and southern latitudes, when one typically shifts from daily activities to nightly activities).

We introduce and define the term *nightways* as the role of night in society. Nightways refers to the cross-disciplinary study of nocturnal customs, behaviors, habits, and items of a group of people to understand the anthropological complexity of nycthemeral practices. Nightways deal with the interconnected ideas, values, formalized behaviors, and material objects that are organized and reenacted through the performance of social roles and tasks related to experiences of the night. While nighttime is a regularly occurring period of darkness, its cultural meanings and symbolism are tightly involved in constructing and maintaining social and ideological relationships in specific contexts. Within any setting, various nightways can be found—they are not single overarching structures or frameworks but a plurality of patterns or aspects of cultural systems to be understood with models that differ according to the scale of analysis.

The study of ancient nightways includes the recovery of realia, including the material remains of lighting and quotidian nightly activities. Analysis of the evidence of production, distribution, consumption, and disposal of night-associated items contributes to the interpretation of social processes and

TABLE 0.1. Major time periods highlighted in the volume

Maya	
Diego de Landa, bishop of the Yucatan, burns the books and images of the Maya outside the church at Mani	July 12, 1562 CE
Late Postclassic	1250–1540 CE
Early Postclassic	1000–1250 CE
Terminal Classic	900–1000 CE
Late Classic	600–900 CE
Early Classic	250–600 CE
Late Preclassic	300 BCE–250
Middle Preclassic	1000–300 BCE
Early Preclassic	2000–1000 BCE
Archaic period	7000–2000 BCE
Teotihuacan	
Aztec	1150–1500 CE
Postclassic	900–1150 CE
Epiclassic	600–900 CE
Classic	150–600 CE
Formative	1 BCE–150 CE
Aztec	
Colonial	1521–1821 CE
Cortés conquers Tenochtitlan	August 13, 1521 CE
Cuauhtémoc	1521–1525 CE
Death of Motecuhzoma II	June 30, 1520 CE
Cuitláhuac briefly reigns	1520 CE
Motecuhzoma II receives Cortés	November 1519 CE
New Fire Ceremony	1507 CE
Motecuhzoma II	1502–1520 CE
Templo Mayor completed	1487 CE
Ahuitzotl	1486–1502 CE
Tizoc	1481–1486 CE
Axayacatl	1469–1481 CE
New Fire Ceremony	1455 CE
Motecuhzoma I	1440–1469 CE

continued on next page

TABLE 0.1—*continued*

Aztec	
The Triple Alliance formed	1428 CE
Itzcoatl	1427–1440 CE
Chimalpopoca	1417–1426 CE
New Fire Ceremony	1403 CE
Huitzilihuitl	1396–1417 CE
Acamapichtli	1375–1395 CE
New Fire Ceremony	1351 CE
Tenochtitlan founded	1345 CE
Volcanic Eruptions	
Pacaya eruption	830–930 CE
Almolonga eruption	750–850 CE
El Chichón eruption	680–880 CE
El Chichón eruption	490–690 CE
Loma Caldera eruption, buries Cerén	660 CE
Ilopango eruption, causes evacuation of Zapotitán Valley	539 (440–550) CE
Amatitlan eruption	380–1300 CE

actions that underlay nightways in antiquity. By studying familiar questions from a different angle—the nocturnal angle—we can better understand culture and its influence on behavior, identity, and the role of the natural world on lifeways. This parallax perspective has been effective in enriching our understanding of numerous ancient lifeways (Gonlin and Nowell 2018b, 6).

Recently, the concept of "abundance" has been introduced into archaeology to consider the agrarian state (Winter 2007), food (Gremillion 2011, 93–114), urban economies (Smith 2012), and myriad other economic, social, and political features (Smith 2017a). This concept relates to both natural and cultural situations (Smith 2017b, 10–12). Nighttime is one of the most natural states of abundant darkness, tempered by meteorological and seasonal phenomena and technology, in the past and present. An abundance of darkness can be found in other circumstances and places beyond but sometimes associated with the night, such as tombs and burials (Lopiparo, this volume), volcanic eruptions (Egan, this volume), eclipses (Aveni 2018), caves (Moyes 2012), interior rooms of buildings (Isbell 2009), under the deep dark depths of water, *temazcales* (Olson; Sheets and Thomason, both this volume), blindfolds (Klein, this volume), and mines (James 2016). Evidence for both ancient nightly practices and experiences of darkness at night and in such a variety of dark locations has been recently identified in the archaeological record (Dowd and Hensey 2016b; Gonlin and Nowell 2018a). The abundance of artifacts, features, and sites attributable to these concepts substantially improves and expands our understanding and interpretations of the past (Coltman, this volume).

Artificial darkness can occur intentionally by human actors intent on creating an atmosphere that is psychologically charged from a liminal state to one of permanence. The liminality created by wearing a blindfold is evaluated in Cecelia Klein's chapter (this volume). The placement of a jade mask over the face of the deceased ensures darkness, as does covering the body with earth or a sarcophagus lid; death permanently ensconces one in the dark. Jeanne Lopiparo (this volume) discusses how inhabitants of the Ulúa Valley entangled death with ancestors. One of the most famous Mesoamerican examples of this behavior was recovered at the Classic Maya site of Palenque by Dr. Alberto Ruz Lhuillier (1973). The long-lived Ahau K'inich Janaab Pakal I (603–683 CE), buried in the Temple of the Inscriptions, was elegantly dressed for the afterworld with a mask, ear flares, a collar, a pectoral, and bracelets—all made of jade and collectively weighing several pounds (Marken 2007; Ruz Lhuillier and Mason 1953; Tiesler and Cucina 2006).

Artificial darkness is also accomplished through actively engaging with the landscape. The Classic Maya conception of the watery underworld was deep and dark in the depths of water. Shells associated with water (Nagao 2014), such as the conch shells on Temple 11 at the Classic Maya city of Copan (Schele and Miller 1986, 122–123), evoked this dangerous place. Cenotes, water-filled sinkholes in limestone topography, were likewise perceived as portals to a watery underworld and a haven of the Moon Goddess during the day (Iwaniszewski 2016, 39).

BACKGROUND

The premise of this volume was developed out of Pre-Columbian Nights in Mexico and Central America, a session that was organized by Nancy Gonlin for the 82nd Annual Meeting of the Society for American Archaeology held in Vancouver in 2017. Eureka, or "ah-ha," moments rarely happen during a career. Sometimes the moment occurs when previously unconsidered issues suddenly come to mind. In other instances, the discovery of a residence or grave provides the moment. Here, the senior editor was enjoying an evening of reading and refreshment when it occurred to her that we seem to focus on only issues of "daily" behaviors when studying the past or in building our social theories (Gonlin 2018, xxix). Scholars indirectly, if ever, consider the night separately or in conjunction with the day in reconstructions. Yet we spend a tremendous part of our lives performing nightly activities and, by consequence, in various levels of darkness. While the study of daily activities was never meant to exclude nightly activities or those that occur in dark conditions, it does fail to incorporate explicit nocturnal and dark aspects. In this volume, authors apply a variety of frameworks to explore nightways and darkways and how humans in antiquity behaved during or utilized aspects of night and darkness.

An action undertaken during daylight hours often takes on different connotations when that same action is performed in the shadows, in darkened conditions, or during nighttime. In addition, certain activities are associated with the time of day in which they occur. Darkness reveals cultural aspects that scholars take for granted and, as a juxtaposition to the default daytime approach, requires us to evaluate both familiar and new points of analysis. By focusing studies on nocturnal actions, we expand our understanding of how the environment influenced behavior and how nightly associations are cultural constructs that vary over time and space, as well as over variations in social identities.

In the process of researching the topic, we learned that although a few scholars have studied nightly behavior, little anthropological or archaeological research has been done. Apart from cultural astronomers (e.g., Aveni 2008), the few notable exceptions in darkness and nighttime studies are by Jacques Galinier and his colleagues (2010; Becquelin and Galinier 2016; Galinier and Zamudio Vega 2016), with explicit investigations by archaeologists being rare (Dowd and Hensey 2016b). Now, however, this volume stands in companionship with a previously edited volume by the senior editor and April Nowell, *Archaeology of the Night: Life after Dark in the Ancient World* (2018a). In that publication, cultures from several times and places were explored, with three of the chapters pertaining to Mesoamerica. Jeremy Coltman (2018), an epigrapher and iconographer, considered how darkness represented creation, especially among the ancient Maya. Anthony Aveni (2018), a well-known cultural astronomer, elaborated on the meaning of night in day for eclipses that were predicted and experienced by the Classic Maya and others. Nancy Gonlin and Christine Dixon (2018) employed a nighttime household archaeology (Gonlin 2020, 398–399) approach to round out quotidian practices of the Classic Maya at Copan, Honduras, and Joya de Cerén, El Salvador. Integral to those three chapters was the consideration of religion and ideology alongside the material record of daily life. Building on insights gained from a nightways perspective, we dedicate here a volume of explorations into what night and darkness meant to some of the ancient peoples of Mesoamerica.

Historical scholars who have examined aspects of nocturnality and cultures of darkness (Palmer 2000), improved lighting technology, and the spread of the availability of new foods together gave rise to a new nightscape that brought forth major cultural and behavioral changes throughout historical Europe (Baldwin 2012; Bogard 2013; Ekirch 2005; Koslofsky 2011). Many of these aspects are ones we consider commonplace and normal today but that are actually recent modifications to our behavior. For instance, Craig Koslofsky (2011, 1) focused on the nocturnal revolution in early modern Europe, noting that night imposed several limits on daily life while acting "as a many-faceted and evocative natural symbol." Essentially, he identified the transition in public behavior and culture that occurred in the early eighteenth century because of the then newly available artificial domestic lighting, public street lighting, and the non-alcoholic beverages of tea, chocolate, and coffee (2011, 2, 276): "In 1660, no European city had permanently illuminated its streets, but by 1700 consistent and reliable street lighting had been established in Amsterdam, Paris, Turin, London, and Copenhagen, and across the Holy Roman Empire from Hamburg to Vienna" (2011, 2) through the extensive use of oil lamps (or, in Paris, candles) in glass-paned lanterns. Late hours of the day were transformed into times of sociability as cities removed curfews and coffeehouses appeared (2011, 276). The results were that people stayed out late and went to bed late. Sleep patterns were affected and shifted from a "first sleep," a period of an hour or more of wakefulness, and a "second sleep" (Ekirch 2005, 300–301) to a single period (Koslofsky 2011, 6, 276). Social patterns of labor changed as working days were extended much further into the nights ("burning the midnight oil").

BATS, PROWLERS, HOWLERS, PRANCERS, AND PLANTS IN THE DARK

Changes in human nocturnal behaviors alter human experiences and interactions with significant elements of our lives, particularly nocturnal animals, darkness, and even death. There are animals that are associated with the night for numerous reasons, some of which have connections with the underworld (Quirarte 1979) or darkness. Others have nocturnal or crepuscular habits or represent nocturnal celestial bodies. In the Neotropics, there were, and still are, fauna that frequent the night and flourish in the dark. Such creatures include jaguars, dogs, pumas, coyotes, bats, owls, deer, rabbits, toads, and numerous others: "Many animal combinations express a duality in Precolumbian symbolism that is also a duality in nature: predator and prey, captor and captive, above and below. Jaguar and deer are hunter and hunted: they interact in origin myths; [and] they are shown together in art" (Benson 1997, 13). Four of these animals were especially significant to ancient Mesoamerican nights, and the literature is full of material regarding their role in darkness and the night (Benson 1997; Brown 2005; Looper 2019). Below, we discuss a sample of these animals (bats, jaguars, dogs, and deer) and their powerfulness in these contexts, although other animals could be considered as well. These four animals, among others, were incorporated into calendar symbols used by ancient Mesoamericans in their recordkeeping. Sometimes these animals are portrayed with each other, as they share qualities of the night: "In Maya art the deer represented the symbolic inversion of the jaguar, embodying the herbivore versus carnivore, weakness versus strength, and timidity versus fierceness" (Looper 2019, 202).

BATS

Mesoamerican cultures experienced their surrounding world as plagued with mysteries and superhuman strength, and generally interpreted it in light of religious belief. In this context, animals had a prominent role because they possessed physical characteristics and a vital force lacking in humans. In the case of bats, this is markedly obvious due to their capacity to fly, get their bearings at night, and avoid obstacles without needing sight. In this sense, these animals are located within the sphere of the divine, either as deities, representations, or manifestations. (Navarro and Arroyo-Cabrales 2013, 603–604)

One need not have a deep knowledge of bat species to know the basics—these small flying mammals are most active at night and twilight, flying about in search of food through echolocation; they do not need light to see; they hang upside down; and some are hematophagous. In Mesoamerica alone, there are 165 species (*Chiroptera* family) classified along the lines of their diet (Navarro and Arroyo-Cabrales 2013, 583). They are more numerous in iconographic representations from a wide swath of Mesoamerican cultures than in actual physical remains, most likely due to their fragile nature and small size (2013, 586), although a few remains are notable (e.g., Brady 2019). Linguistically, bats are present in every Mesoamerican language, from the *zotz* of Mayan speakers to the *quimichin* of Aztec Nahuatl, though there are more representations of bats in Maya art than any other Mesoamerican culture. The bat's significance to the Maya is illustrated in the Classic Maya emblem glyph (Martin 2005)

FIGURE 0.2. *Emblem glyph (on Stela I/CPN 18) of the Classic Maya city of Copan, Honduras, that incorporates the face of a bat with cross-hatched markings for darkness. Drawn by David M. Reed, after Maudslay (1889–1902) and Schele (1987).*

of the city of Copan, Honduras, whose politicians made use of a bat with its distinctive nose-leaf (figure 0.2) as its fearsome animal protector (see Martin 2020 for an exploration of "emblem" glyphs in Classic Maya polities).

Bat representations in Late Postclassic Mexican codices clearly illustrate the bat deity associated with decapitation and sacrifice (Brady and Coltman 2016, 229; Navarro and Arroyo-Cabrales 2013, 596–599); however, such symbolism is missing from Classic Maya Lowland depictions, contra Eduard Seler (1904) (Brady and Coltman 2016, 229–230). Bats are important symbols in some ethnographically known Mayan-speaking groups, such as the Highland Tzotzil, the people of the bat. James Brady and Jeremy Coltman (2016) aptly summarize the many roles bats play in Maya ideology: bats are emblematic of certain lineages; they are servants and messengers and have a connection with scribes; bats are nocturnal pollinators and critical to agricultural fertility; and they are *wahy* beings (Stuart 2021), potentially bringing disease.

As in Western culture, bats generally have a negative image in Mesoamerica (e.g., bats can bring death). Their connections to caves, darkness, and the night are seen throughout Mesoamerican cultures through time and space (Cajas 2009). However, bats are necessary to agriculture. For example, they have been observed dispersing seeds and pollinating night plants that are vital to the well-being of various cultures: the agave plant and the sacred ceiba tree among them (Brady and Coltman 2016; Navarro and Arroyo-Cabrales 2013). This connection is a strong one for the very positive attributes bats have and may even be considered to be sexy.

JAGUARS

In Mesoamerica, the jaguar (*Panthera onca*), an apex predator, figures prominently in iconography from the Preclassic to the Postclassic periods and beyond. Well-known from the Olmec is the were-jaguar, a human-feline form that was perhaps the royal offspring of Olmec rulers and mythical jaguars (Saunders 2001, 385). From the Popol Vuh, it is known that the jaguar is associated with the sun as it journeys through the underworld at night. The ancient Maya believed many animals had sacred powers, especially the jaguar. In Maya mythology, the second age of the world was the age of the "jaguar sun," when Tezcatlipoca changed into a jaguar (Tozzer and Allen 1910, 358). This crepuscular animal represented rulership, royalty, power, transformation, shamans, warfare, and the night. For instance, from the tomb of Ahau Jasaw Chan Kawil (Burial 116) at Tikal in the Temple of the Jaguar (Temple 1), incising on bones pictures the Paddler Gods transporting the Maize God through the waters of the underworld. At the front of the boat is the Old Jaguar Paddler, marked by the symbol for darkness—*ak'bal*—and at the stern is Old Stingray Paddler, denoted with the *k'in*, or day symbol (Martin and Grube 2008, 46–47). Such a vivid illustration shows the kind of nocturnal (and diurnal) association to be found in a study of ancient Maya beliefs.

Classic Maya rulers were often depicted sitting on jaguar thrones (e.g., Lord Chac of Uxmal [Kowalski 1985]), wearing jaguar pelts (as in the Bonampak murals), and incorporating the Maya name for jaguar, *b'ahlam*, into their own titles, such as Ahau Itzamnaaj B'ahlam II of Yaxchilan, Mexico (father of Bird Jaguar IV [Fitzsimmons 2009, 120]), or "White Eye Jaguar" of Tikal (Stuart 2007). Elsewhere, a dedication of fifteen jaguars beneath Altar Q at Copan, Honduras, stands as one example of jaguar sacrifices that were used to mark auspicious occasions. Altar Q is a square monument that illustrates the succession of rulers from the dynasty founder, K'inich Yax K'uk' Mo', through the sixteenth king, Yax Pasaj Chan Yopaat.

In Postclassic Aztec society, the highest-ranking military were members of either the elite jaguar society or the eagle society. The regalia of Aztec rulers, like Maya royalty, included jaguar pelts. Nicholas Saunders (1994, 113) noted that the Aztec and Maya consistently used jaguar iconography for "warfare and status-related situations." Therefore, we see that the jaguar and its associations (e.g., spotted skin, paws, and behaviors) held nocturnal qualities that ran deep in ancient Mesoamerican supernatural beliefs, mythology, and psyche and symbolized power and military prowess. Notably, Seler (1902–1903, 172) translates from the Codex Telleriano-Remensis a passage describing jaguars as the demons of darkness, thus an animal specifically associated with a symbol of darkness, the interior of the earth, and the earth itself throughout ancient Mesoamerica.

Dogs

Another animal with Precolumbian ties to night and darkness is the dog (*Canis familiaris*). Death is a form of darkness, and its symbolism is tied to canines: "The dog's association with the dead is almost worldwide" (Benson 1997, 24). Given the natural behaviors of these carnivores, Elizabeth Benson (1997, 24) concludes:

> Dogs are appropriate escorts for the dead. They walk with their noses to the ground. They dig in the earth, bury bones, and hunt in burrows. They eat carrion and make themselves smell of it. They have night vision; they howl at night; they know what is there in the darkness. Relating to the earth, to dead things, to sounds and smells that are imperceptible to humans, dogs have esoteric knowledge and special connections with the underworld.

Justin Kerr (2001) writes about "the Last Journey" (figure 0.3) of an individual's funerary procession that is featured on a pottery vessel known as the Ratinlinxul vase. His retainers and servants accompany and carry him, while a dog escorts the procession to Xibalba, the underworld. Elizabeth Hill Boone (1994, 137) writes that "dogs filled functional and symbolic roles in Aztec culture. They were kept for food, but also were often buried with the dead in the belief that their spirits could lead the deceased on the hazardous journey through the underworld."

Dogs played many roles in ancient Mesoamerica. As early as the Preclassic period, particular breeds were used for food, some were traded, while others were used as sacrifices (Sharpe et al. 2018). Matthew Looper (2019, 32) considers it possible that dogs were utilized by the ancient Maya for hunting, based on Mary Pohl's work (1985), a reasonable supposition given the widespread use of dogs in such capacity cross-culturally. Both the Maya and the Aztec considered dogs as psychopomps (Beyer 1908; Neumann 1975; Seler 1902–1903, 157) and believed a dog was responsible for having brought fire to humans (Neumann 1975; Thompson 1930, 151). The Mayan glyph for dog (*tzul*)

FIGURE 0.3. *Classic Maya vase (K0594) depicting a deceased individual in a palanquin with his funerary procession to the underworld, accompanied by his dog. Drawn by Alexandre Tokovinine.*

combines animal ribs with a death sign and sometimes with the symbol for darkness placed above one eye (Neumann 1975). The Aztec god Xolotl, their god of lightning and death, also held similar dog and mythological associations, including forming part of the Nahuatl name for the Mexican hairless dog, the *xōlōitzcuīntli*.

DEER

Deer were the most important species hunted by ancient Mesoamericans throughout time long before writing was invented (see chapters in Götz and Emery 2013). They provided an essential form of protein; they were utilized for their bones and antlers in tool making and stone working; their hides were fashioned into garments; their sinew was necessary for compound tool manufacture; and their antlers were often incorporated into dances and ritual as masks or drum beaters (e.g., a deer mask was recovered at Joya de Cerén [Brown and Gerstle 2002, 99]) (Looper 2019, 39–49). Their ubiquitous presence at sites spanning from Archaic to modern times illustrates the high degree to which Mesoamericans long depended on this animal.

A recent book by Looper (2019) provides an extensive consideration of this ruminant and contextualizes it within Maya culture, past and present. Much of the discussion here is taken from Looper's treatise and is applicable to wider Mesoamerican beliefs and practices. He identifies three species of deer found in the Maya area, each of which carries a distinctive Mayan name (2019, 22), but he notes that it is the white-tailed deer (*Odocoileus virginianus*) that is most commonly portrayed in Classic Maya art (figure 0.4) rather than the red brocket (*Mazama temama*) or the Yucatan brown brocket deer (*Mazama pandora*) (2019, 21).

FIGURE 0.4. *Classic Maya vase (K5204) of two deer with sky band and star glyphs. Deer were a key resource for all Mesoamericans. Note the black background, which may symbolize darkness or night. Permission from Justin Kerr.*

Deer have crepuscular habits and most often feed at dawn and dusk (Looper 2019, 26), which may be opportune times for hunting them (2019, 30) by all kinds of beings, whether human or jaguar. Of the many hunting methods employed by humans, two stand out since they are known to have taken place at night, as recorded in ethnohistoric and ethnographic sources consulted by Looper (2019, 30):

> Night-light hunting takes advantage of the strong reflection of light from the eyes of deer in the dark, making them easier targets (Pohl 1977: 540). In the early twentieth century, split-pine torches were attached to hats for this purpose (Gann 1918: 24).
>
> Waiting on an elevated platform or hammock-like seat is also a well-known technique, often done at dawn or dusk or at night when deer are active. These are located adjacent to the fields, along game trails, or near water sources or fruiting trees, especially from April to July (Jorgenson 1993: 61, 110). Deer were hunted using this method after the fields were burned, when the deer were tempted to lick the saline ashes (Gann 1918: 24).

Hunting, as expressed in Classic Maya art, was a male activity that was portrayed by figures with "dark patches of paint on the body or face (possibly camouflage), broad-brimmed or bowler-style hats, headdresses incorporating the heads of various animals, striated skirts and capes (possibly made of grass), conch shells, and weapons, usually spear-throwers, a typically long-range weapon" (Looper 2019, 33).

Deer are integral to the mythology of Mesoamerica, as relayed by Elizabeth Benson (1997, 24):

> In Oaxaca, the original mythic Mixtec couple was named One Deer (a calendrical name). The Codices Vindobonensis and Bodley show that the original couple had thirty-two offspring, most of which were human; one was a deer. In an Aztec myth a two-headed deer fell from the sky, shot down by a hunting god, Mixcoatl. Forced to cohabit with him, she gave birth to the culture hero and deity Quetzalcoatl ("Quetzal-Serpent").

Dogs and deer are connected through hunting and symbolism, as each can represent death. Deer were essential elements of sacrificial rituals; they symbolized the ancestors, sexuality, fertility, and rain and were associated with junior elites (although not typically rulers) in Classic Maya society (Looper 2019, 48). They also represented the setting sun (Looper 2019). As the sun sets, there is no guarantee that it will rise the following day: these liminal time periods that bookend the night can be dangerous ones for deer and humans alike. Looper (2019, 35) concludes that deer images in Classic Maya society were used as a metaphor for borders, especially those between forest and field. Deer represent disease, enemies, and wilderness—all of which threatened the cosmic order.

Deer may very well have been associated with darkness and the night, as exemplified in Classic Maya culture by the Starry Deer Crocodile, a mythic supernatural creature with deer attributes (Looper 2019, 104–106): "Because its body is sometimes shown studded with stars, it seems to be associated with the night sky" (2019, 105). In central Mexican mythology, "stars are conceptualized as deer and the Morning Star as a hunter (Seler 1996: 218)" (2019, 106). Deer do, however, sport the symbolism of the sun and lack the quintessential Mayan glyph for darkness, *ak'ab*, though they are most associated with the setting sun of the West (2019, 157).

PLANTS IN THE DARK

Perhaps less well-known than the nocturnal animals of Mexico and Central America are the nocturnal plants and the nocturnal uses of plants. Paleoethnobotanist Venicia Slotten, a contributor to this volume, greatly enhances our understanding of ancient nights by including discussion of the nocturnal associations of flora in Mesoamerica. Plants need the night, just as animals do, to function properly. Particular species were adapted to nocturnal blooming, and the uses to which ancient Mesoamericans put plants during the nighttime are bolstered by archaeobotanical, linguistic, ethnohistoric, and ethnographic evidence. Taken together, the neotropical flora and fauna created a landscape that differed for its inhabitants, depending on the time of day one experienced it. The night could be a foreboding place, full of sensations, sights, sounds, tastes, and smells that created an environment unique to the dark, but it also offered opportunities unparalleled by those of the day.

PRECOLUMBIAN SENSE OF TIME

The concept of night is a fundamental component of understandings of time. A basis for conceptualizing how ancient Mesoamericans perceived time can be found through an examination of their mythos. For example, the Aztec and Maya clearly held distinct connotations tied to either the nighttime or the daytime hours. These cultural ideas influenced how, when, and where activities were performed, as well as how ancient Mesoamericans experienced and thought about nighttime. It is little wonder that the ancient Mesoamericans were superb astronomers, as their myths were directly tied in with the dark night sky: "Astronomical events being observed and recorded in hieroglyphic books, in architectural alignments, and in stone monuments were not perceived as objective scientific observations. Rather, they served to tie the present to the recent and distant past, based on patterns and cycles displayed in the sky that were attributed to foundational events undertaken by supernaturals in mythic time" (Vail and Hernández 2013, xxiii). It is no surprise that the sun and moon figured prominently in Maya myths (Chinchilla Mazariegos 2017). Here, we focus primarily on the abundance of published materials on the Aztec and Maya to illustrate the above points, although other Mesoamerican cultures shared similar features.

AZTEC NIGHTS

The ancient Aztec held religious beliefs they connected to qualities of the night. Central to this view was their concept that the cosmos was organized into binary opposites, such as night and day. As told in the origin story of the Legend of the Five Suns, the universe had been created and destroyed four times prior to our present universe. Each creation formed an age called a "sun." The fifth era began in darkness with the gods gathering at Teotihuacan. Two gods sacrificed themselves by jumping into a fire and rising as the sun and the moon, respectively. The remaining gods then sacrificed themselves, their blood setting in motion the sun and moon. From then on, the daily movement of the sun, and therefore the continuation of life itself, depended on the nourishment of the gods with human blood.

One god of the nocturnal sky was Tezcatlipoca, or Lord of the Mirror Smoking, so called because of the black, magical mirror worn in place of a lost right foot. As a deity of Toltec origin, he was associated with the earth and the moon (Bunson and Bunson 1996). Obsidian was his symbol and the jaguar his animal disguise. One alias was Yohualli Ehecatl (Night Wind), for which Tezcatlipoca was the divinity associated with nightly and evil characteristics of the wind (Olivier 2015). Tezcatlipoca's central role in creation myths was the forecasting of the end of eras and announcing the rise of future lords and the emergence of new "suns" or historical epochs (Milbrath 2014).

The jaguar characteristic of Tezcatlipoca, whose spotted skin was compared to the starry sky, is traced to Classic period Teotihuacan, as seen in the Patio of the Net Jaguars of the Palace of the Jaguars. The netted jaguar is considered the precursor to later images showing Tezcatlipoca wearing a netted cape (Anawalt 1996, 198, figure 19). From this observation, a connection with Maya lunar imagery is extended: the Classic Maya moon deity was a lunar jaguar, and a net features prominently in Maya folktales of the moon (Milbrath 1999, 41, 120–145, figures 4.2–4.5).

MAYA NIGHTS

Among the ancient Maya, Tezcatlipoca's counterpart—Kawil—was, intriguingly, associated with vegetation symbols, principally maize (Milbrath 2014). Kawil undergoes numerous transformations over a period spanning more than a thousand years, but his imagery consistently has celestial associations, including sky bands, sky glyphs, and stars. Kawil's mirror may represent the planet Jupiter as an orb shining in the night sky. The study of monuments that record texts with dated events shows an association between Kawil and Jupiter's retrograde period. Jupiter played a significant role, especially in the events recorded in the lives of Classic Maya rulers, many of whom were represented with the insignia of Kawil (2014, 192). Kawil's mirror is linked with smoking axes and burning torches, symbols that may refer to thunder and lightning. Like Kawil, Tezcatlipoca had a connection with planetary cycles and the moon, but his aspect, or manifestation, was more capricious. Tezcatlipoca is a lord of fate who seems connected with astrological cycles linked to the motions of the sun, moon, and planets (2014, 194).

These centuries' long beliefs, with their roots in Toltec, Maya, Teotihuacan, Aztec, and possibly Olmec cultures, indicate that nighttime concepts were as consequential as daytime ones and that nightly activities in tandem with behaviors in the dark or dark places featured prominently in the lives of ancient Mesoamericans. The chapters that follow interweave many of the themes discussed here, as well as other perspectives of the nightways of Ancient Mexico and Central America.

EXPLORING THEMES OF NIGHT AND DARKNESS

The chapters in this volume are examinations of facets of the night and darkness among the ancient, historical, and contemporary peoples of Mexico and Central America (figure 0.1). The authors contribute to nightways research by drawing on archaeology, art history, chronicles, ethnology, geology, palynology, and resource estimation. Rather than limiting the volume to only archaeological studies, the inclusion of historical and contemporary groups, as well as natural phenomena, enriches our understanding of the concepts of darkness and its relationship to the night (table 0.1). Although many themes are explored, this volume is not comprehensive, since the topics of night and darkness are only beginning to be incorporated into Mesoamerican research.[2]

The topics and cultures presented herein were largely determined by scholars willing to step outside of familiar themes and explore new avenues. Brigitte Steger and Lodewijk Brunt (2003) faced similar hurdles in bringing together researchers willing to think differently and write about their unfamiliar topic of night and sleep, as did Gonlin and Nowell (2018a) in their night volume. Scholars in this publication discuss myriad different associations attached to night and darkness when drawing on studies of the Maya, Teotihuacanos, Maya-Ulúa, Otomí, and Aztec. Contributors were able to develop and discover ideas and directions for future research and further thinking on notions of night and darkness in the past. Within these pages we hope you will find encouragement in their attempts and fresh conceptualizations, well beyond simply identifying areas inferred to be places where sleep, an obvious nighttime activity, occurred in buildings.

A major theme that runs through this volume is a nocturnal ecology, of which some parameters were discussed above. Modified and imbued with meaning, the ancient Mesoamericans created their own nightscapes and darkscapes—inscribing various media with their perceptions, engaging in different practices, recording their thoughts about these aspects, and leaving behind the material traces for us to interpret. For example, the ancient

Maya likely had nocturnal associations with food; sociopolitical and economic aspects played key roles through such associations. Practice theory provides a framework for the interplay of power, wealth, and behavior through which one can build a better understanding of nightways in Mesoamerica. Similar to other authors' insights, the integration of archaeology, ethnography, and iconography is instrumental to robust interpretations of nighttime foodways. A nocturnal dimension to consumption is a near cultural universal, but this dimension has not been fully explored for Mesoamericans. The duality of Mesoamerican concepts lends itself to a consideration of nocturnal foodways that conveyed entangled messages that could be read by a wide audience (Reed, Zeleznik, and Gonlin, this volume). The role of consumption in inequality extended to nighttime contexts.

Plants were part of the Mesoamerican worldview and figured prominently in origin myths. A compendium of night plants with which the ancient Maya and other Mesoamericans would have been familiar is produced by Venicia Slotten. Her botanical review of the vines, bushes, and flowers that are active at night gives insight into the nocturnal landscape. Relying on linguistic cues, ethnohistory, ethnology, and archaeology, Slotten discusses medicinal uses of plants that likely occurred only at night, including treating headaches, fevers, stomachaches, night sweats, and myriad other ailments. For example, insomnia had many cures that involved the ingestion of plant substances that were widely available, judging from archaeobotanical remains across the region. For nighttime sleeping, ethnohistorical accounts name specific plants that were chosen for inducing sleep. Some of these species have been recovered archaeologically. Color and fragrance were characteristics to be considered when choosing bedding materials. The ritual uses of plants during the night are many, judging from ethnographic accounts. Going back in time where remains of similar plants are recovered during Classic times, one can speculate that there was a nocturnal element to their use, some even during lunar eclipses. Slotten further connects particular flora to the Maya cosmovision, with the sacred tree of life embodied in the ceiba. The remains of charcoal, as commonly recovered from archaeological sites, indicate that the woody taxa would have been used in nighttime capacities for torches, hearths, cooking, and rituals. A multitude of known flora of the Mesoamerican past is thus reinterpreted through the lens of nocturnality.

Darkness does not arise only from the onset of the night. There are other natural phenomena that bring on darkness during the day, such as a total solar eclipse (e.g., Aveni 2018) or massive dust storms. Astronomical events were accurately predicted by ancient Mesoamericans. For decades, scholars have studied how and what features of the sky the ancient Maya and Aztec found of interest (e.g., Aveni 1975). Stargazing is surely one of the oldest natural sciences (Sari 2016, 11), and many ancient settlements are best viewed in relationship to their night skies (Ashmore and Sabloff 2002). Nuria Sari (2016, 11) advocates this viewpoint for the island of Cozumel and the preservation of its heritage. The political geography of ancient Mesoamericans included the dark, night sky and all its wonders, yet most scholars do not consider darkness an explicit and essential element in our theories and re-creations of the past. Still, we readily accept that Mesoamericans aligned their architecture according to the stars, planets, and calendars (e.g., Galindo Trejo 2016).

However, another type of natural event was unpredictable: an explosive volcanic eruption with its hallmark plume of smoke and ash shooting high into the sky. The tectonically active landscape of Mexico and Central America has numerous volcanoes, some of which have exploded during our own lifetime. Rachel Egan informs us about explosive eruptions and the "volcanic nights" they produce. Such nights have their own characteristics that engage the senses. Egan describes the smells associated with a volcanic eruption that would have been distinct to this phenomenon. It is known that ancient inhabitants experienced explosive eruptions, yet curiously, reference to such events by literate peoples, such as the Classic Maya, has not been found. Research on volcanic eruptions furthers our understanding of migrations, political economies, and collective and individual responses to such catastrophes that created an unnaturally dark world.

Illumination and the dark have gone hand in hand throughout human existence. Our first recorded success with fire stretches back millennia, possibly even prior to the dawn of *Homo sapiens* (Gowlett 2016). The anthropological study of luminosity was inspired by Mikkel Bille and Tim Flohr Sørensen's (2007) seminal article on this topic, as well as by lychnology, the study of pre-modern lighting devices (Micheli and Santucci 2015; Strong 2018, 2021).[3] Sociocultural dimensions of light and darkness are explored through the natural landscape, sources of artificial lighting, and aspects of the built environment. Remains from the ancient Maya city of Copan, Honduras, and the ancient agricultural community of Joya de Cerén, El Salvador, provide concrete evidence as well as possibilities for ancient lighting technologies through Nancy Gonlin and Christine Dixon-Hundredmark's research. The role that hearths, torches, candles, ceramics, mirrors, and even fireflies may have played in illumination is considered, as well as the symbolic aspects of these objects. Inequality existed across the social spectrum in terms of how one experienced the night through access to such technologies and the type of house in which one spent the night. A reconsideration of mundane artifacts in terms of the night is in order so we can expand our understanding of the Late Classic Maya way of life and encompass all of the social spectrum (Lohse 2014).

The technology of illuminance is used to make an entrée into Teotihuacan nights. The investigation of night lighting in the Early Classic period Highland Mexican metropolis, which perhaps as many as 125,000 residents called home, contributes to sensory archaeology. Jesper Nielsen and Christophe Helmke (2018, figure 4.2) identify a number of icons portraying unlit, smoking, and lit torches at this grand city, providing us with concrete evidence of their use. One can envision, hear, and smell the city at night, the crackling of the torches going strong. One of the residents' major concerns would have been obtaining fuel for a variety of purposes, including illumination. From where the population obtained fuel sources, what those sources were, and how much fuel was available are addressed. Firewood was needed for other activities as well, such as heating the cool night air, cooking, rituals, and craft activities. But perhaps the largest amount of fuel would have been used for lime production. The sights, noises, and aromas of ancient urban life were many; some pertained to activities that were subversive in nature. Nocturnal illumination facilitated a range of activities, legal and illicit. By applying ethnohistorical data from the Codex Mendoza and the Florentine Codex and ethnographic insights to supplement the archaeological data, Randolph Widmer enlivens the bustling city of Teotihuacan to the extent that we can easily picture nightlife in this ancient, crowded nightscape.

It is well-known that as the sense of sight diminishes in darkness for humans, other senses rise to the fore. It is common for humans to have enhanced hearing in dark places, and one of those is the inside of the temazcal, a structure and activity readily identified with Mesoamericans in the past and present and across the geographic extent of this culture area. An understudied characteristic of this built environment is an appreciation of its acoustic properties, as reported by Payson Sheets and Michael Thomason who studied Structure 9, the sweat bath, at Cerén, El Salvador. This Classic Maya community was preserved by volcanic ash around 660 CE and exhibits extraordinary preservation of structures, artifacts, features, and other aspects of the built landscape. The acoustical studies were made possible by using a replica of the sweat bath that was created for visitors to this World Heritage site. Human voices are enhanced and amplified, adding to the mystical qualities of the darkness. The temazcal itself plays a major role in this experience through its unique resonances. The members of Household 2, who were likely the caretakers of the temazcal, could engage the community in darkness by maintaining and protecting this essential element of their lives. Jan Marie Olson delves into the deep meanings and the darkness of the temazcal to reveal its place in Aztec life and their dualistic philosophy. Its functional uses cannot be separated from its non-material attributes, and we should not isolate the medicinal from the religious, as was the case for Spanish colonizers. Balance could be achieved by way of the sweat bath for men and women, and those who were ill could become well again. Nighttime was ideal for seeking the healing powers of night forces, feminine goddesses, the temazcal, and human healers. The sweat bath is gendered, as the feminine space represents the womb and an entrance into the Earth, just as caves do. Women go to the sweat bath to give birth and to cleanse in contemporary societies, and it is likely that we can extend these practices into ancient times. Symbolic re-birth also occurred in the sweat bath, whether one was attempting to cleanse physical or mental ailments (a false dichotomy for many peoples). Just as central as the structure itself is the associated firebox. A study of structural variations in Late Aztec period temazcales is revealing, as shape and location loosely correlate with each other. Given the fact that Europeans of the sixteenth century rarely bathed (Classen, Howes, and Synnott 1994, 70–71), it is no wonder that daily bathing among the Aztecs was misunderstood by the colonizers and many sweat baths were destroyed. Despite those acts of destruction, numerous temazcales have been recovered in the archaeological record, and they illuminate these dark spaces and often nightly practices of the past.

Rituals, ancestors, darkness, the underworld, and the night are all connected in the Mesoamerican cultures. The ancients used glyphs and iconography to express these connections, and in this volume, they are illustrated in case studies of the Classic Maya, peoples of the Ulúa Valley, the Otomí, and the Aztecs. The concept of primordial darkness is necessary to better understand what darkness meant to ancient Mesoamericans. Jeremy Coltman presents a foundation for the Classic Mayan *ch'een* glyph that symbolizes caves but also wells, cisterns, dark interiors, or burials. Represented by a motif of cross-bones and eyeballs and set against either a dark or a cross-hatched background, this symbol first appears in the Preclassic at the ancient Maya city of Holmul, Guatemala. In his chapter, Coltman explores how ch'een is used to imbue primordial darkness and the wild untamed forest. An association of ch'een with leafy arbors and bowers furthers this interpretation. This glyph was utilized by ancient Mesoamericans to show the power of deities. The skull and cross-bones motif may be most familiar from Aztec iconography, but a clear argument is made for its precursor among the Classic Maya. Coltman's chapter builds on his previous publications on the night where he explores darkness, creation, and the ancient Maya worldview (Coltman 2018).

The underworld in Mesoamerican cosmology is intrinsically connected with the night, death, the landscape, and ancestors. To illustrate these vital connections, Jeanne Lopiparo provides an example from Late to Terminal Classic sites (ca. 600–1000 CE) at communities in the central alluvium of the Ulúa Valley (household sites [CR-80, CR-103, and CR-381] and the larger center of Currusté [CR-32]). Household renewal rituals manifested in structured deposits and were often closely associated with human burials. The interaction of the living and the dead was an integral part of existence. These shared practices transcended hundreds and in some cases thousands of years of occupation. Concepts of renewal and regeneration were expressed materially through polychrome vessels, figural artifacts, and structured deposits. Relying on archaeology, iconography, epigraphy, ethnohistory, ethnography, and analogy with the Classic Maya, Lopiparo presents a robust case for the interpretation of the built landscape and the daily and nightly journey of the sun and other celestial bodies.

Numerous nocturnal rituals were associated with fire, but perhaps the best-known one from ancient Mesoamerica is the Aztec New Fire Ceremony, which occurred every fifty-two years to coincide with the meshing of the Mesoamerican ritual and solar calendars. On the night of this ominous date, household and temple fires were extinguished throughout the empire and priests gathered outside Tenochtitlan at Citlaltepetl, as described by Kirby Farah. Such descriptions are well-known from ethnohistorical sources that highlight the Aztec version. However, this ceremony was practiced before the existence of the Aztec Triple Alliance. Evidence from the northern Basin of Mexico Otomí capital of Xaltocan informs us about variation in ideology and sociopolitical organization and that Early Postclassic polities conquered by the Aztecs often retained their own identities through the maintenance of rituals. Archaeological evidence for the New Fire Ceremony has been uncovered at central Mexican sites. Kirby uses these data to examine dynamics of evolving power, politics, and practices. Similarities and differences between the pre-Aztec New Fire ritual at Xaltocan and the New Fire Ceremony that defined the Aztec Empire are indicative of both continuity and identity. The element of darkness was essential, as the appropriate time for such rituals was during the night.

Cecelia Klein offers a deep exploration of the use of the blindfold (*ixqui-milli*) among the Aztecs and its association with darkness. Hampered by non-indigenous interpretations of this device, colonial explanations relied on a Christian heritage that incorrectly associated the blindfold with guilt and sin. Klein proposes that the blindfold did indeed symbolize that a transgression had occurred but also that the wearing of it could make amends, since the wearer was returned to the darkness of Creation when dressed in the blindfold. The generative aspect of darkness the Aztecs assigned to the blindfold was thus used for healing. Only two deities in the painted manuscripts wear blindfolds, Tezcatlipoca ("Mirror Smoking") and Tlazolteotl ("Divine Filth"), both of whom have the ability to erase errors and are associated with the night and the wind. The propitious hour of midnight was ideal for donning the blindfold for naked clients to petition the deities to erase the damage. This practice recalls the rituals of many other cultures, both ancient and modern and across Mesoamerica and beyond.

We are fortunate to have Julia Hendon synthesize and reflect on night and darkness in the Mesoamerican past. Her prolific work has focused on social practices of ancient cultures, and her insights afford additional reflection on the significance and meaning of the night and darkness to the ancient peoples of Mexico and Central America. Hendon effectively concludes the volume by highlighting the centrality of the night and considers why archaeologists have not paid more attention to it. She offers directions for further research, as we do, below.

INTO THE FUTURE

In past and recent scholarship, night has often been, at best, implicit with interpretations considered within the context of daily or daylight behavior. There has been a bias toward day and daytime activities research; a diecentrism has existed, as Steger and Brunt (2003) indicate. Theories almost invariably focus on that which is perceived during daylight; thus night and darkness remain underexplored themes. Here, we propose a research agenda aimed at explicitly discovering such influences on behavior. The authors in this volume have begun to rectify our knowledge of these missing components—nighttime and darkness—in their many motifs, and, by extension, ramifications are assessed in some ancient Mesoamerican cultures. The intentions are to delineate and illustrate how adding a nightways dimension augments archaeological issues within an anthropological framework where the aspect has been previously neglected. The results demonstrate that the concepts of night and darkness enrich and strengthen anthropological and humanistic explanations of behavior, ecology, power, economy, ideology, and the supernatural—thus working toward a more holistic, encompassing anthropological discourse of the study of humanity. Night and darkness are constituent parts of the human experience and our behaviors. In a similar way to Robert Shaw (2015), we propose considering the experiences of levels and types of darkness in greater detail in archaeology, with attention to the nuances of dark and light, to the relationships between lit and unlit spaces and objects within those spaces, to luminosity following Bille and Sørensen (2007), to the role of shadows, and to the exploration of the behaviors involved. We seek new boundaries in understanding darkness beyond those found in cave archaeology, where scholars such as Charles Faulkner (1988) explicitly discuss the quality of light as an interpretative issue and the identification of *dark zones*. Paul Pettitt (2016) emphasizes the ways light and darkness figured in ancient belief systems, and Holley Moyes's (2012) edited collection on the ritual use of caves provides new insights. Our authors go beyond the human experiences and perceptions that have been explored only recently by art critics and urban sociologists (Garcia-Ruiz and Nofre 2020), geographers (Edensor 2013, 2015a, 2015b, 2017; Morris 2011; Segre 2020), and historians (Ekrich 2005; Koslofsky 2011).

Nighttime, when discussed in archaeology, is nearly always in association with astronomy, where incredible insights into the past have resulted. The night sky was as essential to ancient peoples as their economic or political organization. Heritage strategies that incorporate the nightscape do greater justice to the past, and as advocated for the island of Cozumel, "the preservation of dark skies would allow for development of archaeological and astronomical research projects that would support making nocturnal landscapes another exceptional attraction" (Sari 2016, 16). In our research as archaeologists, we must consider the local communities affected and the context in which archaeological remains were situated, and that pursuit includes the preservation of archaeological remains as well as dark nights.

Systematic studies of the anthropological aspects of nightways remain open directions of research. Our current theories neglect to directly address nocturnal elements and thus require revisions; rarely is more than a passing mention made of nocturnal behaviors. This volume is a continuation of the theme of the archaeology of the night (Gonlin and Nowell 2018a), but it also expands on the concept of darkness (Dowd and Hensey 2016b) and luminosity (Bille and Sørensen 2007). By re-imagining the vast records many of us Mesoamericanists already have, we can use those data to great effect in creating an understanding of the role of night, darkness, and luminosity among ancient peoples of Mexico and Central America.

ACKNOWLEDGMENTS

We thank April Nowell and Christine Dixon-Hundredmark for their careful reading of the ideas presented in this introductory chapter, for their substantive edits, and for helping us clarify our thoughts on many points. Insights from Matthew Looper and Gabrielle Vail are much appreciated. Three anonymous reviewers provided critical feedback.

NOTES

1. Such sources of light include the moon, the stars, the Milky Way, natural gas flares, magma and lightning from volcanoes, auroras, wildfires, and bioluminescent organisms. https://www.nasa.gov/mission_pages/NPP/news/earth-at-night.html.

2. In 2010, the Pre-Columbian Society of Washington, DC, held a symposium titled Under Cover of Darkness: The Meaning of Night in Ancient Mesoamerica. Six presentations were made, but these papers were not published. One of the presenters, Cecelia Klein, expanded her original paper, which is included in this volume.

3. http://www.lychnology.org/.

REFERENCES

Anawalt, Patricia. 1996. "Aztec Knotted and Netted Capes: Colonial Interpretations vs. Indigenous Primary Data." *Ancient Mesoamerica* 7 (2): 187–206.

Ashmore, Wendy, and Jeremy A. Sabloff. 2002. "Spatial Orders in Maya Civic Plans." *Latin American Antiquity* 13 (2): 201–215.

Aveni, Anthony F. 1975. *Archaeoastronomy in Pre-Columbian America*. Austin: University of Texas Press.

Aveni, Anthony F., ed. 2008. *Foundations of New World Cultural Astronomy*. Boulder: University Press of Colorado.

Aveni, Anthony F. 2018. "Night in Day: Contrasting Maya and Hindu Responses to Total Solar Eclipses." In *Archaeology of the Night: Life after Dark in the Ancient World*, ed. Nancy Gonlin and April Nowell, 139–154. Boulder: University Press of Colorado.

Baldwin, Peter C. 2012. *In the Watches of the Night: Life in the Nocturnal City, 1820–1930*. Chicago: University of Chicago Press.

Becquelin, Aurore Monod, and Jacques Galinier, eds. 2016. *Las cosas de la noche: Una mirada diferente*. Mexico City: Centro de Estudios Mexicanos y Centroamericano. https://doi.org/10.4000/books.cemca.4201.

Benson, Elizabeth P. 1997. *Birds and Beasts of Ancient Latin America*. Gainesville: University Press of Florida.

Beyer, Herman. 1908. "The Symbolic Meaning of the Dog in Ancient Mexico." *American Anthropologist* New Series 10 (3): 419–422.

Bille, Mikkel, and Tim Flohr Sørensen. 2007. "An Anthropology of Luminosity: The Agency of Light." *Journal of Material Culture* 12 (3): 263–284.

Bogard, Paul. 2013. *The End of Night: Searching for Natural Darkness in an Age of Artificial Light*. New York: Little, Brown.

Boone, Elizabeth Hill. 1994. *The Aztec World*. St. Remy Press and Smithsonian Books: Montreal and Washington, DC.

Brady, James E. 2019. "Evidence of Bat Sacrifice in Ancient Maya Cave Ritual." *Archaeological Discovery* 7: 84–91.

Brady, James E., and Jeremy D. Coltman. 2016. "Bats and the Camazotz: Correcting a Century of Mistaken Identity." *Latin American Antiquity* 27 (2): 227–237.

Brown, Linda A. 2005. "Planting the Bones: Hunting Ceremonialism at Contemporary and Nineteenth-Century Shrines in the Guatemalan Highlands." *Latin American Antiquity* 16 (2): 131–146.

Brown, Linda A., and Andrea Gerstle. 2002. "Structure 10: Feasting and Village Festivals." In *Before the Volcano Erupted: The Ancient Cerén Village in Central America*, ed. Payson Sheets, 97–103. Austin: University of Texas Press.

Bunson, Margaret R., and Stephen M. Bunson. 1996. *Encyclopedia of Ancient Mesoamerica*. New York: Facts on File.

Cajas, Antonieta. 2009. "Bats in Maya Art." *FLAAR* (June): 1–10.

Chinchilla Mazariegos, Oswaldo. 2017. *Art and Myth of the Ancient Maya*. New Haven, CT: Yale University Press.

Christenson, Allen J. 2007. *Popol Vuh: Sacred Book of the Quiché Maya People*. Norman: University of Oklahoma Press.

Classen, Constance, David Howes, and Anthony Synnott. 1994. *Aroma: The Cultural History of Smell*. London: Routledge.

Coltman, Jeremy D. 2018. "Where Night Reigns Eternal: Darkness and Deep Time among the Ancient Maya." In *Archaeology of the Night: Life after Dark in the Ancient World*, ed. Nancy Gonlin and April Nowell, 201–222. Boulder: University Press of Colorado.

Conkey, Margaret. 2018. "Afterword: A Portal to a More Imaginative Archaeology." In *Archaeology of the Night: Life after Dark in the Ancient World*, ed. Nancy Gonlin and April Nowell, 387–390. Boulder: University Press of Colorado.

Dowd, Marion, and Robert Hensey. 2016a. "Background and Acknowledgements." In *Darkness: Archaeological, Historical, and Contemporary Perspectives*, ed. Marion Dowd and Robert Hensey, xi–xii. Oxford: Oxbow Books.

Dowd, Marion, and Robert Hensey, eds. 2016b. *Darkness: Archaeological, Historical, and Contemporary Perspectives*. Oxford: Oxbow Books.

Edensor, Tim. 2013. "Reconnecting with Darkness: Gloomy Landscapes, Lightless Places." *Social and Cultural Geography* 14 (4): 446–465.

Edensor, Tim. 2015a. "The Gloomy City: Rethinking the Relationship between Light and Dark." *Urban Studies* 52 (3): 422–438.

Edensor, Tim. 2015b. "Introduction to Geographies of Darkness." *Cultural Geographies* 22 (4): 559–565.

Edensor, Tim. 2017. *From Light to Dark: Daylight, Illumination, and Gloom.* Minneapolis: University of Minnesota Press.

Ekirch, A. Roger. 2005. *At Day's Close: Night in Times Past.* New York: W. W. Norton.

Evans, Susan Toby. 2013. *Ancient Mexico and Central America: Archaeology and Culture History*, 3rd ed. London: Thames and Hudson.

Faulkner, Charles H. 1988. "Painters of the 'Dark Zone.'" *Archaeology* 41 (2): 30–35.

Fitzsimmons, James L. 2009. *Death and the Classic Maya Kings.* Austin: University of Texas Press.

Fogelin, Lars. 2019. *An Unauthorized Companion to American Archaeological Theory.* https://arizona.academia.edu/LarsFogelin.

Galindo Trejo, Jesús. 2016. "Calendric-Astronomical Alignment of Architectural Structures in Mesoamerica: An Ancestral Cultural Practice." In *The Role of Archaeoastronomy in the Maya World: The Case Study of the Island of Cozumel*, ed. Nuria Sanz, Chantal Connaughton, Liza Gisbert, José Pulido Mata, and Carlos Tejada, 21–36. Paris: United Nations Educational, Scientific, and Cultural Organization.

Galinier, Jacques, Aurore Monod Becquelin, Guy Bordin, Laurent Fontaine, Francine Fourmaux, Juliette Roullet Ponce, Piero Salzarulo, Philippe Simonnot, Michèle Therrien, and Iole Zilli. 2010. "Anthropology of the Night: Cross-Disciplinary Investigations." *Current Anthropology* 51 (6): 819–847. https://doi.org/10.1086/653691.

Galinier, Jacques, and Mario A. Zamudio Vega. 2016. *Una noche de espanto: Los otomíes en la obscuridad.* Mexico City: Tenango de Doria UICEH, Universidad Cultural del Estado de Société d'Ethnographie Centro de Estudios Mexicanos y Centroamericanos.

Gann, Thomas William Francis. 1918. *Maya Indians of Southern Yucatan and Northern British Honduras.* Bureau of American Ethnology Bulletin 64. Washington, DC: Bureau of American Ethnology.

Garcia-Ruiz, Manuel, and Jordi Nofre, eds. 2020. *ICNS Proceedings.* Lisboa: ISCTE Instituto Universitario de Lisboa.

Geoscience Australia, Canberra. 2018. "Astronomical Definitions." http://www.ga.gov.au/scientific-topics/astronomical/astronomical-definitions.

Gonlin, Nancy. 2018. "Preface." In *Archaeology of the Night: Life after Dark in the Ancient World*, ed. Nancy Gonlin and April Nowell, xxix–xxx. Boulder: University Press of Colorado.

Gonlin, Nancy. 2020. "Household Archaeology of the Classic Period Lowland Maya." In *The Maya World*, ed. Scott R. Hutson and Traci Ardren, 389–406. New York: Routledge.

Gonlin, Nancy, and Christine C. Dixon. 2018. "Classic Maya Nights at Copan, Honduras and El Cerén, El Salvador." In *Archaeology of the Night: Life after Dark in the Ancient World*, ed. Nancy Gonlin and April Nowell, 45–76. Boulder: University Press of Colorado.

Gonlin, Nancy, and April Nowell, eds. 2018a. *Archaeology of the Night: Life after Dark in the Ancient World*. Boulder: University Press of Colorado.

Gonlin, Nancy, and April Nowell. 2018b. "Introduction to the Archaeology of the Night." In *Archaeology of the Night: Life after Dark in the Ancient World*, ed. Nancy Gonlin and April Nowell, 5–24. Boulder: University Press of Colorado.

Götz, Christopher M., and Kitty F. Emery, eds. 2013. *The Archaeology of Mesoamerican Animals*. Atlanta: Lockwood.

Gowlett, John A.J. 2016. "The Discovery of Fire by Humans: A Long and Convoluted Process." *Philosophical Transactions of the Royal Society of London, Series B: Biological Sciences* 371 (1696): 20150164. https://doi.org/10.1098/rstb.2015.0164.

Graulich, Michel. 1983. "Myths of Paradise Lost in Pre-Hispanic Central Mexico." *Current Anthropology* 24: 575–588.

Gremillion, Kristen J. 2011. *Ancestral Appetites: Food in Prehistory*. Cambridge: Cambridge University Press.

Hanson, Dirk. 2014. "Drowning in Light." *Nautilus* 11: 4–22.

Hensey, Robert. 2016. "Past Dark: A Short Introduction to the Human Relationship with Darkness over Time." In *Darkness: Archaeological, Historical, and Contemporary Perspectives*, ed. Marion Dowd and Robert Hensey, 1–10. Oxford: Oxbow Books.

Isbell, William H. 2009. "Huari: A New Direction in Central Andean Urban Evolution." In *Domestic Life in Prehispanic Capitals: A Study of Specialization, Hierarchy, and Ethnicity*, ed. Linda R. Manzanilla and Claude Chapdelaine, 197–219. Memoirs of the Museum of Anthropology 46. Ann Arbor: Museum of Anthropology, University of Michigan.

Iwaniszewski, Stanislaw. 2016. "Time and the Moon in Maya Culture: The Case of Cozumel." In *The Role of Archaeoastronomy in the Maya World: The Case Study of the Island of Cozumel*, ed. Nuria Sanz, Chantal Connaughton, Liza Gisbert, José Pulido Mata, and Carlos Tejada, 39–55. Paris: United Nations Educational, Scientific, and Cultural Organization.

James, Sian. 2016. "Digging into the Darkness: The Experience of Copper Mining in the Great Orme, North Wales." In *Darkness: Archaeological, Historical, and Contemporary Perspectives*, ed. Marion Dowd and Robert Hensey, 75–83. Oxford: Oxbow Books.

Jorgenson, Jeffrey Paul. 1993. "Gardens, Wildlife Densities, and Subsistence Hunting by Maya Indians in Quintana Roo, Mexico." PhD thesis. University of Florida, Gainesville.

Kerr, Justin. 2001. "The Last Journey." http://www.mayavase.com/jour/journey.html.

Koslofsky, Craig. 2011. *Evening's Empire: A History of the Night in Early Modern Europe*. Cambridge: Cambridge University Press. https://doi.org/10.1017/CBO 9780511977695.

Kowalski, Jeff Karl. 1985. "Lords of the Northern Maya: Dynastic History in the Inscriptions of Uxmal and Chichén Itzá." *Expedition* 27 (3): 50–60.

Lohse, Jon C. 2014. "Alienating Ancient Maya Commoners." *Archaeological Papers of the American Anthropological Association* 23 (1): 81–94.

Looper, Matthew. 2019. *The Beast Between: Deer in Maya Art and Culture*. Austin: University of Texas Press.

Marken, Damien B, ed. 2007. *Palenque: Recent Investigations at the Classic Maya Center*. Lanham, MD: Altamira.

Martin, Simon. 2005. "Of Snakes and Bats: Shifting Identities at Calakmul." *PARI Journal* 6 (2): 5–13.

Martin, Simon. 2020. *Ancient Maya Politics: A Political Anthropology of the Classic Period 150–900 CE*. Cambridge: Cambridge University Press.

Martin, Simon, and Nikolai Grube. 2008. *Chronicle of the Maya Kings and Queens*, 2nd ed. London: Thames and Hudson.

Maudslay, A. P. 1889–1902. "Archaeology Plate 65." In *Biologia Centrali-Americana, or, Contributions to the Knowledge of the Fauna and Flora of Mexico and Central America: Archaeology*, vol. 1: *Plates*, 65, ed. F. Ducane Godman and Osbert Salvin. London: R. H. Porter and Dulau.

Micheli, Maria Elisa, and Anna Santucci, eds. 2015. *Lumina: Convegno Internazionale di Studi Urbino 5–7 guigno 2013*. Pisa, Italy: Edizione ETS.

Milbrath, Susan. 1999. *Star Gods of the Maya: Astronomy in Art, Folklore, and Calendars*. Austin: University of Texas Press.

Milbrath, Susan. 2014. "The Maya Lord of the Smoking Mirror." In *Tezcatlipoca: Trickster and Supreme Deity*, ed. Elizabeth Baquedano, 163–196. Boulder: University Press of Colorado.

Morris, Nina J. 2011. "Night Walking: Darkness and Sensory Perception in a Nighttime Landscape Installation." *Cultural Geographies* 18 (3): 315–342.

Mothrè, Ève, and Aurore Monod Becquelin. 2016. "La Profundidad de la Noche Maya." In *Las cosas de la noche: Una mirada diferente*, ed. Aurore Monod Becquelin and Jacques Galinier, 99–112. Mexico City: Centro de Estudios Mexicanos y Centroamericano. https://doi.org/10.4000/books.cemca.4201.

Moyes, Holley, ed. 2012. *Sacred Darkness: A Global Perspective on the Ritual Use of Caves*. Boulder: University Press of Colorado.

Nagao, Debra. 2014. "An Interconnected World? Evidence of Interaction in the Arts of Epiclassic Cacaxtla and Xochicalco, Mexico." PhD thesis, Columbia University, New York City, NY.

Nagao, Debra. 2020. "Proscenium of the Dark: Darkness and Liminality in Pre-Columbian Mesoamerica." In *México Noir: Rethinking the Dark in Contemporary Writing and Visual Culture*, ed. Erica Segre, 1–25. Bern, Switzerland: Peter Lang.

"NASA-NOAA Satellite Reveals New Views of Earth at Night." https://www.nasa.gov/mission_pages/NPP/news/earth-at-night.html.

Navarro, Laura, and Joaquin Arroyo-Cabrales. 2013. "Bats in Ancient Mesoamerica." In *The Archaeology of Mesoamerican Animals*, ed. Christopher M. Götz and Kitty F. Emery, 583–605. Atlanta: Lockwood.

Neumann, Franke J. 1975. "The Dragon and the Dog: Two Symbols of Time in Nahuatl Religion." *Numen* 22 (1): 1–23.

Nielsen, Jesper, and Christophe Helmke. 2018. "'Where the Sun Came into Being': Rites of Pyrolatry, Transition, and Transformation in Early Classic Teotihuacan." In *Smoke, Flames, and the Human Body in Mesoamerican Ritual Practice*, ed. Vera Tiesler and Andrew K. Scherer, 77–107. Washington, DC: Dumbarton Oaks Library and Research Collection.

Olivier, Guilhem. 2015. "Enemy Brothers or Divine Twins? A Comparative Approach between Tezcatlipoca and Quetzalcoatl, Two Major Deities from Ancient Mexico." In *Tezcatlipoca: Trickster and Supreme Deity*, ed. Elizabeth Baquedano, 59–82. Boulder: University Press of Colorado.

Palmer, Bryan D. 2000. *Cultures of Darkness: Night Travels in the Histories of Transgression (from Medieval to Modern)*. New York: Monthly Review Press.

Pettitt, Paul. 2016. "Darkness Visible: Shadows, Art, and the Ritual Experience of Caves in Upper Palaeolithic Europe." In *Darkness: Archaeological, Historical, and Contemporary Perspectives*, ed. Marion Dowd and Robert Hensey, 11–23. Oxford: Oxbow Books.

Pohl, Mary D. 1977. "Hunting in the Maya Village of San Antonio, Rio Hondo, Orange Walk District, Belize." *Journal of Belizean Affairs* 5: 52–63.

Pohl, Mary D. 1985. "The Privileges of Maya Elites: Prehistoric Vertebrate Fauna from Seibal." In *Prehistoric Lowland Maya Environment and Subsistence Economy*, ed. Mary D. Pohl, 133–145. Papers of the Peabody Museum of Archaeology and Ethnology 77. Cambridge, MA: Peabody Museum, Harvard University.

Quirarte, Jacinto. 1979. "The Representation of Underworld Processions in Maya Vase Painting: An Iconographic Study." In *Maya Archaeology and Ethnohistory*, ed. Norman Hammond and Gordon R. Willey, 116–148. Austin: University of Texas Press.

Ruz Lhuillier, Alberto. 1973. *El Templo de las Inscripciones, Palenque*. Mexico City: Instituto Nacional de Antropología e Historia.

Ruz Lhuillier, Alberto, and J. Alden Mason. 1953. "The Mystery of the Temple of the Inscriptions." *Archaeology* 6 (1): 3–11.

Sari, Nuria. 2016. "The Cultural Landscape of the Sky as Heritage and Development." In *The Role of Archaeoastronomy in the Maya World: The Case Study of the Island of Cozumel*, 11–19. Paris: United Nations Educational, Scientific, and Cultural Organization.

Saunders, Nicholas J. 1994. "Predators of Culture: Jaguar Symbolism and Mesoamerican Elites." *World Archaeology* 26 (1): 104–117.

Saunders, Nicholas J. 2001. "Jaguars." In *Archaeology of Ancient Mexico and Central America: An Encyclopedia*, ed. Susan Toby Evans and David L. Webster, 385–386. New York: Garland.

Schele, Linda. 1987. "Drawing of Inscriptions on Three Sides of Stela: CPN 18." Black ink on mylar. Schele Drawing Collection. Object no. SD-1012. www.collections.lacma.org.

Schele, Linda, and Mary Ellen Miller. 1986. *The Blood of Kings: Dynasty and Ritual in Maya Art*. New York: George Braziller.

Schnepel, Burkhard, and Eyal Ben-Ari. 2005. "Introduction: 'When Darkness Comes . . .': Steps Toward an Anthropology of the Night." *Paidemua: Mitteilungen zur Kulturkunde* Bd. 51: 153–164.

Segre, Erica, ed. 2020. *México Noir: Rethinking the Dark in Contemporary Writing and Visual Culture*. Bern, Switzerland: Peter Lang.

Seler, Eduard. 1902–1903. *Codex Vaticanus no. 3773 (Codex Vaticanus B): An Old Mexican Pictorial Manuscript in the Vatican Library, Published at the Expense of His Excellency the Duke of Loubat, Elucidated by Dr. Eduard Seler*. English edition by A. H. Keane. Facsimile. Berlin: T. and A. Constable.

Seler, Eduard. 1904. "The Bat God of the Maya Race." *Bureau of American Ethnology, Bulletin* 28: 231–241. Washington, DC.

Seler, Eduard. 1996. *Eduard Seler: Collected Works in Mesoamerican Linguistics and Archaeology*, vol. 5. Culver City, CA: Labyrinthos.

Sharpe, Ashley, Kitty F. Emery, Takeshi Inomata, Daniela Triadan, George D. Kamenov, and John Krigbaum. 2018. "Earliest Isotopic Evidence in the Maya

Region for Animal Management and Long-Distance Trade at the Site of Ceibal, Guatemala." *Proceedings of the National Academy of Sciences* 115 (14): 3605–3610.

Shaw, Robert. 2015. "Controlling Darkness: Self, Dark, and the Domestic Night." *Cultural Geographies* 22 (4): 585–600.

Smith, Monica L. 2012. "Seeking Abundance: Consumption as a Motivating Factor in Cities Past and Present." *Research in Economic Anthropology* 32: 27–51.

Smith, Monica L., ed. 2017a. *Abundance: The Archaeology of Plentitude*. Boulder: University Press of Colorado.

Smith, Monica L. 2017b. "The Archaeology of Abundance." In *Abundance: The Archaeology of Plentitude*, ed. Monica L Smith, 3–22. Boulder: University Press of Colorado.

Spitschan, Manuel, Geoffrey K. Aguirre, David H. Brainard, and Alison M. Sweeney. 2016. "Variation of Outdoor Illumination as a Function of Solar Elevation and Light Pollution." *Scientific Reports* 6: 26756.

Spitschan, Manuel, Geoffrey K. Aguirre, David H. Brainard, and Alison M. Sweeney. 2017. "Erratum: Variation of Outdoor Illumination as a Function of Solar Elevation and Light Pollution." *Scientific Reports* 6: 26756; doi: 10.1038/srep26756.

Steger, Brigitte, and Lodewijk Brunt, eds. 2003. *Night-time and Sleep in Asia and the West: Exploring the Dark Side of Life*. London: Routledge.

Strong, Meghan E. 2018. "A Great Secret of the West: Transformative Aspects of Artificial Light in New Kingdom Egypt." In *Archaeology of the Night: Life after Dark in the Ancient World*, ed. Nancy Gonlin and April Nowell, 249–264. Boulder: University Press of Colorado.

Strong, Meghan E. 2021. *Sacred Flames: The Power of Artificial Light in Ancient Egypt*. Cairo: American University in Cairo Press.

Stuart, David. 2003. "On the Paired Variants of TZ'AK." http://www.mesoweb.com/stuart/notes/tzak.pdf.

Stuart, David. 2007. "'White Owl Jaguar': A Tikal Royal Ancestor." https://decipherment.wordpress.com/2007/11/04/white-owl-jaguar-a-tikal-royal-ancestor/.

Stuart, David. 2021. "The *Wahys* of Witchcraft: Sorcery and Political Power among the Classic Maya." In *Sorcery in Mesoamerica*, ed. Jeremy D. Coltman and John D. Pohl, 179–205. Louisville: University Press of Colorado.

Thompson, J. Eric. 1930. *Ethnology of the Mayas of Southern and Central British Honduras*. Field Museum of Natural History, Publication 274, Anthropological Series 17, no. 2. Chicago: Field Museum Press.

Tiesler, Vera, and Andrea Cucina, eds. 2006. *Janaab' Pakal of Palenque: Reconstructing the Life and Death of a Maya Ruler*. Tucson: University of Arizona Press.

Time and Date AS. 2018. "Twilight, Dawn, and Dusk." https://www.timeanddate.com/astronomy/different-types-twilight.html.

Tozzer, Alfred M., and Glover M. Allen. 1910. *Animal Figures in the Maya Codices*. Papers of the Peabody Museum of American Archaeology and Ethnology, Harvard University 4, no. 3. Cambridge: Salem Press.

Turner, Victor. 1969. *The Ritual Process: Structure and Anti-Structure*. New York: Transaction.

Vail, Gabrielle, and Christine Hernández. 2013. *Re-Creating Primordial Time: Foundation Rituals and Mythology in the Postclassic Maya Codices*. Boulder: University Press of Colorado.

Winter, Irene J. 2007. "Representing Abundance: A Visual Dimension of the Agrarian State." In *Settlement and Society: Essays Dedicated to Robert McCormick Adams*, ed. Elizabeth C. Stone, 117–138. Los Angeles: Cotsen Institute of Archaeology.

1

Sociopolitical differences among the Classic Maya are examined in this chapter through the power of food and feasting, with a consideration of nocturnal practices. The Late Classic Maya (600–900 CE) of Mexico and Central America (see figure 0.1 and table 0.1) organized themselves into polities with divine rulers (Houston and Stuart 1996). One of the measures of inequality manifests in consumption practices. People in present and past societies consumed certain foods at particular times of the day, and while these foods symbolize quotidian practices, they are loaded with sociopolitical meanings: food functions as a vehicle beyond its nutritional value, and mealtimes or food events serve as occasions to reinforce culturally appropriate behaviors. Direct evidence for nighttime foodways remains sparse for the ancient Maya; this chapter is not about the certain kinds of foods consumed at night, but, as we discuss, nocturnal associations existed and held vital roles in society. We take a multi-pronged approach to integrate ethnographic, archaeological, and iconographic evidence with theory that proposes that nocturnal consumption was steeped in symbolism and a vehicle for social distinction and political power. We discuss food systems and foodways, not food as an item. The thread of the chapter is not night, darkness, or light per se but how the injection of those components into the overlapping and interacting spheres of politics, wealth, and theory relates to food systems—which in turn encompass and influence the management of

Classic Maya Social Distinctions and Political Power

Inserting a Nocturnal Dimension into the Hierarchy of Consumption

DAVID M. REED,
W. SCOTT ZELEZNIK,
AND NANCY GONLIN

DOI: 10.5876/9781646421879.c001

resources (including fuel for cooking food), pottery production, pottery use and purpose, and events that can come only as a result of the influence of night and the underlying support structures and systems.

In general, the term *food* refers to any nutritious substance that consists of calories, proteins, fats, minerals, or carbohydrates, which can be metabolized by people or animals to maintain life and growth. Because of food's vitalness for sustenance, it is a powerful semiotic device for other aspects of life. The foods people consume reflect not only available resources but also the cultures and circumstances in which they are eaten, that is, foodways. Food systems refer to the totality of foods available to a group, how foods are managed from production to consumption, and what resources are involved in the production of consumed plants and animals (hence, fuels, processing, agricultural technologies, transportation, storage, cooking, i.e., food economics). The study of culture-specific aspects of foods, such as the social rules about eating and the foods deemed appropriate for certain individuals or at particular times (i.e., the psychology of food choice), should include a nocturnal dimension.

Food acts as symbolic capital within the foodways that influence cultural identity. Anthropologists have long considered how food preparation, its distribution, and its consumption authenticate social order, cultural values, morals, and aesthetic beliefs. Members of society imbue kinds and qualities of food with moral, sentimental, religious, and health-related meanings (Ochs and Shohet 2006). Eating can be as much a political or religious act as a process of nourishment. Gastro-politics operate in the everyday processes of who produces food, who prepares food, and who is given precedence in the serving and eating of food (Appadurai 1981). Pierre Bourdieu (1984) noted that food habits have been associated with class distinctions in many societies. Consumption patterns, preferences, and practices are simultaneously classed and classifying, both reflecting and re-inscribing class distinctions. For example, David Reed and W. Scott Zeleznik (2016) have shown for the Late Classic Copan Maya of Honduras that food was a marker of social distinction through paleodietary reconstructions, production technologies, bioarchaeological analyses, and glyphic readings. Here, we explore how nighttime foodways contain aspects of social distinction for the Lowland Maya.

First, we briefly review the relationship among social status, wealth, and consumption and then move on to a consideration of the ethnohistoric and ethnographic records that reveals details about the nocturnal dimension of foodways. Feasting was integral to establishing and maintaining social status and is considered anew with the nocturnal dimension of this practice highlighted. Feasting and food in Classic Maya society are revealed through iconography and epigraphy as well as archaeological indicators of foodways. We arrive at an enhanced understanding of social distinctions and their expressions in Late Classic Maya society and contribute to a more inclusive view of the past.

SOCIAL STATUS, WEALTH, AND CONSUMPTION

When we speak of resources and power, we generally think of manipulating wealth—wealth as both tangible and non-tangible goods related to subsistence and some cultural idea of a standard of living. Wealth, as manifested in material objects, including food, forms the foundation of political and economic capital. It is a central and indispensable component of status and distinction. Elites (and others seeking to advance themselves) use many means at their disposal to maintain and further their interests by building other forms of capital (symbolic and cultural) that they then hope to translate into political and economic capital. Because food is such a vital part of human subsistence, it is a primary target for manipulation to build capital.

Practices (and the objects of these practices) are used to distinguish individuals and to build symbolic capital that may be directly or clearly related to economic capital. The degree to which elites can ultimately translate symbolic capital into socioeconomic capital is a measure of their long-term success. For example, deer hunting and consumption of deer meat were integral to elite identity. but in the interim and with the temporal and spatial fragments that we as archaeologists view, we need to understand the richness of the fields of symbolic capital that are constructed concordantly with those of economic capital because they do define social distinction. Moreover, material objects like food and their containers (e.g., ceramic plates and vessels) are frequently employed to further social and economic relationships through their exchange; they may stand for other, less tangible objects such as land or labor, or they may represent a more salient bond between individuals or social groups, with the tableaux themselves acting as portable proclamations of prestige and power (Reents-Budet 2006, 213). For example, examine the tributary scenes shown on vessels K1563, K1790, and K2800, wherein the delivery of tribute in the form of food appears to be taking place (Boot 2014; García Barrios 2017). These scenes record events while simultaneously acting as a visual and material tool for sociopolitical propaganda. We must remember that material objects are not magic wands themselves that confer status and power; the act of displaying, pre-stating, or giving objects to other individuals—investing in relationships—creates dominance relationships (Helms 1998; Mauss 1967; Sahlins 1972).

While elites vie for wealth and power, they must also act to maintain political and economic support among their constituents—individuals of lower status. Hence, they must maintain some ideological and cultural connections with the society at large. A feast is a celebration with foods, perhaps served only for the occasion, in unique and sacred containers (Fernandes 2006). Feasting, with its salient display and consumption of special and abundant foods, may have been one way to connect with supporters while simultaneously reinforcing status differences (Hayden and Gargett 1990). Indeed, Maya royalty were clearly attempting to accrue symbolic capital and transfer it into economic capital. However, this move gave them a tenuous hold on political power in the Classic period and may have ultimately backfired, leading to their demise (Webster 2002).

In our view, sociopolitical organization is a broad term referring to the conjunction of the structure of social and political power relationships in a society and the rules and norms that characterize them. Relative power can be distinguished by the level of resources and forms of sanctions brought to bear in a social relationship when a single individual's desires are perceived as increasingly contrary to another individual's desires (Giddens 1979, 93). Resources, including foods that were rare or difficult to acquire or that carried a heavy symbolic load, form the "basis or vehicle of power, comprising structures of domination" (1979, 69); they are "the media through which power is exercised, and structures of domination are reproduced" (1979, 91). Power is transformed into political power when it is made public, as in feasting—when it becomes of interest to the greater society. As a society-wide concern, it falls under the sanctions (rules and norms)[1] of the society, which inherently reinforce the particular forms of inequality in the society (e.g., economic or kinship-based). This position is not to say that all political power relationships are sanctioned by society, but, as society-wide concerns, they are judged in relationship to these norms and may derive authority from them. Eric Wolf (2001, 384–385) refers to this type of power as structural power.

For example, it was clear that elites at Copan were building symbolic capital in numerous ways. One way that stands out is how they seem to have had sole access to features associated with cultural and ritual knowledge. Glyphic representations, rare religious objects, and foods (cacao [McNeil 2006], deer meat [Looper 2019]) were significant in our analysis in distinguishing elites from commoners and other elites (Reed and Zeleznik 2016). The degree to which the use of these items was translated into political or economic capital is more difficult to assess (Lucero 2003).

DAVID M. REED, W. SCOTT ZELEZNIK, AND NANCY GONLIN

Food is both a symbol and an agent. Because everyone must eat, then what and how one eats, with whom one eats, how food is prepared, how food is served, who prepares the food, when food is prepared, and the timing of eating become symbolic and define social divisions. Every meal contains numerous messages. When and where one eats is as central as what one eats in presenting the message. A true measure of power is the ability to control the provision, production, and consumption of food. Food is a medium for distinction, connection, and exchange.

Erell Hubert (2016, 2) notes that studies of the engagement of people with the material world "have stressed . . . moving beyond purely symbolic or economic interpretations of material culture to exploring the way human experiences and the material world are mutually produced through interactions between people and things." People imbue and manipulate material items to create, idealize, negotiate, transform, and reinforce social concepts (Bourdieu 1984). Therefore, we suggest that food items and their associated objects reflect identity and participate in constructing identities through their use as well as the timing of their use (day or night).

Thus an array of agents acts together to create social identity and distinction in Maya society with respect to nocturnal foodways. These agents include the people or actors, the food, the acquisition of the food and its timing, the tools used in the preparation of the food (e.g., ritual manos and metates or ceremonial knives), objects used in the serving or presentation of food (e.g., pottery containers), the location of the food and its consumption, and the timing of associated events (day or night) (Ardren 2020).

Continuing further, if one posits that darkness, like light, is more than just a medium and that it evokes agency (Bille and Sørensen 2007), then darkness can also have a material dimension. From this position, one can investigate the ways darkness and nighttime are used socially regarding experiences and materiality in culturally specific ways. In a similar vein, the anthropology of luminosity includes consideration of the source of light as object and agent or, alternatively, the materiality of the lumen. Exploring how light (or the lack of light) is used in relation to social identity depends on the roles different modes of light (e.g., bright light, dim light) have, on the purpose that types of light (e.g., sunshine, firelight, or moonlight) are used to answer what, why, and how light and darkness are socially manifested and experienced (Bille and Sørensen 2007) (see chapters by Gonlin and Dixon-Hundredmark; Widmer; and Sheets and Thomason, this volume). The intersection of the consumption of food and light with social class and time of day reveals much about Classic Maya hierarchy.

ETHNOHISTORIC AND ETHNOGRAPHIC EVIDENCE FOR NOCTURNAL FOODWAYS

The following few examples show that context and the type of food, in addition to the timing of its acquisition and consumption, are indeed significant for the historical and contemporary Maya. Fray Diego de Landa notes that "*guisados*" (ragouts or stews) were consumed at night, and rules of hospitality indicate that guests were offered drinks during the day but meals at night: "In the morning they take their warm drink with pepper, as has been said, and in the daytime they drink the other cool drinks and eat their stews at night" (in Tozzer 1941, 91). While we do not know the ingredients of the stews or exactly what consisted of meals at night, a distinction between daytime and nighttime food is therefore posited.

Among ethnographies of the Maya, we can perceive a few of their long-held perspectives on the agency of the night. For instance, in his Yucatec Mayan Oral Literature, Allan Burns (1983, 31) tells that "Mayan people often refer to the events of the 'nighttime' world as the converse of those found in the 'daytime' world." Most relevant here, we are told that "the nighttime world is also the realm of deer and other animals[,] which are hunted." Charles Wisdom (1941, 71) recorded that deer were normally hunted at night by the Ch'orti' of Guatemala, after the proper ritual had been performed. Given the centrality of deer to the Maya, as evidenced by zoological remains and epigraphic illustrations (Looper 2019), we infer that this species retained some of its nocturnal symbolic aspect regardless of the event-specific symbolism embodied in its consumption (cf. Brown and Emery 2008).

Who Eats at Night?

Charles Wagley observed that the Mam Maya of Chimaltenango celebrate All Saints Day (November 1), when the souls of the dead are thought to return to Earth. Early in the morning, people go to the cemetery to place fruits, meat, tortillas, and flowers on the graves of deceased relatives. After about 10:00 p.m., the crowd at the cemetery disperses. The food and flowers are left for the dead, who are thought to return during the night to eat, drink, and pass the time (Wagley 1949). Here, the aspect of nocturnal timing is notable since the night is an ominous time for actions performed or imagined with the foods involved in an event.

Other beings consume at night as well. The contemporary and Classic Maya have *wahy*, animal companion spirits or co-essences. In the tales, myths, and dreams of the contemporary Maya of Zinacantán, Robert Laughlin and Carol

Karasik (1988, 66) report that "our animal souls need to be fed. Every night the hunters go out with lassos to catch the animals' food." The *wahy* glyph (Houston and Stuart 1989) is prominent in Maya epigraphy and iconography and is often featured on painted vessels from the Classic period indicating co-essences of supernaturals or humans.

While the preferred interpretation for the **WAY** glyph in the 1990s was as a reference to supernatural animal companion spirits, in 2005 David Stuart suggested that these horrific entities should be viewed as incarnations or personifications of particular ailments and diseases (Miller and Taube 1993, 72, 78; Stuart 2005; see also Helmke 2013; Helmke and Nielsen 2009; Stuart 2021). The *wahy* glyph is now interpreted as the embodiment of disease, witchcraft, demons, transforming wizards, animal spirits, and dark forces—all associated with the night (Looper 2019; Stuart 2015). The possessive constructions involving the term *wahy* in the Classic period should be seen as references to the supernatural entities, spiritual counterparts one could access in one's sleep, and embodiments of particularly malign ailments, wielded as curses. Maya rulers and elites made use of *wahyob* "as a way of terrorizing their enemies" (Looper 2019, 171).

Certain animals eat at night, such as deer (Looper 2019) and bats (Brady and Coltman 2016; Navarro and Arroyo-Cabrales 2013), and have been viewed as carrying disease. Bats, which are mainly active during twilight and at night, held strong symbolic meaning to the Maya. Bats were linked to night, darkness, and the underworld, not only because of their nocturnal behavior but because caves were considered portals to the underworld and a frequent location for ceremonies. Throughout the Maya area, bat imagery abounds, including molded figurines, figures on pottery, bat head glyphs, noble titles, the month name, *tzotz*, and place names, such as found in Copan's emblem glyph (figure 0.2). Bats were viewed as nocturnal counterparts of birds (especially hummingbirds), which were messengers of the gods and were likely *wahy* beings with ties to caves, sorcery, and darkness (see introduction, this volume, for more on deer and bats).

Nighttime Consumption of Food and Beverage

Humoral theory seems to have evolved independently in the Americas and the Old World (López Austin 1986), though there is debate about its origins (Foster 1994). In chapter 7 (this volume), Jan Olson discusses these competing reconstructions regarding ethnomedicine and agrees with the position of humoral theory that is in alignment with the duality of Mesoamerican ideology. The sweat bath, a structure and practice that dates back centuries, is a prime example of how hot and cold were (and continue to be) utilized by indigenous Mesoamerican groups.

Although classificatory schemes show geographical differences, some foods tend to be consistently classified as *hot*, while others are consistently classified as *cold*. Among the Zapotec, it has been noted that *cold* items make one ill if taken at night, while *hot* items do not. The digestive effects of food items, rather than intrinsic properties, may serve as the guide for classification. *Cold* items include plants such as avocados, raw sugarcane, and cactus leaves or game hunted in the *cold* forest, such as peccary (Looper 2019, 161). In contrast, *mezcal* (distilled from the blue agave) is considered *hot* (Castillo Cocom and Luviano Saúl 2012; Gonzalez 2001).

Among the Tzeltal Maya of Chiapas, Aguacatenango, Duane Metzger (1964) noted that two drinking cycles were observed for events. Both the ceremonial and informal drinking cycles lasted about eight hours. Both types of drinking cycles tended to occur in the daytime, although ceremonial drinking associated with certain circumstances like marriage ceremonies, curing rituals, and funerals often occurred at night. Again, a relationship exists between the time of day and how or what foods belong to the activity. Nocturnal associations are distinct from diurnal ones.

We have previously shown for the ancient Maya that food was indeed a marker of social distinction, whether for energy replenishment or ritual purposes, and we expand on previous work to begin to understand the sustenance of the Maya diet and how nocturnal eating was distinguished from consumption at other times of the day. Feasting may have been one such nighttime event. Stephen Houston and colleagues (2006, 104) suggested that "dining at royal courts of the Classic Maya was probably far more about abundance and variety of foods than about an avid, private savoring of taste. There is thus an almost transitional quality to what we know about Classic cuisine. It seemed to emphasize quantity over the presence of especially rare preparations." Feasting occurred among the Classic Maya and numerous other cultures (see Kassabaum 2019 for a recent article on detecting feasting in archaeological contexts).

ICONOGRAPHY AND EPIGRAPHY OF FOOD AND FEASTING

The topic of feasting plays a significant role in the archaeology of food (Hastorf 2017; Kassabaum 2019). There are tantalizing indications of foods and their uses in Classic Maya hieroglyphic texts. Pictorial scenes on panels,

FIGURE 1.1. *Photograph of the Piedras Negras Lintel 3, 782 CE, which discusses a feast (Morley 1937).*

monuments, murals, and painted ceramics (plates, bowls, and platters) have been found that identify foods consumed (e.g., tamales) and special activities encompassing their use. At least one of these has been read to have been a nighttime consumption. David Stuart (2004) identified glyphic elements likely representing eat, drink, and feast. Erik Boot (2005) suggested that there is a glyphic element standing for "meal."

Panel 3 at Piedras Negras, Guatemala (figure 1.1), was carved in 782 CE and presents a pictorial narrative centered on the life of the grandfather of the current ruler when he celebrated the completion of the first twenty years of his reign in 749 CE. The anniversary took place in the presence of former archrivals from Yaxchilan. A group of subsidiary lords are pictured sitting in front of a ruler on his throne and high-ranking members of his court, including his heir. According to the panel's main text, two days after the anniversary, the ruler of Piedras Negras danced at midnight and then drank "hot" or "inebriating" cacao (Tokovinine 2016, 15). Furthermore, similar texts have been noted as indicating that food and drink occur mostly as tokens of bounty, with the ruler receiving food but not offering it to others (Houston, Stuart, and Taube 2006).

The event depicted and described on Panel 3 includes consumption of a special pulque drink and is part of a larger set of rituals (Tokovinine 2016). The nighttime (*yik'in*) occurrence of consumption or the time when there was a notable transition of calendrical significance implies that special foods held symbolic aspects of either holy or hierarchical reaffirming rituals, the night, or specific

FIGURE 1.2. *Rollout photograph showing a palace scene from Guatemala with an offering of tamales below the ruler.* © *Museum Associates/Los Angeles County Museum of Art Conservation, by Yosi Pozeilov.*

calendric times. Pulque, the fermented sap of the agave plant, was a potentially exotic drink for some regions of the Classic Maya area, although it was common among the Aztecs (Evans 2005, 2013, 543). Textual evidence for its ritual use can be found at many sites. Examples from Copan include texts carved on altars. One such inscription states that the penultimate ruler of Copan "drank pulque." Another inscription on Altar U mentions that the same lord impersonated the god of drinking in the act of drinking pulque. A third example, on Altar K, reports pulque drinking by the twelfth king of Copan (Tokovinine 2016).

The formal display and consumption of drinks and food by Classic Maya royalty in visual and written narratives suggest that some of these events were feasts (figure 1.2). Drinking, apart from a natural and everyday activity of quenching thirst, is central to socializing and hospitality. Repeated, ritualized, and communal drinking often acts to mark similarities or differences between social groups. Alcoholic forms of drink are generally consumed for cultural (social) rather than physiological reasons. Furthermore, drinking, especially of alcohol, creates and builds social identity. It can be used to mark or affirm differences and similarities among groups, thus acting as a tool for maintaining and reinforcing group identities. The location and time of consumption become as central in defining identities as the beverage itself. Rules regarding drinking habits are a component of Bourdieu's habitus, just as objects are used to affirm social, personal, or group identities (Hayne 2016).

For example, the archaeobotanical remains from a Late Classic (750 and 805 CE) feasting deposit excavated at La Corona, Petén, Guatemala indicate that the feasts were made from both wild and domesticated ingredients, and some may have had medicinal properties (Cagnato 2018). This event appears to have included those of elite and lower social status, who came together to celebrate a special event near Structure 10 at La Corona. Elsewhere at the site, ceramic and animal bone feasting refuse was found. Polychrome pottery fragments with texts that include royal titles of La Corona and Calakmul personages imply that the area served as a venue for feasting (Baron 2013, 2016).

Another example of feasting comes from excavations of agricultural areas near Joya de Cerén, where intensive manioc cultivation in elevated planting beds was uncovered (Dixon 2013). From evidence recovered from Structure 10, the feasting building, Payson Sheets and colleagues (2012) suggest that fermented manioc beer was consumed during a harvest feast at the time of the Loma Caldera eruption that most likely occurred in the evening, before residents had gone to bed.

The discard patterns of specific vessels, such as vases for cacao drinks (e.g., Lucero 2001; however, see Loughmiller-Cardinal 2019), platters for tamales, small bowls for holding *atole*, and similar pottery forms, as well as numerous grinding stones, serve archaeologists in identifying areas used for the preparation of festival foods. It has been suggested that a signature set of three polychrome ceramic shapes was essential to feasts and ritual events, largely for presentation but not preparation. This ternary assemblage included the *uchib* (drinking cup), the *lak* (shallow dish), and the *hawate* (tripod plate) (Foias 2007). Remains of similar feasting wares, culinary sets, and other feasting assemblages appear in epigraphic scenes and have been found in deposits at Altun Ha, Buenavista del Cayo, Calakmul, Cerén, Copan, La Corona, Piedras Negras, and elsewhere (Bray 2003; Cagnato 2018; Farahani et al. 2017; Hayden 2014; Hendon 2003; Muñoz 2006; Pollock 2015; Reents-Budet 2000, 2006; Reents-Budet et al. 2000, 2010; Ting, Graham, and Martinón-Torres 2014). Cross-culturally, feasting is observed ethnographically and archaeologically across the globe (Bray 2003; Dietler and Hayden 2001; Hayden and Villenueve 2011; Knudson, Gardella, and Yaeger 2012; LeCount 2001; Staller and Carrasco 2010).

Dogs were one of the most important ritual animals of the ancient Maya. Dogs, with their association with death and the journey to the underworld, have been linked to feasting activities through archaeological evidence and paleodietary isotopic analysis (Koželsky 2005; Shaw 1991; White et al. 2001). As inferred from the distribution of dog remains in elite contexts at sites such as Kaminaljuyu, they were likely valued as a status resource and sometimes used for food, particularly during feasts and funerals (Emery et al. 2013). However, dogs were not commonly used by the ancient Maya as a food source, as determined by zooarchaeological analysis by Petra Cunningham-Smith and colleagues (2020).

Late Classic feasting references imply a vital role for food display and sharing. Feasting acted as a statement about political and social rank and of establishing or maintaining social and political networks. Houston and colleagues (2006, 128) write:

> It has become a commonplace [belief] among scholars that the Maya practiced formal commensality . . . that involved [ingestion by] relatively large numbers of people outside the immediate domestic unit and sets of formal behaviors beyond the scope and scale of ordinary repasts. Specifically, most scholars see evidence for redistributive or Dietler's "patron-role" feasts (1996, 2001), in that such repasts would have been expected as ways of gratifying retainers and subjects or as a means of recruiting labor for civic works (Reents-Budet 2000).

Julia Hendon (2003, 207) argues that although "feasting cycles . . . would have been a focus of elite energy, the organization of Maya social groups into Houses argues for the importance of feasts that cross-cut status lines." Furthermore, feasts are events used to create and maintain social relations (Kan 1989), whereby hosts repay social debts and create new ones. Furthermore, feasts act as vehicles for the exchange of material goods (Mauss 1967; Thomas 1991). Alfred M. Tozzer (1941, 92) notes that Maya nobles "at the end of the repast, were accustomed to give a manta to each [guest] to wear, and a little stand and vessel, as beautiful as possible." Reciprocity does not necessarily put people on an even plane but may serve to palliate, even as it reinforces, a rigid stratification (Keating 2000).

Beyond the food itself, items considered to have been under elite control formed a part of a political economy based on prestige goods and were needed in support of these events. Ritualized exchange of pottery, prestige goods, and certain foods or drinks during feasting events, weddings, accession ceremonies, politico-religious celebrations, or calendrical observances may have served to symbolize and maintain social ties, create social indebtedness, secure alliances, reinforce patron-client relationships, validate hierarchies, consolidate support, or amass tribute. Thus these items act as sociopolitical currency. Surely, some of these auspicious events occurred during the night, which further enhanced their sacredness and inscribed inequality on the event.

CONCLUSIONS

By attaching materialistic and agency elements to nighttime food, associated items (such as serving vessels) and events provide a framework for understanding how aspects of Classic Maya social hierarchy were created, maintained, and reinforced. Food and other substances (e.g., tobacco [Loughmiller-Cardinal and Eppich 2019]) and their participation in events signified and symbolized relationships beyond their nutritional or sustenance values, often with ties to the night, darkness, and the underworld. Social relations are expressed and produced in the form of structured occasions of commensality. Through its consumption in a communal context (feasting), food is transformed into social capital. Goods and wealth are therefore reincorporated into the social system as signifiers of specific interpersonal relationships and obligations (Gell 1986). Although Mesoamericans shared many foodways, such as the obvious emphasis on maize, beans, and squash, we caution that given the vast array of cultures and chronological depth of this culture area, one must analyze foodways within a specific cultural and chronological context as accurately as possible. In particular, incorporating the aspects of night and darkness enriches our understanding of lifeways by identifying neglected dimensions of analysis.

Food played a central role in social distinction among the ancient Maya. The kinds of food, their quantity, the location, and the timing of their presentation and consumption are all interlinked to create and reinforce social distinction and hierarchy. Foods that likely held at least partial nocturnal connotations included deer, puma, panther, "cold" forest animals, pulque, fermented honey, manioc beer (alcoholic beverages), exotic cacao mixtures, and avocados. Several types of events, such as funerals, marriages, and royal anniversaries, and attendant items, such as commemorative pottery or specially decorated serving vessels, were imbued with nocturnal aspects due to the timing of their consumption or use and occurrences.

In closing, we leave you to consider many directions for future research. Our imagination should not be limited to envisioning daily practices but extended to include nightly practices and those that took place in the dark. Clues to nocturnal feasting should be explicitly sought, with the material record open to reinterpretation. Linda Schele (Schele and Freidel 1990) liked to speculate about theatrical aspects of royal proceedings—did any of them contain a required nocturnal or dark aspect? Some ceremonial pottery appears to have been produced for an event and then disposed of, as described for La Corona deposits. There may be similar deposits elsewhere for which we can discern their purpose. A focus on the night has furthered our understanding of the

Classic Maya, and we hope to see future research that incorporates this component of the past.

ACKNOWLEDGMENTS

Portions of this research were undertaken by the senior author while at Dumbarton Oaks on a Summer Fellowship in 2015. Gratitude is due to Bellevue College for its support of Nan Gonlin's research. Unfortunately, our coauthor, friend, and colleague W. Scott Zeleznik passed before the publication of this volume. We are indebted to him for his contribution and insightfulness into ancient Maya sociopolitical structure and its anthropological underpinnings.

NOTE

1. Rules are codified, explicit, or announced actions, while norms are accepted standards that may not be expressed as laws.

REFERENCES

Appadurai, Arjun. 1981. "Gastro-Politics in Hindu South Asia." *American Ethnologist* 8: 494–511.

Ardren, Traci, ed. 2020. *Her Cup for Sweet Cacao: Food in Ancient Maya Society*. Austin: University of Texas Press.

Baron, Joanne Parsley. 2013. "Patrons of La Corona: Deities and Power in a Classic Maya Community." PhD dissertation, University of Pennsylvania, Philadelphia.

Baron, Joanne Parsley. 2016. *Patron Gods and Patron Lords*. Boulder: University Press of Colorado.

Bille, Mikkel, and Tim Flohr Sørensen. 2007. "An Anthropology of Luminosity: The Agency of Light." *Journal of Material Culture* 12 (3): 263–284.

Boot, Erik. 2005. "A Vessel Fit for a Feast: Kerr no. 3091." Unpublished manuscript. http://www.mayavase.com/FitforaFeast.pdf.

Boot, Erik. 2014. "'Out of Order!' Or Are They? A Textual and Visual Analysis of Two Dedicatory Texts on Classic Maya Ceramics." *PARI Journal* 15 (2): 15–37.

Bourdieu, Pierre, trans. Richard Nice. 1984. *Distinction: A Social Critique of the Judgement of Taste*. Cambridge, MA: Harvard University Press.

Brady, James E., and Jeremy D. Coltman. 2016. "Bats and the Camazotz: Correcting a Century of Mistaken Identity." *Latin American Antiquity* 27 (2): 227–237.

Bray, Tamara L., ed. 2003. *The Archaeology and Politics of Food and Feasting in Early States and Empires*. New York: Kluwer Academic/Plenum.

Brown, Linda, and Kitty Emery. 2008. "Negotiations with the Animate Forest: Hunting Shrines in the Guatemalan Highlands." *Journal of Archaeological Method and Theory* 15 (4): 300–337.

Burns, Allan Frank. 1983. *Epoch of Miracles: Oral Literature of the Yucatec Maya*. Austin: University of Texas Press.

Cagnato, Clarissa. 2018. "Sweet, Weedy, and Wild: Macrobotanical Remains from a Late Classic (8th Century AD) Feasting Deposit Discovered at La Corona, an Ancient Maya Settlement." *Vegetation History and Archaeobotany* 27 (1): 241–252.

Castillo Cocom, Juan A., and Ríos Luviano Saúl. 2012. "Hot and Cold Politics of Indigenous Identity: Legal Indians, Cannibals, Words, More Words, More Food." *Anthropological Quarterly* 85 (1): 229–256.

Cunningham-Smith, Petra, Ashley E. Sharpe, Arianne Boileau, Erin Kennedy Thornton, and Kitty F. Emery. 2020. "Food, Friend, or Offering: Exploring the Role of Maya Dogs in the Zooarchaeological Record." In *Her Cup for Sweet Cacao: Food in Ancient Maya Society*, ed. Traci Ardren, 161–187. Austin: University of Texas Press.

Dietler, Michael. 1996. "Feasts and Commensal Politics in the Political Economy: Food, Power, and Status in Prehistoric Europe." In *Food and the Status Quest: An Interdisciplinary Perspective*, ed. Polly Wiessner and Wulf Schiefenhövel, 87–125. Oxford: Berghahn Books.

Dietler, Michael. 2001. "Theorizing the Feast: Rituals of Consumption, Commensal Politics, and Power in African Contexts." In *Feasts: Archaeological and Ethnographic Perspectives on Food, Politics, and Power*, ed. Michael Dietler and Brian Hayden, 65–114. Washington, DC: Smithsonian Institution Press.

Dietler, Michael, and Brian Hayden, eds. 2001. *Feasts: Archaeological and Ethnographic Perspectives on Food, Politics, and Power*. Washington, DC: Smithsonian Institution Press.

Dixon, Christine C. 2013. "Farming and Power: Classic Period Maya Manioc and Maize Cultivation at Cerén, El Salvador." PhD dissertation, University of Colorado, Boulder.

Emery, Kitty E., Erin Kennedy Thornton, Nicole R. Cannarozzi, Stephen Houston, and Héctor Escobedo. 2013. "Archaeological Animals of the Southern Maya Highlands: Zooarchaeology of Kaminaljuyu." In *The Archaeology of Mesoamerican Animals*, ed. Christopher M. Götz and Kitty E. Emery, 381–416. Atlanta: Lockwood.

Evans, Susan Toby. 2005. "Men, Women, and Maguey." In *Settlement, Subsistence, and Social Complexity*, ed. Richard E. Blanton, 198–228. Los Angeles: Cotsen Institute of Archaeology, University of California.

Evans, Susan Toby. 2013. *Ancient Mexico and Central America: Archaeology and Culture History*, 3rd ed. London: Thames & Hudson.

Farahani, Alan, Katherine L. Chiou, Rob Q. Cuthrell, Anna Harkey, Shanti Morell-Hart, Christine A. Hastorf, and Payson D. Sheets. 2017. "Exploring Culinary Practices through GIS Modeling at Joya de Cerén, El Salvador." In *Social Perspectives on Ancient Lives from Paleoethnobotanical Data*, ed. Matthew P. Sayre and Maria C. Bruno, 101–120. Cham, Switzerland: Springer International Publishing.

Fernandes, Luci. 2006. "Food." In *Encyclopedia of Anthropology*, ed. H. James Birx, 979–980. Thousand Oaks, CA: Sage.

Foias, Antonia E. 2007. "Ritual, Politics, and Pottery Economies in the Classic Maya Southern Lowlands." In *Mesoamerican Ritual Economy: Archaeological and Ethnological Perspectives*, ed. E. Christian Wells and Karla L. Davis-Salazar, 167–194. Boulder: University Press of Colorado.

Foster, George McClelland. 1994. *Hippocrates' Latin American Legacy: Humoral Medicine in the New World*. Lausanne, Switzerland: Gordon and Breach.

García Barrios, Ana. 2017. "The Social Context of Food at Calakmul, Campeche, Mexico: Images Painted on the Pyramid of Chiik Nahb'." In *Constructing Power and Place in Mesoamerica: Pre-Hispanic Paintings from Three Regions*, ed. Merideth Paxton and Leticia Staines Cicero, 171–190. Albuquerque: University of New Mexico Press.

Gell, Alfred. 1986. "Newcomers to the World of Goods: Consumption among the Muria Gonds." In *The Social Life of Things: Commodities in Cultural Perspective*, ed. Arjun Appadurai, 110–138. Cambridge: Cambridge University Press.

Giddens, Anthony. 1979. *Central Problems in Social Theory: Action, Structure, and Contradiction in Social Analysis*. Berkeley: University of California Press.

González, Roberto Jesús. 2001. *Zapotec Science: Farming and Food in the Northern Sierra of Oaxaca*. Austin: University of Texas Press.

Hastorf, Christine A. 2017. *The Social Archaeology of Food: Thinking about Eating from Prehistory to the Present*. Cambridge: Cambridge University Press.

Hayden, Brian. 2014. *The Power of Feasts: From Prehistory to the Present*. Cambridge: Cambridge University Press.

Hayden, Brian, and Rob Gargett. 1990. "Big Man, Big Heart? A Mesoamerican View of the Emergence of Complex Society." *Ancient Mesoamerica* 1 (1): 3–20.

Hayden, Brian, and Suzanne Villenueve. 2011. "A Century of Feasting Studies." *Annual Review of Anthropology* 40: 433–439.

Hayne, Jeremy. 2016. "Drinking Identities and Changing Ideologies in Iron Age Sardinia." In *Creating Material Worlds: The Uses of Identity in Archaeology*, ed. Elizabeth Pierce, Anthony Russell, Adrián Maldonado, and Louisa Campbell, 107–134. Oxford: Oxbow Books.

Helmke, Christophe. 2013. "Mesoamerican Lexical Calques in Ancient Maya Writing and Imagery." *PARI Journal* 14 (2): 1–15.

Helmke, Christophe, and Jesper Nielsen. 2009. "Hidden Identity and Power in Ancient Mesoamerica: Supernatural Alter Egos as Personified Diseases." *Acta Americana* 17 (2): 49–98.

Helms, Mary W. 1998. *Access to Origins: Affines, Ancestors, and Aristocrats.* Austin: University of Texas Press.

Hendon, Julia A. 2003. "Feasting at Home: Community and House Solidarity among the Maya of Southeastern Mesoamerica." In *The Archaeology and Politics of Food and Feasting in Early States and Empires*, ed. Tamara L. Bray, 203–233. New York: Kluwer Academic/Plenum.

Houston, Stephen D., and David Stuart. 1989. *The Way Glyph: Evidence for "Co-Essences" among the Classic Maya.* Research Reports on Ancient Maya Writing 30. Washington, DC: Center for Maya Research.

Houston, Stephen D., and David Stuart. 1996. "Of Gods, Glyphs, and Kings: Divinity and Rulership among the Classic Maya." *Antiquity* 70: 289–312.

Houston, Stephen, David Stuart, and Karl A. Taube. 2006. "Ingestion." In *The Memory of Bones: Body, Being, and Experience among the Classic Maya*, by Stephen Houston, David Stuart, and Karl A. Taube, 102–133. Austin: University of Texas Press.

Hubert, Erell. 2016. "Figuring Identity in Everyday Life." *Journal of Anthropological Archaeology* 44: 1–13.

Kan, Sergei. 1989. *Symbolic Immortality: The Tlingit Potlatch of the Nineteenth Century.* Washington, DC: Smithsonian Institution Press.

Kassabaum, Megan C. 2019. "A Method for Conceptualizing and Classifying Feasting: Interpreting Communal Consumption in the Archaeological Record." *American Antiquity* 84 (4): 610–631.

Keating, Elizabeth. 2000. "Moments of Hierarchy: Constructing Social Stratification by Means of Language, Food, Space, and the Body in Pohnpei, Micronesia." *American Anthropologist* 102 (2): 303–320.

Knudson, Kelly J., Kristin R. Gardella, and Jason Yaeger. 2012. "Provisioning Inka Feasts at Tiwanaku, Bolivia: The Geographic Origins of Camelids in the Pumapunku Complex." *Journal of Archaeological Science* 39 (2): 479–491.

Koželsky, Kristin L. 2005. "Identifying Social Drama in the Maya Region; Fauna from the Lagartero Basurero, Chiapas, Mexico." Master's thesis, Florida State University, Tallahassee.

Laughlin, Robert M., and Carol Karasik, transl. 1988. *The People of the Bat: Mayan Tales and Dreams from Zinacantán.* Washington, DC: Smithsonian Institution Press.

LeCount, Lisa J. 2001. "Like Water for Chocolate: Feasting and Political Ritual among the Late Classic Maya at Xunantunich, Belize." *American Anthropologist* 103 (4): 935–953.

Looper, Matthew. 2019. *The Beast Between: Deer in Maya Art and Culture*. Austin: University of Texas Press.

López Austin, Alfredo. 1986. "La pólemica sobre la dicotomía fríocalor." In *La medicina invisible: Introduccíon al estudio de la medicina tradicional de México*, ed. Xavier Lozoya and Carlos Zolla, 73–90. Mexico City: Folios Ediciones, S.A.

Loughmiller-Cardinal, Jennifer. 2019. "Distinguishing the Uses, Functions, and Purposes of Classic Maya 'Chocolate' Containers: Not All Cups Are for Drinking." *Ancient Mesoamerica* 30 (1): 13–30.

Loughmiller-Cardinal, Jennifer A., and Keith Eppich, eds. 2019. *Breath and Smoke: Tobacco Use among the Maya*. Albuquerque: University of New Mexico Press.

Lucero, Lisa J. 2003. "The Politics of Ritual: The Emergence of Classic Maya Rulers." *Current Anthropology* 44 (4): 523–558.

Mauss, Marcel. 1967. *The Gift: Forms and Functions of Exchange in Archaic Societies*. New York: Norton.

McNeil, Cameron L., ed. 2006. *Chocolate in Mesoamerica: A Cultural History of Cacao*. Gainesville: University Press of Florida.

Metzger, Duane. 1964. "Interpretations of Drinking Performances in Aguacatenango." PhD dissertation, University of Chicago, IL.

Miller, Mary, and Karl Taube. 1993. *The Gods and Symbols of Mexico and the Maya*. New York: Thames and Hudson.

Morley, Sylvanus Griswold. 1937. "Plate 146: Piedras Negras, Lintel 3." In *The Inscriptions of Peten*, vol. 5, part 1: *Plates*. Publication 437. Washington, DC: Carnegie Institution of Washington.

Muñoz, Arturo René. 2006. "Power, Production, and Prestige: Technological Change in the Late Classic Ceramics of Piedras Negras, Guatemala." PhD dissertation, University of Arizona, Tucson.

Navarro, Laura, and Joaquín Arroyo-Cabrales. 2013. "Bats in Ancient Mesoamerica." In *The Archaeology of Mesoamerican Animals*, ed. Christopher M. Götz and Kitty E. Emery, 583–605. Atlanta: Lockwood.

Ochs, Elinor, and Merav Shohet. 2006. "The Cultural Structuring of Mealtime Socialization." *New Directions for Child and Adolescent Development* 111: 35–49.

Pollock, Susan, ed. 2015. *Between Feasts and Daily Meals: Towards an Archaeology of Commensal Spaces*. Berlin: Exzellenzcluster Topoi der Freien Universität Berlin und der Humboldt–Universität zu Berlin.

Reed, David M., and W. Scott Zeleznik. 2016. "The Maya in the Middle: An Analysis of Sub-Royal Archaeology at Copan, Honduras." In *Human Adaptation in Ancient Mesoamerica*, ed. Nancy Gonlin and Kirk D. French, 175–208. Boulder: University Press of Colorado.

Reents-Budet, Dorie J. 2000. "Feasting among the Classic Maya: Evidence from the Pictorial Ceramics." In *The Maya Vase Book*. vol. 6, ed. Justin Kerr, 1022–1037. New York: Kerr Associates.

Reents-Budet, Dorie. 2006. "The Social Context of *Kakaw* Drinking among the Ancient Maya." In *Chocolate in Mesoamerica: A Cultural History of Cacao*, ed. Cameron L. McNeil, 202–223. Gainesville: University Press of Florida.

Reents-Budet, Dorie, Ronald L. Bishop, Jennifer T. Taschek, and Joseph W. Ball. 2000. "OUT OF THE PALACE DUMPS: Ceramic Production and Use at Buenavista Del Cayo." *Ancient Mesoamerica* 11 (1): 99–121.

Reents-Budet, Dorie, Sylviane Boucher Le Landais, Ronald L. Bishop, and M. James Blackman. 2010. "Codex-Style Ceramics: New Data Concerning Patterns of Production and Distribution." Paper presented at the 24th Symposium of Archaeological Investigations in Guatemala. Museo Nacional de Arqueología e Etnología, Guatemala City, July 19–24.

Sahlins, Marshall. 1972. *Stone Age Economics*. Chicago: Aldine-Atherton.

Schele, Linda, and David Freidel. 1990. *A Forest of Kings: The Untold Story of the Ancient Maya*. New York: William Morrow.

Shaw, Leslie Carol. 1991. "The Articulation of Social Inequality and Faunal Resource Use in the Preclassic Community of Colha, Northern Belize." PhD dissertation, University of Massachusetts, Amherst.

Sheets, Payson, David Lentz, Dolores Piperno, John Jones, Christine Dixon, George Maloof, and Angela Hood. 2012. "Ancient Manioc Agriculture South of the Ceren Village, El Salvador." *Latin American Antiquity* 23 (3): 259–281.

Staller, John Edward, and Michael Carrasco, eds. 2010. *Pre-Columbian Foodways: Interdisciplinary Approaches to Food, Culture, and Markets in Ancient Mesoamerica*. New York: Springer.

Stuart, David. 2004. *Understanding Early Classic Copan*. Philadelphia: Museum of Archaeology and Anthropology, University of Pennsylvania.

Stuart, David. 2005. "The Way Beings." In *Sourcebook for the 29th Maya Hieroglyph Forum*, ed. David Stuart, 160–165. Austin: Department of Art and Art History, University of Texas.

Stuart, David. 2015. "Birth of the Sun: Notes on the Ancient Maya Winter Solstice." On Maya Decipherment. https://mayadecipherment.com/2015/12/29/birth-of-the -sun-notes-on-the-ancient-maya-winter-solstice/.

Stuart, David. 2021. "The *Wahys* of Witchcraft: Sorcery and Political Power among the Classic Maya." In *Sorcery in Mesoamerica*, ed. Jeremy D. Coltman and John D. Pohl, 179–205. Louisville: University Press of Colorado.

Thomas, Nicholas. 1991. *Entangled Objects: Exchange, Material Culture, and Colonialism in the Pacific*. Cambridge, MA: Harvard University Press.

Ting, Carmen, Elizabeth Graham, and Marcos Martinón-Torres. 2014. "Molding the 'Collapse': Technological Analysis of the Terminal Classic Molded-Carved Vases from Altun Ha, Belize." In *Craft and Science: International Perspectives on Archaeological Ceramics*, ed. Marcos Martinón-Torres, 53–63. UCL Qatar Series in Archaeology and Cultural Heritage. Doha, Qatar: Bloomsbury Qatar Foundation.

Tokovinine, Alexandre. 2016. "'It Is His Image with Pulque': Drinks, Gifts, and Political Networking in Classic Maya Texts and Images." *Ancient Mesoamerica* 27 (1): 13–29.

Tozzer, Alfred M., transl. 1941. *Landa's Relación de las Cosas de Yucatan*. Papers of the Peabody Museum of American Archaeology and Ethnology, Harvard University, 18. Cambridge, MA: Harvard University Press.

Wagley, Charles W. 1949. *The Social and Religious Life of a Guatemalan*. Menasha, WI: American Anthropological Association.

Webster, David. 2002. *The Fall of the Ancient Maya: Solving the Mystery of the Maya Collapse*. London: Thames & Hudson.

White, Christine D., Mary E.D. Pohl, Henry P. Schwartz, and Fred J. Longstaffe. 2001. "Isotopic Evidence for Maya Patterns of Deer and Dog Use at Preclassic Colha." *Journal of Archaeological Science* 28 (1): 89–107.

Wisdom, Charles. 1941. *The Chorti Indians of Guatemala*. Chicago: University of Chicago Press.

Wolf, Eric R. 2001. *Pathways of Power: Building an Anthropology of the Modern World*. Berkeley: University of California Press.

2

The ancient Mesoamerican landscape has been extensively researched archaeologically, with the field of paleoethnobotany allowing for a greater understanding of what plants ancient people valued agriculturally and in their economic, ritual, medicinal, and other *daily* practices. But what about *nightly* practices? How has the nighttime left its mark on the ethnographic, ethnohistoric, and paleoethnobotanical records of Mesoamerica? The ancient Maya (see figure 0.1 and table 0.1) associated much of their environment with night-related practices, or *nightways*. In this chapter, I explore the connections between ethnobotanical studies and archaeobotanical investigations. Ethnobotanical data can be used to help illuminate how the ancient inhabitants interacted with and viewed their nocturnal environment. Such interactions will be explored through the rituals, cultural practices, medicinal applications, Mayan linguistic connections, and natural, nocturnal phenomena of the landscape.[1] These emphases all lead to addressing the inquiry of what the plants of the nighttime had to offer ancient Mesoamericans.

LINGUISTIC CONNECTIONS TO NOCTURNAL PLANTS

Names and characteristics of some plants in Mesoamerica share many linguistic connections with the night and darkness. Some of these names are in

Mesoamerican Plants of the Night

Ethnographic and Paleoethnobotanical Perspectives

Venicia Slotten

DOI: 10.5876/9781646421879.c002

Spanish, while others are in Mayan languages, such as Yucatec, Lakantun, Ch'orti', and Itzaj. The study of a culture's local names for its flora can reveal culture-specific concepts of cosmology, life, illnesses, and more. In these cases, how the flora were related to nightly activities and concepts becomes clearer when the terms used to describe them are assessed. Often, plants used to treat certain conditions incorporate the name of that illness into the common name.

Many names refer to the characteristic that most of the plants I discuss in this section share: they bloom when it is dark, most often during the night. Typically, flowers open up during the day to take advantage of diurnal insects that can aid in transferring pollen to another plant. Alternatively, plants that bloom as darkness descends have evolved to successfully attract nocturnal pollinators such as moths or bats and therefore do not need bright colors to attract insects during the daytime. This rhythm means they usually have a strong fragrance to attract pollinators and white-colored flowers that reflect well in the moonlight, subsequently illuminating in the dark—characteristics that have typically evolved to attract birds, bees, and other insects. Many of the species have white petals, whose bright luminous reflections of the moonlight attract night pollinators and help the plant reproduce. However, it wasn't just the local fauna that paid attention to the unique characteristics these plants share and exhibit more profoundly in the dark of night. Many ancient Mesoamericans referred to the plants accordingly and even utilized them in manners associating them with their nightly appearance. Even though many of the names are in the Spanish language, all of them have been recorded in ethnographic studies of indigenous populations of the region and are likely translated from Mayan languages.

For example, *Ipomoea alba* L., a variety of morning glory, has Spanish names related to the night such as "flor de luna," "luna blanca," and "galán noche" (Williams 1981), which respectively translate to "moon-flower," "white moon," and "nightlong." This vine often resides in moist thickets, secondary growth, and rocky banks (Standley and Williams 1970). Mayan terms for this species include *huchuk ts'aan* (hiccup vine), *naxh* (hiccup), *haapolin* (of water origin), and *xutub* or *sutup* (something that spirals) (Austin 2002). The flor de luna has a strong fragrance, contrary to most other night-blooming species, but more important, it has large flowers that open quickly in the evening and stay open throughout the night, attracting large nocturnal moths. Its names not only refer to *I. alba*'s peak activity during the evening but also to the fact that its petals form a round shape resembling the moon in the night sky. It may not be night-related, but the plant also had a significant role in ancient

Mesoamerican production of rubber; its milky sap was combined with *Castilla elastica* Cerv. (*kikche*) to coagulate latex and enhance the elasticity of rubber balls. This process is still practiced in Chiapas, Mexico, and was recorded by the Spaniards in the sixteenth century (Hosler, Burkett, and Tarkanian 1999). *I. alba* and *C. elastica* are often found together, with the *I. alba* vine twining on the tree for support. Other related species (such as *I. tricolor*, what is known as *tlitliltzin* in Nahuatl) were used in rituals by the Aztecs and Zapotecs for their psychoactive properties (Carod-Artal 2015; Schultes 1941).

Two vines, *Sarcostemma clausum* (Jacq.) Schult. and *Clematis dioica* L., and a small shrub *Palicourea tetragona* (Donn.Sm.) C.M. Taylor (formerly *Psychotria chiapensis* Standl.) have in common the Spanish name "*dama de noche*," or night-lady, as well as night bloom (Balick, Nee, and Atha 2000; Williams 1981). All three of these plants have white flowers that specifically bloom at night, but none as large as *I. alba* and its luminous moon-shaped petal arrangement. Both *S. clausum* and *C. dioica* are vines abundant along streams and in wet to dry thickets, open forests, and second growth (Standley and Steyermark 1946–1976; Standley and Williams 1969), whereas *P. tetragona* is a small shrub common in the wet lowlands (Standley and Williams 1975). Some of these plants have been found archaeobotanically as seeds or charcoal at sites such as Cobá, Mexico, Cihuatán, El Salvador, and Tikal, Guatemala (Beltran Frias 1987; Lentz, Dunning, and Scarborough 2015; Miksicek 1988). Many researchers recorded them with the suggestion that they were utilized medicinally, as discussed below.

Another tropical plant, *Cestrum nocturnum* L., has intriguing linguistic ties to the night in several languages. In English, two common names for this plant are night jessamine and queen of the night. The Spanish common name is *huele de noche* (smell of the night), a name indicating that *C. nocturnum* is especially aromatic during the nighttime. This woody shrub has slender, tubular greenish-white flowers and round berries favored by birds. It is common in moist forests and disturbed areas (Gentry and Standley 1974). The blossoms are in fact quite fragrant, releasing a sweet perfume mostly at night; however, the fruit is poisonous to humans. The Itzaj Mayan term for this plant, *ix-'aka~jaway*, means "contagious night." This moniker likely refers to both the toxicity of the plants' fruits and the fact that the flowers' lingering scent at night can cause headaches, nausea, respiratory problems, and sneezing in humans (Atran, Ximena, and Ucan Ek' 2004). The Yucatec Maya used *C. nocturnum* in sweat baths and as a treatment for "night sweats" (Shaista and Amrita 2016) (see chapters 6 and 7, this volume, for more on sweat baths).

Another example of a white-flowered Mesoamerican herb with linguistic connections to the night is *Blechum pyramidatum* (Lam.) Urb., whose Spanish name *"yierba-de-noche"* translates to "weed of the night" or "night-herb." Mayan terms for the plant include *x akab xiu* and *xaka xiu* (Kunow 2012). It is a small vine that blooms white flowers in April and May in damp or wet thickets, mixed forest, and pastures and along streams (Standley, Williams, and Gibson 1974). Not only is this plant's name night-related, but so is its medicinal use. The Maya in the Yucatan use it to treat night sweats or night fever by washing a child with its leaves that have been boiled in water (Kunow 2012).

Mexican marigold, or *Tagetes erecta* L., is a widely cultivated flowering plant in the Asteraceae family from the Americas that is common in moist or dry thickets and open fields (Nash and Williams 1976). The Itzaj name for the species, *ix-tupuj*, translates to say that the flower had the ability to "extinguish the moon" or to "illuminate." The flower petals are so colorful that they are said to resemble flames so bright that they could compete with the moonlight. So, it is little wonder that its name reflects this characteristic. The ancient Aztecs gathered this wild plant and cultivated it for medicinal applications, as a ceremonial incense, and for decorative purposes. Aztec nobles showcased the species in their elaborate gardens and possibly considered it a sacred or rare plant (Granziera 2001). Both Nahua and Ch'orti' speakers strongly associate the flower with the dead and believe it can dispel contaminations of the body after one attends a funeral (Kufer 2009). Charred achenes of *Tagetes erecta* have been recovered from an early dry-cave site in Guerrero, Mexico, called Oxtotitlan. Numerous Olmec paintings are found in the cave, and the plant material recovered may have been associated with ritual activity related to those paintings. Perhaps the vivid colors of the flowers led to the plant's incorporation into ritual activities in dark caves such as at Oxtotitlan, making use of the petals' luminous qualities in an otherwise darkened space.

Another creeping herb or weed is *Mimosa pudica* L. (*ix-wenel*) (figure 2.1). It is part of the Fabaceae family and grows mostly in undisturbed shaded areas. *Ix-wenel*, due to its sensitive nature, is deemed "the sleeper." The leaves of this weed appear to sleep when disturbed, touched, or shaken by another organism. Its compound leaves immediately fold inward and droop, a reaction that defends the plant from harm, causing it to appear wilted to herbivores. The leaves also naturally fold inward each evening and reopen at dawn, further emphasizing that the plant has the ability to sleep. The Maya clearly recognized this quality, as indicated by their naming of the plant and its medicinal uses, which will be discussed below.

FIGURE 2.1. Ix-wenel (*Mimosa pudica*) *leaves can be seen folding inward as if they are asleep. This "sleeper" plant has been used by the Maya medicinally as a sedative. Picture taken by the author at the University of California Botanical Garden, Berkeley.*

MEDICINAL APPLICATIONS OF
MESOAMERICAN PLANT SPECIES

Many Mesoamerican flora that are associated with the night either linguistically or because of their nocturnal characteristics were applied medicinally, according to their night-related qualities. In this section, medicinal concoctions involving botanical remains are discussed. These curatives have been shown ethnobotanically to have been applied or prepared only during the nighttime.

An example is *Bursera simaruba* (L.) Sarg. (*chacah*), a tree species that flourishes in dry to moist secondary forests, in fence rows, and often in the mangrove ecoregions in Mesoamerica (Standley and Steyermark 1946–1976). Present-day Maya use a decoction created from *B. simaruba* leaves to relieve fatigue. There is a practice of leaving the chacah leaves out in the open overnight to freshen with the dew and then to be subsequently utilized to relieve headaches (Atran, Ximena, and Ucan Ek' 2004). This ritual provides one view of ancient Maya nightly medicinal preparation activities. The species has been widely recovered from archaeological excavations, including sites in Belize (Cuello, Pulltrouser Swamp), Guatemala (Dos Pilas), Mexico (Cobá), and El Salvador (Santa Leticia) (Beltran Frias 1987; Lentz 1994; Miksicek 1983, 1986; Miksicek, Wing, and Scudder 1991). Archaeological investigators suggest that the tree was utilized mainly as firewood, for construction, and for medicinal purposes (likely to relieve fever, headache, and fatigue). Ethnographically, the tree has been shown to serve as the wood in fence posts and the resin for incense and glue, and the leaves have been incorporated into baths to cure headaches, malarial fevers, and skin irritations (Atran, Ximena, and Ucan Ek' 2004; Standley and Steyermark 1946–1976).

Hamelia patens Jacq., or *ix-kanan*, is a plant that ethnographers report is ingested for numerous medicinal purposes. One use stands out because it is prescribed to be taken during the night, according to folk knowledge in the Petén (Atran, Ximena, and Ucan Ek' 2004). The branches and leaves, which treat an inflamed stomach, are incorporated into a tea to be drunk at night. *Ix-kanan* has been recovered during paleoethnobotanical studies of several Mesoamerica sites, including Cerén, Cuello, Pulltrouser Swamp, and Santa Leticia (Lentz and Ramírez-Sosa 2002; Miksicek 1983, 1986; Miksicek, Wing, and Scudder 1991). All reports indicate that the species was valued as a source of fuel (Lentz 1999). A plaster cast of this medicinal shrub was recovered at Cerén in the dooryard of Structure 4 of Household 4, from which the researchers concluded that the inhabitants valued its medicinal properties enough to keep it alongside their residence (Lentz and Ramírez-Sosa 2002).

PLANTS THAT ASSIST WITH SLEEPING

Many Neotropical plant species have recorded medicinal uses to assist in inducing sleep or as a narcotic to relieve restlessness. Recall that the plant the Itzaj Maya termed "contagious night," or *C. nocturnum*, has a name relating to its remedial use. When a handful of the leaves from this bush are dissolved and combined with a Rutaceae plant called *ix-ruud'aj*, the resulting foam can be used to bathe a sleepless child (Atran, Ximena, and Ucan Ek' 2004). Furthermore, *ix-tupuj* (*Tagetes erecta*) has a medicinal application where the flowers are made into a tea to relieve night sweats in children (Breedlove and Laughlin 2000). Similar uses are seen for *ix-wenel*, the sleeper plant (*Mimosa pudica*), which has a traditional use as a treatment for epilepsy and sleeplessness. An Itzaj tradition says to boil the leaves of *ix-wenel* and then wipe them over a child for nine Fridays in a row or to place nine dry leaves under the head child's at night to induce sleep (Atran, Ximena, and Ucan Ek' 2004).

Contemporary Maya in Belize use the plant as a sedative through various preparations (Arvigo and Balick 1993; Duke 2009). Either the leaves are sprinkled onto food as powder or the branches are boiled and incorporated into a tea. *Mimosa* seeds have been recovered from a domestic structure at Cihuatán in El Salvador, reflecting that the plant would have been incorporated into the regular lifestyle of the ancient inhabitants (Miksicek 1988).

The mixture of leaves of *Mimosa pudica*, *Erythrina standleyana* Krukoff, and *Gliricidia sepium* (Jacq.) Walp. is used to bathe a child who is suffering from insomnia (Atran, Ximena, and Ucan Ek' 2004). Charcoal from these plant species has been recovered from the archaeobotanical remains of elite contexts at Tikal and Dos Pilas, thus showing that these species were utilized in ancient as well as modern times (Cavallaro 2013; Lentz, Dunning, and Scarborough 2015).

X-holom-x-al (Yucatec) is a herbaceous plant with purple-blue flowers that grows to half a meter tall and is found throughout Central America (Ming 1999; Roys 1931). Maya in the Yucatan employ the plant (*Ageratum conyzoides* L.) to cure night fevers in nursing women. The entire plant is boiled and then bathed in for three consecutive days. It is also taken internally (Kunow 2012).

Extracts of the leaves and bark of *Piscidia piscipula* (L.) Sarg. (known as *aj-b'ox jab'in* to the Lakantun Maya) are well-known as a sedative or narcotic for humans, helping one rest at night. Itzaj Maya ethnographic records (Atran, Ximena, and Ucan Ek' 2004) show that this plant is used to help tired children when combined with *Gossypium hirsutum* L. (cotton) and *Cymbopogon citratus* (DC.) Stapf (lemongrass). The tree typically favors coastal conditions and low, wetland forests. Charcoal from this medium-sized deciduous tropical tree has been recovered from archaeobotanical studies of both Maya and Olmec sites, such as Barton Creek Cave, Actun Chapat, Dos Pilas, San Andres, and Late Classic Tikal (Cavallaro 2013; Lentz, personal communication, 2015; Lentz, Dunning, and Scarborough 2015; Morehart 2011).

Common curing practices described in ethnographic studies of the Maya say that curers often learned from dreaming what plants or words to use in their prayers during sleep (Kunow 2012). These many examples reveal that the ancient Maya turned to their environment and landscape at night to solve their sleeplessness. The remedies discussed here could have been dreamt about during the night in a vision that revealed their narcotic qualities to a shaman.

Nightly Sleeping Arrangements

Ancient Mesoamericans aptly treated insomnia with plants but also depended on them to provide the physical area and objects on which to spend the night.

Ethnohistoric accounts indicate that Maya families slept together in one room on beds made of small rods (saplings) on top of a mat that was covered with cotton cloths (Sharer and Traxler 2006). Mats or bedding woven from *Cyperus canus* J.Presl & C.Presl (*tule* or *pojp*) and *Plumeria rubra* L. (*sak pojp*) are widely used throughout Mesoamerica as cool, comfortable surfaces on which to rest in a hot climate. The culms (hollow stems) of these sedges are also used to weave baskets and fans (Williams 1981). The site of Tula of the Toltecs is named after this plant. Tule is a perennial grass-like sedge that can be found in damp thickets, in wet fields, or along streambeds and rivers (Standley and Steyermark 1946–1976). However, the plant is scarce in its wild state, meaning it is usually intentionally planted. The use of *P. rubra* by the Ch'orti' demonstrates that bedding materials were also chosen for their fragrance and vivid white coloration (Kufer 2009). *C. canus* fibers have been recovered in an archaeological context, on the floor of a commoner dwelling at Dos Pilas (Cavallaro 2013)—possibly the remnants of a former mat, bedding, or hammock.

The woven symbol of the sleeping mats, known as *pojp* in Ch'orti', can be seen across the Maya region and spanning several time periods. The symbol is thought to have transcended the simple notion of a sleeping mat—it can also represent rulership, royal authority, or a seat of power. Archaeologists have identified the woven mat symbol on ancient architecture at sites such as Copan, Kaminaljuyu, Nakbe, and Uaxactun (Kufer 2009; Sharer and Traxler 2006).

Yucatec Maya regularly place a series of protective plants around their sleeping areas (Kunow 2012). One of these species is the bright red achiote (*Bixa orellena* L.), which produces seeds (*kuxub* in Yucatec) said to help disperse measles. The perennial shrub is often cultivated but also grows abundantly in wet or dry lowland thickets, reaching up to 9 meters in height and blooming white or pink flowers (Raddatz-Mota et al. 2017; Standley and Williams 1961). "Achiote" is derived from the Nahuatl word "*achiotl*," meaning shiny seed. Ancient Mesoamericans did more than just place this plant in sleeping areas for protection; they also valued achiote's natural color by using it as a pigment in food products and body paints (Raddatz-Mota et al. 2017). Both the Aztec and the Maya used achiote as an additive to flavor cacao beverages and to add a deep red color (Wyatt 2003). The cone-shaped achiote seeds are covered with a viscous reddish-orange aril that is used to produce vivid pigments or dyes. Archaeobotanical achiote charcoal has been recovered from an elite floor context at Dos Pilas (Cavallaro 2013) and inside a container (likely storage for paint or coloring) in a ceremonial gathering building at Cerén (Farahani et al. 2017). These contexts provide evidence that the small shrub also had ritual significance in the past.

Wood from the *tancaz che* tree (*Zanthoxylum*) is placed around a sleeping area as a protectant to guard one from the evil winds. Interestingly, one of the local Spanish names for *Zanthoxylum* in Guatemala is *duerme-lengua* (Standley and Steyermark 1946–1976), or "sleep-tongue," likely referring to the numbing properties of the plant when chewed. *Ficus* (fig) leaves are often placed around the bed to prevent one from snoring. This widely distributed wood species is recovered from many Mesoamerican archaeobotanical contexts. Present-day Yucatec curers have a practice of calming a sleepless child by cutting up *Nopalea* cacti pads and arranging them around sleeping areas, one in each of the four corners and a fifth piece suspended over the center, a pattern related to the axis mundi and known as a quincunx (Kunow 2012).

NIGHT-RELATED RITUALS: THE MOON
AND MESOAMERICAN PLANTS

Plants held symbolic meanings for the Maya, where nightly conditions determined their management strategies and even foretold the fate of the world. For instance, chaya, *ix-chay* (Itzaj) or *ch'atat* (Ch'orti') (*Cnidoscolus aconitifolius* [Mill.] I.M.Johnst.)—a large, fast-growing perennial shrub with small white flowers that grows in moist or dry thickets, open forests, and open rocky places—has a name reflecting this quality because "chay" means to increase or multiply in Itzaj Maya (Standley and Steyermark 1949). Chay also serves as a generic term for plants in Yucatec Maya (Ross-Ibarra and Molina-Cruz 2002). The plant regenerates easily from fallen parts, grows quickly, and is eaten as a nutritious leafy vegetable today by many Maya groups (Ross-Ibarra and Molina-Cruz 2002). It is well adapted to the region's tropical climate, making the shrub especially useful because it is available throughout the dry season with minimal irrigation and supplies fresh, edible leaves with high levels of Vitamin A (Kufer 2009). *Ix-chay* has succulent stems that reveal a milky sap when cut. The *itz*, or sap, is usually a whitish color, and the Itzaj Maya have a folktale regarding this characteristic. During an eclipse, *chib'al k'in*, when the moon blocks the sun and the world goes into darkness, the stems of chaya are cut. If it is an abnormally red sap, that color symbolizes that the world may end. Today, it is widely believed in Mesoamerica that one should ask the plant for permission before it is harvested, often in the late evening, to avoid harm from its spines (Ross-Ibarra and Molina-Cruz 2002). The plant is thought to wake up early in the morning, so harvesting during the evening would prevent one from being stung. Archaeologically, chaya roots have been tentatively identified at Pulltrouser Swamp from raised agricultural fields (Miksicek 1983), an indication that the plant was grown for consumption purposes in ancient times.

Another example, *Leptocoryphium lanatum* (Kunth) Nees, a species in the Poaceae family whose common names (*zacate de sabana* and *u-su'uk-il-chäk'an*) translate to mean "savanna grass," is utilized in making adobe when mixed with mud. What is curious is that ethnographic evidence shows that this grass should be cut and harvested only during a full moon (Atran, Ximena, and Ucan Ek' 2004; Kufer 2009). This observation means the ancient Maya perhaps purposefully left some of their daily activities to be conducted at night during certain times of the lunar cycle.

COSMIC WORLDVIEWS AND PLANTS

Ancient Mesoamericans had an extensive understanding of their night sky. Once it was dark, they would observe the movements and patterns of the celestial bodies to keep track of time and agricultural cycles, as well as to tell the story of creation (Freidel, Schele, and Parker 1993). The manner in which ancient Mesoamericans referred to elements in the night sky directly associated them with the surrounding vegetation.

On clear dark nights, the Milky Way is visually prominent. When it runs north-south in relation to the ecliptic, the Classic Maya depicted it in their art as the world tree. The world tree portrays directional aspects of one's surroundings, a symbolic axis mundi. The great tree of life rises toward the sky to support the celestial realm and the sky. This tree of life is often depicted as a giant ceiba tree (known as *yaxche* in Yucatec) (figure 2.2), linking this species with motifs of the Milky Way, the night, and the world of the gods. In this way, the Maya not only depicted time in their art (Freidel, Schele, and Parker 1993) but also connected time to the plant world.

Today, the Quiche Maya view the Pleiades—a constellation of stars near the zenith in the tropics—as a handful of seeds, particularly *Zea mays* kernels. This set of stars sits close to the horizon in the highlands when it is time to plant maize in March (Tedlock 1985), symbolizing the sowing of the seeds as the stars soon slip from sight past the horizon.

Relating cosmic bodies, such as the Milky Way and the Pleiades, to their local flora is a way to make sense of their nightly world and the drastic visual changes in scenery, and it reveals how much significance the ancient Mesoamerican inhabitants placed on certain plants. Maize was a staple food in their diet and the ceiba tree a prominent and impressing figure on their landscape. Such values were so strong that their relevance must have been

FIGURE 2.2. *The ceiba tree, known as the tree of life. Author photo.*

present in the inhabitants' minds during their nocturnal activities and when observing the night sky.

BRINGING LIGHT INTO THE NIGHT: THE USE OF FIREWOOD IN MESOAMERICA

Ancient Mesoamericans would have supplemented moonlight with firelight to navigate a darkened landscape (see chapters by Gonlin and Dixon, and Widmer, this volume, for more on sources of lighting). A large variety of woody taxa have been recovered and identified from archaeological excavations in Mesoamerica, reflecting the high diversity of wood flora in the tropics. Over sixty species were utilized as firewood by the ancient inhabitants, many of which may have been consumed on a nightly basis in hearths or as torches. This statement is not to suggest that all recovered charcoal samples of woody species were used in this manner. However, wood would have been the primary source of fuel for ancient Mesoamericans to cook their food (see chapter by Reed and colleagues, this volume), enact rituals that require burning, create lime plaster, and perform many other activities.

The dynamic ecological contexts of Mesoamerica could have led to a practice of varied sections (explained below) (Robinson and McKillop 2013). The diverse assemblage of trees that were selected as timber suggests that Mesoamericans made efforts to conserve the local biodiversity. Ancient Mesoamericans were skilled conservators of their environment by employing a wide variety of management practices (Dunning and Beach 1994; Ford and Nigh 2015; Lentz and Hockaday 2009; Lentz et al. 2012; McNeil 2011; McNeil, Burney, and Piggott Burney 2010). Up until the Late Classic period, it appears that resources were carefully managed so that stands of primary forests were conserved. However, as ancient populations grew, such stands of preferred wood resources were exhausted and alternative resources were pursued (Lentz and Hockaday 2009). Today, overexploitation of such a precious and essential resource has impacted the local climate and agricultural productivity (Lentz, Dunning, and Scarborough 2015). For example, elders from Ch'orti' communities have recalled the deliberate preservation of areas of land to encourage reforestation, avoid overexploitation, and provide their descendants with enough trees to build homes (Kufer 2009, 199). Prehistorically, such overexploitation of forest patches resulted in a change in forest composition and subsequent adaptation of wood selection behavior among Classic Maya at Paynes Creek (Robinson and McKillop 2013). Alternatively, the diverse assemblage of woods used as fuel in the area could be indicative of earlier exploitation where the preferred size or type of wood for construction or fuel was in short supply or not readily available.

Pine (*Pinus* sp., or *ocotl* in Itzaj) is one of the most ubiquitous wood species recovered archaeobotanically in the region as charcoal remains, often found in ceremonial caches (Lentz et al. 2005, 2016; Morehart, Lentz, and Prufer 2005). The hero twins of the Popol Vuh navigated their way into the Dark House of the lords of the underworld using pine torches (Tedlock 1985, 119). The notion that pine was preferentially used for torches is supported archaeobotanically (Graham, McNatt, and Gutchen 1980; Morehart 2011; Morehart, Lentz, and Prufer 2005; Stone 1997). Most of the pine remains recovered from cave sites have been interpreted as remnants of torches used in caves (Graham, McNatt, and Gutchen 1980). Oak (*Quercus* sp.) is another wood species preferred as fuel since it is a slow-burning firewood (Schlesinger 2001). Many of the paleoethnobotanical remains recovered from Mesoamerican cave sites can be interpreted as symbolic offerings (Morehart 2011). Wood charcoal and other botanical food remains such as copal incense, various flowers, many tree fruits, and domesticates like maize, beans, and squash were often included in burned ritual offerings that brought light into the darkness of a cave.

CONCLUSIONS

There are many uncertainties when attempting to link together archaeo-botanical and ethnographic data of specific linguistic groups in Mesoamerica. Yet the abundance of plants discussed in this chapter has been retrieved in archaeological contexts. From these occurrences, I suggest that many of the linguistic connections and cultural practices have deep roots in prehistoric times. Ethnographers have noted that even people who are not known as healers are knowledgeable about plant remedies. Oral traditions pass on the knowledge of the plant resources to all who make use of them. From this custom, the night-related uses discussed here could have been widely acknowledged and practiced in ancient times.

The series of plants presented represents just some examples of how both the ancient and present-day Maya actively interacted with their landscape throughout the day and night. Certain medical concoctions involving plants were specifically intended for use during the night, whether it was the collection, preparation, or application of a species to relieve a variety of health issues. At night, humans engaged in activities that differed significantly from those conducted during daylight hours. Normally, one would assume that the main activity people engaged in at night was sleep. In fact, the ancient Maya likely utilized their knowledge of the landscape and vegetation to assist in achieving slumber, since many species recovered from archaeological sites have sleep-inducing properties. This tradition certainly involved collecting and gathering plant materials in the dark at night.

Ethnobotanical data and paleoethnobotanical remains combine to help reveal what the ancient Maya would have experienced in their environment while traversing their local nocturnal landscape and what behaviors occurred during this time while dealing with the darkness of nighttime. As farmers ventured into the night to harvest savanna grass for mixing with mud for adobe walls, they looked up at the full moon to confirm that the time was right to collect this prized material. Brightly colored and illuminated flowers would have lit up their view, reflecting the bright moonlight and, in a way,

TABLE 2.1. Plant species that have medicinal, morphological, cultural, or linguistic traits relating to nighttime in Mesoamerica

Scientific Name	Family	Common Names (English)	Common Names (Spanish)	Common Names (Indigenous)
Ageratum conyzoides	Asteraceae	chick weed, whiteweed, billygoat weed	yerba de chivo	*x holom x al, x-ta-ulum, x-ta-ulumil, zac-mizib*
Bixa orellena	Bixaceae	annatto, lip-stick bush	achiote, cuajachote	*k'uxub', kiwi', vo'ox, oox, xayau, tlaa-palachiyotl, achiotl*
Blechum pyramidatum	Acanthaceae		contra hierba, yierba de la noche, frondosa	*akab xiu, sam-ak-ách, xaka xiu*
Bursera simaruba	Burseraceae	birchwood, gumbo-limbo, torchwood	indio desnudo, palo mulato, palo jiote, chaca piocha, chinacuite	*chaklaj, tasi pom, chäkaj, nab'an che', säk chikaj, sac chacah, xaka, cajha, chacai, chocohu-ite, copalli, jicote, tacamahaca*
Ceiba sp.	Bombacaceae	ceiba, white cotton tree	Ceiba de lana, huimba	*yaaxche, jaxche, piim, ch'ooj, p'iitz', xiloxochitl, pachote*
Cestrum nocturnum	Solanaceae	night jes-samine, queen of the night	huele de noche, yerba de bruja	*ak'ab' jom, ix-'aka~jaway*
Clematis dioica	Ranunculaceae	night bloom, tietie	barba de viejo, dama de noche, hierba de mendigo	
Cnidoscolus aconitifolius	Euphorbiaceae	tree spinach	copapapa, chi-chicaste, chaidra, chicasquil	*chaya, chayok, chayo, chimchim chay, ix-chay, ix-ya'ax, ch'atat, tzimchay, tzah, sakil la*
Cymbopogon citratus	Poaceae	lemongrass	zacate limon, sakate limon	*aj/ix-su'uk`limoon*
Cyperus canus	Cyperaceae	tule		*pojp*
Erythrina standleyana	Fabaceae	coral bean tree, tiger wood	pito rojo	*chak-ch'ob'en, chakmo'ol che', aj/ix-pito-che', mo'te'*

continued on next page

TABLE 2.1—*continued*

Scientific Name	Family	Common Names (English)	Common Names (Spanish)	Common Names (Indigenous)
Ficus sp.	Moraceae	fig	amate, chilamate, higueron, mata-palo, leche de oje	*ixkopo', ju'un, ak'jun, chu jun*
Gliricidia sepium	Fabacaeae	madrigal, pea tree, quick stick	cacao de nance, madre cacao, canté, cansina, madera negra, yaité	*hotz, k'ante', kuchu-nuk, sakyab', zacyab, aj/ix-k'än-te', cacahuanantl*
Gossypium hirsutum	Malvaceae	cotton	algodón	*tinam, tänäm, ajtaman, tsiin*
Hamelia patens	Rubiaceae	scarlet bush, firebush, redhead	canudo, cigua-pate, chichipin, coralillo, aguatillo, achiotillo	*ix-kanan, ix-känal, canan, chactoc, chi-chipince, neanan*
Ipomoea alba	Convolvulaceae	moon-flower, good-night flower, nightbelle, moonvine	flor de luna, luna blanca, galán noche, bejuco de tabaco, gamuza, guamol, pañal de niño	*huchuk ts'aan, haapolin, nacta, naxh, sutup, xpeten, xutub*
Leptocoryphium lanatum	Poaceae	panicgrass	zacate de sabana	*u-su'uk-il-chäk'an*
Mimosa pudica	Fabaceae	sensitive plant, shame weed, humble plant, touch-me-not	dormilones, dorme maria, arranhhadeiras, sensitiva	*ix-wenel, ixmu-mutz', ixmutz'il, guara k'ish*
Nopalea sp.	Cactaceae	prickly pear, nopal	tunas	*x pakam, tzacam*
Palicourea tetragona	Rubiaceae	night bloom, white wood, wild lime	casada, palo verde, clavel	*yaxcanan*
Pinus sp.	Pinaceae	pine, pitch pine	pino, ocote	*'okootej, ocotl, hub-bub, huhub, sachaj, tahte, tajte', tikte'*
Piscidia piscipula	Fabaceae	dogwood, may bush, fishpoison tree	jabin, barbasco, borracho, cahu-inga, frijolillo, palo de zope	*aj b'ox jab'in, aj säk jab'in, jebe, haabi, habim, chijol, tiaxib, tzijol, zopilocuave*

continued on next page

TABLE 2.1—*continued*

Scientific Name	Family	Common Names (English)	Common Names (Spanish)	Common Names (Indigenous)
Plumeria rubra	Apocynaceae	red jasmine, frangipani	palo de flor blanca, palo de mayo, candelero, nicte de monte, súchil	*sak pojp*, *cacaloxochitl*
Sarcostemma clausum	Asclepiadaceae	night bloom	mata-torsalo, bejuco de pescado, dama de noche	
Tagetes erecta	Asteraceae	garden marigold, Aztec marigold	flor de muerte, clavel de los muertos, rueda de arado, ruda amarilla	*ixp'ak kan, ixpa'jul, ixpujuk, ix-tupuj, xpuhuc, tutz, cot tus, cempoalxochitl, kaqi tus, antzil vo'tus, sampwer*
Zanthoxylum sp.	Rutaceae	prickly wood, prickly ash	duerme-lengua, palo de alacrán	*sina'an che', tamcaz che, ix tancaz che*

competing with the moon as a light source, "extinguishing" its beauty with their brilliantly shining petals. *C. nocturnum* flowers would have bloomed in the darkness and emitted a strong yet slightly poisonous fragrance, causing passersby to sneeze or develop a headache if they stepped too close. Night-feeding insects and bats would have flown through the air, taking advantage of the late-blooming or nocturnal flowers with strong sweet-smelling scents. *Ix-wenel* leaves would have shuddered and collapsed into a slumber as the ancient inhabitants wandered through torch-lit pathways and gardens, likely bumping into the herbs that were reminding them that it was time to be asleep, just as the plant's actions demonstrated. In the distance, they could see the flames of a bountiful harvest of food ritually offered, perhaps in a cave. Once back in their residences, the farmers would have dispersed a particular set of seeds, leaves, and other objects around their woven sleeping mats to protect them throughout the night from evil winds and keep their minds at ease.

The night for ancient Mesoamericans was not just viewed as a time to sleep; it was a time to collect and interact with local vegetation. By approaching the study of ancient cultures from the dark perspective of the night, we can learn a great deal more about how ancient humans fully operated throughout their lives, not just how they conducted their lives during the day.

NOTE

1. For reference, all scientific and common names of plants discussed in the chapter are listed in table 2.1.

REFERENCES

Arvigo, Rosita, and Michael Balick. 1993. *Rainforest Remedies: 100 Healing Herbs of Belize*. 2nd ed. Twin Lakes, WI: Lotus.

Atran, Scott, Lois Ximena, and Edilberto Ucan Ek'. 2004. *Plants of the Petén Itza' Maya: Plantas de Los Maya Itza' del Petén*. Memoirs of the Museum of Anthropology 38. Ann Arbor: University of Michigan.

Austin, Dan. 2002. "Moonvine: Discovering Florida's Ethnobotany." *Palmetto* 21 (4): 10–15.

Balick, Michael J., Michael H. Nee, and Daniel E. Atha. 2000. *Checklist of Vascular Plants of Belize*. Memoirs of the New York Botanical Garden 85. New York: New York Botanical Garden.

Beltran Frias, Luis. 1987. "Subsistencia y aprovechamientio del medio." In *Cobá, Quintana Roo analisis de dos unidades habitaciones Mayu*, ed. Linda Manzanilla, 213–232. Mexico City: Universidad Nacional Autónoma.

Breedlove, Dennis E., and Robert M. Laughlin. 2000. *The Flowering of Man: A Tzotzil Botany of Zinacantán*. Washington, DC: Smithsonian Institution Press.

Carod-Artal, Francisco. 2015. "Hallucinogenic Drugs in Pre-Columbian Mesoamerican Cultures." *Neurologia* 30 (1): 42–49.

Cavallaro, Dana A. 2013. "Reconstructing the Past: Paleoethnobotanical Evidence for Ancient Maya Plant Use Practices at the Dos Pilas Site, Guatemala." MA thesis, University of Cincinnati, OH.

Duke, James A. 2009. *Duke's Handbook of Medicinal Plants of Latin America*. Boca Raton, FL: CRC Press.

Dunning, Nicholas P., and Timothy Beach. 1994. "Soil Erosion, Slope Management, and Ancient Terracing in the Maya Lowlands." *Latin American Antiquity* 5 (1): 51–69.

Farahani, Alan, Katherine L. Chiou, Anna Harkey, Christine A. Hastorf, David L. Lentz, and Payson Sheets. 2017. "Identifying 'Plantscapes' at the Classic Maya Village of Joya de Cerén, El Salvador." *Antiquity* 91 (358): 980–997.

Ford, Anabel, and Ronald Nigh. 2015. *The Maya Forest Garden: Eight Millennia of Sustainable Cultivation of the Tropical Woodlands*. New York: Routledge.

Gentry, Johnnie L., and Paul C. Standley. 1974. *Flora of Guatemala*. Fieldiana, Botany Series 24, part 10. Chicago: Field Museum of Natural History.

Graham, Elizabeth, Logan McNatt, and Mark A. Gutchen. 1980. "Excavations in Footprint Cave, Caves Branch, Belize." *Journal of Field Archaeology* 7 (2): 153–172.

Granziera, Patrizia. 2001. "Concept of the Garden in Pre-Hispanic Mexico." *Garden History* 29 (2): 185–213.

Hosler, Dorothy, Sandra L. Burkett, and Michael J. Tarkanian. 1999. "Prehistoric Polymers: Rubber Processing in Ancient Mesoamerica." *Science* 284 (5422): 1988–1991.

Kufer, Johanna. 2009. "Ajk'opot Gente: The Unrecognized Keepers of the Maya Plant Lore." In *The Ch'orti' Maya Area Past and Present*, ed. Brent E. Metz, Cameron L. McNeil, and Kerry M. Hull, 198–213. Gainesville: University Press of Florida.

Kunow, Marianna A. 2012. *Maya Medicine: Traditional Healing in Yucatan*. Albuquerque: University of New Mexico Press.

Lentz, David. L. 1994. "Paleoethnobotanical Evidence for Subsistence Practices and Other Economic Activities in the Petexbatun Region during the Classic Period." Paper presented at the 93rd American Anthropological Association Meeting, Atlanta, GA, November 30–December 4.

Lentz, David L. 1999. "Plant Resources of the Ancient Maya: The Paleoethnobotanical Evidence." In *Reconstructing Ancient Maya Diet*, ed. Christine D. White, 3–18. Salt Lake City: University of Utah Press.

Lentz, David L., Nicholas P. Dunning, and Vernon L. Scarborough, eds. 2015. *Tikal: Paleoecology of an Ancient Maya City*. Cambridge: Cambridge University Press.

Lentz, David L., Elizabeth Graham, Xochitl Vinaja, Venicia Slotten, and Rupal Jain. 2016. "Agroforestry and Ritual at the Ancient Maya Center of Lamanai." *Journal of Archaeological Science: Reports* 8: 284–294.

Lentz, David L., and Brian Hockaday. 2009. "Tikal Timbers and Temples: Ancient Maya Agroforestry and the End of Time." *Journal of Archaeological Science* 36 (7): 1342–1353.

Lentz, David L., and Carlos R. Ramírez-Sosa. 2002. "Cerén Plant Resources: Abundance and Diversity." In *Before the Volcano Erupted: The Ancient Cerén Village in Central America*, ed. Payson Sheets, 33–42. Austin: University of Texas Press.

Lentz, David L., Sally Woods, Angela Hood, and Marcus Murph. 2012. "Agroforestry and Agricultural Production of the Ancient Maya at Chan." In *Chan: An Ancient Maya Farming Community*, ed. Cynthia Robin, 89–109. Gainesville: University Press of Florida.

Lentz, David L., Jason Yaeger, Cynthia Robin, and Wendy Ashmore. 2005. "Pine, Prestige, and Politics of the Late Classic Maya at Xunantunich, Belize." *Antiquity* 79 (305): 573–585.

McNeil, Cameron L. 2011. "Deforestation, Agroforestry, and Sustainable Land Management Practices among the Classic Period Maya." *Quaternary International* 249: 19–30.

McNeil, Cameron L., David A. Burney, and Lida Pigott Burney. 2010. "Evidence Disputing Deforestation as the Cause for the Collapse of the Ancient Maya Polity of Copán, Honduras." *Proceedings of the National Academy of Sciences* 107 (3): 1017–1022.

Miksicek, Charles H. 1983. "Macrofloral Remains of the Pulltrouser Area: Settlements and Fields." In *Pulltrouser Swamp: Ancient Maya Habitat, Agriculture, and Settlement in Northern Belize*, ed. Billie L. Turner and Peter D. Harrison, 94–104. Austin: University of Texas Press.

Miksicek, Charles H. 1986. "Paleobotanical Identifications." In *The Archaeology of Santa Leticia and the Rise of Maya Civilization*, ed. Arthur Demarest, 199–200. New Orleans: Tulane University Press.

Miksicek, Charles H. 1988. "Man and Environment and Cihuatan." In *Cihuatan, El Salvador: A Study in Intrasite Variability*, ed. Jane H. Kelly, 149–155. Nashville: Vanderbilt University Press.

Miksicek, Charles H., Elizabeth S. Wing, and Sylvia J. Scudder. 1991. "The Ecology and Economy of Cuello." In *Cuello: An Early Maya Community in Belize*, ed. Norman Hammond, 70–84. Cambridge, MA: Harvard University Press.

Ming, Lin C. 1999. "Ageratum Conyzoides: A Tropical Source of Medicinal and Agricultural Products." In *Perspectives on New Crops and New Uses*, ed. Jules Janick, 469–473. Alexandria, VA: American Society for Horticultural Science Press.

Morehart, Christopher T. 2011. *Food, Fire, and Fragrance: A Paleoethnobotanical Perspective on Classic Maya Cave Rituals*. Oxford: Archaeopress.

Morehart, Christopher T., David L. Lentz, and Keith M. Prufer. 2005. "Wood of the Gods: The Ritual Use of Pine (*Pinus* spp.) by the Ancient Lowland Maya." *Latin American Antiquity* 16 (3): 255–274.

Nash, Dorothy L., and Louis O. Williams. 1976. *Flora of Guatemala*. Fieldiana, Botany Series 24, part 11/14. Chicago: Field Museum of Natural History.

Raddatz-Mota, Denise, Laura J. Pérez-Flores, Fernando Carrari, José A. Mendoza-Espinoza, Fernando Díaz de León-Sánchez, Luis L. Pinzón-López, Gregorio Godoy-Hernández, and Fernando Rivera-Cabrera. 2017. "Achiote (Bixa orellana L.): A Natural Source of Pigment and Vitamin E." *Journal of Food Science and Technology* 54 (6): 1729–1741.

Robinson, Mark E., and Heather I. McKillop. 2013. "Ancient Maya Wood Selection and Forest Exploitation: A View from the Paynes Creek Salt Works, Belize." *Journal of Archaeological Science* 40: 3584–3595.

Ross-Ibarra, Jeffrey, and Alvaro Molina-Cruz. 2002. "The Ethnobotany of Chaya (*Cnidoscolus aconitifolius* ssp. *aconitifolius* Breckon): A Nutritious Maya Vegetable." *Economic Botany* 56 (4): 350–365.

Roys, Ralph L. 1931. *The Ethno-botany of the Maya*. New Orleans: Middle American Research Institute.

Schlesinger, Victoria. 2001. *Animals and Plants of the Ancient Maya: A Guide*. Austin: University of Texas Press.

Schultes, Richard E. 1941. "Economic Aspects of the Flora of Northeastern Oaxaca." PhD dissertation, Harvard University, Cambridge, MA.

Shaista, Amin, and Parle Amrita. 2016. "Delicate, Fragrant, Lady of the Night—A Medicinal Gift." *Journal of Medicinal Plants Studies* 4 (6): 13–17.

Sharer, Robert J., and Loa P. Traxler. 2006. *The Ancient Maya*, 6th ed. Redwood City, CA: Stanford University Press.

Standley, Paul C., and Julian A. Steyermark. 1946–1976. *Flora of Guatemala*. Fieldiana, Botany. Chicago: Field Museum of Natural History.

Standley, Paul C., and Julian A. Steyermark. 1949. *Flora of Guatemala*. Fieldiana, Botany Series 24, part 6/1. Chicago: Field Museum of Natural History.

Standley, Paul C., and Louis O. Williams. 1961. *Flora of Guatemala*. Fieldiana, Botany Series 24, part 7/1. Chicago: Field Museum of Natural History.

Standley, Paul C., and Louis O. Williams. 1969. *Flora of Guatemala*. Fieldiana, Botany Series 24, part 8/4. Chicago: Field Museum of Natural History.

Standley, Paul C., and Louis O. Williams. 1970. *Flora of Guatemala*. Fieldiana, Botany Series 24, part 9/1–2. Chicago: Field Museum of Natural History.

Standley, Paul C., and Louis O. Williams. 1975. *Flora of Guatemala*. Fieldiana, Botany Series 24, part 11/1–3. Chicago: Field Museum of Natural History.

Standley, Paul C., Louis O. Williams, and Dorothy N. Gibson. 1974. *Flora of Guatemala*. Fieldiana, Botany Series 24, part 10/3–4. Chicago: Field Museum of Natural History.

Stone, Andrea. 1997. "Precolumbian Cave Utilization in the Maya Area." In *Human Use of Caves*, ed. Clive Bonsall and Christopher Tolan-Smith, 201–206. British Archaeological Reports International Series 667. Oxford: Archaeopress.

Tedlock, Dennis. 1985. *Popol Vuh: The Definitive Edition of the Mayan Book of the Dawn of Life and the Glories of Gods and Kings*. New York: Simon and Schuster.

Williams, Louis O. 1981. "The Useful Plants of Central America." *Ceiba* 24 (1–2); Index, 343–381. *Ceiba* 24 (3–4). Tegucigalpa, Honduras: Escuela Agricola Panamericana.

Wyatt, Andrew R. 2003. "Mexico and Central America, Pre-Columbian." In *The Encyclopedia of Food and Culture*, ed. Solomon H. Katz and William Woys Weaver, 497–502. New York: Charles Scribner's Sons.

dense blackness loomed behind us like a torrent
poured out over the earth

    —Pliny the Younger (Gilman 2007, 33)

Extending the Notion
of Night and Darkness

Volcanic Eruptions in
Ancient Mesoamerica

Rachel Egan

The recent research on archaeological evidence for nightly practices has profoundly shaped interpretations of the past (Gonlin and Nowell 2018). As scholars begin to investigate this rarely examined portion of ancient life, it is essential to include associations of the night and darkness beyond the time of day. One such avenue is the exploration of phenomena that produce experiences of darkness similar to night, such as volcanic eruptions. These geological phenomena strongly influenced life throughout ancient Mesoamerica and provide an alternative avenue of investigation into ancient experiences of a form of darkness created by the rainfall of tephra. Volcanic eruptions, particularly those of significant size such as mega-eruptions, are known for ejecting tephra into the atmosphere, creating darkness even at the height of daylight, and, in some cases, initiating what are termed "dark ages of history" (Dull et al. 2001; Grattan and Torrence 2007; Gunn 2000; Keys 2000; Rampino, Self, and Stothers 1988). While fundamentally different from regular nighttime, how people perceived and experienced "volcanic night" is still a fundamental part of addressing the myriad ways darkness impacted life in ancient Mesoamerica. Volcanic night and its unusual qualities must have demanded explanation and interpretation.

DOI: 10.5876/9781646421879.c003

In this chapter, I explore the relationships among night, darkness, and volcanoes. First, I address what is volcanic night and to what extent people may have experienced it in ancient Mesoamerica. Second, I explore the affective nature of volcanic night with particular attention to the ephemeral and emotional impacts of such events. Third, I explore how people may have understood and explained such an unusual phenomenon. Finally, I consider what volcanic night means for how we reconstruct past disasters as well as future directions of hazard and disaster research.

VOLCANIC NIGHT

Volcanoes are some of the earth's most dramatic processes. They have played a significant role in culture and culture change throughout human history. Effects of eruptions can range from globally induced nuclear winters to small-scale local perturbations. They have buried cities, darkened skies, triggered drought and famine, and played a role in the collapse of civilizations (Costanza, Graumlich, and Steffen 2007; Gunn 2000; Keys 2000). While there are different types of volcanic eruptions, each capable of triggering a range of effects and responses, the explosive eruptions are the focus of this chapter. An explosive eruption is defined as "an energetic eruption that produces mainly ash, pumice, and fragmental ballistic debris [tephra]" (US Geological Survey 2015). This eruption type has the capability to produce large quantities of ascending tephra (a term for the ejected debris) and gas, forming an ash cloud (also known as a plume or an eruptive column) that rises directly above a volcanic vent. During an explosive eruption, it is possible for the ash cloud to reach the Earth's stratosphere where it can then circle the planet, impacting global climate. Such was the case for the 1883 eruption of Krakatoa, one of the largest and most deadly eruptions in human history (Thornton 1997). Even smaller-scale eruptions can cause significant disturbances on grand scales, such as the 2010 eruption of the Eyjafjallajökull volcano in Iceland that triggered a major disruption in air travel (and the economy) for much of Europe (Gudmundsson et al. 2010).

Explosive eruptions are destructive. But beyond the ash, lava, and other material products lies an equally devastating set of effects—the hard to measure sensory experience of an eruption. For example, many of the reports of the 1883 Krakatoa eruption focused on the sensory effect of such an explosive eruption; 3,000 miles away people heard a sound "coming from the eastward, like the distant roar of heavy guns" (Symons 1888, 79). Nearer to the eruption there was a smell of sulfur so strong that it was hard to breathe (1888, 445). For those under the shadow of the ash cloud, it turned daylight into complete darkness, in some areas for over twenty-four hours. The darkness triggered by an eruption is no ordinary darkness. It has unusual qualities and a particular feel to it. The Krakatoa eruption produced a local night that was "blacker than the blackest night" and "deeper than that of night" (1888, 328). Beyond the local extent of the darkness, this eruption triggered a hazy sky accompanied by the dimming and blurring of the celestial bodies, which persisted long after the initial eruption. Also known as a "dry fog," such an event occurs when ejected ash and gasses stay suspended for prolonged periods of time, effectively absorbing incoming solar radiation and then scattering it back out into space (Stothers 1984, 1999). The Krakatoa dry fog was remarked upon the world over for producing an unusual blue or green appearance to the sun and moon, bright sunrises and sunsets, rings around the sun, and dark or disappearing celestial bodies (Rampino, Self, and Stothers 1988). The sky itself appeared to change, with references to the colors of copper and lead juxtaposed against a blue-green sun and moon (Symons 1888, 203). The alteration to the atmosphere and the appearance of the sky are not unusual with volcanic eruptions, especially for those living under the plume where ash, dust, and aerosols backscatter light (Stothers 1996). Together, the darkness and haziness radiating outward from the source of an explosive eruption constitute what will be referred to as "volcanic night." It is this powerful yet understudied phenomenon that this chapter will address.

VOLCANIC ERUPTIONS IN ANCIENT MESOAMERICA

Thus far, no native texts have been recovered that reference the occurrence of volcanic night in the pre-Hispanic Mesoamerican world. However, Mesoamerica—the culture area that is part of the Central American Volcanic Arc, a 1,100 km region stretching from the Isthmus of Mexico to northern Panama and running parallel to the Pacific Ocean (Ford and Rose 1995)—is one of the most geologically active areas in the world. Formed by the subduction of the Oceanic Plate under the southern edge of the North American Plate and the western edge of the Caribbean Plate, the arc is home to hundreds of volcanoes (figure 0.1), some of which reach 4,000 m in height (e.g., Tajumulco in Guatemala is 4,203 m) (Kimberly 2011). During the pre-Hispanic period in Mesoamerica, there were at least eight active volcanoes in Mexico, six active volcanoes in Guatemala, and two active volcanoes in El Salvador (figure 3.1).

Many of these volcanoes produced substantial eruptions, ranging from 2 through 6 on the Volcanic Explosivity Index (VEI), a relative logarithmic

FIGURE 3.1. *Locations of volcanoes that were active during the pre-Hispanic period in Mesoamerica, as discussed in this chapter. This list was compiled using the Volcanoes of the World (VOTW) database by the Smithsonian Institution and should be considered preliminary. Volcanoes highlighted in gray are those that produced a VEI 4 or higher eruption in the pre-Hispanic era.*

scale that measures the volume and type of ejected materials to gauge destructiveness (Newhall and Self 1982). The atmospheric effects of these eruptions are hard to ascertain, as many factors play a role in their nature, duration, and severity—including volcanic composition, direction and force of prevailing winds, and the size of the eruptive column. Because volcanic night and dry fogs leave no tangible, material trace in either the archaeological or geological record, scholars must rely on proxies to identify when such an event may have occurred. However, because volcanic night is produced by the injection of aerosols into the stratosphere, eruptions that rank 4 or higher on the VEI scale are generally considered explosive and thus are more likely to produce atmospheric effects (1982).

To determine the number of eruptions with the potential to have triggered a volcanic night, the Volcanoes of the World (VOTW) database was searched (Global Volcanism Program 2013). This database provides a catalog of volcanoes and eruptions from the past 10,000+ years. For the time period from 3000 BCE through 1500 CE in Mesoamerica, sixteen active volcanoes and seventy-two eruptions were identified (see tables 0.1 and 3.1). Only eruptions that had clear radiocarbon ages were included. Of these potential eruptions, eleven rank VEI 4 or higher. Table 3.1 summarizes what is known about each of the eruptions, including the volcano name, location, eruptive age, VEI rank (if known), volcano type, and evidence.

The question, then, is: To what extent were the impacts of the eleven documented VEI 4+ eruptions experienced within the Mesoamerican world? It is reasonable to conclude that these volcanic eruptions produced extensive effects, including local perturbations to the skies, pyroclastic flows, extensive tephra-fall, shaking, loud noises, and unusual smells. For example, the analogous VEI 5–1982 eruption of El Chichón in Mexico caused perturbations to the global atmosphere, with tephra-fall from the eruption reaching all the way to the northern Yucatan town of Merida—a distance of 551 km (Carey and Sigurdsson 1986; Grattan 2006; Nooren 2017). Looking at the map (figure 3.1), a wide area of Mesoamerica had the potential to be impacted by these eruptions. While current evidence does not allow us to ascertain if any of these eruptions conclusively triggered a volcanic night, many people in ancient Mesoamerica, especially those living near the volcanic arc, likely experienced some degree of perturbation from volcanic events. Assuming that at least one, if not all, of the eleven eruptions produced some degree of alteration to the atmosphere (volcanic night), how people experienced it is the subject of the next section.

THE AFFECTIVE NATURE OF VOLCANIC NIGHT AND ITS DARKNESS

What was the emotional impact of volcanic night and the darkness that occurred with it? Currently, there is little evidence for major cultural breaks following eruptive events in Mesoamerica (Grattan 2006), perhaps apart from the Ilopango eruption sometime during the fifth or sixth century (Dull et al. 2010; Sheets 2012; Sigl et al. 2015). Rather, the story appears to be one of persistence and success despite the repetitive and occasionally catastrophic eruptions. But this chapter is about more than the immediate and easily measured effects and responses to volcanic eruptions. Numerous historical records extend beyond the damaging immediate physical impacts to reference the darkness from eruptive columns, the haziness of the sun and moon, and the changing colors that can occur in the wake of eruptions (Rampino, Self, and Stothers 1988). Instead, I want to shift focus to intangible, ephemeral aspects of volcanic night and the emotional responses these powerful events can trigger.

Drawing on historical literature pertaining to volcanic eruptions from around the world, a consistent pattern of volcanoes as harbingers of fear and anxiety emerges. For example, in response to the VEI 6–1883 Krakatoa

TABLE 3.1. Table of identified volcanic eruptions in Mesoamerica between 3000 BCE and 1500 CE. The table was compiled using the Volcanoes of the World (VOTW) database. Eruptions that rank VEI 4 or higher are highlighted in gray.

Name	Country	Volcano Type	VOTW #	Eruption Year	VEI	Evidence
Michoacán–Guanajuato	Mexico	Pyroclastic cone(s)	341060	1140 BCE ± 865 years		Radiocarbon (corrected)
				1880 BCE ± 150 years	3	Radiocarbon (uncorrected)
				2050 BCE (?)		Anthropology
				2750 BCE ± 200 years	3	Radiocarbon (uncorrected)
Ceboruco	Mexico	Stratovolcano	341030	1567 CE		Historical observations
				1542 CE		Historical observations
				930 CE ± 200 years	6	Radiocarbon (uncorrected)
Chichinautzin	Mexico	Volcanic field	341080	400 CE ± 100 years	3	Radiocarbon (corrected)
				200 CE ± 100 years	3	Radiocarbon (corrected)
				2238 BCE ± 1413 years	3	Radiocarbon (corrected)
El Chichón	Mexico	Lava dome(s)	341120	1360 CE ± 100 years	5	Radiocarbon (corrected)
				1190 CE ± 150 years	4	Radiocarbon (corrected)
				780 CE ± 100 years	5	Radiocarbon (corrected)
				590 CE ± 100 years	3	Radiocarbon (corrected)
				480 CE ± 200 years		Radiocarbon (corrected)
				190 CE ± 150 years		Radiocarbon (corrected)
				20 BCE ± 50 years		Radiocarbon (corrected)
				700 BCE ± 200 years		Radiocarbon (corrected)
				1340 BCE ± 150 years		Radiocarbon (corrected)
				2030 BCE ± 100 years	5	Radiocarbon (corrected)

continued on next page

TABLE 3.1—*continued*

Name	Country	Volcano Type	VOTW #	Eruption Year	VEI	Evidence
Colima	Mexico	Stratovolcano	341040	1519 CE	3	Historical observations
				1110 CE ± 200 years		Radiocarbon (corrected)
				730 CE ± 100 years		Radiocarbon (uncorrected)
				540 CE ± 150 years		Radiocarbon (corrected)
				650 BCE ± 200 years		Radiocarbon (corrected)
				1140 BCE (?)		Radiocarbon (uncorrected)
				1170 BCE ± 200 years		Radiocarbon (corrected)
				1320 BCE (?)		Radiocarbon (uncorrected)
				1450 BCE ± 100 years		Radiocarbon (uncorrected)
				1890 BCE ± 75 years		Radiocarbon (uncorrected)
				1940 BCE ± 300 years		Radiocarbon (corrected)
				2370 BCE ± 150 years	4	Radiocarbon (uncorrected)
				2800 BCE ± 100 years		Radiocarbon (corrected)
Popocatépetl	Mexico	Stratovolcano	341090	1504 CE	2	Historical observations
				1488 CE	2	Historical observations
				[1363] CE	2	
				1354 CE	2	Historical observations
				1345 CE	2	Historical observations
				823 Mar 1 CE ± 90 days	4	Ice core
				250 CE (?)		Radiocarbon (uncorrected)
				200 BCE ± 300 years	5	Radiocarbon (uncorrected)
				1890 BCE ± 75 years		Radiocarbon (uncorrected)

continued on next page

TABLE 3.1—*continued*

Name	Country	Volcano Type	VOTW #	Eruption Year	VEI	Evidence
San Martín	Mexico	Shield	341110	890 CE ± 40 years		Radiocarbon (uncorrected)
				480 CE ± 50 years		Radiocarbon (uncorrected)
				380 CE ± 75 years		Tephrochronology
				120 CE ± 200 years		Radiocarbon (uncorrected)
				150 BCE ± 300 years		Tephrochronology
				750 BCE ± 40 years		Radiocarbon (uncorrected)
				1320 BCE ± 300 years		Radiocarbon (uncorrected)
				2130 BCE ± 50 years		Radiocarbon (uncorrected)
Tacaná	Mexico	Stratovolcano	341130	30 CE ± 40 years		Radiocarbon (uncorrected)
				70 CE ± 100 years	4	Radiocarbon (corrected)
Acatenango	Guatemala	Stratovolcano	342080	1080 BCE ± 150 years		Radiocarbon (corrected)
				1450 CE ± 50 years		Anthropology
				90 CE ± 100 years		Radiocarbon (uncorrected)
				260 BCE ± 75 years		Radiocarbon (uncorrected)
				370 BCE ± 200 years		Radiocarbon (uncorrected)
				2710 BCE ± 75 years		Radiocarbon (uncorrected)
Almolonga	Guatemala	Stratovolcano	342040	800 CE ± 50 years	3	Radiocarbon (corrected)
Atitlan	Guatemala	Stratovolcano	342060	1020 BCE ± 150-years		Radiocarbon (uncorrected)
Fuego	Guatemala	Stratovolcano	342090	970 CE ± 50 years		Radiocarbon (uncorrected)
				900 CE ± 75 years		Radiocarbon (uncorrected)
				590 CE ± 75 years		Radiocarbon (uncorrected)
				1580 BCE ± 75 years		Radiocarbon (uncorrected)

continued on next page

TABLE 3.1—continued

Name	Country	Volcano Type	VOTW #	Eruption Year	VEI	Evidence
Pacaya	Guatemala	Complex	342110	1360 CE ± 75 years	3	Radiocarbon (uncorrected)
				1160 CE ± 75 years	3	Radiocarbon (uncorrected)
				880 CE ± 500 years	3	Tephrochronology
				400 CE ± 50 years	2	Radiocarbon (uncorrected)
Tecuamburro	Guatemala	Stratovolcano	342120	960 BCE ± 75 years		Radiocarbon (uncorrected)
Ilopango	El Salvador	Caldera	343060	450 CE ± 30 years*	6	Radiocarbon (corrected)
San Salvador (Loma Caldera)	El Salvador	Stratovolcano	343050	1200 CE (?)	4	Anthropology
				640 Aug CE ± 30 years	3	Radiocarbon (corrected)

*The dates for the Ilopango eruption have been revised to 440–550 CE (Dull et al. 2010).

eruption, a document by a Mr. Verbeek stated that "terror and dismay reigned everywhere, and darkness had settled over the land" (quoted in Symons 1888, 94). Likewise, the far-reaching darkness from the VEI 7–1815 eruption of Tambora, which produced what is known as the "year without summer," inspired numerous responses focused on darkness and death, including Mary Shelly's *Frankenstein* (De Boer 2002; De Boer and Sanders 2002; Rampino and Self 1982). In another case, the great dry fog of 536 CE (most likely triggered by a volcanic eruption) led many people to cite the devastation and fear. In Rome, Cassiodorus remarked "how fearful it is, then, to endure for so long what will terrify a people," in response to the "blue-colored sun" and a moon "shorn of its natural splendor" (quoted in Young 2000, 35). The accounts by Pliny of the VEI 5–79 CE eruption of Vesuvius detail the nature of the eruption as well as the devastating effects it had on those who witnessed the dramatic eruption. The terror of this event is unmistakable in a letter Pliny wrote, which states:

> You could hear the shrieks of women, the wailing of infants, and the shouting of men . . . People bewailed their own fate or that of their relatives, and there were some who prayed for death in their terror of dying. Many besought the aid of the gods, but still more imagined there were no gods left, and that the universe was plunged into eternal darkness for evermore . . . I could boast that not a groan or cry of fear escaped me in these perils, but I admit that I derived some poor consolation in my mortal lot from the belief that the whole world was dying with me and I with it. (quoted in Radice 2003, 6.16)

Looking to ancient Mesoamerica, similar accounts emerge. In 1835, the VEI 5 Coseguina eruption in Nicaragua was described by a nearby ship officer, who stated that the eruption "enveloped everything in the greatest darkness, so that the nearest objects were imperceptible. The melancholy howling beasts, the flocks of birds of all species, that came to seek . . . asylum among men, the terror which assailed the latter, the cries of the women and children, and the uncertainty. Everything combined to overcome the stoutest soul and fill it with apprehension" (Sheets 1971, 27).

Likewise, ethnohistoric records for the Aztec reference the "Smoking Mountain," also known as Popocatzin, as a source of anxiety because it produced smoke and flames several times a day (Plunket and Uruñuela 2008, 112). In many Mesoamerican belief systems, extending back in time, volcanoes and volcanic eruptions were linked to the cosmological order, often thought to have played a role in the destruction of previous worlds (Freidel, Schele, and Parker 1993; Plunket and Uruñuela 2008). Volcanoes, in Mesoamerica and around the world, are clearly powerful things, capable of producing not only extreme destruction but also emotional turmoil, anxiety, and fear.

However, references to volcanic night and other optical phenomena have not been identified in pre-Hispanic Mesoamerica. Therefore, we must look to other similar phenomena to parse out how this unusual quality may have impacted peoples living in the region. Perhaps the best analogous events are eclipses, which have notable similarities in appearance to volcanic nights (Stothers 1984, 344). Eclipses occur when a celestial body moves into the shadow of another celestial body. During a lunar eclipse, the moon, either totally or partially, passes through the earth's shadow, giving the moon a reddish hue. During a solar eclipse, the moon moves between the sun and the earth, blocking the light from the sun. As a result, the sun appears dark, and the horizon often takes a reddish hue. However, the darkness outside of daytime caused by an eclipse is still somewhat different from volcanic night in terms of duration (an eclipse tends to last minutes, whereas volcanic night can be prolonged from days to months) and extent (solar eclipses occur over a small area, whereas volcanic night can produce optical phenomena on a global scale). Nevertheless, because eclipses were documented and discussed in pre-Hispanic Mesoamerica, they provide a starting point for understanding volcanic night.

Many lunar and solar eclipses occurred in pre-Hispanic Mesoamerica. Extensive knowledge of the skies and celestial bodies as well as the creation of detailed calendar systems allowed people to document and even predict when eclipses would occur (Milbrath and Dowd 2015). For the Colonial and contemporary Maya, eclipses were seen as a time of danger and were considered bad omens that were met with anxiety and fear. The sun was believed to be the giver of life, so its disappearance could be catastrophic, even for a short duration (Milbrath 1999). Some people thought it could cause blindness or disfigurement and could harm a pregnant woman or her unborn child. Eclipses are also associated with world-ending events in Maya mythology (see the Paris Codex, the Popol Vuh, the Chumayel text in the Books of Chilam Balam, and the Dresden Codex) (Dowd and Milbrath 2015, 184). Based on expanding archaeological evidence, it is becoming clearer that while these mythologies were influenced by contact with the Spanish, they have antecedents dating back to the pre-Hispanic period.

Likewise, the Aztec also saw eclipses as powerful events. According to Aztec belief, the decapitations of females were linked to celestial events and tied to political metaphors. The goddess Cihuacoatl represented a decapitated deity tied to solar eclipses and was a threat to the sun and the Aztec.

In contrast, the goddess Coyolxauhqui represented the full moon eclipsed by the sun and therefore the triumph of the sun over the moon as well as the triumph of the Aztec state (Milbrath 1997). Themes of turmoil, violence, political upheaval, and the world ending are also associated with solar eclipses among Aztec beliefs.

Clearly, the actions of the sun and moon were remarked upon throughout Mesoamerica. Moreover, alterations to the hue and brightness of the celestial bodies caused by eclipses could have wide-ranging ramifications. While we do not know if Mesoamerican groups recorded volcanic night, we cannot discount that it had significant affective power to overwhelm the senses and trigger psychological distress, creating a climate conducive to emotions such as fear and anxiety (Meskell 1994; Tarlow 2000, 2012). This effect was likely exacerbated when an eruption was catastrophic or unexpected, as the trauma can shake the very foundations of a person's faith (Cashman and Cronin 2008, 407). Therefore, we must ask whether volcanic night was regarded as a similar, powerful event and how peoples in Mesoamerica might have explained such phenomena.

EXTENDING THE NOTION OF NIGHT

Given the capacity to evoke fear and anxiety, how did people in Mesoamerica understand such events? Around the world, volcanic night has often been described in terms of its nocturnal qualities. For example, in reference to the Vesuvius eruption, Pliny the Younger described the eruption as producing a darkness "blacker and denser than any ordinary night" (quoted in Gilman 2007, 31), one that was "not the darkness of a moonless or cloudy night but as if a lamp had been put out in a closed room" (2014, 33). Many other such descriptions exist. The ways volcanic night has been referenced around the world reflect the similarity in terms of optical qualities of volcanic night and nighttime. However, volcanic night, much like eclipses, refuses "categorization in the ordinary epistemological and temporal framework" of nighttime in the Western world (Aveni 2018, 141). This complexity does not mean that volcanic night was not tied into nighttime and darkness in the Mesoamerican worldview. To address whether people in Mesoamerica similarly framed volcanic night as related to nighttime, we must first unpack night in Mesoamerica (see chapter 1 for a consideration of this relationship as well). Here I want to focus on the ancient Maya as a case study for understanding the relationship between nighttime and volcanic night.

The Maya were astute observers of the natural world and had a series of elaborate calendars to track the movements of the celestial bodies, of which the sun was perhaps the most significant. The Maya went to great lengths to record and track precise movements of the sun, including the timing and position of sunrises and sunsets, equinoxes, solstices, zenith and nadir passages, and even degrees and positions of sunlight and shadows. The necessity for knowing the length of night and degree of darkness stems from the Maya worldview that the movement of the celestial bodies within the supernatural world (where these bodies resided) affected the natural world and human actions within it. Thus by knowing the move-

FIGURE 3.2. *The AK'AB glyph. Redrawn by the author based on the drawing by John Montgomery (2002.)*

ment and phases of celestial bodies, the Maya could predict events on Earth. This knowledge was then recorded in all levels of Maya society, from daily rituals to the architecture and layout of cities (Aveni 2003).

Within the cosmological order was the passage of time, tracked by the movement of the sun. The base unit of time in the Maya calendar system was the day. Night, in this context, was the period between sunset and sunrise when the sun deity transitioned from the daily journey across the sky (day) into the underworld (night). The Classic period glyph for night was "AK'AB." This glyph translates to night, darkness, or both (figure 3.2). When placed within a cartouche, AK'AB became the third day sign in the 260-day count (the Tzolkin calendar). When placed in opposition to K'IN (the day sign), it could denote the specific period between sunset and sunrise.

In addition to time, night was also conflated with darkness, as supported by the iconographic and hieroglyphic record. The AK'AB sign could also represent darkness as an attribute of nature. When the sign appeared with other place signs, AK'AB referenced the dark nature of the place, such as the sweat bath (see Sheets and Thomason, and Olson, this volume), interiors of temples, the underworld (Schele and Mathews 1998), caves (both natural and constructed; see Coltman, this volume), and eclipses (Aveni 2018). When the sign was placed with people or the supernatural, it denoted their characteristics associated with night or darkness. For example, the appearance of the AK'AB glyph with the sun deity denoted the location of the sun in the underworld and its embodiment of its nocturnal personality. Likewise, objects could be shown to

have dark hues when associated with **AK'AB** (Stone and Zender 2011). Finally, when placed with the signs for West, the glyph represented both the direction and the color black. Clearly, the Maya understood night to be more than just a specific period of a day. Therefore, the association between night and darkness begs the question as to whether volcanic night was conceived of as part of the framework of "night" and "darkness" within the Maya cosmological order.

One clue that supports the close relationship between volcanic night and night/darkness comes from the way the Maya described eclipses. For the Maya, solar eclipses, which also produce darkness outside the context of nighttime, appear to have been associated with night, darkness, or both. When the **K'IN** sign was shown as half black (darkness)

FIGURE 3.3. *The winged K'IN sign translated as an eclipse glyph. The cross across the sun is formed by two eyeballs. Page 56b of the Dresden Codex. Author drawing.*

and half white surrounded by winged features, it is translated as an eclipse (figure 3.3). Likewise, when the sun was shown as having dark qualities during the day, it is again thought to reference an eclipse event (figure 3.4) (Milbrath 1995, 494). The association of night and darkness in imagery and text with eclipses among the pre-Hispanic, Colonial, and contemporary Maya shows that these events were also conceptualized in similar terms (García Velásquez 2006).

These examples illustrate that the Maya conflated night and darkness, at least as metaphorically interchangeable in some respects. Night could be a period of time, a personal or material quality, a location within the landscape, or a specific celestial event. Therefore, night and, by extension, darkness extended far beyond the traditional definition of night as a specific period between sunset and sunrise. In this respect, night and darkness were woven into every aspect of the cosmological order. It is therefore reasonable to assume that

FIGURE 3.4. *The Codex Telleriano-Remensis, page 40v, Los Angeles County Museum of Art. The sun disk is shown surrounded by stars, representing day as night. Author drawing.*

volcanic night in the wake of an eruption was likely conceptualized as linked to night and darkness. However, one quality would have rendered its occurrence as necessitating explanation and action: its unpredictability.

EXPLAINING VOLCANIC NIGHT

Based on Classic Maya astronomical knowledge of the celestial, it is likely that on any given evening, those with knowledge of the calendars could have predicted the length and luminosity of the night (see Gonlin and Dixon, this volume, on Maya luminosity). When the sun appeared outside of its normal iridescence, it would have been noted by anyone observing the sky. Thus the darkness and other optical phenomena that can accompany volcanic eruptions would have been significant in their ability to render the predictable temporarily unpredictable. The appearance of night/darkness outside of nighttime would have been of note to those who experienced it.

Even with modern instruments, volcanic eruptions and their impacts are difficult to predict. Mesoamericans would not have been able to forecast the timing, severity, or length of volcanic night. It is difficult to reconstruct how people explained events such as volcanic night, especially when those impacted were unknowledgable of the causes. While we know now that eruptions can produce a range of sensory effects such as unusual feelings, sights, sounds, and smells, the ability to link complex effects to specific triggers was problematic even a few decades ago (Grattan and Torrence 2007). However, the Maya did not need to understand that volcanic night and other optical phenomena were the products of the interaction between tephra and aerosol gasses emitted during volcanic eruptions to grasp the gravity of their occurrence. What is clear is that these events must have demanded explanation and interpretation.

So, how did people in Mesoamerica explain the occurrence of volcanic night? Given the affective nature of volcanic night and the need for human response in the wake of its occurrence, why is it not referenced in Mesoamerican texts, imagery, and architecture? It is possible that it simply has yet to be discovered. Alternatively, scholars *may* have interpreted volcanic night and altered hues of celestial bodies caused by volcanic eruptions as eclipses due to the similarity between the phenomena. In fact, numerous scholars have noted that some eclipse dates do not match actual eclipse events (Aveni 2003; Aveni and Calnek 1999; Dowd and Milbrath 2015; García Velásquez 2006; Hofling and O'Neil 1992; Milbrath 1995, 1999), an idiosyncrasy worth exploring in the future.

While no records (yet) exist that firmly document the occurrence of volcanic night for the pre-Hispanic Mesoamerican world, ethnohistoric and contemporary Maya accounts offer some potential insights. The idea that the astronomical was astrological (Thompson 1974) pervades many such accounts, and common themes relating the abandonment of the social order linked to the actions of both humans and the celestial bodies can be found. It is likely that these themes have antecedents tying back to the pre-Hispanic era. Based on these accounts, three potential explanations are proposed: (1) waning power or health of the sun deity; (2) failure, illegitimacy, or death of a ruler; or (3) misconduct of the people (Egan 2017). The following paragraphs review the archaeological, ethnohistoric, and contemporary data to support these possible explanations.

The sun, conceptualized as a deity, was a dynamic force in the Maya world. The successful daily journey of the sun was vital for world functioning; and the actions of the deity were closely tied to maize, fertility, and health (Sharer and Traxler 2006). The sun deity and his daily cycle of birth (rising), life (daylight), and death (setting) was responsible for bringing both light and darkness to the world. Like many of the Maya deities, the sun could embody positive and negative traits, depending on its manifestation. Every day the sun went on the journey through the world levels. Colonial and contemporary Maya groups describe the sun's journey differently; some reference birth and death in an endless cycle, while others say the sun goes to its house or a cave or is eaten at night. But all interpretations involve nightly transformation during the journey in the underworld (Freidel, Schele, and Parker 1993). Thus this deity is integral to understand nighttime and darkness in the Maya worldview.

Anything that prevented the successful daily journey of the sun was often regarded as a bad omen by the Maya. For example, among Colonial and contemporary Maya groups, the disappearance of the sun during a solar eclipse was explained as a sign that the sun had (briefly) lost its fecundity, that the body of the deity was ill, or that the sun had died—sometimes as the result of a battle in the heavens (Aveni 2018; Milbrath 1999, 27). It is plausible that similar explanations existed for the disappearance or dimness of the sun following a volcanic night. However, since the pre-Hispanic Maya predicted eclipses using their knowledge of the movement of the sun and moon in relation to the earth, volcanic night must have been exceedingly more worrisome due to its unpredictability and irregularity. Volcanic night was in essence something about which one (even the best astronomers) could not warn others.

The failure, illegitimacy, and death of a ruler have also been invoked as causes of disruption to the sun and other celestial bodies. Rulers, as "divine lords," served as intermediaries between the human and the supernatural. They were believed to possess the power of deities with the ability to call on them to witness auspicious events, and through sacrifice they were responsible for appeasing supernatural forces (Houston and Stuart 1996). In addition, Maya rulers could legitimize their power by adopting the name of the sun god—K'inich—into their title, thus identifying themselves with that deity's potency (Colas 2003). Thus the ability to predict events, such as eclipses, was a source of power. As intermediaries, their failure to predict celestial events, such as volcanic night, would have undermined their authority and legitimacy to the title of K'inich.

Likewise, the occurrence of unusual celestial events, such as eclipses and volcanic night, could be portents for the lives of rulers and other high-status people, such as astronomers and priests. For instance, for the Mexica, a Postclassic Mesoamerican culture, eclipses were conceptually tied to the death of a ruler because the ruler was the embodiment of the sun (Milbrath 1995). A similar concept is present among the Classic period Maya, an indication that they, too, may have viewed eclipses as omens for or causes of the death of a ruler (Colas 2003).

Last, the actions of everyday people in the Mesoamerican world could be the harbingers of unusual and worrisome phenomena. Eclipses, earthquakes, and other unusual events have been linked to the improper actions of people in Colonial and contemporary Maya myths. For the Lacandón, a contemporary Maya group, solar eclipses are believed to be a warning, meant to signal the watching eye of the creator deity. If it was observed that people were misbehaving, the deity could be given permission to enact destruction on the earth (Reilly 1997, 135). Likewise, earthquakes are thought to be caused by the four gods at the corners of the world shaking the pillars that hold up the earth to remind people to behave (Cline 1944). Many Maya groups, in the past and present, believe that the proper following of daily ritual ensures triumph over darkness (Aveni 2018, 148). Because events in the natural world could be attributed to human action, one can infer that volcanic night may have also been attributed to the improper behavior of people.

CONCLUSIONS

The catastrophic power of darkness in the wake of volcanic eruptions lies in its ability to render the ordered and predictable world temporarily unpredictable—triggering anxiety, fear, and emotional unrest. Volcanic night and the altered optical properties of the skies and celestial bodies following an eruption could extend for months or even years beyond the initial triggering eruption (Cooper and Sheets 2012; Grattan 2006; Gunn 2000; Sheets 2008; Stothers 1999; Torrence and Grattan 2002). Because the movement and nature of the celestial bodies could have real-time consequences for the world of the living and vice versa, the appearance of night and darkness outside of the usual boundaries must have demanded action and explanation (Houston and Taube 2000). It is possible that volcanic night may have been regarded as the product of action (or inaction) of deities, rulers, or people, with its occurrence necessitating response to be mediated. How people understood such events, what they meant, and what actions they prescribed would have had a direct impact on societal functioning. Volcanic night must have served as a reminder, for those who experienced it, of the power of the supernatural and the fragility of the social order. How people coped with it and with the other sensory aspects of volcanic eruptions, as well as what stories they told and actions they took in its wake, warrant further exploration.

We are only just beginning to understand the many ways people in the past engaged with night and darkness and what those concepts meant. This chapter took steps to address volcanic night, the darkness, and altered optical phenomena that can accompany large, explosive volcanic eruptions. For Mesoamericans, several large volcanic eruptions during the pre-Hispanic era had the potential to produce such phenomena. While relatively unusual, volcanic night must have provided a rare sensory experience, especially for those under the shadow of an eruption. Like sweat baths, interiors of temples, the underworld, caves, and eclipses, volcanic night reinforces the idea that for people in Mesoamerica, night and darkness were experienced beyond the nighttime. These nightscapes and darkscapes are equally essential in the larger narrative of how people experienced, engaged with, and explained night and dark in the pre-Hispanic Mesoamerican world.

FUTURE DIRECTIONS

As archaeologists seek to find new ways to study disasters, it is hoped that more complex and multifaceted approaches to reconstructing past disasters and how they have intersected with human population through time will emerge. Already, recent trends in disaster research have taken a more inclusive approach to disaster studies by framing them as social phenomena and by incorporating long-term time scales. This orientation has yielded surprising results about the resilience of human communities (Grattan and Torrence 2007; Sheets 2012). This case study took steps toward highlighting the hard to measure, incorporeal, and ephemeral aspects of volcanic eruptions. Eruptions are more than their measurable and quantifiable aspects, such as ashfall and pyroclastic flows that can devastate populations located in the path of destruction (often with high visibility to archaeologists at such well-known sites as Pompeii and Cerén); equally significant is the feeling of an eruption and its ability to produce unusual sights, sounds, and smells. The affective nature of eruptions and their sensory experience are a vital part of how people experience them. By expanding archaeological research on ancient disasters toward archaeologies of the senses and emotions (Fleisher and Norman 2016; Houston, Stuart, and Taube 2006; Joyce 2005; Tarlow 2012), we can begin to critically address the role of the immaterial and the hard to measure products of eruptions. While challenging to see archaeologically, these aspects are no less difficult to imagine (Hamilakis 2014, 4). The awesome power of volcanic night to inspire fear and awe has been remarked upon throughout history. As Lord Byron (2001) wrote in his 1816 poem "Darkness" in response to an eruption:

> The bright sun was extinguish'd, and the stars
>> Did wander darkling in the eternal space,
>> Rayless, and pathless, and the icy earth
>> Swung blind and blackening in the moonless air.

ACKNOWLEDGMENTS

This chapter stems from the session Night and Darkness in Pre-Columbian Mexico and Central America organized by Dr. Nancy Gonlin at the 2017 Society for American Archaeology Annual Meeting. I am very grateful for Dr. Gonlin and Dr. Christine Dixon for encouraging me to explore the intersecting topics of night, volcanoes, and Mesoamerica. Much of this research has been supported by Dr. Payson Sheets, without whom I would not have discovered my interest in volcanic eruptions and the Maya. I would also like to thank Dr. Brian McKee for his unwavering support.

REFERENCES

Aveni, Anthony F. 2003. "Archaeoastronomy in the Ancient Americas." *Journal of Archaeological Research* (11) 2: 149–191.

Aveni, Anthony F. 2018. "Night in Day: Contrasting Maya and Hindu Responses to Total Solar Eclipses." In *Archaeology of the Night: Life after Dark in the Ancient World*, ed. Nancy Gonlin and April Nowell, 139–154. Boulder: University Press of Colorado.

Aveni, Anthony F., and Edward E. Calnek. 1999. "Astronomical Considerations in the Aztec Expression of History: Eclipse Data." *Ancient Mesoamerica* 10 (1): 87–98.

Byron, Baron George Gordon. 2001. *Selected Poetry of Lord Byron*, ed. Leslie A. Marchand. New York: Modern Library.

Carey, Steven, and Haraldur Sigurdsson. 1986. "The 1982 Eruptions of El Chichón Volcano, Mexico (2): Observations and Numerical Modelling of Tephra-Fall Distribution." *Bulletin of Volcanology* 48 (2–3): 127–141.

Cashman, Katharine V., and Shane J. Cronin. 2008. "Welcoming a Monster to the World: Myths, Oral Tradition, and Modern Societal Response to Volcanic Disasters." *Journal of Volcanology and Geothermal Research* 176 (3): 407–418.

Cline, Howard. 1944. "Lore and Deities of the Lacandon Indians, Chiapas, Mexico." *Journal of American Folklore* 57 (224): 107–115.

Colas, Pierre Robert. 2003. "K'inich and King: Naming Self and Person among Classic Maya Rulers." *Ancient Mesoamerica* 14 (2): 269–283.

Cooper, Jag, and Payson Sheets, eds. 2012. *Surviving Sudden Environmental Change: Answers from Archaeology*. Boulder: University Press of Colorado.

Costanza, Robert, Lisa J. Graumlich, and Will Steffen, eds. 2007. *Sustainability or Collapse? An Integrated History and Future of People on Earth*. Cambridge, MA: MIT Press.

De Boer, Jelle Zeilinga, and Donald Theodore Sanders. 2002. *Volcanoes in Human History: The Far-Reaching Effects of Major Eruptions*. Princeton, NJ: Princeton University Press.

Dowd, Anne S., and Susan Milbrath, eds. 2015. *Cosmology, Calendars, and Horizon-Based Astronomy in Ancient Mesoamerica*. Boulder: University Press of Colorado.

Dull, Robert, John Southon, Steffen Kutterolf, Armin Freundt, David Wahl, and Payson Sheets. 2010. "Did the Ilopango TBJ Eruption Cause the AD 536 Event?" Paper presented at the American Geophysical Union Fall Meeting, San Francisco, CA, December 13–17.

Dull, Robert, John Southon, and Payson Sheets. 2001. "Volcanism, Ecology and Culture: A Reassessment of the Volcán Ilopango TBJ Eruption in the Southern Maya Realm." *Latin American Antiquity* 12 (1): 25–44.

Egan, Rachel. 2017. "Extending the Notion of Night: Volcanic Eruptions in Mesoamerica." Paper presented at the Society for American Archaeology Annual Conference, Vancouver, BC, March 30–April 3.

Fleisher, Jeffrey, and Neil Norman, eds. 2016. *The Archaeology of Anxiety: The Materiality of Anxiousness, Worry*. New York: Springer.

Ford, Anabel, and William I. Rose. 1995. "Volcanic Ash in Ancient Maya Ceramics of the Limestone Lowlands: Implications for Prehistoric Volcanic Activity in the Guatemala Highlands." *Journal of Volcanology and Geothermal Research* 66 (1–4): 149–162.

Freidel, David A., Linda Schele, and Joy Parker. 1993. *Maya Cosmos: Three Thousand Years on the Shaman's Path*. New York: William Morrow.

García Velásquez, Erik. 2006. "The Maya Flood Myth and the Decapitation of the Cosmic Caiman." *PARI Journal* 7 (1): 1–10.

Gilman, Benedicte. 2007. *Ashen Sky: The Letters of Pliny the Younger on the Eruption of Vesuvius*. Los Angeles: Getty Publications.

Global Volcanism Program, 2013. *Volcanoes of the World*, vol. 4.8.0., ed. Edward Venzke. Smithsonian Institution. https://doi.org/10.5479/si.GVP.VOTW4 2013.

Gonlin, Nancy, and April Nowell, eds. 2018. *Archaeology of the Night: Life after Dark in the Ancient World*. Boulder: University Press of Colorado.

Grattan, John. 2006. "Aspects of Armageddon: An Exploration of the Role of Volcanic Eruptions in Human History and Civilization." *Quaternary International* 151 (1): 10–18.

Grattan, John, and Robin Torrence. 2007. "Beyond Gloom and Doom: The Long-Term Consequences of Volcanic Disasters." In *Living under the Shadow. Cultural Impacts of Volcanic Eruptions*, ed. John Grattan and Robin Torrence, 1–18. London: Routledge.

Gudmundsson, Magnús T., Rikke Pedersen, Kristín Vogfjörd, Bergthöra Thorbjar-nardóttir, Steinunn Jakobsdóttir, and Matthew J. Roberts. 2010. "Eruptions of Eyjafjallajökull Volcano, Iceland." *Eos, Transactions of the American Geophysical Union* 91 (21): 190–191.

Gunn, Joel. 2000. *The Years without Summer: Tracing AD 536 and Its Aftermath*. British Archaeological Reports. Oxford: BAR Publishing.

Hamilakis, Yannis. 2014. *Archaeology and the Senses: Human Experience, Memory, and Affect*. Cambridge: Cambridge University Press.

Hofling, Charles A., and Thomas O'Neil. 1992. "Eclipse Cycles in the Moon Goddess Almanacs in the Dresden Codex." In *The Sky in Mayan Literature*, ed. Anthony F. Aveni and Russell B. Colgate, 102–132. Oxford: Oxford University Press.

Houston, Stephen, and David Stuart. 1996. "Of Gods, Glyphs and Kings: Divinity and Rulership among the Classic Maya." *Antiquity* 70 (268): 289–312.

Houston, Stephen, David Stuart, and Karl Taube. 2006. *The Memory of Bones: Body, Being, and Experience among the Classic Maya*. Austin: University of Texas Press.

Houston, Stephen, and Karl Taube. 2000. "An Archaeology of the Senses: Perception and Cultural Expression in Ancient Mesoamerica." *Cambridge Archaeological Journal* 10 (2): 261–294.

Joyce, Rosemary A. 2005. "Archaeology of the Body." *Annual Review of Anthropology* 34: 139–158.

Keys, David. 2000. *Catastrophe: An Investigation into the Origins of the Modern World*. New York: Ballantine.

Los Angeles County Museum of Art. *The Codex Telleriano-Remensis*. Ancientamericas.org. http://ancientamericas.org/codex/codex-telleriano-remensis.

Meskell, Lynn. 1994. "Dying Young: The Experience of Death at Deir el Medina." *Archaeological Review from Cambridge* 13 (2): 35–45.

Milbrath, Susan. 1995. "Eclipse Imagery in Mexica Sculpture of Central Mexico." *Vistas in Astronomy* 39 (4): 479–502.

Milbrath, Susan. 1997. "Decapitated Lunar Goddesses in Aztec Art, Myth, and Ritual." *Ancient Mesoamerica* 8 (2): 185–206.

Milbrath, Susan. 1999. *Star Gods of the Maya: Astronomy in Art, Folklore, and Calendars*. Austin: University of Texas Press.

Milbrath, Susan, and Anne S. Dowd. 2015. "An Interdisciplinary Approach to Cosmology, Calendars, and Horizon-Based Astronomy." In *Cosmology, Calendars, and Horizon-Based Astronomy in Ancient Mesoamerica*, ed. Anne S. Dowd and Susan Milbrath, 3–18. Boulder: University Press of Colorado.

Montgomery, John. 2002. "Drawing of the AK'AB Glyph." In *Dictionary of Maya Hieroglyphs*. FAMSI. http://www.famsi.org/mayawriting/dictionary/montgomery/mainindex.htm.

Newhall, Christopher G., and Stephen Self. 1982. "The Volcanic Explosivity Index (VEI): An Estimate of Explosive Magnitude for Historical Volcanism." *Journal of Geophysical Research: Oceans* 87 (C2): 1231–1238.

Nooren, Kees, Wim Z. Hoek, Hans Van Der Plicht, Michael Sigl, Manfred J. van Bergen, Didier Galop, Nuria Torrescano-Valle, Gerald Islebe, Annika Huizinga, and Tim Winkels. 2017. "Explosive Eruption of El Chichón Volcano (Mexico) Disrupted 6th Century Maya Civilization and Contributed to Global Cooling." *Geology* 45 (2): 175–178.

Plunket, Patricia, and Gabriela Uruñuela. 2008. "Mountain of Sustenance, Mountain of Destruction: The Prehispanic Experience with Popocatépetl Volcano." *Journal of Volcanology and Geothermal Research* 170 (1): 111–120.

Radice, Betty. 2003. *The Letters of the Younger Pliny*. London: Penguin Books.

Rampino, Michael R., and Stephen Self. 1982. "Historic Eruptions of Tambora (1815), Krakatau (1883), and Agung (1963), Their Stratospheric Aerosols, and Climatic Impact." *Quaternary Research* 18 (2): 127–143.

Rampino, Michael R., Stephen Self, and Richard B. Stothers. 1988. "Volcanic Winters." *Annual Review of Earth and Planetary Sciences* 16 (1): 73–99.

Reilly, F. Kent, III. 1997. "Ancient Maya Astronomy and Cosmology in Lacandon Maya Life." *Journal of Latin American Lore* 20 (1): 125–142.

Schele, Linda, and Peter Mathews. 1998. *The Code of Kings: The Language of Seven Sacred Maya Temples and Tombs*. New York: Scribner.

Sharer, Robert J., and Loa P. Traxler. 2006. *The Ancient Maya*. 6th ed. Stanford, CA: Stanford University Press.

Sheets, Payson D. 1971. "An Ancient Natural Disaster." *Expedition* 14 (1): 24–31.

Sheets, Payson D. 2008. "Armageddon to the Garden of Eden: Explosive Volcanic Eruptions and Societal Resilience in Ancient Middle America." In *El Niño, Catastrophism, and Culture Change in Ancient America 2008*, ed. Daniel H. Sandweiss and Jeffrey Quilter, 165–186. Washington, DC: Dumbarton Oaks.

Sheets, Payson D. 2012. "Responses to Explosive Volcanic Eruptions by Small to Complex Societies in Ancient Mexico and Central America." In *Surviving Sudden Environmental Change, Understanding Hazards, Mitigating Impacts, Avoiding Disasters*, ed. Jago Cooper, Payson D. Sheets, and David Abbott, 43–63. Boulder: University Press of Colorado.

Sigl, M., M. Winstrup, J. R. McConnell, K. C. Welten, G. Plunkett, F. Ludlow, U. Büntgen, M. Caffee, N. Chellman, D. Dahl-Jensen, H. Fischer, S. Kipfstuhl,

C. Kostick, O. J. Maselli, F. Mekhaldi, R. Mulvaney, R. Muscheler, D. R. Pasteris, J. R. Pilcher, M. Salzer, S. Schüpbach, J. P. Steffensen, B. M. Vinther, and T. E. Woodruff. 2015. "Timing and Climate Forcing of Volcanic Eruptions for the Past 2,500 Years." *Nature* 523: 543–549.

Stone, Andrea, and Marc Zender. 2011. *Reading Maya Art: A Hieroglyphic Guide to Ancient Maya Painting and Sculpture*. London: Thames & Hudson.

Stothers, Richard B. 1984. "Mystery Cloud of AD 536." *Nature* 307 (5949): 344–345.

Stothers, Richard B. 1996. "The Great Dry Fog of 1783." *Climatic Change* 32 (1): 79–89.

Stothers, Richard B. 1999. "Volcanic Dry Fogs, Climate Cooling, and Plague Pandemics in Europe and the Middle East." *Climatic Change* 42: 713–723.

Symons, George James. 1888. *Eruption of Krakatoa, and Subsequent Phenomena: Report of the Krakatoa Committee of the Royal Society*. Cambridge, MA: Harvard University Press.

Tarlow, Sarah. 2000. "Emotion in Archaeology." *Current Anthropology* 41 (5): 713–746.

Tarlow, Sarah. 2012. "The Archaeology of Emotion and Affect." *Annual Review of Anthropology* 41: 169–185.

Thompson, John Eric Sidney. 1974. "Maya Astronomy." *Philosophical Transactions of the Royal Society of London: Series A, Mathematical and Physical Sciences* 276 (1257): 83–98.

Thornton, Ian W. 1997. *Krakatau: The Destruction and Reassembly of an Island Ecosystem*. Cambridge, MA: Harvard University Press.

Torrence, Robin, and John Grattan. 2002. "The Archaeology of Disasters: Past and Future Trends." In *Natural Disasters and Culture Change*, ed. Robin Torrence and John Grattan, 1–18. London: Routledge.

US Geological Survey. 2015. "Volcano Hazards Program Glossary: Explosive Eruption." https://www.usgs.gov/volcanoes/glossary.

Young, Bailey K. 2000. "Climate and Crisis in Sixth-Century Italy and Gaul." In *The Years without Summer: Tracing AD 536 and Its Aftermath*, ed. Joel D. Gunn, 35–42. Oxford: Archaeopress.

4

The ancient Maya peoples of Mexico and Central America (see figure 0.1) lived in a Neotropical environment where bright moonlight, the stars, and the Milky Way were part of the nightscape and their mythology and perception of time (Vail 2017; Vail and Hernández 2013). We can begin to understand how the Late Classic (600–900 CE) Maya navigated the night in terms of illumination and what the roles of darkness and light were in Late Classic society by considering a historical ecology of this natural environment with the advantages and challenges of living in it (introduction, this volume). This chapter focuses on material evidence for the sources of lighting during Mesoamerican Classic times and the metaphorical role some lighting sources, such as hearths and torches, played in Classic Maya culture (Scherer and Tiesler 2018).

The explicit study of light and lighting in anthropology is recent but has already enhanced our understanding of social interactions. An anthropology of luminosity as put forth by Mikkel Bille and Tim Flohr Sørensen (2007, 265) presents this type of anthropological study as "an examination of how light is used socially to illuminate places, people and things, and hence affect the experiences and materiality of these, in culturally specific ways . . . how light, as matter in itself, may be manipulated and used in social and material practices." Luminosity, in their words, refers to "luminous qualities of the relationship between light and sight" (2007, 266). Cross-cultural linguistic expressions demonstrate

Illuminating Darkness in the Ancient Maya World

Nocturnal Case Studies from Copan, Honduras, and Joya de Cerén, El Salvador

NANCY GONLIN AND CHRISTINE C. DIXON-HUNDREDMARK

DOI: 10.5876/9781646421879.c004

how the fundamental concepts of light and dark are interwoven through metaphors, idioms, myths, and experiences into the consciousness of humanity through time and space: "Light is more than just a medium: it evokes agency" (2007, 264). The myriad socio-cultural dimensions to ideas and experiences of light and darkness make for fertile anthropological ground of inter- and intra-cultural comparisons. For example, consider who has access to lighting; how lighting and shadow are used to highlight or obscure; the role of lighting in safety, mischief, or resistance; or the way lighting can be used in displays of power and politics or entertainment. Understanding the cultural implications underlying and agencies involved in these examples, among others, can add dimensions for comprehending anthropological practices and interactions in the present and the past. Examinations of lighting and its role in the built environment further our understanding of the variation of human experiences (e.g., Griffiths 2016; Moyes and Papadopoulos 2017) and conceptions of nighttime and darkness, as well as broaden our consideration of the diversity of such perspectives, including how nocturnal illumination varied from house to house along the social spectrum and along the rural-urban continuum.

We all are familiar with, make sense of, and experience night and darkness; however, we do not all share the same perspectives and embodiments of these phenomena through time, space, or social position. Lychnologists, scholars who formally study luminosity, have made progress in our understanding of nocturnal and dark experiences through their study of lighting in the ancient world (e.g., Micheli and Santucci 2015; Popkin 2022; Strong 2018). Archaeological researchers have begun to direct intentional focus on understanding darkness (Dowd and Hensey 2016; Moyes 2012; introduction, this volume) and ancient nights (Gonlin and Nowell 2018), in particular, ancient Maya nights (Aveni 2018; Coltman 2018; Gonlin and Dixon 2018; see chapters by Coltman; Reed, Zeleznik, and Gonlin; Sheets and Thomason, this volume). As our inquiry expands, so, too, must our archaeological imaginings of the types of material culture employed in the dark and at night.

One ubiquitous component of night is darkness, varying globally by latitude but nonetheless experienced by humans the world over. We humans created various lighting mechanisms to overcome darkness or to emphasize it. This chapter explores the potential evidence in the archaeological record of the ancient Maya for tools of illumination, both materially and symbolically, by focusing on two different sites (Copan, Honduras, and Joya de Cerén, El Salvador). In the tropical region where the ancient Maya thrived, nights are relatively consistent in length throughout the calendar year. Fortunately, many lighting practices and evidence for the use of fire leave material traces in the archaeological record, as is the case for torches, hearths, and lamps the world over (e.g., Micheli and Santucci 2015; Torrell 2016). The study of lighting encompasses much more than such material items; it includes phenomenological experiences of light and darkness in space and of metaphorical expressions, phrases, and idioms woven into language and expressed in other symbolic media.

While ancient light has long since faded, information about the methods and tools used to illuminate darkness can be detected from several sources, including evidence contained in realia such as artifacts and features, the remains of writing and other symbols, the use of ethnohistoric documents, historical recordings, and the critical use of ethnographies. Thus archaeologists must draw inferences from varied sources to extract the material dimension of lighting rather than measuring the materiality of light itself—the lumen (Bille and Sørensen 2007, 269).

Among the array of Classic period Maya cultures (Beyyette 2017), a range of sources is available to provide information about the light and illumination mechanisms of the past. Beyond the simple documentation that lighting was used, the study of light can inspire new questions and dimensions of understanding, creating a pseudo-language that we can decipher and interpret. The varied historical uses for which lighting was utilized raise many research questions not directly considered before. Jeremy Coltman (2018, this volume) has explicitly considered what the role of light and darkness was in Late Classic society. We can examine how light was used as an agent in sociopolitical interactions. In a complex society, we would expect to find status differences in illumination, as Randolph Widmer (this volume) has found to be the case at Teotihuacan, Mexico. There very well may have been age, class, and gender dimensions to producing lighting. How lighting was used for safety, craft production, navigation, ritual, politics, and other symbolically laden activities should be investigated as one aspect of these habits. How vital was illumination to the nightly practices of the ancient Maya, given our current situation of nocturnal life? If ancient cities or outlying areas were lit at night, how was this illumination accomplished, and whose efforts and labor went into creating and tending lighting throughout the night? And what protections or vulnerabilities might such lighting afford? While many of the complexities of ancient uses of lighting might elude the archaeological gaze, as with other aspects of archaeological research we can examine and interrogate various lines of evidence to better understand these practices. We can investigate to what degree the ancient Maya engineered their structures with the aspect of lighting in mind. Such a bounty of new research avenues leads to productive

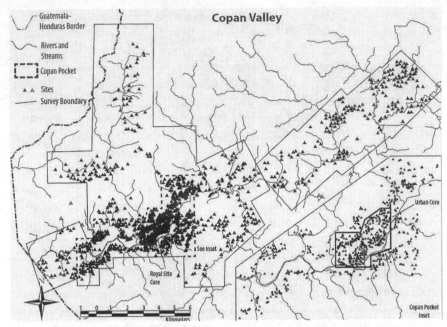

FIGURE 4.1. *Plan map of the Classic Maya site of Copan, Honduras, and the Copan Valley settlement. The Main Group and urban neighborhoods are shown in detail in the inset. Courtesy, David M. Reed.*

and exciting new considerations of the Classic period Maya, but interpretations must be grounded in archaeological data. One avenue of inquiry is to begin by considering the types of lighting technology employed and how to identify this evidence in the archaeological record.

Luminosity is addressed for the Late Classic Maya with the majority of evidence from two World Heritage sites: Copan, Honduras (figure 4.1), and Joya de Cerén, El Salvador (see figure 6.1). These two sites were chosen for a number of reasons. The first author (Gonlin) has conducted research at both locales, and the second author (Dixon-Hundredmark) excavated at Cerén for several field seasons (Dixon 2013). Second, excavations at Copan and Cerén have taken place over decades, creating a rich database for both sites. Third, these two sites provide contrasting degrees of preservation (Webster, Gonlin, and Sheets 1997), with Copan exhibiting remains typical of the tropics, while Cerén was a farming community with extraordinary preservation of organic materials and in situ remains. The sudden burial of Cerén beneath meters of volcanic ash in 660 CE has preserved remarkably detailed aspects of ancient lifeways, such as thatch roofs, the hollows where agricultural plants had existed, a painted gourd, a sweat bath (see Sheets and Thomason, this volume), and incredibly, even rolled-up woven sleeping mats in the rafters of the roofs. Such preservation was made possible by the nature of the volcanic phases of the Loma Caldera eruption that buried the site. Examination of these two different locations in the context of the archaeology of darkness and the night affords a range of evidence of lighting as we initiate focused consideration of ancient Maya lighting practices. We begin this exploration by briefly considering ecological dimensions of lighting before turning to cultural innovations in an array of illumination sources. We then address the relationship of lighting to the built environment before concluding with suggestions for future research.

LIGHTSCAPES OF THE TROPICS—LANDSCAPE CONSIDERATIONS

"Light is important because it is the only natural tool that allows us to visually perceive space; only through the contrast between light and shadow can we read a space and understand it correctly" (Cesario et al. 2016, 1). Sunlight and moonlight are two obvious natural sources of lighting experienced by humans the world over and through time (Alley 2017), and they can be manipulated in various ways. The Central American countries and much of Mexico lie within the Neotropics, where the average strength of the sun per day is greater due to nearly equal nighttime and daylight lengths year-round than in more northern or southern latitudes. The sun is literally more intense the nearer one gets to the equator (Harris 2017). These observations have well-known effects on the lightscapes of the tropics. While the intensity of the sun nearer the equator is often readily recognized, less often considered is that the amount of light the moon gives off is similarly affected by several factors.[1] The sun and the orbit of the moon taken together determine the brightness of the moon, but the difference is not perceptible to the human eye. Pollutants dim the brightness of all astronomical objects, as do clouds. During the agricultural season when fields are prepared and burning commences or other cultural practices are undertaken, such as lime production (Hansen et al. 2002; Seligson, Ortiz Ruiz, and Barba Pingarrón 2019), the moon's visibility is greatly diminished by smoky skies. Likewise, rainy season weather obscures the day sky with its grayness and the nighttime with its cloud cover. So, like our own night skies, the darkness of night would have varied from evening to evening for the ancient occupants of the Maya region. Thus natural phenomena and cultural practices were influences for the varied observance of the moon and the night sky of the past, as they are in the present: "Creating *lightscapes* are [*sic*] about recognizing the luminosity and materiality of the light source, and in the extended agency it offers to its surroundings" (Bille and Sørensen 2007, 274, original emphasis).

Beyond the larger geographical influences on the experiences of night, we must further consider the localized variation of individual perception of darkness and light. One aspect of light perception involves biological and cultural influences of individual human eyesight. Biologically, photoreceptors, the cones and rods in our eyes, will affect perception of light (Buser and Imbert [1992] and McIlwain [1996], quoted in Kamp and Whittaker 2018). Because the number of photoreceptors varies from individual to individual, each of us has, in effect, one's own unique lightscape. Color perception is as much a matter of culture as it is of cones and rods, as linguists well attest (Rowe and Levine 2012). Furthermore, suitable and preferred lighting is highly culturally patterned. In the archaeological record, it is difficult for us to see the degree of cultural considerations of how darkness is quantified. While we may not know the differences of individuals' photoreceptors or the specific cultural logic related to the categorization and appraisal of light perception, we can begin to think of how different social positions of members of Classic Maya society might have influenced various personal nightscapes and experiences.

The nighttime sky of the Classic Maya would have been immensely dark (darker than the nights witnessed by the majority of humans today) whether one lived in rural or urban areas of the Lowlands. There is no comparison to the past of the tremendous amount of light that currently pollutes the skies. Most modern humans do not appreciate the brightness of the moonlight, as the ancient Maya did (Christenson 2007, 79), because we often cannot detect it among the artificial sources of nocturnal lighting. In the context of examining ancient lighting practices, it is helpful to adopt a relativistic perspective and to recognize the lumicentric culture of the twenty-first century. However, in the context of darker nights, in a world less populated, and before the advent of electricity, the ancient Maya people—like other societies on earth at that time—would have been acclimated to dark nights and perhaps have been more sensitive to forms of light that modern humans might find rather dull in comparison to contemporary lighting techniques. Sensitivity to different phases of the moon, planning around these phases, and imbuing them with cultural meanings existed in Classic times (Landau, Hernandez, and Gonlin 2022). The creation of solar and lunar deities in innumerable cultural mythologies attests to the extreme significance afforded these astronomical bodies. The ancient Maya used the nocturnal lightscape of the tropics to great effect.

Contemporary Maya peoples are known to adhere to a lunar cycle in planting and harvesting, and modern Maya farmers have relayed observations on how moonfall and rainfall correlate (Landau, Hernandez, and Gonlin 2022). In a study that combines Classic Mayan inscriptions for accession dates at eleven major cities with the lunar cycle, Kristin Landau, Christopher Hernandez, and Nancy Gonlin (2022) detected a statistically significant pattern in which it was more likely for a king to come to power during either a full moon or a new moon, both of which are auspicious calendrical times. Given the immense astronomical knowledge of the Maya and the fact that divine rulership and agricultural productivity were intricately intertwined, it is no surprise that this correspondence has been found.

Another example of a royal event and the phase of the moon comes from a Classic Maya city along the Usumacinta River in Guatemala: Yaxchilan. Structure 23 sported numerous lintels, and one of them shows the queen, Lady Xoc, engaging in a bloodletting ceremony with her husband, King Shield Jaguar (Miller and Martin 2004; Schele and Miller 1986). The large torch used to illuminate the scene and the blue background may indicate that this ritual took place at night (Gonlin and Dixon 2018, 62). On the date of this performance, October 24, 709 CE, the waxing gibbous moon could have supplied additional lighting, since this celestial body was 89.94 percent illuminated at that time (2018, 62). How one uses light can have great social, political, and economic influence; and "light and shadows can be a way of permeating the boundary between public and private" (Bille and Sørensen 2007, 273). Below, we consider the experiences and effects of lighting in a review of the material evidence for how the ancient Maya illuminated their world and symbolic meanings attributed to such lighting sources.

TECHNOLOGIES AND SYMBOLISM OF ARTIFICIAL LIGHTING

Apart from natural sources of light (sun and moon) briefly considered above, there are many technologies to illuminate the dark that ancient people invented and utilized to great effect. Some of these technologies are portable—such as torches, lamps (Moullou 2015), a variety of ceramic forms that held fire, candlefish (Hough 1926, 199–201), and kukui (Van Gilder 2018)—while others are not (e.g., hearths, wall sconces). The lighting of fires has particular significance in Maya religion (Stuart 1998). Given the numerous hieroglyphic Classic Mayan passages that pertain to burning events, David Stuart (1998, 403) concludes that "burning and bloodletting went hand-in-hand as modes of spiritual and ritual expression." So, while our main focus in this section is the archaeological evidence for lighting practices, the symbolism of such technology should be simultaneously considered, as the two are conflated. Anthropologists have long challenged Western society's tendencies to prioritize binary divisions of secular and sacred domains by noting the inappropriateness for many cultures of the world to mark any distinction between the two. Given such a predisposition in our own culture, we are aware as we discuss the more mundane, utilitarian ideas of illumination technology that such tools would have been potentially employed and interwoven with significant symbolic meaning by the ancient Maya (Hamann 2002) and other cultures (Bille and Sørensen 2017).

It is essential to acknowledge the limitations of archaeological preservation for many types of illumination that would have relied heavily on perishable materials. Despite this constraint, much evidence remains from the Maya area regarding lighting technologies. Below, we consider the role that hearths, torches, candles, ceramic forms, mirrors, and fireflies played in the dark. While most of these sources of illumination are artifacts and by definition are portable, the hearth, as a feature, is not. Once we explicitly look for the tools and contexts of ancient light, only then do they become highly visible, in many cases having already been waiting in plain archaeological sight.

Hearths

Hearths have been the center of life for ancient peoples for eons (Nowell 2018) and comprise a substantial category of the cross-cultural archaeological record. Two of the best-known and most readily archaeologically visible forms of ancient Maya lighting were hearths and torches, one used in situ while the other was readily transportable. "As in many Maya homes today, the fire and hearth, generally surrounded by the three stones for cooking[,] are the center of life's activities. In the cosmic sense as well, the three stones are the center of the universe," as reported by Mark Pitts (2011, 12). Iconographically, the hearth is represented by three stones, as at Ceibal, Guatemala (Josserand and Hopkins 2011, 85). Karl Taube (1998, 436) reports that "large, worked stone spheres have been found over much of the Maya area," so we can surmise that these objects may be indicative of hearths. For the Maya, the three-stone hearth goes back centuries. At the Preclassic site of Yaxnohcah in the Yucatan, Kathryn Reese-Taylor (personal communication, July 23, 2019) and colleagues recovered in the plaza of the Grazia complex a hearth associated with a three-stone arrangement under an altar.[2] Both Joya de Cerén and Copan provide evidence for the significance of hearths. At Cerén, a number of hearths have been documented within their wider community context: the hearth found in the kitchen (Structure 11) of Household 1 is a rarity because it was intact, with three large stones used to support vessels that contained remains of ash from the fires of cooking below. At Cerén, many such features are found outdoors, such as the one along the western wall of a domicile, Structure 2, and two other hearths located in an area utilized for food preparation along the north exterior corridor of Structure 10, a religious community center. It is likely that feasts occurred at this building, according to Linda Brown's work (2001). Likewise, in rural Copan, from a small sample of completely excavated farmsteads (Gonlin 1993), the only indoor hearth was associated with a kitchen (Structure 3 at 7D-6–2), whereas others were found along exterior wall lines (e.g., 7D-3–1). Cooking and food preparation were part of every household's production. In summarizing both urban and rural Copan neighborhoods, Julia Hendon (2009, 119) remarks that "these quintessential activities of daily life took place in outdoor locations in the patio, on the terraces, or in roofed areas that were not fully enclosed rooms." We can envision nocturnal activities centered around the heat of the hearth easily taking place outdoors in the refreshing cool of the tropical night.

The demands for wood would have been substantial during Classic Maya times (Lentz et al. 2014; Robinson and McKillop 2013), perhaps enough to cause anthropogenic changes to the environment. Charcoal from pine and oak is very frequently recovered in archaeological contexts (see Slotten, this volume). Hearths are often associated with the heat of cooking activities, yet undoubtedly some hearths were lit to produce light itself in a set location.

While some fires were used for lighting nocturnal activities, others were lit for manufacturing purposes. Hearths were employed in a range of applications including heat, cooking, protection, and manufacture of plaster and pottery, among others. In the Maya world, a great deal of lime was produced for nixtamalization of maize, and hence lime and maize tie in with hearths where maize was cooked in various forms. Other types of lime production were necessary for plaster manufacture for construction (Abrams 1994, 116–117; Hansen et al. 2002; Russell and Dahlin 2007; Seligson 2016; Seligson, Ortiz Ruiz, and Barba Pingarrón 2019; Villaseñor 2010). As a result, numerous fires for burning limestone were necessary. It is worthwhile to consider whether lime manufacture was a nocturnal activity (see Widmer, this volume, for lime production at Teotihuacan), due to the high heat required to produce the end product. Hearths were a localized and fixed source of light and heat. Much more evidence for lighting techniques of the Maya world is found from mobile lighting sources, as described below. Portable hearths were created in ceramic vessels.

FIGURE 4.2. *Classic Maya ceramic cylinder vessel (K1278). Note the torches in the palace scene, which indicate that the activities portrayed likely took place in the dark and perhaps at night. Note also the mirror resting in a vessel on the floor. Photograph © Justin Kerr file no. K1278.*

TORCHES

The Late Classic Maya portrayed the torch, or "burning spear" (in reference to the torch held by King Shield Jaguar on Lintel 24, Structure 23 at Yaxchilan, Mexico [Miller and Martin 2004, 100]), in many different art forms. Evidence that torches were devices commonly employed by everyone in society includes media, such as the lintel representation and elite Classic Maya cylindrical vessels (figure 4.2); ethnographic observations and the wide range of uses of torches from quotidian to ceremonial contexts; and torch remains in domestic, ritual, and cave locations. Epigraphic evidence reinforces the widespread usage of torches through the existence of the Classic Mayan glyphs for fire (**K'AHK'**), spark (**TOK**), and torch (**TAAJ**) (Stone and Zender 2011). Torches were employed in other Mesoamerican societies as well, such as Teotihuacan (Nielsen and Helmke 2018; Widmer, this volume).

Ethnohistoric records provide insights into potential analogous practices throughout the Maya area. Charles Wisdom (1940, 21) reports many instances of torch use among the indigenous groups of Guatemala: "The Tunuco Indians, who live in the middle highlands . . . produce nearly all the pine torches sold in the markets, since the best pines for this purpose grow only in the middle highlands." Ch'orti' guests routinely received a provision of pine torches along with food and a bed, and in fact Wisdom recorded that "every family keeps a supply of torches in its kitchen to give to travelers to light their trail when caught by nightfall before getting home" (1940, 25). The documentation of torches provided for guests indicates the degree of widespread use for this material type and illustrates cultural patterns of hospitality. In addition to providing safe passage, torches were essential to night hunting of deer. Torches were used to blind the deer (1940, 71), making a deer in the torchlight an easier target (see Looper 2019 for a full treatment of deer by the Classic Maya). Torches also serve an essential role in the preparation of planting (Stone and Zender 2011, figure 66.4). Historically, John Lloyd Stephens (1843) and Frederick Catherwood, in their travels through Mexico and Central America in the mid-1800s, made note of the use of torches by their guides. Torches were clearly embedded in symbolism, as relayed by Andrea Stone and Marc Zender (2011, 161): "Given that fire played a pivotal role in Maya thought, the torch had complex symbolic dimensions. A torch could stand for solar heat and drought or the light of a firefly." Torches, especially those made of pine, had great utilitarian uses but were often essential elements of rituals (Morehart, Lentz, and Prufer 2005).

It has proven difficult to find remains of torches in residential contexts because of their perishable nature. The more one uses a torch, the less of it remains; when spent, a torch may simply be dropped in its location of disuse. Keith Prufer and Peter Dunham (2009, 305) noted that "poor preservation of organic materials at surface sites has likely masked evidence of an important relationship between the Maya ritual and pine in a variety of contexts, though remains of these materials are preserved in caves." Protected venues throughout the Maya Lowlands have produced remains of torches through careful excavations (2009, 297, 304; Stone and Brady 2012, 487) or the fired clay handles used in some cases to support the torch material (Brady 1989, 257–258).

Images on pottery vessels portray the ancient Maya using torches to light up palaces (figure 4.2) and perhaps large courtyards where nocturnal rituals were performed (Miller and Martin 2004, 21–22); just as likely, torches could have illuminated late night gatherings of common folk outside their banausic architecture. The perishable nature of torches makes preservation unlikely, unless in atypical situations. The Cerén site in El Salvador affords a rare opportunity to investigate ancient Maya life in a farming community and just such atypical preservation. The first phase of the Loma Caldera eruption coated the site with a fine ash that prevented initial burning of some perishable materials, such as thatch roofs; thus if the inhabitants had used torches at Cerén, these items potentially would have been preserved. To date, no torches have been identified in the inventory of the community's possessions (Sheets 2002). Despite the remarkable preservation of this site, there is surprisingly minimal evidence for lighting practices. Perhaps torches were less important at Cerén, perhaps they were used in contexts or locations not yet identified in this community, maybe their flammable nature resulted in their ignition and burning during the eruption, or possibly the inhabitants (who have not yet been found) ran away from the eruption with torches in hand. No torch holders were found built into or fastened to the walls of Cerén's structures, further suggesting that perhaps torches were used in other contexts, more limitedly, or not at all. However, we may consider anew the "cord holders" constructed from loop handles that have broken off from their vessels. Such loop handles were implanted in Cerén's architecture (Gonlin and Dixon 2018, 55; Sheets 2006) and may very well have been strong enough to support a small torch. Without charcoal marks in evidence as on stone structures, this scenario is not plausible on structures with thatched roofs. Despite the current lack of direct evidence for torches at Cerén, other forms of lighting technologies have left a mark, and one of the most significant is the hearth, as described above.

CANDLES

Another type of material culture useful in lighting is wax, a substance that has many uses—one of the most common of which is for candle making (Widmer, this volume), though remains of the actual substance are rare. Stone and Zender (2011, 161) and many others concur that wax candles and oil lamps were not found among the ancient Maya, a conclusion based on the lack of evidence. Apiaries, though difficult to detect archaeologically, have recently been recovered (Źrałka et al. 2018). Interestingly, an assemblage of artifacts from Cerén might suggest that some communities of the ancient Maya had the potential to manufacture and use wax candles. At Cerén in Structure 4, a storehouse/workshop for Household 4, excavations revealed a ball of beeswax about the size of a baseball (Payson Sheets, personal communication, March 31, 2017). Inhabitants placed the wax on a high shelf that paralleled the building's partition wall, and it was kept safe there along with many other items, including a censer decorated with an animal head (Gerstle and Sheets 2002, 78). Cotton, grown at Cerén (Lentz and Ramírez-Sosa 2002, 35–37), was a "vital crop" and one that could have been used for the manufacture of candle wicks (Wisdom 1940, 64). These components of the archaeological assemblage—beeswax,[3] a ceramic vessel, and cotton—could have been combined to form candle lighting for the Cerén community, or they may have each had very different separate functions.

Beyond the Classic Maya, there is no evidence for candle use in Mesoamerica pre-hispanically. Later in time, the Franciscan friar Bernardino de Sahagún (1963 [1569], book 10, 91) documented in the Florentine Codex an Aztec man

FIGURE 4.3. *Aztec man making candles. Depiction from the Florentine Codex, book 10, page 91 (Dibble and Anderson 1961 [1569]). Image in the public domain.*

making candles (figure 4.3). This figure is wearing a costume of Nahuatl and Spanish elements, and the process portrayed is that of tallow dipping.[4] Such candle makers and candle sellers were noted in the marketplace of Aztec society (Nichols 2013); *candelanamacac* is the hybrid term from the Spanish *candela* with a Nahuatl ending.[5] It is most likely, then, that candle making and candle using did not take place in Mesoamerica before the arrival of the Spaniards, pending further evidence and interpretations (Peterson 2003).

POTTERY FORMS

Evidence for lighting practices is also visible through pottery remains, a type of material abundant in the archaeological record. Ceramics are ideal vessels for retaining heat and containing fire, whether they are censers (*incensarios*), braziers, or shallow open dishes (Stone and Zender 2011, 155). While we typically think about dishes in terms of food consumption, these receptacles served to warm up, smoke up, and perhaps light up the night. One type of pottery vessel, the censer, is connected to hearths in the Maya area. Taube (1998, 434–435) reminds us that "aside from actual hearths, three-pronged *incensarios* probably also indicate the widespread occurrence of three-stone hearths by at least Late Formative times . . . these censers function much like portable three-stone hearths." Some of these vessels are fairly fancy and ornate, while others are plain. Their distribution varies, but they are found at most households in the Maya region distributed across the social spectrum. At Cerén, every household had at least one censer (Beaudry-Corbett and Bishop 2002,

121–122), as did rural Copan households (Gonlin 1993, 377–378). From this wide distribution of censers in non-elite settings, we can infer that censers were a part of ancient Maya life—day and night. The amount of light emanating from these incense-holding vessels, however, would be minimal to our modern eye.

The practice of incense burning was widespread across the ancient Maya world and, indeed, all of Mesoamerica. The Mayan glyph for incense was written as either "**POM**" or "**CH'AAJ**" (Scherer and Houston 2018). For Cerén, Payson Sheets (2006, 53) reports that each household had an incensario and burned copal. Copal, or *pom* in numerous Mayan languages (e.g., Laughlin 1975, 282), is a natural resin produced from a number of different trees, primarily of the *Bursera* and *Protium* genera (Case et al. 2003, 191), but this material may also come from *Pinus* spp. (2003, 194). A recent test of *Protium copal* incense by Zul Merali and colleagues (2018) examined this substance for its anxiolytic properties using animal models (rats) that were exposed to the incense for five minutes. It appears that even in that short exposure, a few minutes is enough to increase social interactions and has a calming effect. The burning of copal, as recorded in ethnographic contexts (Case et al. 2003, 190–191), drives away insects and is used as a remedy for numerous maladies (2003; Merali et al. 2018). Copal is symbolically tied to creation and is a prime offering for the gods. Smoke is intimately tied to ritual practices for numerous ancient Mesoamerican cultures (Scherer and Tiesler 2018). The nocturnal uses of copal could have been many. Apart from the calming effect the inhalation of the smoke would have had, its insect-scattering properties would have been most welcome in the tropics. In an everyday sense, one must wonder whether the burning of copal in storehouses and kitchens was a routine practice to make offerings to the deities while simultaneously keeping away pests. Perhaps other resins were used for more mundane purposes, though the censers from Cerén may indicate otherwise.

Candeleros (figure 4.4a) have been recovered in small numbers in rural Copan (Gonlin 1993) and areas just outside its urban core (Landau 2016) but were more numerous in urban zones (Willey et al. 1994, 308). These little pots are not typically found in high numbers in the Maya Lowlands (Landau 2016, 266) but were manufactured in abundance by people who lived in Copan, in areas east of Copan (Douglass 2007; Hendon, Joyce, and Lopiparo 2014; Urban and Smith 1987), and in the great Classic city of Teotihuacan in the Basin of Mexico (Carballo et al. 2019; Cowgill 2015; Foley 2017; Kolb 1988; Richey 2018). Although these enigmatic mini-containers elude functional classification, it is a misnomer to call them "candeleros," a Spanish word for "candleholder" or "candlestick." Per the discussion of candles above, it may be unlikely that candeleros were used to hold candles, although many sport burn marks and we know that beeswax was available to Mesoamericans. Another reason their use eludes us is that residue analysis has not been routinely performed on them (Richey 2018). Jennifer Foley (2017, 272) notes that "there are reports of the Aztecs using *candeleros* to hold blood, which was then absorbed by strips of paper and burned with copal incense on the altars of temples (Linné 2003 [1934]:113–114)." Candeleros come in a wide variety of shapes and quality of manufacture, from the simplest pinch pots to elaborately incised and punctated specimens. Some have one hole while other types have several, although most are small in size. Given this diversity, it is unlikely that all of them were used in similar fashion.

Although no candeleros have been recovered from Cerén, a small number of miniature pots have been found that are about the same size as Copan's fancy candeleros from the urban neighborhood of Las Sepulturas (figure 4.4b). Marilyn Beaudry-Corbett (1990, 157), who analyzed numerous Cerén ceramics, refers to these diminutive vessels as "miniature pigment pots" with good reason, observing that each contains the remains of powdered red pigment. Interestingly, she notes that "the rim diameters were extremely consistent in size (2.5 cm) and finish (a flattened lip), suggesting a stand[ard]ized production procedure such as fashioning them around a cylindrical form" (1990, 157). John Longyear (1952, 101–102) noted a similar manufacturing process for the Copan candeleros by forming the clay around a stick. The Cerén miniature pot illustrated in figure 4.4b sports appliquéd elements that perhaps form the shape of a turtle. This specimen resembles items recovered at Copan that are called bottle-shaped candeleros (figures 155–158 in Willey et al. 1994). No pigment or wax has been recovered from the Copan candeleros; however, it is unknown whether they were tested for residue.

While these types of small pots were not likely instrumental in lighting technology, as with censers, archaeologists associate candeleros with ritual activities (Hendon 1987; Hendon, Joyce, and Lopiparo 2014, 132), and smoke was a significant aspect of such behaviors. Patricia Urban and colleagues (2015) have hypothesized that candeleros from the Naco Valley, Honduras, were all about producing smoke. The distribution of candeleros at Naco sites is such that both residences and storehouses contain the greatest numbers. Fumigation of structures holding perishable materials could be accomplished with candeleros. Whether candeleros were used in nocturnal rituals or cleansing (fumigation) remains to be seen, although these two activities are not mutually exclusive, conceptually or otherwise.

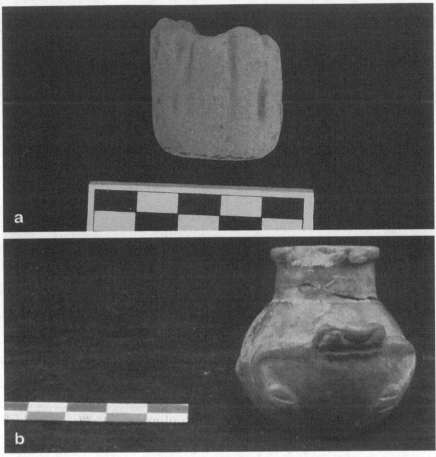

FIGURE 4.4. *(a) A Classic Maya candelero from San Lucas, Copan, Honduras. Courtesy, Kristin V. Landau. (b) Miniature pot (Specimen 295-5-18) from Cerén, El Salvador. Courtesy, Payson Sheets. Note the similarity in size (~2.5 cm) and shape of the aperture. Such small ceramics could have functioned as candleholders, for burning incense, and for holding pigments or other substances.*

Jennifer Loughmiller-Cardinal (personal communication, July 22, 2019) notes that most candeleros are not tested for residues, and when washed, any traces of wax could be destroyed.[6] For the sample of candeleros Loughmiller-Cardinal examined, she determined the remains of carbon, which indicates that something was burned inside of them, but those remains do not tell us exactly what was burned. Her future research involves testing candeleros and flasks for crossover residues of hallucinogens, perhaps those from *Bufo marinus* and copal (see Loughmiller-Cardinal and Zagorevski 2016). Clearly, the catchall label of "candeleros" encompasses a multi-use category that residue analysis can help refine. Whether the uses correlate with form is of interest and an avenue to be further explored, as Loughmiller-Cardinal (2019) has done for cylindrical Classic Maya vessels. Archaeologists are becoming increasingly sophisticated in distinguishing among use, purpose, and function (2019, 22–25; Loughmiller-Newman 2012) with the analytical tool of residue analysis and the consideration of context.

MIRRORS

A form of reflectivity could have been employed in illumination practices to enhance the potential of lighting. A mirror might not be the first object that comes to mind when considering illumination technology for the Late Classic Maya, but for eons, mirrors have been used "to enhance the effects of candlelight" (Brox 2010, 14) or light from any source. Mirrors are abundant in Mesoamerica and have been well studied (Gallaga and Blainey 2016). The Classic Maya recorded this object with the glyph **NEHN** (Stone and Zender 2011, 73). Their distribution at Copan is found in different contexts and in the remains of houses of all social statuses, from elite residences (Willey et al. 1994, 251–252) to the humblest abodes (Gonlin 1993, 406). To date, though, none have been recovered from Cerén (Payson Sheets, personal communication, August 21, 2017). Inferring from pictures on various media, such as highly decorated ceramic vessels, and from mirrors found in archaeological contexts, their size ranged from small to large (figure 4.2).

Given the wide distribution of mirrors in Mesoamerica, it should be considered whether these mirrors were used in illumination. They are not made of glass, as modern mirrors are, but most are manufactured from polished pyrite, obsidian, or hematite (Gallaga 2016, 4). Referencing the research of Emiliano Gallaga (2016, figure 1.1), the reflection one sees of oneself in a pyrite mirror looks smoky and is unclear. Such mirrors have been found primarily in a number of specific contexts: divination (Taube 1992), ornamentation on dress (Joyce 2002), or in "elite burial and cache contexts" (Blainey 2016, 180). For example, at Copan, two Teotihuacan-style mirrors (Nielsen 2006) were interred with the burial of a royal woman in the Margarita tomb in the central Acropolis (Bell 2002). It may be that mirrors relate to "how light is used in relation to social identity" (Bille and Sørensen 2007, 269). Indeed, Marc Blainey (2016, 184) maintains that iron-ore mirrors, like other shiny objects, could be interpreted as linking humans to the spirit world (Taube 2016, 302) and were "a classic component of the shaman's tool kit within the ancient Maya royal court" (Blainey 2016, 197). The ability to manipulate light and shadow is powerful, so it comes as no surprise that mirrors are often portrayed on pottery vessels depicting royal court scenes (figure 4.2) (see Coltman [this volume], who discusses the symbolism of the Spiral Eye Mirror motif and its connection to darkness).

FIREFLIES

The use of insects has a long history in Mesoamerica that extends from the earliest to contemporary times (Vela 2019). Various species, including bees, grasshoppers, scorpions, and butterflies, among others, have figured in the mythology and subsistence practices of Mesoamericans. Thus we consider another potential lighting source for the ancient world that comes from the realm of insects. Bioluminescent beetles might have played a role in lighting the dark and, to our knowledge, have not been previously considered as a source of lighting among the ancient Maya. Their ability to pierce the darkness, as recorded in the Popol Vuh, is well-known (Schuettler 2006). The substance that glows—luciferin—is also found in algae, bacteria, fungi, and other types of animals, such as jellyfish (Grimaldi and Engel 2005, 383–386). The *Lampyridae* taxonomic family includes many species of fireflies, some of which are referred to as lightning bugs, glowworms, and dark fireflies (Lewis 2016, 8). For fireflies, light is vital for communication, much more so than pheromones: "The duration of the flash, interval of the flash, and the location from where the beetle flashes are species dependent" (Grimaldi and Engel 2005, 384–385) (see also Lloyd 1997; Stanger-Hall, Lloyd, and Hills 2007). These small insects produce an extraordinary amount of light for their size; perhaps one reason is that, according to entomologists, "the light emitted by these insects is unique in being cold. Nearly 100 percent of the energy given off appears as light" (Borror, Triplehorn, and Johnson 1989, 432–433).

Walter Hough, as head curator of the Department of Anthropology of the United States National Museum (later the Smithsonian Institution) during the 1920s and 1930s, wrote a lengthy bulletin titled *Fire as an Agent in Human Culture* (1926). Among the many topics he included in this treatise was a section on fireflies. Fireflies as sources of light were common in both the Americas and the Far East (1926, 196). Hough described the American genus *Pyrophorus* at length, and mention is made of ethnohistorians and their encounter with fireflies (e.g., Herrera). Bernal Diaz is recorded as stating that "in his first experience with the Pyrophorus [he] thought them to be the matchlocks of numerous enemies in the forests and ordered his soldiers to prepare for action" (1926, 196). The light of these insects was apparently bright enough to serve as a sort of flashlight, guiding people through the bush. They were also employed for reading in the dark, lighting up a room, illuminating hunting expeditions (by securing the beetles on one's feet), and as a type of glowing jewelry worn by women.

Although Hough reports on many travelers' observations through Mexico, details are lacking for this part of the world on exactly how fireflies were collected and in what type of container they were stored. He did report on other areas, however (Hough 1926, 198):

> Necessarily in the employment of fireflies as light for various purposes there would arise the need of apparatus for confining the insects. In the West Indies this has taken the form of a lantern with a grating of small rods, like the cages in which the Chinese keep fighting crickets. Another form closer to nature is the calabash perforated with many small holes and furnished with a door. Humboldt describes the latter form used under remarkable circumstances during a voyage from Cumana [Venezuela].

Another type of container was noted "from Java a curious firefly lamp consisting of a small oval wooded box with pivoted lid. The interior is lined with pitch, upon which fireflies are stuck. Reserve fireflies are kept in a cane tube. The apparatus is described as a burglar's dark lantern" (1926, 198). He provides other provocative ideas for the containment of fireflies. Hough (1926, 197) states that "a Chinese student . . . inclosed fireflies in a paper lantern," and in Japan, they were kept in a cage. Only the lightest of materials would have been necessary to confine these little non-aggressive beetles, and of note is the fact that all of the materials are perishable.

The Classic Maya created a glyph for firefly (Lopes 2004; Stone and Zender 2011, 189) (figure 4.5). The iconography of the firefly or lightning bug (**KUHKAY**?) has been studied by Luís Lopes (2004, 6), who states that there is "evidence indicating their association with the underworld, with both Classic and Postclassic deities, and with several important Maya myths. In particular, fireflies seem to be equated with stars in some of these myths." In the Popol Vuh, fireflies are mentioned in the section describing the descent of the Hero Twins, Hunahpu and Xbalanque, into the Underworld, Xibalba. They are given a torch and two cigars, which they are to return to the Xibalbans: "As for the cigars, they just put fireflies on their tips. All night they would glow brilliantly because of them" (Christenson 2007, 153). Clearly, the prominent characteristic and potential of this bioluminescent beetle were realized by the Classic Maya, although we admittedly lack direct evidence for the beetle's utilization as a light source of any significance. Much of the lighting technology that may have been employed by them involves a reconsideration of the evidence already available to archaeologists. Our task is to evaluate anew the potential of various technologies and consider the possibilities, even those from unexpected sources such

FIGURE 4.5. *The Classic Maya firefly glyph* ***KUHKAY?***. *Drawing courtesy of Jeremy Coltman, digitized by David M. Reed.*

as fireflies. Today, fireflies are experiencing a decline in numbers and species due to diminishing habitats and light pollution (firefly.org). Perhaps as a result of few encounters with fireflies and readily available brighter light sources, modern humans are not likely to consider the firefly a source for illumination, but records show that fireflies have been used for a long time by peoples throughout the world to light up dark spaces.

LIGHTING AND THE BUILT ENVIRONMENT

Maya building design and layout afford insight into ancient considerations of lighting. Bille and Sørensen (2007, 270–272; 2017) study luminosity through the combined effect of light, architecture, and space—all of which are aspects frequently considered in architectural studies of built environments. Archaeologists have categorized architectural differences of the built Maya world based on perceived functions into temples, residences, ball courts, roads (*sacbeob*), plazas, sweat baths (*temazcales*), ancillary structures such as kitchens and warehouses, and special purpose buildings such as the community structures at Cerén (Gerstle and Sheets 2002) and the *popol na* at Copan (Fash 2011; Stomper 2001). We can examine different lighting choices in a variety of architectural settings to evaluate the mental templates of architecture and lighting. Of special relevance are structures typically categorized as residential buildings because of their domiciliary role in nightly activities and their association with artificial light (Moullou 2015).

At Copan, numerous residences have been completely excavated that run the gamut from the spectacular to the humble. Located outside the main ceremonial core but within the urban neighborhood of Las Sepulturas is the "House of the Bacabs," or 9N-8 (Webster 1989). Residents lived in several patio groups in 9N-8, the central and largest of which is Patio A, encompassing several structures (Structures 80–84) where the scribe himself lived. Inhabiting a house constructed entirely of stone had its advantages, to be sure, but it would have been naturally dark inside during the day and even more so at night. As has been noted for residential architecture in other cultures (e.g., Isbell 2009, 212; Jameson 1990, 98), illumination would have been essential in such dark spaces. Copan affords hints of elite lighting practices from burn marks visible on the floor of Structure 83. It is possible that such marks were made by braziers that provided warmth in the night. These ceramics have openings that would have allowed small amounts of light to escape and just might have been enough to enhance one's night vision, perhaps functioning as an early take on the night light. Alternatively, the use of shallow open dishes for lighting (per above) may have made their mark on the white plastered surface of the floor (see Widmer, this volume, for the use of such vessels at Teotihuacan). Such functional aspects of their use should not be separated from but viewed in conjunction with their ritual use. Undoubtedly, there was a strong connection between ritual use and fire. While there was sanctity to a fire's light, fire was also functionally an essential part of lighting the dark and the night. According to Stone and Zender (2011, 157), "Because of the transformative and cleansing aspects of fire, the act of fire-drilling came to be seen as a divine one, akin to the creation of the sun and the world." Thus whatever the container for flames, the light, smoke, and shadows may have held supernatural significance.

In Patio H of 9N-8 (Structures 64, 110, and 76), residents performed craft activities indoors, possibly by day and night as impending deadlines loomed for these artists. Among the many remains Widmer (2009) recorded in Room 110B was Vessel 3, a censer that contained only charcoal and lots of it. Widmer (2009, 182) surmised that "this censer functioned as either a light source for the room, as a container for a torch, or else for burning incense as part of the ritual prescription for artifact manufacture, perhaps both." Window slots in this structure would have allowed the penetration of natural light, whether from the sun or the moon. Such windows are not large but exist in other stone buildings in the Maya region. Kenneth Hirth (2009, 53) notes for the Highland Mexico site of Xochicalco that evidence for where lithic specialists conducted their craft was found "in the doorways of rooms that opened onto lighted areas." Given the sharpness of lithic debris, one would be able to see the glistening shards much easier in bright light and, it was hoped, retrieve as much as possible for safety's sake. Thus it appears that in addition to lighting choices, ancient Mesoamericans sensibly utilized areas of natural lighting such as doorways that allow natural light into spaces (for comparison, see Shepperson [2017] for a study of doorway light in ancient Mesopotamian domestic spaces). At Cerén, evidence for obsidian blade manufacture has not been found, but scrapers were re-sharpened by members of Household 1 by the ramada structure (Structure 5; see figure 6.1) (Payson Sheets, personal communication, September 1, 2019). This provenience further associates lighted areas and activities involving sharp tools.

Given the outdoor tropical lifestyles of ancient Mesoamericans, courtyards were fashioned as open areas for work but were essential for letting in light to the structures placed around them. Courtyards were also built to serve as marketplaces or focal nodes (Hutson 2016, 115) and were used for public events, among other functions (Inomata and Tsukamoto 2014); they could also serve as unrestricted areas where stargazing could take place (see Lopiparo, this volume). For structures that did not have windows or those with small ones (Healan 2009, 74), as noted above for 9N-8, open spaces were essential. Hendon's (2009, 120) comments on Room 110B of Patio H are instructive:

> The shell working in Copan's Structure 9N-110B Room 2 takes place in the most enclosed and least visible location considered here. It is the most private location, in the sense of being the most controllable by the participants and the least subject to intrusion by others. This privacy, which suggests a desire to keep hidden what was being produced or the process of production itself, comes at a cost: the only natural light comes from the doorway into Room 1, which in turn has only one doorway onto the terrace. Artificial light may have been provided by burning material in the two pots, but the amount of illumination would not be great. Thus, this was not an easy place to cut, scrape, and shape brittle shells into complicated shapes and objects. The other rooms, with their direct access to the outside, would have been better lit and still fairly private if the workers stayed inside and did not take advantage of the large terrace, but not nearly as conducive to secrecy.

Moving away from Copan's stone structures and away from elite contexts, thousands of urban and rural dwellers built their small abodes with cobble foundations and topped them with perishable materials of wattle and daub or thatch, materials that are well-suited to the tropics.[7] Unlike the dark, dank stone interiors of elite housing, these residences breathed; and exterior light sources, such as the sun and moon or the light produced from an outdoor hearth, could penetrate them. One consideration of internal lighting in perishable structures that are not solidly built is that at night, as Kristin Landau (personal communication, December 5, 2016) has highlighted, any light inside would showcase interior activities and people's figures would be visible to those who are outside the house. Thus while these perishable structures are easier to light up than their stone counterparts, such lighting would come at the cost of some internal privacy. Hendon (2009, 116) sums up these architectural differences by stating:

> Stone walls are less permeable to sound and light, confining what is said or done inside them more effectively than walls of wood or clay. At the same time, stone walls limit the occupants' observation of people's comings and goings to what can be seen through the doorway (if not closed off by a mat or curtain). The more permeable wood and clay walls change the experience of inside and outside and afford greater opportunity for continued interaction between people working outside and inside the house (Robin 2002). People inside the wattle-and-daub houses in rural and urban Copan, such as those found at practically all groups considered here, would have been able to note what was happening outside more readily than their neighbors in stone buildings.

At the farming community of Cerén, residents chose a range of building materials with different implications for lighting: wattle and daub (e.g., Structure 2), pole and thatch (e.g., Structure 11), and adobe (e.g., Structure 3). Adobe would have functioned similarly to stone architecture in that both materials would keep out light and sound yet retain interior coolness through the hot hours of the day. Structure 3 at Cerén is the largest known structure in the community and was a public building, likely used for political and community meetings. The use of adobe would have allowed for additional privacy and coolness during the days and evenings. Inhabitants wisely built their kitchen (Structure 11) from pole and thatch materials that allowed for the flow of air when cooking. Storehouses, located close to domiciles, were necessary for keeping the family's possessions safe during the night (Hendon 2000, 2010; Isbell 2009, 212), and at Cerén, these structures were typically built with wattle and daub. Domiciles were likewise constructed of wattle and daub, allowing for some privacy and some natural lighting during bright moonlit nights. Thus the construction materials of buildings in the ancient Maya world were selected in part with a consideration of lighting needs and were likely varied based on the function and social context of the building.

From indoor lighting and workspaces, we next consider outdoor work areas, many of which have been commonly recorded throughout other Neotropical areas. In Peru, William Isbell (2009, 212) has found Huari architectural engineering at Moraduchayuq, where "patio group courtyards had plaster floors, with drains connected to canals beneath them. Each floor was raised along its edges, about 15 to 25 cm, forming a stone-faced bench usually a little more than a meter wide. This kept rainwater out of the lateral rooms, and I suspect that the elevated benches were covered by long eaves projecting from roofs over lateral rooms. Consequently, these benches were securely sheltered, but well lighted, making them excellent work and living space."

Another cross-cultural example hails from Europe. At the Classical (fifth and fourth centuries BC) Greek town of Olynthos, Michael Jameson (1990, 97–98) considers environmental factors, the use of the courtyard, and the orientation of domestic structures:

> In the Mediterranean climate, where most of the known Greek houses are located, the court was in fact one of the chief living areas of the house. The rooms opening directly off the court, as most did, were extensions of the court's living area. Porches shading one or more sides of the court increased the utility of the court as living space; they might extend into the court area or be a recessed space off the court. (Porches supported by pillars on all four sides of the court, forming a peristyle, were rare before the Hellenistic period.) A porch was most useful on the north side of the court. Ancient writers recommended south-facing living rooms to gain sun in the winter while being shaded from the higher sun of summer; where the site permitted, as on the north hill of Olynthos, south-facing living rooms do in fact predominate.

These two examples afford cross-cultural insights into the ways architecture, including indoor and outdoor spaces, was constructed to facilitate lighting, heating, and household activities during the day and the night.

NAVIGATING THE NIGHT WITH THE COLOR WHITE

Other lighting technologies might have been used in the ancient Maya world. The color white (*saq*) reflects well, and materials with this color were often chosen by the ancient Maya for construction. In a number of Mayan languages, "The term often means something 'artificial' or something devised by human arrangement or skill" (Houston et al. 2009, 33). It is no surprise, then, that a constructed road is called a *sacbe* (meaning "white way"), one of which was built at Cerén and many of which were built at Copan and other Maya cities, such as Chunchucmil (Hutson 2016) and Uci (Hutson and Welch 2021). A less typically preserved aspect of illumination present at Cerén is the ground surface itself. Cerén is constructed on and with the very light tephra of the previous Ilopango eruption, called Tierra Blanca Joven (TBJ), named for the young white nature of the soil that formed from Ilopango ash. Cerénians would have recognized that the fine granules of the TBJ ash made for excellent construction material that could be compacted to form a surface with a cement-like hardness. Pozzolanic plasters (which incorporate volcanic ash and glass), similar to TBJ, are known from other areas of the Maya Lowlands, namely Calakmul, Mexico, and Lamanai, Belize (Villaseñor 2010; Villaseñor and Graham 2010). Such plasters may have increased glimmer to catch the moonlight (Meghan Strong, personal communication, December 12, 2017). At Cerén, this TBJ ash was used as the living surface, for construction of buildings and agricultural beds, and for the creation and maintenance of the sacbe at the site. In construction of the sacbe, the whitest of the TBJ ash was selected for its uppermost layer. Inhabitants would have appreciated the reflective nature of such light-colored ash, and perhaps that characteristic was one motivation for using the lightest ash to coat the top layer of the sacbe, apart from its pozzolanic properties. This white coating would have allowed light from the moon and stars to reflect off its surface. While not totally illuminating the way, a lighter path through agricultural fields and into the community center would have resulted. After evening gatherings near Structure 10, this same path might have been used by those living further from the core of the community to safely navigate their way home. The lighter ash used throughout the construction of Cerén would have contributed to greater reflectivity of the entire landscape of the built environment, further aiding nightly navigation in the dark. Similarly, throughout the Maya area, plaster was a common substance used to coat plaza floors, benches, buildings, and sacbeob. While much of this plaster was often painted bright blue and red, white plaster would have had a similar effect as the TBJ surface at Cerén, providing a reflective surface that would create better visibility in the very dark ancient Maya nights.

At the ancient city of Chunchucmil in Mexico's Yucatan Peninsula, Scott Hutson and Jacob Welch (2016, 120–122) discuss the dozens of *chichbes* that were built by urban inhabitants. These features were slightly elevated pathways lined with parallel stone walls. Their predominance throughout the city may have been vital for nighttime navigation. The glimmering limestone of the Yucatan Peninsula provided raw material for construction but also, by default, for enhanced pathways for those who were out and about in the darkness. Consider that such pathways would have been able to easily guide nighttime celebrants who were safely returning home from observance of royal rituals in the city center. This type of infrastructure would have enabled residents to go where they wanted to go even in the dark of night by guiding them home (Smith 2019, 140).

CONCLUSIONS

In this chapter, we have provided an initial exploration of the evidence for luminosity in the ancient Maya world and brought together a variety of sources of potential lighting that would have been available. It is unknown whether the ancient Maya purposely lit their cities continuously through dark nights or periodically as needed for special activities that took place in the dark or at night, but populated areas undoubtedly sparkled from the light given off by the dying embers of outdoor fires or the shimmering reflections of moonlight off white plastered sacbeob and buildings.

We have touched on the ways the Maya lit up the night and how they managed their built environment to better utilize low, natural lighting sources. Among the artificial lighting sources, fire was by far the most ubiquitous, but rarely did it leave obvious archaeological evidence, leaving us to wonder about its potential manipulation and economic requirements. We should consider whether niches in monumental stone buildings were receptacles for lighting devices and whether receptacles that could hold torches or other sources of light were placed at intervals to light pathways. The round of activities involved in sustaining the multitudes of fires requires us to look at how the fires were fed, who collected resources, and from where. Lychnologists look at evidence for lamps and the production of vegetable oils or animal fats that could be used as illuminants (Meghan E. Strong, personal communication, December 12, 2017). The cost of firewood and producing charcoal would have been phenomenal, as Widmer (this volume) reveals for Teotihuacan. In the Maya area, firewood, collected by children and adults, was an essential part of daily and nightly life—critical for cooking, making plaster, craft activities, ceramic production, heat, safety, deer hunting, and many more pursuits. Some have suggested potential environmental impacts of massive fire practices, such as those required for production of the limestone plaster that covered the cities of the ancient Maya landscape. As archaeologists increasingly tease apart evidence for ancient nightly practices from the material record, it is essential to carefully consider the vast array of artifacts, features, epigraphy, iconography, and historical records that potentially hold information for connecting the night, darkness, and illumination. However the ancient Maya lit up the dark, the symbolism of doing so was inescapable and likely provided as much comfort as the light itself.

ACKNOWLEDGMENTS

Thanks to Bellevue College entomologist Jason Fuller for many resources and illuminating discussions on lightning bugs and to Jeremy Coltman who drew **KUHKAY?** (figure 4.5) and David Reed who digitized it. David Reed composed figure 4.1, Justin Kerr provided figure 4.2, and Kristin Landau allowed use of the photo of the candelero from her Copan excavations (figure 4.4a), as did Payson Sheets from his Cerén excavations (figure 4.4b). We appreciate Venicia Slotten for sharing her expertise on paleoethnobotany and resources on the anxiolytic properties of copal. Cecelia Klein kindly contacted Kevin Terraciano, Jeanette Peterson, and Lisa Sousa; and all four readily provided their expertise on art history, colonial manuscripts, history, and linguistics. We are indebted to Jennifer Loughmiller-Cardinal for sharing her work and insights on candeleros, as well as to Geoff McCafferty's assistance in tracking down and sharing undergrad research on candeleros by his student Kate Richey. Kathryn Reese-Taylor informed us about remains of Preclassic hearths. Gratitude is due to K. Viswanathan, David M. Reed, Kristin V. Landau, and Meghan E. Strong for their insightful edits and comments, as well as to three anonymous reviewers who provided critical feedback.

NOTES

1. "Why Do the Size and Brightness of the Full Moon Change?" 2021.

2. Many thanks to Kathryn Reese-Taylor who generously shared unpublished data with us (July 23, 2019) on the striking ritual assemblage, which included the hearth, three-stone arrangement, and altar at Yaxnohcah dated to the Middle Preclassic.

3. Kevin Terraciano kindly conveyed to us, through Cecelia Klein (July 23, 2019), that there is a "distinction between wax made from bees and tallow in the Mixteca, and different entries in the Mixtec Vocabulario for both." Furthermore, "Molina gives *xicocuitlatl* for *cera*, combining *xicotli* (bee) and *cuitlatl* (excrement) (f. 34 1st num.). Molina gives both the indigenous term and the loanword under *candela de cera* and *candela de sebo*." See Terraciano 2001.

4. This observation came from Jeannette Peterson, through Cecelia Klein (personal communication, July 18, 2019), and is very much appreciated.

5. We are indebted to Jeannette Peterson who conveyed to Cecelia Klein that "two other bits of evidence that candle making was primarily colonial come from language and image in the Florentine. The text calls candles by their Spanish, not Nahuatl, name: a candle seller is *candelanamacac*—a hybrid term from the Spanish which is *candela*—used in the parallel translation of the Florentine. This suggests there was no Nahuatl term" (personal communication, July 18, 2019). In this same communique, Lisa Sousa observed that in Colonial documents, "people [were] 'getting fire' from their neighbors to start a hearth fire for cooking, heat, and light. Seems candles were used mainly in churches, or Spanish homes."

6. Jennifer Cardinal-Loughmiller very helpfully responded to our query regarding residue analysis of candeleros and allowed us to report preliminary findings. While some of these vessels have been examined, much work remains to be done (personal communication to Gonlin, July 22, 2019).

7. Observations of wattle and daub housing in modern Copan (Gonlin during the 1980s and Kristin Landau during the 2000s) reveal that these structures are constructed in such a fashion that walls are not uniform and gaps exist between the chunks or blocks of daub. Solid uniform walls are not the norm for this type of construction.

REFERENCES

Abrams, Elliot M. 1994. *How the Maya Built Their World: Energetics and Architecture*. Austin: University of Texas Press.

Alley, Bobbye. 2017. "Stages of the Sun and Moon." http://sciencing.com/stages-sun -moon-6874673.html.

Aveni, Anthony F. 2018. "Night in Day: Contrasting Ancient and Contemporary Maya and Hindu Responses to Total Solar Eclipses." In *Archaeology of the Night: Life after Dark in the Ancient World*, ed. Nancy Gonlin and April Nowell, 139–154. Boulder: University Press of Colorado.

Beaudry-Corbett, Marilyn. 1990. "Joya de Cerén Ceramics: Classification and Preliminary Analysis of Household Inventories." In *1990 Investigations at the Cerén Site, El Salvador: A Preliminary Report*, ed. Payson D. Sheets and Brian R. McKee, 154–172. Boulder: Department of Anthropology, University of Colorado.

Beaudry-Corbett, Marilyn, with contributions from Ronald L. Bishop. 2002. "Ceramics and Their Use at Cerén." In *Before the Volcano Erupted: The Ancient Cerén Village in Central America*, ed. Payson Sheets, 117–138. Austin: University of Texas Press.

Bell, Ellen E. 2002. "Engendering a Dynasty: A Royal Woman in the Margarita Tomb, Copan." In *Ancient Maya Women*, ed. Traci Ardren, 89–104. Walnut Creek, CA: Altamira.

Beyyette, Bethany J. 2017. "Introduction: On Constructing a Shared Understanding of Historical Pasts and Nearing Futures." In *"The Only True People": Linking Maya Identities Past and Present*, ed. Bethany J. Beyyette and Lisa J. LeCount, 3–23. Boulder: University Press of Colorado.

Bille, Mikkel, and Tim Flohr Sørensen. 2007. "An Anthropology of Luminosity: The Agency of Light." *Journal of Material Culture* 12 (3): 263–284.

Bille, Mikkel, and Tim Flohr Sørensen. 2017. "In Visible Presence: The Role of Light in Shaping Religious Atmospheres." In *The Oxford Handbook of Light in*

Archaeology, ed. Holley Moyes and Costas Papadopoulos, 1–27. Oxford: Oxford University Press.

Blainey, Marc G. 2016. "Techniques of Luminosity: Iron-Ore Mirrors and Entheogenic Shamanism among the Ancient Maya." In *Manufactured Light: Mirrors in the Mesoamerican Realm*, ed. Emiliano Gallaga and Marc G. Blainey, 179–206. Boulder: University Press of Colorado.

Borror, Donald J., Charles A. Triplehorn, and Norman F. Johnson. 1989. *An Introduction to the Study of Insects*, 6th ed. Philadelphia: Saunders College Publishing.

Brady, James E. 1989. "An Investigation of Maya Ritual Cave Use, with Special Reference to Naj Tunich, Peten, Guatemala." PhD dissertation, University of California, Los Angeles.

Brown, Linda A. 2001. "Feasting on the Periphery: The Production of Ritual Feasting and Village Festivals at the Cerén Site, El Salvador." In *Feasts: Archaeological and Ethnographic Perspectives on Food, Politics, and Power*, ed. Michael Dietler and Brian Hayden, 368–390. Washington, DC: Smithsonian Institution Press.

Brox, Jane. 2010. *Brilliant: The Evolution of Artificial Light*. New York: Houghton Mifflin Harcourt.

Buser, Pierre, and Michel Imbert. 1992. *Vision*. Cambridge, MA: MIT Press.

Carballo, David M., Kenneth G. Hirth, Daniela Hernandez Sarinana, Gina M. Buckley, Andres G. Mejia Ramon, and Douglass J. Kennett. 2019. "New Research at Teotihuacan's Tlajinga District, 2012–2015." *Ancient Mesoamerica* 30 (1): 95–113.

Case, Ryan J., Arthur O. Tucker, Michael J. Maciarello, and Kraig A. Wheeler. 2003. "Chemistry and Ethnobotany of Commercial Incense Copals, Copal Blanco, Copal Oro, and Copal Negro, of North America." *Economic Botany* 57 (2): 189–202.

Cesario, Ernesto, Roberta Cocci Grifoni, Angela Leuzzi, and Davide Paciotti. 2016. "Light Design in Historical Buildings, Parameters and Prototypes: Comparisons of Façade Behavior: Metal Meshes vs. High-Tenacity Composite Meshes." Paper presented at the International Conference on Environment and Electrical Engineering. Florence, Italy, June 6–8.

Christenson, Allen J., trans. 2007. *Popol Vuh: Sacred Book of the Quiché Maya People*. Electronic version of original 2003 publication. Mesoweb: www.mesoweb.com /publications/Christenson/PopolVuh.pdf.

Coltman, Jeremy D. 2018. "Where Night Reigns Eternal: Darkness and Deep Time among the Ancient Maya." In *Archaeology of the Night: Life after Dark in the Ancient World*, ed. Nancy Gonlin and April Nowell, 201–222. Boulder: University Press of Colorado.

Cowgill, George L. 2015. *Ancient Teotihuacan: Early Urbanism in Central Mexico*. New York: Cambridge University Press.

Dibble, Charles E., and Arthur J.O. Anderson. 1961 [1569]. *The Florentine Codex*, Book 10: *The People*. Salt Lake City: University of Utah Press.

Dixon, Christine C. 2013. "Farming and Power: Classic Period Maya Manioc and Maize Cultivation at Cerén, El Salvador." PhD dissertation, University of Colorado, Boulder.

Douglass, John G. 2007. "Smoke, Soot, and Censers: A Perspective on Ancient Commoner Household Ritual Behavior from the Naco Valley, Honduras." In *Commoner Ritual and Ideology in Ancient Mesoamerica*, ed. Nancy Gonlin and Jon C. Lohse, 123–142. Boulder: University Press of Colorado.

Dowd, Marion, and Robert Hensey, eds. 2016. *Darkness: Archaeological, Historical, and Contemporary Perspectives*. Oxford: Oxbow Books.

Fash, Barbara W. 2011. *The Copan Sculpture Museum: Ancient Maya Artistry in Stucco and Stone*. Cambridge, MA: Peabody Museum Press and David Rockefeller Center for Latin American Studies, Harvard University.

Firefly.org. "Firefly Conservation and Research."

Foley, Jennifer Marie. 2017. "When Worlds Collide: Understanding the Effects of Maya-Teotihuacán Interaction on Ancient Maya Identity and Community." PhD dissertation, Vanderbilt University, Nashville, TN.

Gallaga, Emiliano. 2016. "Introduction." In *Manufactured Light: Mirrors in the Mesoamerican Realm*, ed. Emiliano Gallaga and Marc G. Blainey, 3–24. Boulder: University Press of Colorado.

Gallaga, Emiliano, and Marc G. Blainey, eds. 2016. *Manufactured Light: Mirrors in the Mesoamerican Realm*. Boulder: University Press of Colorado.

Gerstle, Andrea, and Payson Sheets. 2002. "The Civic Complex." In *Before the Volcano Erupted: The Ancient Cerén Village in Central America*, ed. Payson Sheets, 74–80. Austin: University of Texas Press.

Gonlin, Nancy. 1993. "Rural Household Archaeology at Copan, Honduras." PhD dissertation, The Pennsylvania State University, University Park.

Gonlin, Nancy, and Christine C. Dixon. 2018. "Classic Maya Nights at Copan, Honduras and El Cerén, El Salvador." In *Archaeology of the Night: Life after Dark in the Ancient World*, ed. Nancy Gonlin and April Nowell, 45–76. Boulder: University Press of Colorado.

Gonlin, Nancy, and April Nowell, eds. 2018. *Archaeology of the Night: Life after Dark in the Ancient World*. Boulder: University Press of Colorado.

Griffiths, David Gareth. 2016. "The Social and Economic Impact of Artificial Light in the Roman World." PhD dissertation, University of Leicester, School of Archaeology and Ancient History, Leicester, UK.

Grimaldi, David, and Michael S. Engel. 2005. *Evolution of the Insects*. Cambridge: Cambridge University Press.

Hamann, Byron. 2002. "The Social Life of Pre-Sunrise Things: Indigenous Mesoamerican Archaeology." *Current Anthropology* 43 (3): 351–382.

Hansen, Richard, Steven Bozarth, John Jacob, David Wahl, and Thomas Schreiner. 2002. "Climatic and Environmental Variability in the Rise of Maya Civilization: A Preliminary Perspective from the Northern Peten." *Ancient Mesoamerica* 13 (2): 273–295.

Harris, Amy. 2017. "Sun Intensity vs. Angle." http://sciencing.com/sun-intensity-vs-angle-23529.html.

Healan, Dan M. 2009. "Household, Neighborhood, and Urban Structure in an 'Adobe City': Tula, Hidalgo, Mexico." In *Domestic Life in Prehispanic Capitals: A Study of Specialization, Hierarchy, and Ethnicity*, ed. Linda R. Manzanilla and Claude Chapdelaine, 67–88. Memoirs of the Museum of Anthropology 46. Ann Arbor: Museum of Anthropology, University of Michigan.

Hendon, Julia A. 1987. "The Uses of Maya Structures: A Study of Architecture and Artifact Distribution at Sepulturas, Copán, Honduras." PhD dissertation, Harvard University, Cambridge, MA.

Hendon, Julia A. 2000. "Having and Holding: Storage, Memory, Knowledge, and Social Relations." *American Anthropologist* 102 (1): 42–53.

Hendon, Julia A. 2009. "Maya Home Life: Daily Practice, Politics, and Society in Copan, Honduras." In *Domestic Life in Prehispanic Capitals: A Study of Specialization, Hierarchy, and Ethnicity*, ed. Linda R. Manzanilla and Claude Chapdelaine, 101–125. Memoirs of the Museum of Anthropology 46. Ann Arbor: Museum of Anthropology, University of Michigan.

Hendon, Julia A. 2010. *Houses in a Landscape: Memory and Everyday Life in Mesoamerica*. Durham, NC: Duke University Press.

Hendon, Julia A., Rosemary A. Joyce, and Jeanne Lopiparo. 2014. *Material Relations: The Marriage Figurines of Prehispanic Honduras*. Boulder: University Press of Colorado.

Hirth, Kenneth G. 2009. "Household, Workshop, Guild, and Barrio: The Organization of Obsidian Craft Production in a Prehispanic Urban Center." In *Domestic Life in Prehispanic Capitals: A Study of Specialization, Hierarchy, and Ethnicity*, ed. Linda Manzanilla and Claude Chapdelaine, 43–65. Ann Arbor: Museum of Anthropology, University of Michigan.

Hough, Walter. 1926. *Fire as an Agent in Human Culture*. Bulletin 139. Washington, DC: Smithsonian Institution, Government Printing Office.

Houston, Stephen, Claudia Brittenham, Cassandra Mesick, Alexandre Tokovinine, and Christina Warriner. 2009. *Veiled Brightness: A History of Ancient Maya Color.* Austin: University of Texas Press.

Hutson, Scott R. 2016. *The Ancient Urban Maya: Neighborhoods, Inequality, and Built Form.* Gainesville: University Press of Florida.

Hutson, Scott R., and Jacob Welch. 2016. "Chapter 4: Neighborhoods at Chunchucmil." In *The Ancient Urban Maya: Neighborhoods, Inequality, and Built Form,* by Scott R. Hutson, 97–138. Gainesville: University Press of Florida.

Hutson, Scott R., and Jacob Welch. 2021. "Roadwork: Long-Distance Causeways at Uci, Yucatan, Mexico." *Latin American Antiquity* 32 (2): 310–330.

Inomata, Takeshi, and Kenichiro Tsukamoto. 2014. "Gathering in an Open Space: Introduction to Mesoamerican Plazas." In *Mesoamerican Plazas: Arenas of Community and Power,* ed. Kenichiro Tsukamoto and Takeshi Inomata, 3–15. Tucson: University of Arizona Press.

Isbell, William H. 2009. "Huari: A New Direction in Central Andean Urban Evolution." In *Domestic Life in Prehispanic Capitals: A Study of Specialization, Hierarchy, and Ethnicity,* ed. Linda R. Manzanilla and Claude Chapdelaine, 197–219. Memoirs of the Museum of Anthropology 46. Ann Arbor: Museum of Anthropology, University of Michigan.

Jameson, Michael H. 1990. "Domestic Space in the Greek City-State." In *Domestic Architecture and the Use of Space: An Interdisciplinary Cross-Cultural Study,* ed. Susan Kent, 92–113. Cambridge: Cambridge University Press.

Josserand, J. Kathryn, and Nicholas A. Hopkins. 2011. "Maya Hieroglyphic Writing: Workbook for a Short Course on Maya Hieroglyphic Writing." *FAMSI.* Tallahassee: Jaguar Tours. http://www.famsi.org/mayawriting/hopkins/MayaGlyphWritingWrkBk.pdf.

Joyce, Rosemary A. 2002. "Beauty, Sexuality, Body Ornamentation, and Gender in Ancient Mesoamerica." In *In Pursuit of Gender,* ed. Sarah Nelson and Miriam Rosen-Ayalon, 81–92. Walnut Creek, CA: Altamira.

Kamp, Kathryn, and John Whittaker. 2018. "The Night Is Different: Sensescapes and Affordances in Ancient Arizona." In *Archaeology of the Night: Life after Dark in the Ancient World,* ed. Nancy Gonlin and April Nowell, 77–94. Boulder: University Press of Colorado.

Kolb, Charles C. 1988. "Classic Teotihuacan Candeleros: A Preliminary Analysis." In *Ceramic Ecology Revisited, 1987: The Technology and Socioeconomics of Pottery, Part ii,* ed. Charles C. Kolb, 449–645. Vol. 436(ii) of the BAR International Series. Oxford: British Archaeological Reports.

Landau, Kristin V. 2016. "Maintaining the State: Centralized Power and Ancient Neighborhoods in Copán, Honduras." PhD dissertation, Northwestern University, Evanston, IL.

Landau, Kristin V., Christopher Hernandez, and Nancy Gonlin. 2022. "Lunar Power in Ancient Maya Cities." In *After Dark: The Nocturnal Urban Landscape and Lightscape of Ancient Cities*, ed. Nancy Gonlin and Meghan E. Strong. Louisville: University Press of Colorado. In press.

Laughlin, Robert M. 1975. *The Great Tzotzil Dictionary of San Lorenzo Zinacantán*. Smithsonian Contributions to Anthropology 19. Washington, DC: Smithsonian Institution Press.

Lentz, David L., Nicholas P. Dunning, Vernon L. Scarborough, Kevin S. Magee, Kim M. Thompson, Eric Weaver, Christopher Carr, Richard E. Terry, Gerald Islebe, Kenneth B. Tankersley et al. 2014. "Forests, Fields, and the Edge of Sustainability at the Ancient Maya City of Tikal." *Proceedings of the National Academy of Sciences of the United States of America* 111 (52) (December 30): 18513–18518.

Lentz, David L., and Carlos R. Ramírez-Sosa. 2002. "Cerén Plant Resources: Abundance and Diversity." In *Before the Volcano Erupted: The Ancient Cerén Village in Central America*, ed. Payson Sheets, 33–42. Austin: University of Texas Press.

Lewis, Sara. 2016. *Silent Sparks: The Wondrous World of Fireflies*. Princeton, NJ: Princeton University Press.

Linné, Sigvald. 2003 [1934]. *Archaeological Researches at Teotihuacan, Mexico*. Tuscaloosa: University of Alabama Press.

Lloyd, James E. 1997. "Firefly Mating, Ecology, and Evolution." In *The Evolution of Mating Systems of Insects and Arachnids*, ed. Jae C. Choe and Bernard J. Crespi, 184–192. Cambridge: Cambridge University Press.

Longyear, John M. 1952. *Copán Ceramics: A Study of Southeastern Maya Pottery*. Washington, DC: Carnegie Institution of Washington.

Looper, Matthew. 2019. *The Beast Between: Deer in Maya Art and Culture*. Austin: University of Texas Press.

Lopes, Luís. 2004. "Some Notes on Fireflies." http://www.mesoweb.com/features/lopes/Fireflies.pdf.

Loughmiller-Cardinal, Jennifer. 2019. "Distinguishing the Uses, Functions, and Purposes of Classic Maya 'Chocolate' Containers: Not All Cups Are for Drinking." *Ancient Mesoamerica* 30 (2): 13–30.

Loughmiller-Cardinal, Jennifer A., and Dmitri Zagorevski. 2016. "Maya Flasks: The 'Home' of Tobacco and Godly Substances." *Ancient Mesoamerica* 27 (1): 1–11.

Loughmiller-Newman, Jennifer. 2012. "The Analytic Reconciliation of Classic Mayan Elite Pottery: Squaring Pottery Function with Form, Adornment, and Residual Contents." PhD dissertation, State University of New York, Albany.

McIlwain, James T. 1996. *An Introduction to the Biology of Vision*. Cambridge: Cambridge University Press.

Merali, Zul, Christian Cayer, Pamela Kent, Rui Liu, Victor Cal, Cory S. Harris, and John T. Arnason. 2018. "Sacred Maya Incense, Copal (*Protium copal*—Burseraceae), Has Anti-Anxiety Effects in Animal Models." *Journal of Ethnopharmacology* 216: 63–70.

Micheli, Maria Elisa, and Anna Santucci, eds. 2015. *Lumina: Convegno Internazionale di Studi Urbino 5–7 guigno 2013*. Pisa, Italy: Edizione ETS.

Miller, Mary, and Simon Martin. 2004. *Courtly Art of the Ancient Maya*. San Francisco: Fine Arts Museums of San Francisco and Thames and Hudson.

Morehart, Christopher T., David L. Lentz, and Keith M. Prufer. 2005. "Wood of the Gods: The Ritual Use of Pine (Pinus Spp.) by the Ancient Lowland Maya." *Latin American Antiquity* 16 (3): 255–274.

Moullou, Dorina. 2015. "Lighting Night-Time Activities in Antiquity." In *Lumina: Convegno Internazionale di Studi Urbino 5–7 guigno 2013*, ed. Maria Elisa Micheli and Anna Santucci, 199–212. Pisa, Italy: Edizione ETS.

Moyes, Holley, ed. 2012. *Sacred Darkness: A Global Perspective on the Ritual Use of Caves*. Boulder: University Press of Colorado.

Moyes, Holley, and Costas Papadopoulos, eds. 2017. *The Oxford Handbook of Light in Archaeology*. Oxford: Oxford University Press.

Nichols, Deborah L. 2013. "Merchants and Merchandise: The Archaeology of Aztec Commerce at Otumba, Mexico." In *Merchants, Markets, and Exchange in the Pre-Columbian World*, ed. Kenneth G. Hirth and Joanne Pillsbury, 49–84. Washington, DC: Dumbarton Oaks Research Library and Collection.

Nielsen, Jesper. 2006. "The Queen's Mirrors: Interpreting the Iconography of Two Teotihuacan Style Mirrors from the Early Classic Margarita Tomb at Copan." *PARI Journal* 6 (4): 1–8.

Nielsen, Jesper, and Christophe Helmke. 2018. "'Where the Sun Came into Being': Rites of Pyrolatry, Transition, and Transformation in Early Classic Teotihuacan." In *Smoke, Flames, and the Human Body in Mesoamerican Ritual Practice*, ed. Vera Tiesler and Andrew K. Scherer, 77–107. Washington, DC: Dumbarton Oaks Research Library and Collection.

Nowell, April. 2018. "Upper Paleolithic Soundscapes and the Emotional Resonance of Nighttime." In *Archaeology of the Night: Life after Dark in the Ancient World*, ed. Nancy Gonlin and April Nowell, 27–44. Boulder: University Press of Colorado.

Peterson, Jeanette Favrot. 2003. "Crafting the Self: Identity and the Mimetic Tradition in the *Florentine Codex*." In *Sahagún at 500: Essays on the Quincentenary of the Birth of Fr. Bernardino de Sahagún*, ed. John Frederick Schwaller, 223–253. Berkeley: Academy of American Franciscan History.

Pitts, Mark. 2011. "A Brief History of Piedras Negras as Told by the Ancient Maya: History Revealed in Maya Glyphs." *The Aid and Education Project, Inc. FAMSI.* http://www.famsi.org/research/pitts/pitts_piedras_negras_history.pdf.

Popkin, Maggie L. 2022. "Illuminating the Mysteries of the Great Gods at Samothrace, Greece." In *After Dark: The Nocturnal Urban Landscape and Lightscape of Ancient Cities*, ed. Nancy Gonlin and Meghan E. Strong. Boulder: University Press of Colorado. In press.

Prufer, Keith M., and Peter S. Dunham. 2009. "A Shaman's Burial from an Early Classic Cave in the Maya Mountains of Belize, Central America." *World Archaeology* 41 (2): 295–320.

Richey, Kate. 2018. "The Enigmatic Function of Candeleros." Honours thesis, University of Calgary, Alberta, Canada.

Robin, Cynthia. 2002. "Outside of Houses: The Practices of Everyday Life at Chan Noohol, Belize." *Journal of Social Archaeology* 2: 245–268.

Robinson, Mark E., and Heather I. McKillop. 2013. "Ancient Maya Wood Selection and Forest Exploitation: A View from the Paynes Creek Salt Works, Belize." *Journal of Archaeological Science* 40 (10) (October 1): 3584–3595. doi: 10.1016/j.jas.2013.04.028.

Rowe, Bruce M., and Diane P. Levine. 2012. *A Concise Introduction to Linguistics*, 3rd ed. Boston: Prentice-Hall.

Russell, Bradley, and Bruce Dahlin. 2007. "Traditional Burnt-Lime Production at Mayapán, Mexico." *Journal of Field Archaeology* 32 (4): 407–423.

Sahagún, Bernardino de. 1963 [1569]. *Earthly Things, Book 11 of the Florentine Codex*, Trans. and ann. Charles E. Dibble and A.O.J. Anderson. Santa Fe and Salt Lake City: School of American Research and University of Utah.

Schele, Linda, and Mary Ellen Miller. 1986. *The Blood of Kings: Dynasty and Ritual in Maya Art*. New York: George Braziller.

Scherer, Andrew K., and Stephen Houston. 2018. "Blood, Fire, Death: Covenants and Crises among the Classic Maya." In *Smoke, Flames, and the Human Body in Mesoamerican Ritual Practice*, ed. Vera Tiesler and Andrew K. Scherer, 109–150. Washington, DC: Dumbarton Oaks Research Library and Collection.

Scherer, Andrew K., and Vera Tiesler, eds. 2018. *Smoke, Flames, and the Human Body in Mesoamerican Ritual Practice*. Washington, DC: Dumbarton Oaks Research Library and Collection.

Schuettler, David J. 2006. "Fireflies in the Night: Indigenous Metaphor in Zapatista Folktales." PhD dissertation, Union Institute and University, Cincinnati, OH.

Seligson, Kenneth E. 2016. "The Prehistoric Maya Burnt Lime Industry: Socio-economy and Environmental Resource Management in the Late and Terminal Classic Period Northern Maya Lowlands (650–950 CE)." PhD dissertation, University of Wisconsin, Madison.

Seligson, Kenneth E., Soledad Ortiz Ruiz, and Luis Barba Pingarrón. 2019. "Prehispanic Maya Burnt Lime Industries: Previous Studies and Future Directions." *Ancient Mesoamerica* 30 (2): 199–219.

Sheets, Payson, ed. 2002. *Before the Volcano Erupted: The Ancient Cerén Village in Central America.* Austin: University of Texas Press.

Sheets, Payson. 2006. *The Cerén Site: An Ancient Village Buried by Volcanic Ash in Central America,* 2nd ed. Belmont, CA: Thomson Wadsworth.

Shepperson, Mary. 2017. "Visibility, Privacy, and Missing Windows: Lighting Domestic Space in Ancient Mesopotamia." In *The Oxford Handbook of Light in Archaeology,* ed. Holley Moyes and Costas Papadopoulos, 1–21. Oxford: Oxford University Press. doi: 10.1093/oxfordhb/9780198788218.013.19.

Smith, Monica L. 2019. *Cities: The First 6,000 Years.* New York: Viking.

Stanger-Hall, Kathryn R., James E. Lloyd, and David M. Hills. 2007. "Phylogeny of North American Fireflies (Coleoptera: Lampyridae): Implications for the Evolution of Light Signals." *Molecular Phylogenetics and Evolution* 45: 33–49.

Stephens, John Lloyd. 1843. *Incidents of Travel in Yucatan,* vol. 1. New York: Harper and Brothers.

Stomper, Jeffrey Alan. 2001. "A Model for Late Classic Community Structure at Copán, Honduras." In *Landscape and Power in Ancient Mesoamerica,* ed. Rex Koontz, Kathryn Reese-Taylor, and Annabeth Headrick, 197–230. Boulder: Westview.

Stone, Andrea, and James E. Brady. 2012. "Maya Caves." In *Encyclopedia of Caves,* ed. William B. White and David C. Culver, 486–490. New York: Academic.

Stone, Andrea, and Marc Zender. 2011. *Reading Maya Art: A Hieroglyphic Guide to Ancient Maya Painting and Sculpture.* London: Thames and Hudson.

Strong, Meghan E. 2018. "A Great Secret of the West: Transformative Aspects of Artificial Light in New Kingdom Egypt." In *Archaeology of the Night: Life after Dark in the Ancient World,* ed. Nancy Gonlin and April Nowell, 249–264. Boulder: University Press of Colorado.

Stuart, David. 1998. "'The Fire Enters His House': Architecture and Ritual in Ancient Maya Texts." In *Function and Meaning in Classic Maya Architecture,* ed. Stephen D. Houston, 373–425. Washington, DC: Dumbarton Oaks Research Library and Collection.

Taube, Karl A. 1992. "The Iconography of Mirrors at Teotihuacan." In *Art, Ideology, and the City of Teotihuacan*, ed. Janet C. Berlo, 169–204. Washington, DC: Dumbarton Oaks Research Library and Collection.

Taube, Karl A. 1998. "The Jade Hearth: Centrality, Rulership, and the Classic Maya Temple." In *Function and Meaning in Classic Maya Architecture*, ed. Stephen D. Houston, 427–478. Washington, DC: Dumbarton Oaks Research Library and Collection.

Taube, Karl A. 2016. "Through a Glass, Brightly: Recent Investigations Concerning Mirrors and Scrying in Ancient and Contemporary Mesoamerica." In *Manufactured Light: Mirrors in the Mesoamerican Realm*, ed. Emiliano Gallaga and Marc G. Blainey, 285–314. Boulder: University Press of Colorado.

Terraciano, Kevin. 2001. *The Mixtecs of Colonial Oaxaca: Ñudzahui History, Sixteenth through Eighteenth Centuries*. Stanford, CA: Stanford University Press.

Torrell, Betty R. 2016. "The Hearth as Machine—the Place of the Hearth in the Victorian Middle Class Parlor." Paper presented at the 2016 Victorians Institute Conference, North Carolina State University, Raleigh, October 14–15.

Urban, Patricia, Edward Schortmann, Jacob Griffith-Rosenberger, Reagan Neviska, and Chelsea Katzeman. 2015. "Through a Smoke Cloud Darkly: The Possible Social Significance of Candeleros in Terminal Classic Naco Valley Society." Poster presented at the 80th Annual Meeting of the Society for American Archaeology, San Francisco, CA, April 15–19.

Urban, Patricia A., and Sylvia M. Smith. 1987. "The Incensarios and Candeleros of Central Santa Barbara: Distributional and Functional Studies." In *Interaction on the Southeast Mesoamerican Frontier: Prehistoric and Historic Honduras and El Salvador*, ed. Eugenia J. Robinson, 267–279. BAR International Series 327. Oxford, England: British Archaeological Reports.

Vail, Gabrielle. 2017. "Venus Lore in the Postclassic Maya Codices: Deity Manifestations of the Morning and Evening Star." *Ancient Mesoamerica* 28 (2): 475–488.

Vail, Gabrielle, and Christine Hernández. 2013. *Re-Creating Primordial Time: Foundation Rituals and Mythology in the Postclassic Maya Codices*. Boulder: University Press of Colorado.

Van Gilder, Cynthia L. 2018. "In the Sea of Night: Ancient Polynesia and the Dark." In *Archaeology of the Night: Life after Dark in the Ancient World*, ed. Nancy Gonlin and April Nowell, 155–176. Boulder: University Press of Colorado.

Vela, Enrique, ed. 2019. Special edition 86 on "Insectos en Mesoamérica." *Arqueología Mexicana*.

Villaseñor, Isabel. 2010. *Building Materials of the Ancient Maya: A Study of Archaeological Plasters*. Saarbrücken, Germany: Lambert Academic Publishing.

Villaseñor, Isabel, and Elizabeth Graham. 2010. "The Use of Volcanic Materials for the Manufacture of Pozzolanic Plasters in the Maya Lowlands: A Preliminary Report." *Journal of Archaeological Science* 37: 1339–1347.

Webster, David, ed. 1989. *The House of the Bacabs, Copan, Honduras*. Studies in Precolumbian Art and Archaeology 29. Washington, DC: Dumbarton Oaks Research Library and Collection.

Webster, David, Nancy Gonlin, and Payson Sheets. 1997. "Copan and Cerén: Two Perspectives on Ancient Mesoamerican Households." *Ancient Mesoamerica* 8 (1): 43–61. doi: 10.1017/S0956536100001565.

"Why Do the Size and Brightness of the Full Moon Change?" Ask an Astronomer. 2021. http://curious.astro.cornell.edu/about-us/46-our-solar-system/the-moon/observing-the-moon/129-why-do-the-size-and-brightness-of-the-full-moon-change-intermediate.

Widmer, Randolph J. 2009. "Elite Household Multicrafting Specialization at 9N-8, Patio H, Copán." In *Housework: Craft Production and Domestic Economy in Ancient Mesoamerica*, ed. Kenneth G. Hirth, 174–204. Archaeological Papers of the American Anthropological Association 19. Hoboken, NJ: Wiley.

Willey, Gordon R., Richard M. Leventhal, Arthur A. Demarest, and William L. Fash Jr. 1994. *Ceramic and Artifacts from Excavations in the Copan Residential Zone*. Papers of the Peabody Museum of Archaeology and Ethnology 80. Cambridge, MA: Harvard University.

Wisdom, Charles. 1940. *The Chorti Indians of Guatemala*. Chicago: University of Chicago Press.

Źrałka, Jarosław, Christophe Helmke, Laura Sotelo, and Wiesław Koszkul. 2018. "The Discovery of a Beehive and the Identification of Apiaries among the Ancient Maya." *Latin American Antiquity* 29 (3): 514–531.

5

Teotihuacan was the largest Classic period urban center in Mesoamerica, with a maximum population of around 125,000 (Cowgill 2015, 144) who lived in a dense settlement within 2,200 discrete apartment compounds in the northeast corner of the Basin of Mexico (see figure 0.1 and table 0.1). This chapter will focus on nocturnal characteristics ancient city dwellers faced, with Teotihuacan as a case study. When we envision the sights, smells, and sounds of the ancient nocturnal urban environment, it allows us to perceive the lives of the ancient Teotihuacanos in a richer way, contributing to a sensory archaeology (Day 2013; Hamilakis 2013). One of the challenging aspects of urban life in the city was obtaining fuel for cooking, heating, and lighting, especially for such a large population of residents. Therefore, an analysis of the fuel available for lighting is necessary to include in the discussion of Teotihuacan nighttime activities. Lighting supported nocturnal activities—legitimate, illicit, and subversive, as I will discuss in this chapter.

To provide an example of ancient Mesoamerican nightlife, the Aztec capital Tenochtitlan may provide insights (for more on the Aztecs, see Farah, this volume). The words of a sixteenth-century Spanish chronicler are illustrative, as he describes Tenochtitlan as an almost dead city: "At sunset (around 6 pm) the boom of large drums and conch shell trumpets signaled the end of the working day—and this was not just in Tenochtitlan but in all Aztec towns. All markets closed for the day, local

Teotihuacan at Night

A Classic Period Urban Nocturnal Landscape in the Basin of Mexico

Randolph J. Widmer

DOI: 10.5876/9781646421879.c005

traders upped sticks and headed home, and visitors had to find a bed for the night in local hostels. Chroniclers commented on how a heavy silence fell on the community" (Escalante Gonzalabo 2004; Mursell 2016, 1).

DATA SOURCES

Were the same customs that existed in Tenochtitlan true for Classic period Teotihuacan? Three sources of data can be used to address these activities: archaeological, ethnohistoric, and ethnographic. The first is more direct but is limited in specific application, since there has not been much archaeological excavation and research explicitly focusing on nighttime activities. Ethnohistoric data are "richer" but come from Spaniards who recorded their observations of the Aztecs during the 1500s, and such remarks may be inappropriate when applied to Teotihuacan for a number of reasons. The two ancient cities differ in their ecological location: Tenochtitlan was situated on an island in Lake Texcoco, while Teotihuacan was situated at the head of a river originating from a spring that flowed into the lake. Furthermore, there is a gap of almost 800 years between the times of occupation of the two cities. The wealth of information contained in ethnohistoric documents warrants a judicious use, and we can assume some continuity of cultural traits in the Basin of Mexico. The ethnohistoric sources utilized in this chapter are the Florentine Codex (Dibble and Anderson 1961) and the Codex Mendoza (Berdan and Anawalt 1992). The Florentine Codex, authored by the Franciscan friar Bernardino de Sahagún, consists of thirteen volumes of information on the life, religion, and culture of the Aztecs. It actually represents the first anthropological ethnography; Sahagún invented and used the method of the focus group to obtain his information (León-Portilla 2012). A number of ethnographies are employed to advance plausible reconstructions of Teotihuacan nightlife and activities.

SIGHTS IN THE TEOTIHUACAN NIGHT

A discussion of nocturnal activities conducted at Teotihuacan can be broken down into three sensory aspects: sights, sounds, and smells, the most important of which is sight. The inability to see during nighttime or in darkness can limit many economic activities, but this situation can be mitigated by the use of artificial light (see Gonlin and Dixon-Hundredmark, this volume, for lighting used by the Classic period Maya). A lack of lighting limits the range of activities that could have been conducted at night in Teotihuacan. How much light was available to the inhabitants of Teotihuacan, and in what form was this light available to residents? The answers require an analysis of both fuel availability and the artifacts used in lighting. These questions can be addressed through both archaeological and ethnohistoric data.

The city lies in a valley that is somewhat arid; and the moister wooded areas, where sources of fuel could have been obtained, were largely deforested and replaced with agricultural fields. There were forests containing fuel wood north of the city, but this fuel seems to have been used to slake lime for much-needed plaster rather than been utilized as firewood (Barba and Frunz 1999; Bikowski 2017, 33–34; Carballo 2013). This use is related to the shift through time to finer grinding surfaces of metates, which reduces the amount of cooking time for tortillas, suggesting an increased scarcity of fuel through time (Bikowski 2017, 33). It has been noted that the high cost of fuel consumption was a result of a shift to the production of maize tortillas from other preparations. Tortillas require lime for nixtamalization but less energy for cooking because of their thin shape and direct cooking on comales. Boiled or steamed maize foods, such as atole or tamales, require greater fuel for cooking. In addition, increased fuel consumption may have been a result of the increased production of lime plaster for use in architecture. It has been estimated that the fuel required to produce plaster for Teotihuacan architecture would have constituted 40 percent of the city's total energy requirement (Barba and Frunz 1999; Bikowski 2017, 34).

From research conducted by Carmen Christina Adriano-Morán and Emily McClung de Tapia (2008, 2934), it appears that wood species selected for fuel were trees that were easily cut, quick to ignite, and slow to burn and that produced intense heat. They further note that there does not appear to be any evidence of deforestation and that wood resources were very well managed for cooking, heating, and lighting. The cooking of maize and beans is extremely costly. Martin Bikowski (2017, 33) has suggested a value of 2 kg of fuel per capita for cooking in Classic period Mexican villages and argues that the amount would have been even greater at Teotihuacan because it is a city and not a village. Furthermore, he argues that conspicuous consumption by elites and certain craft activities would have increased per capital fuel consumption at Teotihuacan.

How much more fuel would have been needed for lighting? A strong argument has been made for the management of forest and wood production at Teotihuacan (Adriano-Morán and McClung de Tapia 2008, 2933–2934). Based on the study of charcoal remains, there was a clear preference for oak (*Quercus sp.*), pine (*Pinus sp.*), and cypress (*Taxodium sp.*) as fuel species. In addition, the study results were used to indicate that the residents of Teotihuacan selected firewood based on distinctive burning characteristics (per above) rather than their taxa. This forest management might have involved the practice of coppicing, where the trees are cut about 50 cm above the ground and then allowed to grow from the stump. Oak (*Quercus sp.*) is one of the species that can be coppiced, and it was a favored wood for fuel use at Teotihuacan. This practice is very beneficial because it aids in soil retention and in relatively fast regrowth of forest that can be repeatedly cropped. Coppicing is mentioned as utilized in Highland Mexico village firewood acquisition (Evans 1984, 58) and might even have been reported in the Florentine Codex by Sahagún (Dibble and Anderson 1961, book 10, 81), where he states that the wood cutter "cuts with an axe; he fells trees—cuts them, tops them, strips them, splits them, stacks them." The topping may actually refer to coppicing.

There is a secondary, less desirable category of vegetation that includes shrubs, herbaceous plants, and maize stalks and cobs—an indication of a wide range of fuel choices. These items are not suitable for cooking because they do not produce much heat, they burn out quickly, and they produce smoke (Bikowski 2017, 33).

Most of the wood fuel utilized at Teotihuacan would have been used to produce lime for plaster, which would have been used to stucco architecture, and lime for the nixtamalization of maize. Lime is considered one of Teotihuacan's four major commodities, along with obsidian, cotton, and pottery (Carballo 2013, 121). I would include wood as another important commodity that is necessary for the production of lime. There are three limestone-producing areas near Teotihuacan: one is east in Tepeaca, Puebla, 150 km from Teotihuacan; another is located south of the city near Cuernavaca, Morelos; and the third is the closest to Teotihuacan, situated northwest of the city in the region of Chingú, 9 km east of the site where the Toltecs later built Tula (Hidalgo State). The 60 km distance from Teotihuacan to Tula is estimated to be an eleven-hour trip (Carballo 2013, 126). Chemical analysis of the plaster from the site of Teopancazco, an apartment in Teotihuacan, indicates that the site was plastered with lime from the Chingú area (Barba et al. 2009). There is perhaps another closer secondary source at Zumpango (Murakami 2010, 191–192). The real key to lime production is not the raw limestone from which lime is made but the fuel needed to produce it. Because of the importance of lime for stucco, it is estimated that 600,000 tons of plaster were needed for the temples, plazas, and apartment compounds that covered 12 million m^2 of Teotihuacan (Barba and Frunz 1999). Due to the requirement of wood as fuel for the nixtamalization of maize, less wood would have been available for use as heat and light, or at least wood would have been a resource that had a high cost.

The value of lime as a commodity would clearly bring it under the control of the state, requiring strict and close management of wood as the fuel resource. Since the limestone production area is distant from Teotihuacan, it could be that wood production zones would stretch north, east, and west of the region to meet the city's needs; this importation keeps wood resources near the city sustainable. Therefore, wood itself would become a foreign resource imported into the city and can be considered a fifth trade commodity in David Carballo's (2013, 121) list of commodities that includes obsidian, lime, cotton, and ceramics.

If pine, oak, and cypress were used for cooking and secondary species were used for lighting, then an implication of the differential use would be that lighting was possible because certain other species would be chosen for their ability to produce light from large flames of burning branches rather than heat from coals and embers used primarily for heat. This also leads to the implication that there was economic stratification in the use of fuel, with wealthier households having greater access to higher-quality burning fuel. However, the combination of cooking and lighting can be simultaneously facilitated if performed at night. The gap formed by the space between the three-prong brazier and the vessel resting on the prongs would permit light to emit from this space as well as heat for cooking, thereby efficiently utilizing this fuel for multiple purposes. In chapter 24 of the Florentine Codex, Sahagún (Dibble and Anderson 1961, book 10, 88) states that there were sellers of pine resin and liquid amber, another type of pine resin. Resins are typically used to start larger dense wood fires, but in their burning, they do emit light.

Ironically, the mention of charcoal as a fuel is completely missing from discussions of Teotihuacan's energy needs. Bikowski (2000, 295) mentions that charcoal yields three to four times the amount of energy of wood fuel and would reduce transportation costs but notes that this would result in rapid deforestation. He does not mention charcoal as a Teotihuacan fuel source, an opinion shared by Adriano-Morán and McClung de Tapia (2008). This absence is also echoed in the Florentine Codex, where Sahagún (Dibble and Anderson 1961, book 10, 78) discusses the process of slaking lime: "He places the limestone in the oven, places the firewood, sets the fire, burns the limestone, cools the oven, slakes the lime, carries the lime on his back." There is no mention of charcoal production or selling in the Florentine Codex.

Tapaplatos, shallow matte ceramic bowls with three exterior loop handles (figure 5.1), are currently interpreted as incense burners rather than handled covers for bowls (Cowgill 2015, 130). Their concave interior surfaces are often covered with soot. However, this soot could be a product of the burning of

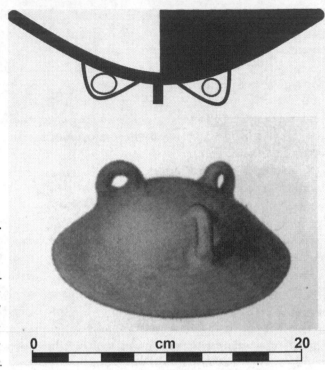

FIGURE 5.1.
Tapaplato *ceramic bowls with three exterior loop handles. It is possible that this type of vessel was used for lighting as well as burning incense.*

0   cm   20

pine pitch for lighting and the burning of incense. It is possible that these vessels served more than one function. Their small size and light weight makes them ideal as a portable source of illumination. Residue analysis would help to clarify their uses. Another portable light source would have been pine torches in iconography from Teotihuacan (Nielsen and Helmke 2018, figure 4.2), on Classic Maya ceramics (Gonlin and Dixon-Hundredmark, this volume), and in the Florentine Codex. Sahagún further relates how the woodcutter sells oak, pine, alder, and madrone, noting that they produce colored flame (Dibble and Anderson 1961, book 10, 81) (see Slotten, this volume, for a discussion of wood species available to ancient Mesoamericans). Therefore, these woods would be usable for lighting, fuel for cooking, and firewood for heating.

Below is a consideration of the possibility that wax candles could have been used for lighting at Teotihuacan, and it provides a cautionary tale about using ethnohistoric sources without further investigation. Beeswax is an important additional energy source that can be used as fuel for lighting (Bogdanov 2016). It is non-vegetative since it is produced by bees. Ethnographic observations from the Yucatan Peninsula (Bianco, Alexander, and Rayson 2017) inform us that a weight of 250–500 g of black beeswax was collected from stingless bees during each harvest, suggesting that wax production was fairly large and could provide for sizable candle production. Perhaps similar collection techniques were used at Teotihuacan.

Beeswax represents another non-wood fuel for providing light. In chapter 25 of the Florentine Codex, Sahagún (Dibble and Anderson 1961, book 10, 91) mentions that the Aztec had cylindrical beeswax candles. These items were produced through an elaborate process of blanching, washing, and boiling to create candles that were white, yellow, and black in color: "A candle maker, prepares beeswax—blanches, washes, boils, purifies, melts, cooks, prepares, bathes it. He forms it into a roll, makes it like a stone column, provides a center for it . . . makes it cylindrical like a wooden roller, places a wick"; in addition, "he sells candles, he sells white, yellow, black ones . . . [candles] overlade with wax, thick-wicked; very smooth, slender; stubby, lumpy, uneven" (1961, book 10, 91). The wax is clearly seen being boiled in a large ceramic basin under a wood fire. The technique described above has been more clearly described. After the honey has been removed from the wax combs, they are broken and placed in a basin of water and allowed to soak for a day or more to soften the pollen, thus allowing for the separation of cocoons. Then, a fire is lit under the vessel until the water boils and the contents are stirred until the wax is melted. The wax that floats to the top is skimmed off and put into another container. When the water cools, the remaining material is pressed with the hands to remove the last of the wax, and the remaining debris is discarded (Cowan 1908, 53–54). One thing that is clear is that candle making is a highly specialized production and incurs some expense. The burning of candles is essential in religious ceremonies of numerous peoples. It seems from this description that two sizes of candles are made: larger cylindrical ones like a wooden roller and slender ones that can be stubby, lumpy, or uneven. So, it might be the case that the Teotihuacan ceramic *candeleros* (figure 5.2) (small, perforated ceramic objects) could actually have held candles instead of incense as suggested by Mesoamerican archaeologists (e.g., Cowgill 2015; Willey et al. 1994, 214) (see Gonlin and Dixon-Hundredmark, this volume, for more on candeleros). Candeleros would have offered a portable source of illumination, useful for nocturnal navigation between rooms in a Teotihuacan apartment compound. Candles at Teotihuacan, if used, may have had standardized sizes consistent with market production and may have been similar to those described for the Aztecs by Sahagún (Dibble and Anderson 1961, book 10, 91). However, it seems that the practice of wax making is Colonial, not pre-Hispanic, based on

FIGURE 5.2. *Teotihuacan ceramic candeleros. The traditional function assigned to them is for burning incense.*

linguistic and historical information (see Gonlin and Dixon-Hundredmark, this volume, for linguistic interpretations). This case illustrates the point that we must be judicious in using ethnohistorical documents, as other evidence points toward candle making as a Colonial innovation. We await further research through residue analysis.

SEEING NIGHTTIME PRACTICES

Here, we rely on ethnohistory to provide us with ideas for activities that may have taken place at Teotihuacan. In addition to the use of controlled portable lighting in tapaplatas and possibly candeleros in providing nocturnal lighting, large fires associated with religious ceremonies by priests conducted throughout the night could possibly have been utilized. Such a practice was recorded in Tenochtitlan, where priests kept the great fires burning in vessels atop the temples throughout the night. It may be reasonable to think that priests at Teotihuacan would have engaged in a similar practice. Smaller-scale rituals likely took place in individual apartment compounds. Although there is no in situ archaeological evidence of household shrines in this household, the number of figurine fragments recovered in the excavations at 33:S3W1 (Tlajinga 33) indicates that ritual activity probably took place (see López Luján et al. 2006 and Manzanilla 1996 for evidence of household shrines at Teotihuacan).

A rite of passage that took place at night among the Aztec, one that might have been held in similar fashion at Teotihuacan, was the marriage ceremony. The Codex Mendoza illustrates a wedding procession showing the bride who is taken to the home of the groom where the wedding takes place (Berdan and Anawalt 1992, folio 61r, pic 3). This ceremony occurs at night in the dark, and the accompanying party members hold pine torches to light the way.

However, not all nocturnal activity required lighting. In fact, astronomy would have benefited from a lack of ambient light. This activity would have been a vital and frequent endeavor that required darkness. Priest-astronomers would have observed the movements of the stars to mark the hours of the night and the changing of the seasons. Again, the Codex Mendoza is instructive: "Head priest who is looking at the stars in the night sky to ascertain the time for services and duties" (Berdan and Anawalt 1992, folio 63r). Stargazing has been recorded in indigenous texts as well. For example, the tracking of Venus is indicated in the Dresden Codex, a Postclassic document of the Maya. The nocturnal work of keeping track of the movements of the planets and stars may have been accompanied by ceremonies involving the playing of drums or other musical instruments.

AROMAS IN THE TEOTIHUACAN NIGHT

A continuation of the nocturnal sensory experience would have been the aromas arising from incense, kitchens, and feasts. One of the most notable smoke-based odors would have been incense, which was burned in public temples and private residences alike. This pleasant scent would have wafted throughout the night air. There would have been the smells of food prepared and eaten at night as household meals or banquets (see Reed, Zeleznik, and Gonlin, this volume, who discuss nighttime food for the Maya). The unmistakable smell of maize, cooked as tortillas, tamales, or pozole, would have dominated the smells of kitchens and spread from there to other parts of the city. Today, the process of nixtamalization creates an intense, distinctive smell that permeates the air, as noted in the streets of modern Mexico City. This aroma would have been a ubiquitous smell throughout the day and night at Teotihuacan, particularly since pozole needs to be soaked and cooked for a long time. There is even the suggestion that the lime-treated water from nixtamalization was poured out onto plastered patio surfaces, an interpretation based on the high concentration of lime found on the surface of the patio.

Among the Aztecs, feasting occurred at night, and this might have been true for the Teotihuacanos as well. Most notable is the feast called Uey tecuilhuitl held during the eighth month. Here, food and drink were consumed over seven days. The feasting went on through the night and was accompanied by singing and dancing from dusk to dawn. Of interest is that at this time, fires were made in huge braziers arranged in six rows of ten each (Dibble and Anderson 1961, book 2, 98). Such braziers are not found at Teotihuacan, and there was an apparent poverty of fancy ceramic serving vessels (Cowgill 2015). Nevertheless, tripod vases and Thin Orange bowls might have been used for such purposes. However, the wear on many Thin Orange bowls indicates a utilitarian purpose because they have ground interior surfaces (2015, 188). Feasting may not have required a special set of luxury ceramics, and it is possible that perishable materials such as *hola santa* (*Piper auritum*) leaves or maguey or agave (*Agave sp.*) leaves were used for the consumption of such meals. During Teotihuacan's rise in the Patlachique phase (100 BCE to 0 BCE), there were fancy serving vessels that might reflect feasting. Why this tradition disappeared later in time is unknown.

TEOTIHUACAN'S NOCTURNAL SOUNDSCAPE

Sounds are a significant sensory media that occurred throughout the night. Examples from Aztec times are illustrative, as they provide insights into what we could reasonably expect to have heard at Teotihuacan. During the Feast of Xilonen, the maize goddess, singing and sacrifice were essential. In the goddess's hand she carried a shield and a magic rattle, a *chicahuaztli*. On the night before the human sacrifice, everybody stayed up, nobody slept, and the women sang the hymns of Xilonen (Dibble and Anderson 1961, book 2, 104). Split log drums and hollow wooden logs with skin heads are depicted in the Florentine Codex, a suggestion for their use at Teotihuacan. Other musical instruments included flutes, drums, whistles, shell trumpets (Cowgill 2015, 181), and long bone rasps, an example of which was recovered from the Tlajinga 33 compound. The city would have been permeated by the sounds of drums and flutes that occurred with the rituals and ceremonies conducted by priests at temples within a compound as well as in larger public temples, many of which were active at night. It is very likely that the barking of dogs was an acoustic feature of the nightscape. Shell trumpets might also have been played at night: "Quetzalcoatl turned the shell into a trumpet by calling worms to drill holes into it, and by calling humming bees to enter it and make it roar. He then shed blood from wounds he inflicted on himself on the retrieved bones, thereby spawning Man. Aztec priests blew shell trumpets five times a night to call people to the bloodletting rites (Heller 2015:307)." Although this reference is specific to the Aztec, it could possibly be relevant to Teotihuacan and the types of soundscapes that characterized the city.

Jacques Soustelle (2002, 35) maintains that the streets of Tenochtitlan were not lit at night, but nonetheless, the night was very important because that is when visiting took place and glowing light from torches would have been seen in doorways with their light and warmth flooding into the inner rooms and courtyards. Feasts and religious services were held at this time, and light emanated from the flames from tripods containing resinous wood. The sounds of gatherings, voices, and music emanated from the compounds.

ILLICIT, SUBVERSIVE, AND PUNISHABLE
NOCTURNAL ACTIVITIES AT TEOTIHUACAN

Not all activities at night were good. Sahagún notes that thievery and sorcery were conducted at night (Dibble and Anderson 1961, book 10, chapter 9, 31, chapter 11, 38–39), which was an ideal time for illicit activities. Thievery would have happened at night when robbers looked through houses with lit torches (Soustelle 2002, 57). Sahagún notes that the thief was a corrupt, poor, miserable, prying individual: "He makes plans, spies, breaks through the walls of one's house, fishes things off with his hands . . . He steals; he makes off with things by trickery. He practices petty theft; he pilfers" (Dibble and Anderson 1961, book 10, chapter 11, 39). In one of the many illustrations in the Florentine Codex, a thief is shown breaking into a house (1961, book 10, figure 66). Did such thievery occur among the urban inhabitants of Teotihuacan? In any large city throughout history, one can plausibly assume that such thefts occurred. It is difficult to obtain archaeological evidence to support such activity, especially petty thefts, but stealing or vandalism on a grander scale may have left its mark.

Prostitution is clearly mentioned by Sahagún with a lengthy entry on the harlot, the carnal woman: "The carnal woman is an evil woman who finds pleasure in her body, who sells her body—repeatedly sells her body" (Dibble and Anderson 1961, book 10, 55). He further describes another trade, that of the "procuress[, the woman] who procures. This aforementioned one [is] a deceiver, a perverter, a deranger, a corrupter, a destroyer of others." She is also a sorcerer who casts spells (1961, book 10, 57), and sorcerers operated at night (1961, book 10, figure 66). Unfortunately, Sahagún does not state when these classes of women practiced their trade with their clients and who their clients were. However, it would seem that such activity would have flourished at night under the cloak of darkness when discretion was helpful for all involved. In a city the size of Teotihuacan, one can conjecture that certain individuals made a living by this trade and that other individuals were inclined to support that occupation.

Other nocturnal activities are mentioned in the Codex Mendoza, which provide us with information about the night among the Aztecs. There is a depiction of a twelve-year-old girl sweeping her house and street at night, indicated by the stars in the scene, as a punishment for disobedience (Berdan and Anawalt 1992, folio 60r, pic 4). As the night was an ominous time, the physical labor combined with the darkness would have seemed like a double reprimand to this young girl. One can only imagine what act of disobedience she had committed to merit such punishment and what, if any, association it had with the night. Whether ancient Teotihuacanos were punished at night cannot currently be determined; however, this information from the codex provides insights into the kinds of nocturnal activities of which we should be aware.

THE SUPERNATURAL CONTEXT OF NIGHT AT TEOTIHUACAN

One aspect of the nocturnal world that cannot be overlooked or under-emphasized is the spiritual realm. Night was an auspicious and dangerous time, and many feasts and ceremonies were performed to reduce this damage and evoke favor from the gods. The dichotomy of night and day played a vital role in the supernatural construct of Aztec religion and undoubtedly extended back in time to the occupation of Teotihuacan, as it did for numerous Mesoamerican cultures. Archaeological evidence in the form of effigy vessels and ceremonial censors appears to depict later deities, so we can infer some of the supernatural and religious contexts from the Classic time period, if not earlier (Carballo 2007). However, scholars agree unanimously that the antecedents of the Aztec Storm God (Tlaloc) and Fire God(s) (Huehueteotl, the Old God, and Xiuhtecuhtli, the Lord of Fire) were present in the Teotihuacano religion (Carballo 2007; Gamio 1922; López Austin and López Lújan 2001; Millon and Drewitt 1961; Pasztory 1997; von Winning 1987). The city's inhabitants probably had ceremonies to honor these deities that may have been similar to those of the Aztecs. These ceremonies would have been influenced by darkness and the night. For the specific information on these ceremonies and attitudes toward these deities, we turn to the Florentine Codex.

Night in Aztec cosmology is considered extremely dangerous. At the end of the fifty-two-year cycle when the solar and ritual calendars meshed together, it was necessary to extinguish all fires and then conduct a New Fire Ceremony where a fire would be lit (see Farah, this volume, on the New Fire Ceremony). If the fire was not lit, the darkness of night would prevail forever and the demons of darkness would descend to eat men. Within the Valley of Mexico, the people gathered in the darkness on their roofs and terraces to watch for the new fire to be reborn on Star Hill (Carrasco 1981, 286). In the Altiplano of Mexico, it was considered a time of evil and fear. Night brought danger. For example, Ciuacoatle (Snake-Woman) brought misery to humans and was an evil omen. By night, she walked weeping and wailing and was an omen of war. Night was also thought to be a time for personal sacrifice. In the Florentine Codex, Sahagún (Dibble and Anderson 1961, book 1, 11) notes that penance was performed naked at night (1961, book 1, 27). At the feast celebrated for the god Macuilxochitl, at midnight, celebrants consumed colored atole with a flower floating on it, which was to evoke favor of the gods thought to be more desirable at this time (1961, book 1, 37).

Of the ceremonies held at night, one was dedicated to Tepicton: modeled images of the mountains Quetzalcoatl, Chalchieutll ycue, Tlaloc, Popocatépetl, Iztac tepetl, Poiauhtecatl, and other mountains. A vigil was held for them by the Aztecs, according to Sahagún. These mountain images were sung to all night, and offerings were provided to them four times during the night. These rituals were done to seek their favor (Dibble and Anderson 1961, book 1, 49).

Another noteworthy ceremony and feast took place at night. On the last day of the twelfth month, there was a great feast—"the arrival of the gods"—at which time all the gods arrived. On the eve of this day, at night, a cheese-shaped cornmeal cake was placed on a mat. All through the night, a priest watched and waited for the cake to be stepped on, indicating that the gods had arrived (Dibble and Anderson 1961, book 2, 21). This nighttime festival is also mentioned in Diego Durán's account. He notes that the footprint was that of an infant (Durán 1967, I: 154). Human sacrifices took place, often at night in front of glowing torches, with throngs of participants and onlookers in the ceremonial center of Tenochtitlan (Carrasco 1981, 282).

Etzalqualiztli, the sixth month, consisted of feasts throughout the month. Fasting was also initiated with the coming of night and took place before the feast in honor of Tlaloc. The fasting began at nightfall, along with offerings, and just before midnight shell trumpets were blown. The celebration of the feast to Tlaloc started at night on top of the Temple of Tlaloc. Trumpets were played, the horizontal drum was beaten, and reed pipes and conch shells were blown. At midnight, captives were sacrificed to Tlaloc (Dibble and Anderson 1961, book 2, 79–88). Conversely, some feasts and ceremonies took place only in daylight and had to end before nightfall, such as the feast to the God of War, Huitzilopochtli.

CONCLUSIONS

Nocturnal activities at Teotihuacan were more varied and extensive than one might initially envision. This urban nightscape was full of sights, sounds, and smells of a large, densely populated city, where everyone from poor residents to lofty rulers contributed to the sensory experience. Recent studies clearly indicate that there was no serious deforestation in the sustaining area of Teotihuacan and that wood resources were well managed. There appears to have been enough fuel, in spite of the demand for cooking, to provide illumination. However, the fact that it operated as a scarce and valuable commodity meant that it had a high cost and was of limited availability to some segments of urban residents. It would have been under commercial market control that was regulated by the state and taxation, as suggested by David Carballo (2013). There was probably a practice of cooking at night to take advantage of fuel for providing illumination as well as energy for cooking.

Another significant outcome of this study is the suggestion that tapaplatos may have functioned as lamps and that their portability was one of the key features allowing residents to move a source of illumination from one room to the next. The potential use of candles, with candeleros serving as receptacles for them, would have facilitated lighting even further, although whether they were manufactured in Precolumbian times is conjectural. Because of the general expense of fuel at Teotihuacan, the ability to light residential compounds was probably a function of wealth, as was the capability for holding feasts. A strategy of affluence may have been to illuminate the compound as much as possible as a visible sign of wealth, a more easily accomplished plan than building improvements, which were limited by urban space restrictions and undoubtedly costlier.

While lighting was necessary for some nocturnal activities, others benefited from the dark. Some of these doings would have been beneficial to society, such as astronomy, when the nocturnal celestial bodies would have been at their greatest visibility. However, other activities, typically undesirable ones that involved treachery, thievery, and prostitution, would have prospered under the cloak of darkness.

The Aztecs said of Teotihuacan that it was the place where time began. Sahagún relates the following: "The time was when there was still darkness.

There all the gods assembled and consulted among themselves who would bear upon his back the burden of rule, who would be the sun. But when the sun came to appear, then all [the gods] died there" (Dibble and Anderson 1961, book 3, 1). The significance of this statement is the association of the beginning of time with darkness, and it was at the time when the sun and its accompanying light appeared that the other gods died. This observation indicates that darkness is not necessarily an evil thing. The night was a sacred time and place filled with the celestial world of the stars and planets whose movements the Teotihuacan priests would have monitored and performed ceremonies and rituals to assure the cosmic order.

REFERENCES

Adriano-Morán, Carmen Cristina, and Emily McClung de Tapia. 2008. "Trees and Shrubs: The Use of Wood in Prehispanic Teotihuacan." *Journal of Archaeological Science* 35 (11): 2927–2936.

Barba, Luis A., and Jose Luis C. Frunz. 1999. "Estudios energéticos de la producción de cal en tiempos teotihuacanos y sus implicaciones." *Latin American Antiquity* 10 (2): 168–179.

Barba Pingarrón, Luis A., Jorge Blancas, Linda Manzanilla, Agustín Ortiz, Donatella Barca, Gino M. Crisci, Dominico Miriello, and Alessandra Pecci. 2009. "Provenance of the Limestone Used in Teotihuacan (Mexico): A Methodological Approach." *Archaeometry* 51 (4): 525–545.

Berdan, Frances, and Patricia Rieff Anawalt. 1992. *The Codex Mendoza*. 4 vols. Berkeley: University of California Press.

Bianco, Briana, Rani T. Alexander, and Gary Rayson. 2017. "Beekeeping Practices in Modern and Ancient Yucatán." In *The Value of Things: Prehistoric to Contemporary Commodities in the Maya Region*, ed. Jennifer P. Matthews and Thomas H. Guderjan, 87–103. Tucson: University of Arizona Press.

Bikowsi, Martin. 2000. "Maize Preparation and the Aztec Subsistence Economy." *Ancient Mesoamerica* 11: 193–206.

Bikowski, Martin. 2017. "Staple Food Preparation at Teotihuacan." *Archaeological and Anthropological Science* 9: 29–38.

Bogdanov, Stefan. 2016. "Beeswax: History, Uses, and Trade." *Bee Product Science* 1–18.

Carballo, David M. 2007. "Effigy Vessels, Religious Integration, and the Origins of the Central Mexican Pantheon." *Ancient Mesoamerica* 18: 53–67.

Carballo, David M. 2013. "The Social Organization of Craft Production and Interregional Exchange at Teotihuacan." In *Merchants, Markets, and Exchange in the*

Pre-Columbian World, ed. Kenneth G. Hirth and Joanne Pillsbury, 113–140. Washington, DC: Dumbarton Oaks Research Library and Collection.

Carrasco, Davíd. 1981. "Templo Mayor: The Aztec Vision of Place." *Religion* 11 (3): 275–297.

Cowan, Thomas William. 1908. *Wax Craft, All about Beeswax: Its History, Production, Adulteration, and Commercial Value.* London: S. Low, Marston.

Cowgill, George. 2015. *Ancient Teotihuacan: Early Urbanism in Central Mexico.* Cambridge: Cambridge University Press.

Day, Jo, ed. 2013. *Making Senses of the Past: Toward a Sensory Archaeology.* Center for Archaeological Investigations, Southern Illinois University, Occasional Paper 40. Carbondale: Southern Illinois University Press.

Dibble, Charles E., and Arthur J.O. Anderson. 1961. *The Florentine Codex.* Salt Lake City: University of Utah Press.

Durán, Diego. 1967. *Historia de las Indias de Nueva España, y islas de la Tierra Firme.* 2 vols. Ed. Angel Maria Garibay K. Mexico City: Editorial Porrua.

Escalante Gonzalabo, Pablo. 2004. *Historia de la Vida Cotidiana en México: 1 Mesoamérica y los Ambitos Indígenas de la Nueva España.* Mexico City: El Colegio de México.

Evans, Margaret I. 1984. *Firewood versus Alternatives: Domestic Fuel in Mexico.* Oxford: Commonwealth Forestry Institute, University of Oxford.

Gamio, Manuel. 1922. *La poblacion del Valle de Teotihuacan: Representativa de las quehabitan las regiones rurales del Distrito Federal y de los estados de Hidalgo, Puebla, Mexico y Tlaxcala*, Tomo 1: *Volumen Primero.* Mexico City: Secretaria de Agricultura y Fomento, Dirección de Antropología.

Hamilakis, Yannis. 2013. *Archaeology of the Senses: Human Experience, Memory, and Affect.* Cambridge: Cambridge University Press.

Heller, Joseph. 2015. "Sacred Sounds from Sea Shells." In *Sea Snails: A Natural History,* ed. Joseph Heller, 307–318. Cham, Switzerland: Springer International.

León-Portilla. Miguel. 2012. *Bernardino de Sahagún: First Anthropologist.* Norman: University of Oklahoma Press.

López Austin, Alfredo, and Leonardo López Lújan. 2001. *Mexico's Indigenous Past.* Norman: University of Oklahoma Press.

López Luján, Leonardo, Laura Filloy Nadal, Barbara W. Fash, William L. Fash, and Pilar L. Hernández. 2006. "The Destruction of Images in Teotihuacan: Anthropomorphic Sculpture, Elite Cults, and the End of a Civilization." *RES: Anthropology and Aesthetics* 49–50: 12–39.

Manzanilla, Linda. 1996. "Corporate Groups and Domestic Activities at Teotihuacan." *Latin American Antiquity* 7 (3): 228–246.

Millon, René, and Bruce Drewitt. 1961. "Earlier Structures within the Pyramid of the Sun at Teotihuacan." *American Antiquity* 26 (3): 371–380.

Murakami, Tatsuya. 2010. "Power Relations and Urban Landscape Formation: A Study of Construction Labor and Resources at Teotihuacan." PhD dissertation, Arizona State University, Tempe.

Mursell, Ian. 2016. "Curfew." http://www.mexicolore.co.uk/aztecs/aztec-life/curfew.

Nielsen, Jesper, and Christophe Helmke. 2018. "'Where the Sun Came into Being': Rites of Pyrolatry, Transition, and Transformation in Early Classic Teotihuacan." In *Smoke, Flames, and the Human Body in Mesoamerican Ritual Practice*, ed. Vera Tiesler and Andrew K. Scherer, 77–107. Washington, DC: Dumbarton Oaks Research Library and Collection.

Pasztory, Esther. 1997. *Teotihuacan: An Experiment in Living*. Norman: University of Oklahoma Press.

Soustelle, Jacques. 2002. *Daily life of the Aztecs*. New York: Courier Corporation.

von Winning, Hasso. 1987. *La iconografía de Teotihuacan: Los dioses y los signos*, vol. 1. Mexico City: Universidad Nacional Autónoma de México.

Willey, Gordon R., Richard M. Leventhal, Arthur A. Demarest, and William L. Fash Jr. 1994. *Ceramics and Artifacts from Excavations in the Copan Residential Zone*. Papers of the Peabody Museum of Archaeology and Ethnology 80. Cambridge, MA: Harvard University.

6

The Sounds in the Dark of the Temazcal at Cerén, El Salvador

Payson Sheets and
Michael Thomason

Perhaps the most intriguing building discovered at the Cerén site (Joya de Cerén in Spanish) in El Salvador is the temazcal, which is a sauna or sweat bath. Situated in a small village in the southeastern Maya area (figure 0.1), the *temazcal* was surprisingly sophisticated in architecture and presumably provided the context for a variety of functions for the people in the community. Here, we review the context of the founding of the village after the Ilopango volcanic eruption (table 0.1), as well as the households and their service relationships to the community, and we then focus on Household 2 and the temazcal. The building has attracted so much attention from scholars and the general public that a precise 1:1 scale replica was built in an area where people could enter the temazcal and experience it. An unanticipated phenomenon is the effect the replica's dome has on the human voice, as noticed by visitors and archaeologists alike. The preliminary analyses of those acoustic phenomena are presented here for the first time.[1] The dark soundscape of the temazcal was clearly part of the experience for participants, adding to the sensations that together created a unique phenomenon, whether we discuss the Maya sweat bath, as in this chapter, or the Aztec temazcal, as written about by Jan Olson in chapter 7. Olson's chapter presents rich and detailed ethnohistoric documentation of Terminal Postclassic temazcal use by the Aztecs and variation of their uses. Unfortunately, there are no comparable ethnohistoric data for the Classic period use of the

DOI: 10.5876/9781646421879.c006

temazcal in El Salvador. Therefore, we must rely on detailed archaeological information. The darkness in the temazcal could be created at any time during the day, whenever needed. Darkness stimulates imagination, mystery, wonder, and transformation. It is likely that all these phenomena were experienced in the temazcal. A wide range of floral species was utilized at the small Maya village, and some of them could well have been used as a part of the ceremonies of curing or connecting with the supernatural domain, as described by Venicia Slotten (this volume).

CULTURAL AND VOLCANOLOGICAL ANTECEDENTS TO CERÉN

What is now El Salvador was densely populated by peoples of the Miraflores ceramic tradition in the first five centuries CE (Dull, Southon, and Sheets 2001). That flourishing culture was abruptly terminated by the catastrophic eruption of the Ilopango volcanic caldera in the 530s CE, most likely in 539 CE. Rachel Egan (this volume) considers the general effects of eruptions on ancient natives, which created a kind of volcanic night and darkness. The Zapotitán Valley received up to 10 m of volcanic ash on the east side, turning it into a white sterile desert overnight and eliminating all flora, fauna, and people. Environmental, ecological, and demographic recovery required a few decades, and the founding of Cerén by a few families occurred in the latter part of the sixth century. The immigrants were Maya from the north (Sheets 2009), who physically and socially constructed a well-functioning community in a short period of time (see Gonlin and Dixon, this volume, for more on Cerén; Gonlin and Dixon 2018).

THE FUNCTIONING VILLAGE OF CERÉN

People lived in the Cerén village for a very brief period, maybe only three generations. In a very real sense, the community functioned between two eruptions of a "volcanological sandwich." The structures were built atop the soils of the Ilopango eruption and then were buried by the Loma Caldera eruption around 660 CE. In spite of its short duration, the sophistication of its architecture, artifacts, adaptations, and social integration is notable (Sheets 2002, 2006). At the center of town is a plaza ringed by public buildings (figure 6.1). Structure 3 was apparently where the village elders met to adjudicate disputes and schedule village events, such as the nighttime harvest ceremony that was being held when Loma Caldera erupted. Structure 13 also faces the plaza and may be where the village musical instruments and other performance

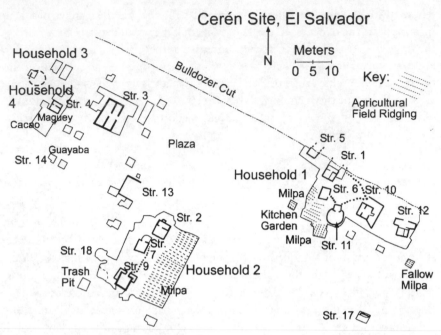

FIGURE 6.1. *Map of the excavated structures of the Cerén site, El Salvador, with inset location map. Note the temazcal (Structure 9) in the southwest area of the site.*

goods were kept, but the area has only been examined with test pits, not full excavations. Another public building is suspected to lie on the plaza's east side, but its existence has not been confirmed with excavation.

Although the sample is very small, each household at Cerén to date had a service relationship to the community as a whole. Each household either maintained a particular structure or two for special use by village members or produced specialty items for widespread consumption. These service relationships are different from the part-time occupational specializations in which each household engaged, to produce something for basic familial functioning in quantities greater than they needed for their own consumption in exchange for items produced by the other households (Sheets 2000). Here, we briefly examine the service relationships of three households to understand how they operated and then turn to the focus of this chapter: darkness and sound in the sauna and Household 2 that serviced the sauna.

Household 1 was typical in that the maize fields surrounding it provided the seed crops (maize, beans, and squash) needed for daily subsistence. Slotten (this volume) documents a wider range of plants available to the residents of the small community. The household members apparently built and maintained a set of household structures including the domicile, the storehouse, and the kitchen (Beaudry-Corbett, Simmons, and Tucker 2002; Sheets 2002, 2006). Their service relationship to the village was in maintaining the two religious structures immediately east of them. They likely performed the upkeep necessary for earthen wattle and daub (*bajareque*) architecture and supported the activities functioning within the structures. They maintained four extra mano and metate sets to grind maize for the annual harvest ceremony in the nearby Structure 10, an event that was actually in progress when the Loma Caldera vent erupted. The mano and floor-mounted metate in their kitchen were grinding stones for processing food for intra-household consumption. Apparently, they also loaned their three deer antler corn huskers to the ceremonial building for the occasion. Antler huskers would not have been stored in the ceremonial building because they would have been chewed by rodents. No husker was found in the household, an unusual situation that is best explained by the loan of them. Very likely, the village elders meeting in Structure 3 made the decision when to hold the harvest ceremony. The household members probably also maintained Structure 12 for the female diviner (shaman), but the evidence is less clear in comparison to the evidence found in the ceremonial structure. Only a small part of the kitchen of Household 3 has been excavated (Sheets 2006), so little can be stated with confidence. The then-fresh spill of large amounts of the bright red pigment "achiote" (*Bixa orellana*) might possibly indicate that this household supplied paint for the harvest ceremony. The pigment could have served as a symbol of human blood. Achiote also has a culinary aspect, and its production might have served as a specialty crop for the community, as a flavoring, a pigment, or both (Slotten, this volume).

Household 4 members differed notably from the others in that they grew and processed a wide variety and volume of specialty crops as a service to the community (Gerstle and Sheets 2002). Three species were grown in such abundance that they were sufficient to supply the entire village's needs. About seventy mature maguey (*Agave americana*) plants were growing southwest of Structure 4. This Central American species produces only fiber, in contrast to its Mexican cousin that is well-known for its use in alcoholic beverages, like pulque. The long *pencas* were de-pulped at a pole in front of the building and then twisted into two-ply strands of string or rope. With seventy plants, the needs of a couple dozen households could have been satisfied. A dense stand of *mirasol* cane (*Tithonia rotundifolia*) was growing just northwest of Structure

4, apparently enough to supply the village with the vertical reinforcing poles for the wattle and daub architecture, as well as the front walls for porches and the swinging doors of buildings (Lentz and Ramirez-Sosa 2002). The third crop produced in abundance that may have been sufficient for the community's needs was chilies. A line of perennial chili plants grew on the west side of the building, perhaps enough for all households, but this is not certain because the boundaries have not yet been found.

A cacao tree was growing in the garden by the building. A considerable amount of processed chocolate was found in the structure, but the volume of production for trade or consumption outside the household is unknown. Cotton seeds were ground on the metate in front of the porch, probably for cotton seed oil, but as with cacao, the volume and destinations are unknown. Growing and distributing specialty crops was an unusual service to the community by members of Household 4, compared to the other households. Household 2, below, was more similar to Household 1 in services.

HOUSEHOLD 2 AND THE TEMAZCAL

The structures of Household 2 were only 45 m from Household 1 (figure 6.1), and that space was filled with mature maize fields and productive trees in an agroforestry adaptation. Household 2's domicile and warehouse (*bodega*) were larger and more solidly built than those of Household 1 and were stocked with relatively more luxury goods (McKee 2002a), making it appear to have been more affluent. Even the daub component of the architecture was more durable, in that the mixture of soil, clay, and volcanic ash resulted in architecture that was sturdier than the structures of Household 1.

The temazcal (figure 6.2) stands only 6 m south of Household 2's storehouse (McKee 2002b), and the hard-packed earth between the two attests to the foot traffic connecting the household members to the functioning structure. The storehouse (Structure 7) held an unusual number of *ollas* (water jars), presumably for pouring over the domed firebox in the middle of the sauna to make steam and for participants to rinse off after exiting. It also held an unusual amount of pine wood, likely used as kindling to start fires in the temazcal's firebox.

Construction details (McKee 2002b) are pertinent here, as the morphology of the structure created darkness any time people used it. Moreover, the inside shape of the walls, bench, firebox, and dome has a notable effect on voices, as noted for the 1:1 scale replica. The first step in construction of the ancient structure was the creation of a solid adobe platform averaging 54 cm in height and

Figure 6.2. *Structures of Household 2, with the domicile building on the left, the storehouse in the center, and the temazcal in the back*

about 5 m long and wide, with a ground-level narrow entrance channel that ends at the firebox (figure 6.3). The effect of water running out of that entrance channel was visible and was clear evidence of people pouring water over the firebox. Part of that platform formed a bench outside of the walls, on both sides of the entrance channel. Inside, the platform forms a bench that surrounds the firebox on all sides except for the entrance. *Lajas* (exfoliated slabs of andesite) were placed on top of the bench and then coated with a thin (1–2 cm) layer of Tierra Blanca Joven (TBJ) volcanic ash from the Ilopango eruption. The walls are thick *"terre pise"* rammed earth, averaging 37 cm in thickness and 1 m in height. A short earthen column at each corner supported horizontal roof beams and poles that supported the grass thatch roof, which protected the earthen dome below it.

The dome was a wattle and daub construction, with *caña india* cane poles radiating from the four walls to meet in the middle and establish reinforcement for the daub. The daub was 5–7 cm thick on each side of the poles. The dome rose 73 cm above the cornice and wall tops. The Loma Caldera volcanic vent, only 600 m to the north, deposited 5 m of tephra on top of the sauna.

FIGURE 6.3. *Cerén Structure 9, the temazcal. The stool is holding up the earthen lintel in the entrance because the wooden lintel had disintegrated.*

The first component of the phreatomagmatic eruption was a lateral blast of fine-grained wet tephra that did no damage to the structure. The second component was a dry phase of vertically falling ash and cinders along with lava bombs. Two lava bombs, on ballistic trajectories from the vent, penetrated the thatch roof and the dome, creating gaping holes. Although the bombs were destructive to the dome, ironically, they were essential to its accurate reconstruction. They created holes large enough for the subsequent phases of the eruption to deposit volcanic ash under the remaining portions of the dome, therefore supporting it until the eruption was finished and for when Brian McKee arrived centuries later to excavate and document it. Had the dome been complete and therefore hollow below and had 5 m of tephra deposited above it, it would have collapsed completely and therefore would not have been reconstructable in a 1:1 scale replica (figure 6.4).

The replica was built recently so visitors to the site could enter and experience it. All who did so noted the complete darkness that enveloped them, as well as the change in one's voice, which resonated and was amplified. Sheets

FIGURE 6.4. *The 1:1 scale replica of the Cerén temazcal, with Salvador "Chamba" Quintanilla*

decided to conduct a preliminary analysis of a human voice outside and inside the temazcal, and some of his personal impressions are provided here. A video voice recording with a Panasonic Lumix DMC-ZS40 was made. The recording was then provided to Michael Thomason, the director of the Physics Learning Labs at the University of Colorado, for analysis. His assistance was enlisted only three weeks before the deadline for chapter submission. His analyses had to be squeezed into his already tight schedule, so they are considered preliminary. Nonetheless, he discovered the natural resonant frequencies of the temazcal's interior. The dominant resonant frequencies are from 80 to 580 Hz, which explains how the dome and interior morphology dramatically lower the tone of one's voice and make it resonate for a long time after speaking. That lowest natural resonance frequency is lower than I can hear, but I strongly sensed it, felt it in my lungs as a strong sensation. Some of the resonances seemed even louder than the initial spoken sound, and that was borne out in the quantitative analysis. This is the first time in my life that I have liked hearing my own voice in a recording; without this effect, my recorded voice seems "tinny" and high pitched to me. It is easy to imagine how a person's voice or singing/chanting in the ancient temazcal, from someone who was leading a ceremony, curation, or other event, could have had an enhanced effect on others, with the greatly lowered pitch and powerfully rich resonances. The effects on music such as that generated by *ocarinas* (whistles) or drums and by singing are yet to be explored. I believe the acoustic effects of such a structure may have been a desired, deliberately constructed, and utilized aspect of bajareque-domed temazcales in the Maya Highlands. As Thomason suggests, such a temazcal can be considered a large constructed musical instrument with its unique natural tones. He identified its five primary natural tones in addition to the powerful lowest one at 18 Hertz.

ACOUSTICAL AND SOUND ANALYSIS OF THE TEMAZCAL REPLICA (BY MICHAEL THOMASON)

The human voices recorded by Sheets demonstrate the compelling acoustic echoes, resonances, and focusing produced inside the temazcal space. Any volume of air enclosed by solid walls will have natural resonances, sometimes referred to as Helmholtz resonance (Helmholtz 1885, 4). The unique sound of the Cerén temazcal replica is due to its interior size, its shape (especially the domed ceiling), and the hardness of the surfaces. The concrete walls of the replica will not perfectly match the acoustic reflectivity of the wattle and daub surfaces of the original. Although no major differences are expected, a complete analysis would include such a comparison.

Sound is a pressure wave, propagating through a medium such as air, water, a taut string, or the body of a musical instrument. When a traveling sound wave reflects from surfaces, the outgoing and reflected waves "interfere" with each other, resulting in certain frequencies, or pitches, which increase in amplitude, or volume, while all other frequencies interfere destructively and decay away. The frequencies that constructively interfere are called standing waves, or the *natural resonant frequencies*.

A source of sound, such as a human voice, may produce a wide range of frequencies. A space such as the interior of the temazcal selects out the highly specific frequencies at which it resonates. The acoustic energy produced by the human voice or a musical instrument couples with those natural resonant frequencies of the room, and the energy driven into a range of frequencies transfers into just the few frequencies at which the room is naturally resonant. This produces the apparent amplification of certain frequencies in the temazcal.

To analyze the audio recording from the temazcal replica, digital audio data were plotted in two different formats. First is a plot of amplitude versus time in kU/second (kU is an arbitrary unit used by the software developer). The second is a three-dimensional plot, called a spectrogram, of frequency versus time versus power, in Hz/second/dB. Power is a value that represents the actual loudness of sound to the human ear. In this plot, the third dimension of power is represented by a color scale from blue to red. Raven Pro 1.5[2] was the software used for this analysis.

While Sheets was speaking in the temazcal, he was exciting, or driving, sound energy with a wide range of frequencies into the space. In fact, Sheets purposely spoke in a musical voice, modulating between high and low pitches, which ensured that a maximum range of resonances was excited. The natural resonant frequencies of the replica were identified by examining brief pauses in the speech, when he was not talking. During these pauses, the sound of the voice continued echoing, primarily at the chamber's natural resonances. In fact, the amplitude at the resonances could actually become briefly louder during the silences—as energy from other frequencies was transferred into the resonances—before decaying away, because sound is gradually absorbed by the surfaces and objects in the room.

As an experimental control, Sheets continued speaking while he exited the temazcal and for some time outside. He purposely maintained the recorder at a constant distance away from his face as he moved around inside the space, as he exited the space, and then as he spoke outside the temazcal. This procedure enabled a comparison of the pauses between speech inside and outside the chamber as a verification of any true differences in the amplitude and spectrogram plots between the inside and outside of the temazcal.

The full audio data include two amplitude plots, Figure 6.5a and 6.5b, and two spectrograms, Figure 6.5c and 6.5d, because Sheets's Panasonic DMC-ZS40 recorded in stereo. Stereo provides valuable data, as the two microphones are configured to record the sound pressure wave approximately 180 degrees out of phase, depending on the frequency. Pressure waves consist of alternating high- and low-pressure zones propagating in a medium. Stereo simultaneously records a high-pressure peak at one microphone and a low-pressure peak at the other microphone and then alternates as the zones arrive at the microphones.

This analysis is preliminary, based on zooming in on brief sections of the recording with the most promising, cleanest data. A complete analysis, second by second, might well reveal other significant phenomena. As an example of sound from inside the temazcal, the data sample chosen is one of the stereo

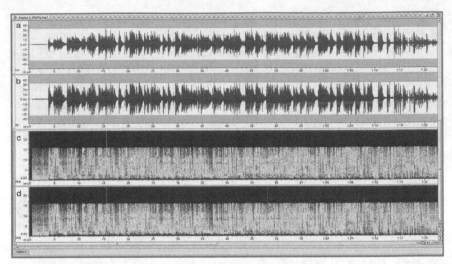

FIGURE 6.5. *Sonogram of temazcal recordings inside under the dome and outside: a and b: amplitude versus time (kU/seconds), left and right stereo channels; c and d: frequency versus time versus amplitude (Hz/seconds/kU), left and right stereo channels.*

channels of Sheets's initial words in the temazcal. The plot of amplitude versus time for the initial phrase, "okay," stretches from 3.89 seconds to 4.158 seconds. Following the initial phrase is a brief pause, 4.158–4.628 seconds, before the beginning of the next word. When the speech stops, the amplitude of sound in the chamber continues, initially at about the same level, then gradually decaying. The sound is still easily audible when the next sound starts at 4.658 seconds.

The plot shows many positive and negative spikes of amplitude. Drawing an imaginary envelope around the maxima of these positive and negative spikes shows a much lower-frequency, gradually decaying oscillation of the sound at about 18 Hertz. This is the lowest natural resonance frequency observed in the temazcal. It would be perceived as a rapid change in loudness.

The word "yea" and the following pause, at 1 minute, 12.425 seconds to 1 minute, 13.7 seconds, is chosen as an example of sound outside the temazcal. Here, the sound amplitude promptly drops to near zero as soon as the speech ends at 1 minute, 13.07 seconds. There are no detectable resonances or reverberation in the amplitude of the background noise recorded outside the temazcal.

The same word "okay" and following pause were examined in the spectrographic data by zooming in to the 580-80 Hz range of frequencies. When the speech ends at 4.158 seconds, it is clear that this frequency band contains the sound energy seen in the figure 6.5a and 6.5b amplitude plots, which continues to reverberate and resonate in the room, gradually fading in amplitude. The entire frequency band is, again, oscillating in amplitude at about 18 Hz, as indicated by dark vertical bands alternating with lighter shaded bands. The vertical bands are actually tilted in a seesaw pattern, indicating that the upper and lower regions of this band are also alternating in amplitude. The resonant amplitude at the position of this microphone is oscillating in phase with the other locations in the temazcal.

TABLE 6.1. Musical tones of the temazcal, and their frequencies in Hertz

Approximate Musical Note	Frequency (Hz)
E3	150
F4	341
C5	512
G#	410
D2	70

The spectrogram shows no equivalent resonance or oscillation in this 580–80 Hz frequency range from speech outside the temazcal. The vocalization of the word "yea" outside the temazcal ends at 1 minute, 13.07 seconds, and there is no subsequent structure in the spectrogram to indicate any resonances or remaining sound energy recorded in this frequency range.

Sound sources in the temazcal induce the space to produce its own musical tones, which reverberate long after the source has stopped. In this sense, the temazcal can be thought of as a musical instrument on its own. To quantify the natural tones, or notes, produced by this instrument, a second analysis was performed. While listening to the recording, the natural resonances were identified by ear, measured using spectral analysis, and checked with a music keyboard and tuning forks. The spectral analysis software used was SignalScope Pro,[3] which produces a real-time plot of sound intensity (dB) versus frequency (Hz). The primary musical tones of the temazcal, in order of their appearance in the recording, are identified in table 6.1. The lowest musical tone, Do, at 18 Hz, identified in the amplitude and spectrogram plots above, was undetectable by ear in the recording and therefore is excluded from this second analysis.

While this analysis is preliminary, the results are intriguing. Several aspects of the temazcal acoustics are worthy of examining in future research. First, use a human voice, a musical instrument, or a signal generator (with continuously variable frequency sound output) to conduct a complete inventory of the room's natural resonances. Second, drive the room with its naturally resonant frequencies to observe the "Q," or quality factor, and "damping" of the room's natural resonances. In other words, at exactly the room's natural resonant frequencies, find the least energy it takes to cause the sound to reverberate. Third, record as a microphone scans around the room to study the two- or three-dimensional standing wave pattern of resonances at different locations and how they alternate in time. Concave surfaces, such as the interior dome of the temazcal, focus sound waves, which could concentrate the sound energy in the center of the room. Fourth, compare sound in the empty room with sound when the room is full of people. When the room is fully occupied, some or much of the sound might be absorbed by the human bodies, substantially damping the resonances and ringing heard in this recording. Fifth, as mentioned previously, test the acoustic reflectivity of wattle and daub surface versus that of concrete. That could be readily achieved, as many original wattle and daub walls are preserved at the site, to be compared to the acoustic reflectivity of the concrete of the replica. Finally, the room's natural resonances constitute the room's own natural musical scale. Commissioning indigenous musicians to compose vocal or native flute music using this natural musical scale and to play the temazcal as its own musical instrument could be worthwhile.

ARCHAEOLOGICAL AND ETHNOGRAPHIC EXAMPLES OF MAYA SWEAT BATHS

Well over a dozen ancient Maya sweat baths, built largely of limestone and located in the lowlands (McKee 2002b, 94), have been reported, but none of them sport a domed roof. Other domed examples may have been common in the volcanic highlands where earthen architecture was more common, and they may have been abundant. However, the usual processes of erosion and decomposition of wattle and daub architecture after site abandonment unfortunately removed all traces of domes, unless unusual circumstances intervene.

McKee (2002b, 94–95) summarized the cases in which ethnographers described Maya sweat baths and their uses. Those examples are concentrated in the highlands and are smaller than Cerén's. They are more associated with a particular family or household instead of being a facility for a community. The use of the sauna and then rinsing afterward results in personal and ritual cleanliness (see Olson, this volume). The feature is also often used for medicinal purposes, such as to alleviate symptoms of respiratory difficulties. Sweat bath use could take on a deeply religious significance as well.

CONCLUSIONS

The domed earthen temazcal at Cerén is at present unique in the Maya area and Mesoamerica in general. However, its design and execution are so sophisticated that it must represent decades or centuries of experience. Further, if preservation were sufficient at other sites, we could know whether it was one of numerous similar functioning temazcales in the Maya area during the Classic period or unique. The structure is so sophisticated that it is difficult to believe it is unique. Rather, it must be the result of generations of Maya experimenting with temazcales built with earthen architecture. It is probable that they were common in towns and villages in the Maya Highlands. The similarities to and differences with the Aztec temazcales are clear (compare this chapter with Olson, this volume). The Spanish and Portuguese are typically credited with bringing domed architecture to the New World, but we now know that it existed centuries before their arrivals.

Ethnographic and ethnohistoric sources record a wide range of functions provided by Maya saunas, including physical cleansing, helping with respiratory problems, post-childbirth healing, and many spiritual or religious aspects (McKee 2002b; Olson, this volume). It is likely that most or all of these pertained to this temazcal in the seventh century. A notable difference is that most saunas recently and today among the Maya are household-specific, while the Cerén sauna was built and used for a wider range of clients. Because it easily seats a dozen people, it must have had multi-familial use, village associations, or uses by numerous men, women, or both sexes for particular purposes and for creating interior darkness at any time of day. Its structural maintenance in fixing cracks and re-thatching and perhaps its original construction were evidently the responsibility of the members of adjacent Household 2. For its functioning, Household 2 personnel provided pine firewood and water to make steam and probably for rinsing off after exiting (Sheets 2006). The nearby storehouse held unusual amounts of pine kindling and water storage jars in comparison to the other storehouses.

After the pine kindling lit the fire in the firebox and other wood was burned, the inside of the temazcal would have been quite hot but laden with dense smoke. The plug in the "donut" could have been removed to allow the smoke to escape and fresh air to enter. Pouring water over the firebox would have steamed up the inside, and after people entered, a pole door would presumably have been pulled over the entrance. The interior of the replica is almost completely dark even without a door, so in ancient times the temazcal with the door shut would have been extraordinarily dark. The darkness would have been utter if the plug were replaced in the "donut." Therefore, use of the Cerén temazcal during the daytime created a darkness of a "Maya night" that could have been the equivalent of illumination of moonlight if no door was pulled shut or, if desired, the utter darkness of an obscured new moon.

As Reed and Gonlin mention in their introduction (this volume), darkness represented creation, and that may have manifested itself in various forms in the temazcal. Someone using it during a successful curing ritual is creating an improved condition. It may well have been used as a rite of passage, a change from an earlier to a different social domain. And the darkness may be symbolic of rebirth. As the microcosm represents the macrocosm, the use of pine kindling as a torch to light the fire in the firebox may reference Kawil's burning torch. As the light from the fire in the firebox is extinguished and the interior of the temazcal goes dark, that could emulate the change from sunlight to a total solar eclipse. As Klein (this volume) mentions, the blindfold on the Aztec returns the wearer to the darkness of creation and therefore healing, thus roughly analogous to the cultural creation of darkness in the temazcal.

Every Cerén household known to date provided a service relationship to the community, and the temazcal was Household 2's contribution. Service relationships are notoriously difficult to document in archaeological contexts but fortunately can be perceived at Cerén. Service relationships must have been a powerful force knitting the social fabric of the functioning town. The residents of Household 2 controlled darkness for others. Those who participated in the sweat house ritual depended on the keepers and the makers of the dark.

NOTES

1. Michael Thomason (physics, University of Colorado–Boulder) wrote the sound analysis section below, and Payson Sheets wrote the other sections of this chapter.

2. http://www.birds.cornell.edu/raven.

3. Faber Acoustical, Inc.

REFERENCES

Beaudry-Corbett, Marilyn, Scott Simmons, and David Tucker. 2002. "Ancient Home and Garden: The View from Household 1 at Cerén." In *Before the Volcano Erupted: The Ancient Cerén Village in Central America*, ed. Payson Sheets, 45–57. Austin: University of Texas Press.

Dull, Robert, John Southon, and Payson Sheets. 2001. "Volcanism, Ecology, and Culture: A Reassessment of the Volcan Ilopango TBJ Eruption in the Southern Maya Realm." *Latin American Antiquity* 12 (1): 25–44.

Gerstle, Andrea, and Payson Sheets. 2002. "Structure 4: A Storehouse-Workshop for Household 4." In *Before the Volcano Erupted: The Ancient Cerén Village in Central America*, ed. Payson Sheets, 74–80. Austin: University of Texas Press.

Gonlin, Nancy, and Christine C. Dixon. 2018. "Classic Maya Nights at Copan, Honduras and El Cerén, El Salvador." In *Archaeology of the Night: Life after Dark in the Ancient World*, ed. Nancy Gonlin and April Nowell, 45–76. Boulder: University Press of Colorado.

Helmholtz, Hermann von. 1885. *On the Sensations of Tone as a Physiological Basis for the Theory of Music*, 2nd English ed., trans. Alexander J. Ellis. London: Longmans, Green.

Lentz, David, and Carlos Ramirez-Sosa. 2002. "Cerén Plant Resources: Abundance and Diversity." In *Before the Volcano Erupted: The Ancient Cerén Village in Central America*, ed. Payson Sheets, 33–42. Austin: University of Texas Press.

McKee, Brian. 2002a. "Household 2 at Cerén: The Remains of an Agrarian and Craft-Oriented Corporate Group." In *Before the Volcano Erupted: The Ancient Cerén Village in Central America*, ed. Payson Sheets, 58–71. Austin: University of Texas Press.

McKee, Brian. 2002b. "Structure 9: A Precolumbian Sweat Bath at Cerén." In *Before the Volcano Erupted: The Ancient Cerén Village in Central America*, ed. Payson Sheets, 89–96. Austin: University of Texas Press.

Sheets, Payson. 2000. "Provisioning the Cerén Household: The Vertical Economy, Village Economy, and Household Economy in the Southeastern Maya Periphery." *Ancient Mesoamerica* 11 (2): 217–230.

Sheets, Payson, ed. 2002. *Before the Volcano Erupted: The Ancient Cerén Village in Central America*. Austin: University of Texas Press.

Sheets, Payson. 2006. *The Cerén Site: An Ancient Village in Central America Buried by Volcanic Ash*, 2nd ed. Belmont, CA: Thomson Learning.

Sheets, Payson. 2009. "Who Were Those Classic Period Immigrants into the Zapotitán Valley, El Salvador?" In *The Ch'orti' Maya Area: Past and Present*, ed. Brent Metz, Cameron McNeil, and Kerry Hull, 61–77. Gainesville: University Press of Florida.

7

The Heat of the Night

*Duality in Aztec Health and
Nocturnal Healing Activities
with a Focus on the Temazcal*

Jan Marie Olson

DOI: 10.5876/9781646421879.c007

In the late 1990s, I had the good fortune of examining a traditional family sweat bath while conducting research in the Guatemalan Cuchumatanes Mountains for the Sombrilla development organization. This stone sweat bath was attached to a large and smoky kitchen where the day's events were discussed. While there, I asked why and how often the sweat bath was used. "Oh," the owner replied, "when I gave birth to my children and to recover from menstrual cramping, and when my husband started to develop arthritis. We used it many times." I noted how small the structure was and yet how efficiently it heated steam for their nighttime customs.

Why was this sweat bath so intriguing? What did it symbolize? The sweat bath, or *temazcal*, represents a variety of ideological relationships that pre-date European contact with the Americas by several thousand years into the Paleo-American era. These Mesoamericans conceptualized life from a dualistic viewpoint, pairing groups of chaos and uniformity, sickness and wellness, female and male, and the ultimate duality—the recurring cycle of night and day (León-Portilla 1990; Maffie 2014). Archaeologists focus much attention on the activities of daytime, but how did ancient people act at night or in darkness? How did the intrinsic value of the dark affect levels of human interaction and, simply, human living? In particular, how did Late Postclassic (1200–1520 CE) central Mexicans (figures 0.1 and table 0.1) relate their dualistic philosophy to the temazcal and thus to concepts of status, personal hygiene, health, and fertility?

Archaeologists, anthropologists, and medical researchers have provided abundant research to show that sweat baths were and are prevalent in Mesoamerica (Alcina Franch 1981; Aparicio Mena and Di Ludovico 2013; Carrasco 1946; Cresson 1938; Ichon 1977; Ortega Cabrera and Álvarez Arellano 2008; Overholtzer 2012; Sheets and Thomason, this volume). Paul Kirchoff (1943), who studied sweat baths around the world, even included it as one of his secondary characteristics of the Mesoamerican culture area. What is clear from this research is that the sweat bath was a multi-functional space for practices such as curing, ritual, hygiene, sexual acts, birthing, and politics. Individual Mesoamerican cultures called the sweat bath by different names, but the Aztecs called it a temazcal from the word *temazcalli*, which in turn is derived from *tema*, "to bathe or sweat," and *calli*, "house" (Cresson 1938, 90; Molina, 2001). The sweat bath, however, stood for more than this physical definition; it was an expression of an entire complex philosophy.

AZTEC PHILOSOPHY OF DUALITY

It is evident from the research of Miguel León-Portilla (1990) and Karl Taube (1993) that the Nahua speakers of Mexico approached their worldview as a complimentary, dialectic, and monistic one (see Klein, this volume, for more on Aztec philosophies). Each aspect of life and the cosmos had an equally important counterpart whose actions alternated endlessly without resolution in a process of interweaving, unifying, intersecting, and balancing (Maffie 2014). This cyclical action was empowered by the main force, Teotl, who was deemed to be the all-encompassing energy. Teotl was simultaneously unity and duality as expressed when the male and female forces merged to create life. The Mesoamerican reality fundamentally rests on this dual metaphor of life force. For example, Peter Markman and Roberta Markman (1989, 137) describe the dual aspects of one of Teotl's children: "As half of a duality, *Tezcatlipoca*, Smoking Mirror, finds his opposite in *Tezcantlanextia*, Mirror Which Illumines. Tezcatlipoca is thus associated with the night and its blurred vision, while [Tezcan]*tlanexti* is linked to the day illuminated by the sun." While they ruled at certain celestial times, they constituted one being.

To comprehend the relationship between day and night, León-Portilla (1990) examined Nahuatl philosophy in part using the poetry of Nezahualcoyotl, the fifteenth-century ruler of Texcoco. León-Portilla wrote that their philosophy depended on the knowledge that all things earthly developed from the *nahualli* (roughly, spirit/soul) of Teotl, recognizing that earth itself was essentially a dreamlike and dangerous place. The Aztec philosophy further emphasized the demonic and tumultuous nature of nighttime when the spirit world, such as shape shifters, gods, and other demons, came alive. The inevitable night was malevolent to humans and opposingly congenial to the gods who battled out the Aztec mythology at every sundown. Even the central myth of the Five Suns began and will eventually end with darkness, when the god Tezcatlipoca will ultimately steal the Fifth Sun.

Individuals in the village of Tecospan in the Valley of Mexico echoed this perception of night as a spirit dreamlike state. In William Madsen's (1960, 1969) ethnography, he wrote that night was a precarious time since the souls, like the "night air" soul, could roam around the earth as nahualli. The term *nahualli* is regularly connected to a sort of modified conscience, soul, or double—often an animal—that is firmly connected to the individual's personality and identity. As the soul roams, any evil or disease that influences the nahualli will also affect their human partners. Therefore, this soul could enter into an individual's dreams and eventually into a person's thoughts, particularly when in an altered state. This frightening dreamlike world helps explain the Nahua ethos that in the words of Burr Cartwright Brundage (1979, 65) approached a "mood of darkness."

The dreamlike state of the night world was repeated in the dreams of people as a supernaturally chaotic and sometimes anarchic time. Dream theory offers some ideas about how perceived chaos can be further enhanced by the physical state of the brain while asleep. According to David Kahn and colleagues (2000), the brain is as active sleeping as it is during waking periods. The dreaming brain, however, "self-organizes differently than the awake brain, not only because the dreaming brain is minimally receptive to outside stimuli, but also because of its changed functional activation patterns and its changed neuromodulation" (2000, 8). Thus in its sleeping state, the brain is acutely reactive to more disorganized internally generated influences, such as feelings and memory. The stabilizing effects of external input are effectively inhibited, and the system flows according to chaos. Sleep and dreaming are necessary revitalizing counterparts to a calmer daytime when human rituals and activities can then be carried out freely.

In a similar sense, the chaos of the sacred night offered strength and power in stability for the Mesoamerican daytime. Michael Mathiowetz and colleagues (2015) noted that native accounts spoke of the first dawn of the first day as the time of mortals, in contrast to the period of the mythical time of creation at night. Many of the gods even changed form as soon as dawn appeared. For example, at the first dawn, when all of the gods were sacrificed at Teotihuacan, Tlahuizcalpantecuhtli turned into the god of stone and of cold.

FIGURE 7.1. *The night god Black Tezcatlipoca from the Fejérváry-Mayer Codex.*

As Tlahuizcalpantecuhtli turned into stone, he was not amenable to human prayers. Therefore, night, when the gods were active and still fleshy, was the best time to converse with and pray to them.

In fact, nightly service to the gods was at least as, if not more, vital than daylight rituals. For instance, the priests offered incense to images of Black Tezcatlipoca four times during the day and six times at night. Brundage cites ethnohistoric accounts that describe the rituals of the priests of the Black Tezcatlipoca. At night, these priests would perform rites and cover their bodies with a black compound consisting of a mixture of "tobacco, narcotic mushrooms, poisonous snakes and scorpions all ground up into a thick paste of soot" (Brundage 1979, 84). Under this guise, the priests would then be impermeable to any tricks the Black Tezcatlipoca could instigate as they went about their devotional duties (Figure 7.1). The goddess Tlazteotl was also associated with these particular night rituals.

THE RITUAL OF BATHING

An essential nightly ritual was bathing. Early descriptions of bathing can be found in the accounts of Aztec scribes and Colonial chroniclers of the fifteenth and sixteenth centuries (Codex Magliabechiano [1970, blade LXXVIII],

Codex Florentine [Sahagún 1970, blades LXXV and CXLVI], Codex Nuttall [Nuttall 1975, blade XVI], and Codex Bodley [Jansen and Perez Jimenez 2005, blade LXXI]).[1]

The Catholic Colonial Spaniards initially considered steam bathing an unhealthy practice and, more despairingly, associated the temazcal rituals with their cultural antagonist, the Moors (Tsikaloudaki et al. 2012). Diego Durán (1971, 269–272) considered it to be the most frightening space of all because inside temazcales, rituals to pagan deities were developed and naked men and women used the space simultaneously. One example of this use can be found in the Codex Magliabechiano (1970): "usaban en estos baños otras vellaquerías nefastas que es bañarse muchos yndios e yndias en cueros y cometían dentro gran fealdad y pecado en este baño."[2] Other writings describe the magic and sorcery surrounding the temazcal, such as the Códice Carolino (1968) where four-day festivals of reverie to Tezcatlipoca and Tontzin are described (de la Serna 1953).

The Christian Spaniards soon prohibited the pagan ritual practices of the temazcales, so King Charles V ordered their destruction. They destroyed mostly elite temazcales in the larger centers, as this is where the Spaniards would have seen the grandest bathing rituals and would also have observed indigenous politicking. The Spanish motive to destroy the temazcales likely had ulterior motives meant to curtail critical elite political relationships and potential elite rebellions. At the end of the seventeenth century, it was still said that the temazcal promoted promiscuity, adultery, male homosexual relations, and incest. In contrast, the Colonial priests and the Spanish Crown were keen on learning about a less controversial function. In both urban and rural centers, they had witnessed the curing abilities of the temazcales and even promoted them. Alejandro Contreras (2001) describes examples in which Colonial hospitals used sweat baths and herbs for curing a variety of ailments, such as coughs and arthritis. Further, Colonial fray Mathias de Escobar commented: "En estos hospitales, como digo, eran curados, todos los enfermos de los pueblos, en los que havía algunos inteligentes herbolarios . . . Sus baños son singulares: para éstos tenían en los hospitales hechos temazcales, que ellos llaman que son unos pequeños hornos, que tomados con debida proporción, causan admirables efectos en la salud"[3] (quoted in Álvarez Amézquita et al. 1960, 184).

What the chroniclers failed to see was that the benefits of sweat bathing came together in a grand syncretism of pleasure, reproduction, body, nature, myth, and health. While Spaniards separated the religious and the medicinal, the Aztec people integrated health and hygiene with their complex cosmovision of duality.

DUALITY IN RESPECT TO THE TEMAZCAL
A Healthy Balance

Health, like all other aspects of Mesoamerican philosophy, was based on a dualistic complementary system in which symbolic energy from their deity Teotl was to keep life in balance. Health was thus conceived as the absence of chaos, that is, an absence of illness and disease and the attainment of full harmony. The necessity of a healthy balance pertained not just to the individual human body but also to the community and the environment. Any imbalance creating "sickness" could take the form of individual illness; community, economic, and political strife; or environmental degradation. Health was tantamount to maintaining corporal stability in individuals and in any larger social circumstances with which they identified (Groark 1997; Ibach 1981).

At one time, specialists in Mesoamerican ethnomedicine agreed that the health system was based on therapeutic conditions as either hot or cold. Now, however, there is an ongoing debate concerning the origin and significance of the "humoral" (hot/cold) system in Latin American ethnomedicine (see Reed, Zeleznik, and Gonlin, this volume). Two basic opinions are spelled out by Alfredo López Austin (1986) who champions an indigenous origin in which the knowledge of humors passed from one specialist to the next. Alternatively, George Foster's (1994) camp argues that the system was transferred from the Colonial Spanish to the general population. More recently, Jacques M. Chevalier and Andrés Sánchez Bain (2003) argued that the "humoral" system is not an appropriate model but that the static hot/cold system should be modified to include a "heliotropic" model, in which the balance of an individual's health has a moving equilibrium.

In this chapter, I agree with López Austin that the indigenous healers of the Americas were highly knowledgeable and capable of creating a humoral system of health that aligned with the Mesoamerican ethos of duality. All plants, animals, and objects were classified according to their hot or cold constitution, as were the various organs found in the human body. Any imbalances would show up as a disruption in normal body health and could affect a particular area of the body to which the curer would apply appropriate measures. There were many mechanisms with which to accomplish balance in health, although Alfonso Aparicio Mena and Francesco Di Ludovico (2013), in their great thesis on Mesoamerican well-being and ethnomedicine, argued that the temazcal was the central device for healing and ensuring good health. They stated that the temazcal was vital in keeping a balance for human health throughout the cycle of death and rebirth. In discussing the goal of wellness and the temazcal, they explained that "the purpose of the *limpia* (bathing) is to re-harmonize the person with that environment, removing and expelling from it the elements (physical, psychological, social and 'symbolic') causing its sickness or influencing it" (2013, 7).

Steam baths were used as a curative measure to treat hot illnesses such as rheumatism, muscular aches, broken bones, coughs, and skin conditions by re-harmonizing the "hot and cold" energies during the sweat (Alcina Franch 1981; Moedano 1977). The *temazcalera*, leader of the bath, would build a fire and throw herb-infused water against the heated rocks to create the steam. In some instances, the fire was external and instead heated the walls of the temazcal. The water would then be thrown on the red-hot wall to create steam. The temazcalera often sped up the recovery from an illness through increasing sweating by thrashing the person's body with twigs and leaves of medicinal plants (see Slotten, this volume). For example, the sweat bath has been used successfully to cure ovarian cysts and cervical fibroids and relieve dysmenorrhea. For these conditions, a vaginal steam is prepared, and the woman is then put to bed under warm covers for at least an hour, primarily at night (Aparicio Mena and Di Ludovico 2013). All of these steps were performed to increase the success in curing an imbalance of heat properties. Once a balance of energies was felt in the client, the temazcalera would end the session.

Because the day was filled with many chores at home and in the field, night was a practical as well as a mythological time for curing. Among the modern Tzetzal and Tzotzil Maya of Chiapas, treatment of illnesses always began at night, roughly one hour after sunset. This time of day connected the individual to the energies associated with the nighttime (Hall 1997).

The Gender Balancing Act

Philosophical duality of the temazcal was also expressed in the relational balance between men and women. Although the male god Tezcatlipoca was revered as a great generating force of the night and the temazcal (Codex Magliabechiano 1970), the sweat bath was mostly considered a female-gender space. Feminine goddesses ruled the temazcal, where life energy and fertility were supported by the Teotl complex of the goddess Toci/Teteoinnan (Ibach 1981). Specifically, it was in her form as Temazcaltoci, "the Grandmother of the Baths," that the mother goddess was revered. She was also referred to as Tlazolteotl (Filth Eater and night goddess), Yoaltícitl (Goddess of the Night), and Xochiquetzal (Flower Quetzal) (Groark 1997, 12) (figure 7.2). As others have observed before, the night is gendered (Gonlin and Nowell 2018).

Tetcu in na.

Capitulo octauo, fo, ibidem

FIGURE 7.2. *Teteoinnan, goddess of the night, fertility, and healing, from the Florentine Codex.*

All the manifestations of this complex were notably connected to fertility, childbirth, midwifery, steam bathing, curing, and the night. Because of these associations, the Aztec worshipped Temazcaltoci before entering the sweat bath and during the cleansing. She was the goddess of medicine and doctors, surgeons, and midwives and was adored by those who had temazcales in their houses (Sahagún 1970). A drawing in the Florentine Codex (1970, book 1, 15–16) shows the image of Temazcaltoci on the front of a temazcal; she was honored and prayed to by those involved in the bathing scene. When a sick person entered the steam bath, it was said that he or she was going to see one of her manifestations, such as Yoaltícitl, "the healer of the night," who could "see the secret things [and] mend that which was disturbed in the bodies of men, fortifying all things tender and delicate" (Carrasco 1946, 740).

Colonial writers also wrote that images of Temazcaltoci were designed in stone or clay and buried beneath the location where the sauna was to be constructed. This deity was consulted by the temazcaleros before choosing the site for a new sweat house. During these ceremonies, offerings of food, alcohol, blood, and incense were given to the statue before people entered (Durán 1971, 271; Sahagún 1950–1982, 33).

Evidence for the integration of the mother goddess complex with the temazcal is also found in more modern contexts. For instance, while working in a central Mexican Nahua village, Gabriel Moedano (1977) wrote of a conceptualized female protector-being of the sweat bath. The women in this village described the bath as a place of uncertainty, with both negative and positive aspects, for which they needed protection and help; for these women, the temazcal philosophically represented a womb, a cave, an underworld oven, and even death. It was unknown to them if the mother goddess would heal or harm, so to overcome uncertainty and influence the outcome in a positive way, offerings were always given.

One modern myth, retold by Kharla García Vargas (2010), tells the story of the protector of the sweat bath and death. In the story, an old woman (likely the moon) was tricked by her two children into entering the forest, where she was later stung by hornets. When she returned home, the children told her to heal the bites in the steam bath. She entered, but they never let their mother out of the temazcal, and her spirit ended up living in the firebox forever. Thus symbolically, the place of death and darkness became the place of renewal in the temazcal.

Sharisse and Geoffrey McCafferty (2008) argued convincingly that caves as well as entrances to temazcales represented portals to the earth mother. Metaphorically, Mesoamericans identified caves and sweat baths with reentering the womb—a dark, closed, and watery space; a sacred feminine space (Brady and Prufer 2005). The cave-womb is where newborns mythically arrived. As an adult, though, individuals could enter the temazcal space, the symbolic womb, to be cleansed and reborn. Caves represented an opening to the underworld where heat and energy could be transmitted to the terrestrial world. This energy or heat was noted in the connection between life and death, as in the resting place of the goddess in the firebox in the previous modern myth. Durán (1967, II, 43–44), though, recounted this same meaning from early Colonial times: "The cave, also means place of the dead. Our mother, our father have gone; they have gone to rest in the water, in the cave." The idea that sweat baths were symbolic of caves (Taube 1986) and caves of sweat baths is further noted in the hamlet of Chamula, Mexico. There, two caves near Chamula are often referred to as the "steambath caves." The Chamulans believe people from past creations used one, while the other cave represented a temazcal for the underworld gods (Groark 1997).

The conflation of caves, sweat baths, and the womb was also noted by Alain Ichon (1977) and Librado Silva Galeana (1984), both of whom stated that the firebox located in the sweat house symbolically represented to Mesoamericans the "navel" or "umbilical cord" of the bath. Interestingly, the sweat bath is also the location where some modern Mesoamericans bury the afterbirth and umbilical cords (Wagley 1957, 129). This act creates a lifelong connection between the temazcal and the individual. As Kevin Groark (1997, 23) aptly stated, "In a very real sense, the sweat bath is an extension of the womb, and continues to nurture and protect the body throughout life."

MENTAL HEALTH

José Alcina Franch (1981) questioned the simple daily hygienic measures of the sweat bath because individuals often came out of the temazcal with sand and herbs stuck to their bodies: they were not clean. Therefore, he argues that the temazcal was more likely used for internal spiritual healing. As is true today, mental illness was considered just as real as bodily illnesses. The gods of the night, Black Tezcatlipoca along with the goddess Tlazteotl, were necessary for cleansing the soul and mind because they could return an individual to a state of mental balance. A priest of these deities would listen to the infractions of the penitent to neutralize the negative state. The ultimate goal of the ritual was for the gods to absorb or eat the *tlazolli*, or "filth," as defined by Louise Burkhart (1989, 110–114). Because these deities were active in the dark, the temazcal was used as the most appropriate place for communication with the gods. Individuals were once again spiritually reborn in the symbolic womb as a balance of mental health was treated.

FERTILITY AND CHILDBIRTH

As spiritual death and birth were enacted in the temazcal, it is not surprising that it was used for actual childbirth. Pregnancy was considered to be a "hot" condition, and thus it was imperative that the mother was kept warm during labor, birth, and postpartum because if she got cold, she could possibly lose her fertility. The sweat bath was used to clean the pregnant woman, in the belief that she should be free of filth and sin before delivery (Bunzel 1967). It was also used to prepare the woman's body for childbirth and to calm her nerves prior to delivery (Sahagún 1970). The Florentine Codex mentions that sweat baths were to be used three or four months into the pregnancy and during labor so the birth would happen quickly. If after a day the woman had not given birth, she was put into the sweat bath again with the midwife (Sahagún 1970, book 6, 159–160). In this case, the new mother returned to the symbolic womb, risking death to give birth, and only then was her fertility reborn through the energy or heat of the temazcal.

In modern central Mexican Nahua communities, women are generally given between one and twelve postpartum cleansings, or *limpias*, from the first day until six months after the delivery to ensure both a healthy balance in the woman's body and milk production (Huber and Sandstrom 2001). The number of limpias a woman received depended on the community in which she lived. Margaret Redfield, who worked alongside her husband, Robert (Redfield 1930), in Tepoztlan, Morelos, in the mid-1900s, was invited to many birthings and recounted the events of one in detail. According to M. Redfield, in the month following the birth of a child, the mother was to take numerous sweat baths. In Tepoztlan, a man carried the mother to a temazcal so her feet did not touch the ground. A midwife and other female relatives followed the two and brought a variety of offerings. The fire was then lit, and an herbal tea was thrown on the heated rocks and ceramic shards. Everyone lay down on mats while the midwife controlled the amount and degree of heat and vapor by waving a fan over the heated rocks. The midwife was very skilled in controlling the heat and the amount of sweating by participants in the temazcal. After the sweat, everyone washed. The new mother was covered in a cloth and laid down so her body temperature did not drop too quickly. This sweat bath would be repeated once a week for two to four weeks. It was imperative that a man bathed with the women so the duality of genders was maintained in balance.

THE TEMAZCAL STRUCTURE

The conventional form of the temazcal is significant in relating to the philosophical aspects of darkness and night. Historical and ethnological accounts of the cosmological symbolism show that Mesoamericans believed humans and their ancestors were born in sweat baths (Child 2007). As mentioned earlier, the dark space of the sweat bath has been associated with fertility and therefore with caves. Caves were not only entrances for the dead to travel to the underworld (Bricker 1973, 114; Taube 1988, 295–296) but were locations where newborns entered the world (Wagley 1949). Thus the sweat bath is a location where one could enter a darkened space (the womb), bathe, and emerge to the light as if one had been reborn (Child 2007). The duality of light and darkness would definitely have been felt by practitioners and users of sweat baths. In the darkness of the temazcal, they would have been able to commune with various deities, particularly those associated with the night and darkness.

Archaeologist Mark Child (2007) documents that the temazcal is often personified as a living entity, likely a deity. The sweat bath in this regard becomes the god who creates the dark space in which the human and the deity can interact. He recounts Esther Katz's work with the Mixteca of Oaxaca where features of sweat houses are given body-part names. For instance, the firebox is equated with the mouth, the entrance as the head, and the ceiling as the back (Katz 1990, 176). This symbolism also can be seen in many of the Aztec codices where temazcal drawings personify the structure. Mark and Jessica Child (2001) show that the two niches above the doorway symbolize the eyes and the doorway as the mouth of the cave.

Codex and Ethnographic Descriptions

Representations of sweat baths vary considerably across Mesoamerica. In the Florentine Codex, Bernardino de Sahagún (1970) describes two types of temazcales: (1) a square-shaped adobe brick structure with the firebox on the outside and (2) a dome-shaped structure with the firebox inside. However, in the Codex Magliabechiano (1970), the temazcal is depicted as a rectangular structure with a flat roof and an exterior firebox. In Durán (1971, 269–272), "These bathhouses are heated with fire and are like small, low huts. Each one can hold ten persons in a squatting position; standing is impossible . . . The entrance is low and narrow. People enter one by one and on all fours. In the back part there is a small furnace which heats the place. The heat is such that it is almost unbearable" (figure 7.3).

In the twentieth century, ethnographic descriptions of sweat baths and their associated rituals exist for much of highland Mesoamerica (summarized in Alcina Franch 1981). Modern temazcales vary tremendously in size, shape, materials of construction, and internal detail—not only across Mesoamerica but within single communities. For example, both square and round temazcales have been found at Milpa Alta, one of the oldest boroughs of Mexico City. Frank Cresson (1938) reported that a square sweat bath was made with stone and wood, while the circular one was made with stone and mud and had a dome-shaped roof (see Sheets and Thomason, this volume, for a description of the temazcal at Cerén with such a roof). Neither had ventilation holes. Cresson (1938) also described the temazcales at San Francisco and San Martin

FIGURE 7.3. *Aztecs praying to the goddess Temazcalteci and preparing for a sweat bath. Typical of Colonial drawings, this temazcal is in a square form. From the Codex Magliabechiano (1970).*

near the town of San Juan Teotihuacan. Both of these types are rectangular with rounded attached fireboxes. His description of a temazcal at Tepoztlan, Morelos, is again different from others. It was built with an upper-level steam chamber and a lower-level doorway and had a gabled roof made of wood and stone and covered by subsequent layers of mud, stone, and tile. In the same community, Robert Redfield (1930, 34) described a rectangular temazcal that was made of stone mortar and was roughly 5 feet high at the center of the structure. The roof peak was fairly low, and the one entrance was built so a person had to enter on hands and knees.

Linton Satterthwaite (1952) summarized many of the attributes a temazcal should have including a firebox, a bench, a drain, and ventilation holes. But there was much diversity. Some structures were made of wood, while others were made of stone and tiles. Some buildings were large enough to hold ten–twelve people and others were smaller, with space for only two–three people. Independent of these characteristics, the most vital structural attribute

FIGURE 7.4. *A typical circular dome-shaped temazcal (modern) from Tlayacapan, Mexico, Morelos.*

was that the temazcal should hold steam, necessitating both a low ceiling and a small doorway (figure 7.4).

ARCHAEOLOGICAL DESCRIPTION OF TEMAZCALES

The identification of archaeological temazcales echoes the variation described in ethnohistoric documents and particularly in ethnographies. Subterranean, semi-subterranean, and at-ground sweat baths of square, rectangular, and circular design have all been described in the academic literature (Child 2007; Houston 1996; McKee 2002; Ruppert 1952; Satterthwaite 1952). Some of the first and most complete discussions of archaeological temazcal structures, though, have come from the Maya Lowland area. Cresson's (1938) seminal work began a systematic analysis of steam bath structures from which a few models have developed.

In the 1950s, Satterthwaite worked at the archaeological site of Piedras Negras in the northern lowlands of Guatemala. With the large number of sweat baths at Piedras Negras, Satterthwaite (1952) was able to build a typology, identify themes, and create a comparative analysis. Part of his findings reasoned that the shape of sweat baths, either rectangular or circular, could identify the class of the users—the former by the elite and the latter by commoners. The largest of the eight temazcales is Structure P-7. This elaborate elite rectangular sweat bath had drains, ventilation holes, numerous stone benches, an adjacent firebox, and a large antechamber that was likely used as a dressing room (1952, 20). These latter attributes list what he felt would have distinguished a structure as a sweat bath. Some structures were made of wood, while others were made of stone and tiles.

Alcina Franch, who worked at Agua Tibia in Guatemala, contributed a comparative rural to urban model to this discussion. He and his collaborators argued that circular structures were more rural in nature than the urban core rectangular structures (Alcina Franch, Ciudad Ruíz, and Iglesias Ponce de León 1980). Later, Groark (1997) separated temazcales, based on status and wealth, into elite and commoner sweat baths. He wrote that most of the elite sweat baths found in ceremonial centers were large and rectangular, except for the oval one from the Maya city Dzibilchaltun. Many of the elite temazcales were constructed with materials similar to those of palaces and temples, while commoners used simpler oval structures. This model is supported by Nuria Desantes (2014, 16) who wrote: "The materiality of the same, as in any Mayan construction, would respond to the user's status and its consequent location. While those located on the periphery of cities or in rural settlements would be built with simple systems and perishable materials, those belonging to the elite, located in the heart of the city, would present greater resistance and durability thanks to the use of more advanced techniques and higher quality materials."

Stephen Houston (1996, 145), in his investigative work at the Palenque Cross Group temples at the Mexican lowland site, argued that these large temples represented sweat baths. While the elite did physically bathe in sweat baths, Houston's translation of the inscriptions carved in the interior walls led him to believe the temples were purely ceremonial and symbolic. More specifically he interprets the temples as rectangular symbolic birth sweat houses for the Palenque Triad, the patron gods of the city. The actual water rituals and bathing of the nobility, though, likely took place in more functional structures at the nearby Otolum spring.

Mark and Jessica Child (2001) extend Stephen Houston's functional/ceremonial model further to explain the symbolism of water fertility as it relates to the site of Palenque. The many water elements at Palenque symbolically equate to essential birthing fluids and caves as birthing passageways. They agree with Houston that the inner sanctums of the Cross Group temples were used ceremonially but stress that the sweat bath was also used for transformative rites, such as those during puberty, adulthood, and marriage. They note that the Palenque king Kan B'ahlam II performed purification rites in the symbolic sweat baths at his coronation in 684 CE.

In her exhaustive study of temazcales, Desantes (2014) also built on Houston's ceremonial versus functional/domestic use model. She noted that rectangular baths were popular in the Classic and earlier times and that the small circular steam baths were more frequent in Postclassic Mesoamerica, particularly that this latter form was more prevalent in the ethnographic literature of Mexico. She argues that this pattern could represent a change in the political structure of elites and communities.

Davide Domenici and his colleagues (2019) developed Satterthwaite's (1952) earlier research and argued convincingly that the use of commoner circular baths was more for functional purposes and that the elite used rectangular structures for purely ceremonial rites. This ceremonial function for rectangular steam baths is supported by the large size of the structures, which suggests that they were used by a collective. Further, these buildings were associated with ball courts of the Maya ballgame, such as at the large ancient cities of Piedras Negras, Chichen Itza, and Tikal. Their argument is supported by Colonial sources and Maya iconographies (Miller 2013, 232) that steam baths were used in purification ceremonies before the ballgame. Elite-attended sweat baths, like their associated ball courts, had impressive masonry structures that were imbued with ideological meaning and status, so much so that the large rectangular sweat bath at Chichen Itza was incorporated right into the ball court structure (Ruppert 1952).

In the lowland Petén jungle of Guatemala sits the ancient city of Nakum. This large site competed with the well-known cities of Tikal, Naranjo, and Yaxha from the Preclassic to Classic periods. Polish archaeologist Jarosław Źrałka (2008, 76–79) defines the rectangular stone Structure 26 at Nakum as a sweat bath for elite families. This private structure served specific families, as it was located in an enclosed area of the South Acropolis.

A final example of a Maya temazcal is thoroughly discussed in chapter 6 of this volume. Payson Sheets and Michael Thomason are able to describe in great depth a rectangular domed sweat bath from the site of Cerén, El Salvador (McKee 1990). The mud and wood structure was covered with volcanic ash and preserved after the Loma Caldera eruption in 660 CE. The researchers note that the temazcal stood close to domestic structures and that a hard-packed earth trail between the two had developed. They conclude that the sweat bath acted as a musical instrument with acoustic properties.

The abundance of sweat bath information coming from the Maya area reveals that to the ancient people, cosmological symbolism and function were central elements for purification rites, transformative rites, wellness, and fertility practices. Symbols of darkness, caves, deities, and fertility/renewal are all present at the sweat baths.

Building on these earlier Maya models, I will attempt to organize Late Aztec period temazcales into semi-rural and urban cases near Tenochtitlan, based on their shape. While there are too few cases to correlate statistically, there is a sense that, like the Maya elite structures, the central Mexicans built rectangular-shaped temazcales in larger urban centers while circular and subterranean ones were constructed in the semi-rural areas.

Urban Temazcales

When Tenochtitlan, in the Valley of Mexico, was initially settled, the Mexica immigrants made a temazcal near what was called Temazcalapan. Everyone was said to have taken part in the bathing ritual to celebrate the founding of their new home (de la Garza 2001). Stories such as this one have added to the sweat bath ethnohistoric data when the archaeology has been notably sparse from the imperial capital. Colonial historian Alva Ixtilxochitl describes many elements of the capital, including the beautiful gardens near Tetzeutzingo. Here, one could find "sumptuous palaces, fountains, canals, ponds, baths and labyrinths, framed by pots and trees brought from various places" (cited in Cabeza 2000, 64). By the 1970s, researcher Edward Calnek (1974) had mapped Tenochtitlan from ethnohistoric resources and found that commoner residences had been grouped around courtyards with shared kitchens, temples, and temazcales (the shapes of the sweat baths are generally unknown). More rectangular sweat baths were located at Tlatelolco and near the modern Palacio de Belles Artes in Mexico City (figure 7.5).

Urban elite sweat baths are located primarily in ceremonial centers and are often associated with temples, royal residences, and ballgame structures (Ortiz Butrón 2005). For example, Aztec period temazcales at Tula were excavated near the exterior east wall of Ballcourt I. Some residential houses were also mapped at the southeast end of this site (Healan 2009). The temazcales had interior/exterior ventilation, along with exterior circular fire pits off the back of the stone structures. A quadrangular temazcal was also built in the center of Ballcourt II (López Luján and López Austin 2007). As mentioned earlier, the relationship between ball courts and sweat baths indicates that players, officials, rulers, and priests participated in purification ceremonies during or after the ballgames (Agrinier 1969; Taladoire 1981, cited in Groark 1997). These temazcales are similar to the image sketched in the Codex Magliabechiano.

During the Epiclassic (700–950 CE), central Mexican temazcales were also built near ceremonial centers. Operation K, adjacent to the ball court and other domestic structures at Xochicalco, shows that elite residents built a rectangular temazcal. Based on architecture and artifact remains, Ronald Webb and Kenneth Hirth (1998) argue that Room 17 of the south patio group was a temazcal. Thus urban temazcales are located near domestic structures

FIGURE 7.5. *A Late Postclassic rectangular stone temazcal from Tlatelolco, Mexico City, Mexico. Thelma Datter, September 7, 2009. Public domain.*

but appear to have a public ceremonial application. For example, entering the temazcales before a ballgame would offer the players or leaders time to commune with the elements of darkness and the energies associated with the womb and rebirth prior to a game. The temazcales located near domestic structures likely functioned in a similar manner to those described in ethnographies and historical documents.

Semi-Rural Temazcales

Rural and commoner sweat baths are less visible in the central Mexican Late Postclassic archaeological record, although some are indeed known from the Maya region (see chapter 6, this volume) (e.g., Haviland 2014; McKee 2002; Webster 2001). Evidence from ethnohistoric documents describing two Chiapan towns, Coapa and Coneta (established in 1554 and abandoned around 1660), confirms that temazcales were the second most common domestic structure. The ratio was an average of one temazcal to every four houses (Lee 1979; Lee and Bryant 1988, 12). Similar ratios are reported for the Totonac region as 1:3 and 1:5 (Ichon 1977) and for Tepoztlan at 1:4 (Redfield 1930). These ratios are so high that surely everyone in the rural community would have had access to sweat baths. However, the archaeological record shows that semi-rural temazcal structures were different than the urban cases. Verónica Ortega Cabrera and Víctor Germán Álvarez Arellano (2008) argue that the further the distance from the urban capital of Tenochtitlan, the less likely that sweat baths are built in rectangular form. Moreover, they state that the rectangular baths drawn in historical books represent the collection bias of the priests and chroniclers who collected most of their evidence from the capital city. To their study, I add these reasons as to why there is a lack of known sweat baths: the nature of salvage work, modern urbanism, reporting around the State of Mexico, difficulties with landowners, and misidentification of structures. Nonetheless, rural temazcales have been located in patio areas of house groupings and near elite palace structures. These temazcales tend to be circular in structure and are constructed of wattle and daub or, alternatively, with *tezontle* (a porous volcanic rock) rather than stone.

In Aztec Late Postclassic (1200–1520 CE) deposits at the central Mexican city of Teotihuacan, two bathing structures were found at the north end of the Pyramid of the Sun (Gomez and Cabrera 2006). The Texapla 1 N3E3 temazcal was a 2.6 m by 2.1 m elliptical structure. It had drains and benches, but, unlike others, it was missing an interior fire chamber. Opposingly, the Cuchitpetanco N4E3 sweat bath was rectangular in shape (2.1 m by 2.5 m), with a concrete and polished stucco floor. It was a subterranean chamber with wide drains and a spot for an internal firebox. It was likely used by the entire community but may have served only the occupants of the adjacent domestic structures. Their locations and constructions attest to the significance of the temazcal for these people.

At the site of Cihuatecpan in the Teotihuacan Valley, Susan Evans found circular temazcal constructions in courtyards at the rear of the main palace building. Here, artifact concentrations showed examples of many of the relationships I have been discussing. Evans and Elliot Abrams (1988) found that 90 percent of the figurines at Cihuatecpan were primarily excavated near domestic structures and sweat baths, a distribution she interpreted as an indication of both domestic and sweat bath ritual. Evans (1996) also noted that the figurines specifically found in and around temazcales were rattles with the "two-prong hairdo." McCafferty and McCafferty (1999) showed that this particular hairstyle depicted Xochiquetzal (a manifestation of the Toci complex) and represented a devotion of adult women to the goddess. Lisa Overholtzer (2012), who also worked at Cihuatecpan, argued that midwives used percussion instruments such as rattles in the temazcales. She suggested that the sound may have relaxed the birthing mother so she could focus on rhythmic sounds to alleviate the pain of childbirth. She further noted that the presence of these rattle figurines implied a "link between figurines and female reproduction and health, since sweat baths were often used for ritual cleansing and healing" (2012, 74). Similarly, a shallow round sweat bath found in the Aztec period rural palace at Chiconautla was made of plastered cobblestone (Elson 1999).

Anomalies in the semi-rural temazcal form do exist, as rectangular structures have been found in the Valley of Mexico at the Aztec III sites of Acozac and the Casa de Morelos in Ecatepec near Mexico City (Garcia Chávez, Gamboa Cabezas, and Saldaña Velez 2003, cited in Gamboa Cabezas and Cobean 2016). Yet even these forms are associated with house structures.

Thus it appears that semi-rural temazcales are more commonly associated with domestic structures of elite or commoner status than with public religious buildings. The population of these rural communities needed access to the medical and hygienic benefits of the temazcal, all the while being watched over by the night-fertility goddesses of the Toci complex.

CONCLUSIONS

The temazcal was an indispensable element in the ritual life and health of Mesoamericans. Many Colonial writers and modern ethnographers have described the structure and the acts or practices associated with sweat bathing. Notably, the temazcal represents an integration of a unique complex combination of images, concepts, and themes that have persisted through time across a very wide geographic area. Resounding in this study are the particular themes of darkness, night, and duality to which the temazcal is the symbolic womb. Elements of these nighttime associations can be inferred from the ritual and philosophical descriptions given in ethnohistoric documents but also from the artifactual remains uncovered within and near bath structures. The temazcal was a place of darkness and spiritual energies where gods and goddesses, midwives, and temazcaleras determined the outcome of fertility and healing. Thus it was within the temazcal that the conceptual nighttime access to the deities and their power was fully sensed and realized.

NOTES

1. The Spanish priests Francisco Clavijero (1945) and Bernardino de Sahagún (1970) wrote that the Aztec people bathed often, sometimes in lakes and rivers and other times in a sweat bath. So often were the sweat baths used that Fray Diego Durán (1967 1, 176) wrote about how the temazcal expanded the social complexity of the elite classes: "había el oficio de corcovados, enanos y de especialistas sopladores para el baño de vapor: Estos sujetos eran reverenciados por su cargo en el barrio, y tenidos por muy honrados. Sus servicios eran remunerados por la familia a los que atendía, con mucha comida, pulque y mazorcas, todo conforme a la calidad de la persona." Translated by author: ". . . there was an office of hunchbacks, dwarfs, and specialist blowers for the steam bath: these subjects were revered for their position in the neighborhood and regarded as very honored. Their services were remunerated by the family they attended, with much food, pulque, and corn cobs, all according to the status of the person."

2. Translated by author: "In these baths they used other wicked homosexuals that bathed many male and female Indians in leather, and they committed inside great ugliness and sin in this bath."

3. Translated by author: "In these hospitals, as I say, they were cured, all the sick of the villages, in those that had some intelligent herbalists . . . Their baths are for a singular person: for the sick they had made temazcales (which they call those with small furnaces) in the hospitals, which taken with due proportion cause admirable effects in health."

REFERENCES

Agrinier, Pierre. 1969. "Excavations at San Antonio, Chiapas, Mexico." *American Anthropologist* 73 (4): 919–920.

Alcina Franch, José. 1981. "El baño de vapor entre los mayas prehispánicos." *Scripta Ethnologica* 6: 41–47.

Alcina Franch, José, Andres Ciudad Ruíz, and Josefa Iglesias Ponce de León. 1980. "El 'temazcal' en Mesoamérica: evolución, forma y función." *Revista Española de Antropología Americana* 10: 93–132.

Álvarez Amézquita, José, Miguel E. Bustamante, Antonio López Picazos, and Francisco Fernández del Castillo. 1960. *Historia de la salubridad y de la asistencia en México*, vol. 3. Mexico City: Secretaría de Salubridad y Asistencia.

Aparicio Mena, Alfonso J., and Francesco L. Di Ludovico. 2013. *The Limpia in the Mesoamerican Ethnomedicines*. Madrid: Bubok.

Brady, James E., and Keith M. Prufer, eds. 2005. *In the Maw of the Earth Monster: Mesoamerican Ritual Cave Use*. Austin: University of Texas Press.

Bricker, Victoria Reifler. 1973. *Ritual Humor in Highland Chiapas*. Austin: University of Texas Press.

Brundage, Burr Cartwright. 1979. *The Fifth Sun: Aztec Gods, Aztec World*. Austin: University of Texas Press.

Bunzel, Ruth Leah. 1967. *Chichicastenango: A Guatemalan Village*. Seattle: University of Washington Press.

Burkhart, Louise M. 1989. *Slippery Earth: Nahua-Christian Moral Dialogue in Sixteenth-Century Mexico*. Tucson: University of Arizona Press.

Cabeza, Alejandro. 2000. "El jardín mexicano hacia el nuevo milenio: Una retrospectiva evolutiva." *Revista de la Universidad de México* 593: 63–68.

Calnek, Edward E. 1974. "Conjunto urbano y modelo residencial en Tenochtitlan." In *Ensayos sobre el desarrollo urbano de México*, ed. Woodrow Borah, Edward E. Calnek, Keith Davies, Luis Unikel, and Alejandra Moreno Toscano, 11–59. Mexico City: Secretaría de Educación Pública.

Carrasco, Pedro. 1946. "El temazcal." In *México Prehispánico: Culturas, Deidodes, y Monumentos*, ed. Jorge A. Viro, 737–741. Mexico City: Emma Hurtado.

Chevalier, Jacques M., and Andrés Sánchez Bain. 2003. *The Hot and the Cold: Ills of Humans and Maize in Native Mexico*. Toronto: University of Toronto Press.

Child, Mark B. 2007. "Ritual Purification and the Ancient Maya Sweatbath at Palenque." In *Palenque: Recent Investigations at the Classic Maya Center*, ed. Damien B. Marken, 233–264. Lanham, MD: Altamira.

Child, Mark B., and Jessica C. Child. 2001. "La historia del Baño de Vapor P-7 en Piedras Negras, Guatemala." In *XIV Simposio de Investigaciones Arqueológicas en Guatemala, 2000*, ed. Juan Pedro Laporte, Ana Claudia Suasnávar, and Bárbara Arroyo, 449–464. Guatemala City: Museo Nacional de Arqueología y Etnología.

Clavijero, Francisco J. 1945. *Historia Antigua de México*. Mexico City: Editorial Porrúa.

Codex Magliabechiano. 1970. 3rd ed. Vol. CLXIII, B.R. 232, folio 155. Ed. Ferdinand Anders. Graz, Austria: Akademische Druck- u. Verlagsanstalt.

Códice Carolino. 1968. *Manuscrito anónimo del siglo XVI en forma de adiciones a la primera edición del vocabulario de Molina*. Estudios de Cultura Náhuatl 7. Mexico City: Universidad Nacional Autónoma de México.

Contreras, Alejandro Tonatiuh. 2001. "Visiones sobre el temazcal mesoamericano: un elemento cultural polifacético." *Ciencia Ergo Sum* 8 (2): 133–144.

Cresson, Frank M., Jr. 1938. "Maya and Mexican Sweat Houses." *American Anthropologist* 40 (1): 88–104.

de la Garza, Mercedes. 2001. "El águila real, símbolo del pueblo mexica." *Caravelle* 76 (1): 105–117.

de la Serna, Jacinto. 1953. *Tratado de las idolatrías, supersticiones, dioses, ritos, hechicerías y otras costumbres gentilicias de las razas aborígenes de México, notas, comentarios y un estudio de Fransisco del Paso y Troncoso*, vol. 10. Mexico City: Ediciones Fuente Cultural.

Desantes, Nuria Matarredona. 2014. "The Architecture of the Steam Bath in the Mayan Culture." *Studies of Mayan Culture* 44: 11–40.

Domenici, Davide, Lorenzo Zurla, Arianna Campiani, and Thomas A. Lee Whiting. 2019. "Baños de vapor en sitios arqueológicos zoques: Nuevos datos desde el occidente de Chiapas." *Estudios de cultura maya* 53: 45–79.

Durán, Diego. 1967. *La Historia de las Indias de Nueva España e Islas de Tierra Firme*. Ed. Angel María Garibay. Mexico City: Editorial Porrúa.

Durán, Diego. 1971. *Book of the Gods and Rites; and the Ancient Calendar*. Ed. and trans. Fernando Horcasitas and Doris Heyden. Norman: University of Oklahoma Press.

Elson, Christina M. 1999. "An Aztec Palace at Chiconautla, Mexico." *Latin American Antiquity* 10 (2): 151–167.

Evans, Susan Toby. 1996. "Cihuatecpan: An Aztec Period Village in the Teotihuacan Valley." In *Arqueología Mesoamericana: Homenaje a William T. Sanders*, ed. Alba Guadalupe Mastache, Jeffrey R. Parsons, and Robert S. Santley, 399–415. Mexico City: Instituto Nacional de Antropología e Historia, Arqueología Mexicana.

Evans, Susan Toby, and Elliot M. Abrams. 1988. "Archaeology at the Aztec Period Village of Cihuatecpan, Mexico: Methods and Results of the 1984 Field Season." In *Excavations at Cihuatecpan*, ed. Susan Toby Evans, 50–234. Vanderbilt University Publications in Anthropology 36. Nashville, TN: Vanderbilt University Press.

Fejérváry-Mayer Codex. 1971. Folio 44. Ed. Ferdinand Anders. Graz, Austria: Akademische Druck- u. Verlagsanstalt.

Foster, George M. 1994. *Hippocrates' Latin American Legacy: Humoral Medicine in the New World*, vol. 1. Langhorne, PA: Gordon and Breach.

Gamboa Cabezas, Luis M., and Robert H. Cobean. 2016. "Comments on Cultural Continuities between Tula and the Mexica." In *The Oxford Handbook of the Aztecs*, ed. Deborah L. Nichols and Enrique Rodrigues Alegria, 53–71. Oxford: Oxford University Press.

García Chávez, Raúl, Luis M. Gamboa Cabezas, and Verónica Saldaña Velez. 2003. *Informe final del Salvamento Arqueológico Circuito Exterior Mexiquense: tramo Ecatepec Peñón*. Mexico City: Archivo Técnico del INAH, Consejo de Arqueología.

García Vargas, Kharla. 2010. "El temazcal curativo y el uso tradicional de las plantas." Master's thesis, Universidad Autónoma de Chapingo, Texcoco, Mexico.

Gomez, Sergio, and Ruben Cabrera. 2006. "Contextos de la ocupacion en teotihuacan." In *El fenomeno Coyotlatelco en el Centro de Mexico: Tiempo, espacio, y significado*, ed. Laura Solar, 231–256. Mexico City: Instituto Nacional de Antropologiá e Historia.

Gonlin, Nancy, and April Nowell. 2018. "Introduction to Archaeology of the Night." In *Archaeology of the Night*, ed. Nancy Gonlin and April Nowell, 5–24. Boulder: University Press of Colorado.

Groark, Kevin. 1997. "To Warm the Blood, to Warm the Flesh: The Role of the Steambath in Highland Maya (Tzeltal-Tzotzil) Ethnomedicine." *Journal of Latin American Lore* 20 (1): 3–96.

Hall, Robert L. 1997. *An Archaeology of the Soul: North American Indian Belief and Ritual*. Urbana: University of Illinois Press.

Haviland, William A. 2014. *Excavations in Residential Areas of Tikal: Non-Elite Groups without Shrines, Analysis and Conclusions*. Tikal Report 20B, University Museum Monographs 140. Philadelphia: University of Pennsylvania Museum of Archaeology and Anthropology.

Healan, Dan M. 2009. "Household, Neighborhood, and Urban Structure in an 'Adobe City': Tula, Hidalgo, Mexico." In *Domestic Life in Prehispanic Capitals: A Study of Specialization, Hierarchy, and Ethnicity*, ed. Linda Manzanilla and Claude Chapdelaine, 67–88. Ann Arbor: University of Michigan and Museum of Anthropology.

Houston, Stephen D. 1996. "Symbolic Sweatbaths of the Maya: Architectural Meaning in the Cross Group at Palenque, Mexico." *Latin American Antiquity* 7 (2): 132–151.

Huber, Brad R., and Alan R. Sandstrom. 2001. "Recruitment, Training, and Practice of Indigenous Midwives: From the Mexico–United States Border to the Isthmus of Tehuantepec." In *Mesoamerican Healers*, ed. Brad R. Huber, 139–178. Austin: University of Texas Press.

Ibach, Thomas J. 1981. "The Temascal and Humoral Medicine in Santa Cruz Mixtepec, Juxtlahuaca, Oaxaca, Mexico." Master's thesis, University of Tennessee, Knoxville.

Ichon, Alain. 1977. "A Late Postclassic Sweathouse in the Highlands of Guatemala." *American Antiquity* 42 (2): 203–209.

Jansen, Maarten, and Gabina Aurora Perez Jimenez. 2005. *Codex Bodley: A Painted Chronicle from the Mixtec Highlands*. Chicago: University of Chicago Press.

Kahn, David, Stanley Krippner, and Alan Combs. 2000. "Dreaming and the Self-Organizing Brain." *Journal of Consciousness Studies* 7 (7): 4–11.

Katz, Esther. 1990. "Des racines dans la 'Terre de la pluie': identité, écologie et alimentation dans le haut pays mixtèque." PhD dissertation, Université de Paris X–Nanterre, Paris, France.

Kirchoff, Paul. 1943. "Mesoamerica, sus limites geograficos, composicion etnica y caracteres culturales." *Acta Americana* 1 (1): 92–107.

Lee, Thomas. 1979. "Coapa, Chiapas: A Sixteenth-Century Coxoh Maya Village on the Camino Real." In *Maya Archaeology and Ethnohistory*, ed. Norman Hammond and Gordon R. Willey, 208–222. Austin: University of Texas Press.

Lee, Thomas, and Douglas Bryant. 1988. "The Colonial Coxoh Maya." In *Ethnoarchaeology among the Highland Maya of Chiapas, Mexico*, ed. Thomas Lee and Brian Hayden, 5–20. Papers of the New World Archaeological Foundation 56. Provo, UT: New World Archaeological Foundation, Brigham Young University.

León-Portilla, Miguel. 1990. *Aztec Thought and Culture: A Study of the Ancient Nahuatl Mind*. Trans. Jack Emory Davis. Norman: University of Oklahoma Press.

López Austin, Alfredo. 1986. "La pólemica sobre la dicotomía fríocalor." In *La medicina invisible: Introducción al estudio de la medicina tradicional de México*, ed. Xavier Lozoya and Carlos Zolla, 73–90. Mexico City: Folios Ediciones, S.A.

López Luján, Leonardo, and Alfredo López Austin. 2007. "The Mexico in Tula and Tula in Mexico-Tenochtitlan." *Estudios de Cultura Náhuatl* 38: 33–83.

Madsen, William. 1960. *The Virgin's Children: Life in an Aztec Village Today*. Austin: University of Texas Press.

Madsen, William. 1969. "The Nahua." In *Handbook of Middle American Indians*, vol. 8: *Ethnology Part 2*, ed. Evon Z. Vogt, series ed. Robert Wauchope, 602–637. Austin: University of Texas Press.

Maffie, James. 2014. *Aztec Philosophy: An Understanding of a World in Motion*. Boulder: University Press of Colorado.

Markman, Peter T., and Roberta H. Markman. 1989. *Masks of the Spirit: Image and Metaphor in Mesoamerica*. Berkeley: University of California Press.

Mathiowetz, Michael, Polly Schaafsma, Jeremy Coltman, and Karl Taube. 2015. "The Darts of Dawn: The Tlahuizcalpantecuhtli Venus Complex in the Iconography of Mesoamerica and the American Southwest." *Journal of the Southwest* 57 (1): 1–102.

McCafferty, Sharisse, and Geoffrey McCafferty. 1999. "The Metamorphosis of Xochiquetzal: A Window on Womanhood in Pre- and Post-Conquest Mexico." In *Manifesting Power: Gender and the Interpretation of Power in Archaeology*, ed. Tracy L. Sweely, 103–125. London: Routledge.

McCafferty, Sharisse, and Geoffrey McCafferty. 2008. "Back to the Womb: Caves, Sweatbaths, and Sacred Water in Mesoamerica." In *Flowing through Time*, ed. Larry Steinbrenner, Beau Cripps, Metaxia Geogopoulos, and Jim Carr, 26–33. Calgary: Chacmool Archaeological Association of the University of Calgary.

McKee, Brian R. 1990. "Excavations at Structure 9." In *Archaeological Investigations at the Cerén Site, El Salvador: A Preliminary Report,* ed. Payson Sheets and Brian R. McKee, 90–107. Boulder: Department of Anthropology, University of Colorado.

McKee, Brian R. 2002. "Structure 9: A Precolumbian Sweat Bath at Cerén." In *Before the Volcano Erupted: The Ancient Cerén Village in Central America,* ed. Payson Sheets, 89–96. Austin: University of Texas Press.

Miller, Catherine Annalisa. 2013. "Earth, Water, Sky: The Liminal Landscape of the Maya Sweatbath." PhD thesis, Virginia Polytechnic Institute and State University, Blacksburg.

Moedano, Gabriel. 1977. "El temazcal y su deidad protectora en la tradicion oral." *Boletín del Departamento de Investigación de las Tradiciones Populares* 4: 5–32.

Molina, Alonso De. 2001. *Vocabulario en lengua castellana y Mexicana.* Part 2, vol. 4, folio 97. Trans. Esther Hernández. Madrid: Ediciones de Cultura Hispánica.

Nuttall, Zelia. 1975. *The Codex Nuttall: A Picture Manuscript from Ancient Mexico.* Intro. Arthur G. Miller. New York: Dover.

Ortega Cabrera, Verónica, and Víctor Germán Álvarez Arellano. 2008. "Dos temazcales aztecas en el área urbana de la antigua ciudad de Teotihuacán." *Arqueología* 38: 65–88.

Ortiz Butrón, Agustín. 2005. "El Temazcal Arqueológico." *Arqueología Mexicana* 13 (74): 52–53.

Overholtzer, Lisa. 2012. "So That the Baby Not Be Formed Like a Pottery Rattle: Rattle Figurines and Aztec Household Social Reproductive Practices." *Ancient Mesoamerica* 23 (1): 69–83.

Redfield, Robert. 1930. *Tepoztlan, a Mexican Village: A Study of Folk Life.* Chicago: University of Chicago Press.

Ruppert, Karl. 1952. *Chichen Itza: Architectural Notes and Plants.* Publication 595. Washington, DC: Carnegie Institution of Washington.

Sahagún, Bernardino de. 1950–1982. *General History of the Things of New Spain,* book 1, 8, ed. Arthur J.O. Anderson and Charles E. Dibble. Santa Fe, NM: School of American Research.

Satterthwaite, Linton. 1952. *Piedras Negras Archaeology: Architecture,* vol. 5. Philadelphia: University Museum, University of Pennsylvania.

Silva Galeana, Librado. 1984. "El Temascal [In Temazcalli]." *Estudios de Cultura Náhuatl* 17: 227–233.

Taladoire, Eric. 1981. *Les Terrains de Jeu de Ball (Mésoamérique et Sud-Ouest des Etats-Unis).* Etudes Mesoaméricaines, series 2; 4: Mexico: Mexico City, ed. Mission Archéologique et Ethnologique Française au Mexique. Mexico City: Centre d'études mexicaines et centraméricaines.

Taube, Karl A. 1986. "The Teotihuacan Cave of Origin: The Iconography and Architecture of Emergence Mythology in Mesoamerica and the American Southwest." *RES: Anthropology and Aesthetics* 12: 51–82.

Taube, Karl A. 1988. "The Ancient Yucatec New Year Festival: The Liminal Period in Maya Ritual and Cosmology." PhD thesis, Yale University, New Haven, CT.

Taube, Karl A. 1993. *Aztec and Maya Myths*. London: British Museum Press.

Tsikaloudaki, Katerina, Öget Nevin Coecen, Kyriaki Tasopoulou, and Ioannis Milonas. 2012. "Daylighting Historic Bathhouses: The Case of Ottoman Hamams." *Metu Journal of the Faculty of Architecture* 30 (1): 45–55.

Wagley, Charles. 1949. *The Social and Religious Life of a Guatemalan Village*. Memoir 71. Menasha, WI: American Anthropological Association.

Wagley, Charles. 1957. *Santiago Chimaltenango: estudio antropológico-social de una comunidad indígena de Huehuetenango*. Ed. José de Pineda Ibarra. Guatemala City: Seminario de Integración Social Guatemalteca.

Webb, Ronald, and Kenneth G. Hirth. 1998. "Rapidly Abandoned Households at Xochicalco, Morelos, Mexico." *Mayab* 13: 88–102.

Webster, David. 2001. "A Rural Sweat Bath from Piedras Negras." Paper presented at the 66th Annual Meeting of the Society for American Archaeology, New Orleans, April 18–22.

Źrałka, Jarosław, 2008. *Terminal Classic Occupation in the Maya Sites Located in the Area of Triangulo Park, Peten, Guatemala*. Krakow: Jagiellonian University Press.

8

The focus of this study is an articulation of symbols—cross-bones, disembodied eyeballs, and spiral eye mirrors that do not reference actual night or darkness per se; there are well-known glyphs and iconographic expressions of such. Instead, this chapter will discuss how this symbolism characterizes dark places and spaces inhabited by nocturnal creatures and beings whose actions may take place under the cover of night—real or symbolic. Much of this symbolism is characterized by nature itself, with mountains, caves, jaguars, altars carved from stone, and arbors fashioned from the leafy forest being thematically related in striking ways.

In contrast to daylight, which in most religious mythologies had to be divinely created, the night was something that had always existed—an inherent darkness that characterized fear and primordial chaos. Rather than a mere empty void, the night and darkness are full of active participants, some menacing and dangerous; hence humans have attempted to understand, tame, and colonize the night (Schnepel and Ben-Ari 2005, 153). People of the ancient world often made a notable distinction between night and darkness in which the evening was quite distinguishable from the primeval night "from which all created nature had its commencement" (Wilkinson 1878, 274).

This kind of darkness or "primeval night" held great interest for the ancient Maya. While the most common form of night and general darkness was signified through the *ak'ab* sign (Stone and Zender 2011, 58), there

The Cave and the Skirt

A Consideration of Classic Maya Ch'een *Symbolism*

Jeremy D. Coltman

DOI: 10.5876/9781646421879.c008

was also an iconographic system that had its roots in the *ch'een* sign whose most general meaning was "cave," "well," "burial," or "cistern" and was frequently depicted as an eyeball or bone set against a cross-hatched or black background (2011, 52). The iconographic variant of this sign is closely related and usually depicted as cross-bones and disembodied eyeballs set against a solid black background indicating the interior darkness of caves and temples (Vogt and Stuart 2005, 157). Ch'een symbolism also decorates the textile garments of many powerful deities and animals associated with the supernatural realm of dreaming, drinking, and the natural environment. With origins among the ancient Maya, the articulation of this symbolism would become one of the more pervasive symbols in the International Style of Late Postclassic Mesoamerica.

In a previous study (Coltman 2018), I noted that the Aztec skull and crossbone motif that appears on skirts and altars had its origins in ancient Maya ch'een symbolism. However, ch'een was also associated with primordial darkness and the chaotic forest wilds that surrounded the domestic and cultivated landscape. In this study, I continue to look at ch'een symbolism and the unique ways it was used to convey multiple meanings. For instance, Classic Maya depictions of leafy arbors denote the ritual forest and sacrificial stone altars that are symbolically anchored to the interior of the earth through the ch'een symbolism that marks them. Ritual structures such as leafy arbors and bowers and low-lying altars are also linked to the world of *wahy* spirits, phantasmagorical creatures of the forest wilds who were often actors in the sacrificial rituals that were associated with these features.

ICONOGRAPHIC VARIANTS OF *CH'EEN*

"Cave" is but only one of the many different meanings of ch'een. In the northern Maya Lowlands, it carries the meaning of "hole, cistern, cave with water" (Barrera Vásquez et al. 1995, 46, 131–133), while in the Tzotzil language, it references "hole, burrow, cave, ravine, cliff" (Laughlin and Haviland 1988, 271, 294, 303, 327; Tokovinine 2013, 25). Any opening or hole in the ground—including caves, cenotes, sinkholes, springs, and grottoes—can be ch'een (Brady 1997; Laughlin 1975, 132; Tokovinine 2013, 25). Explicit references to the ch'een reading in Mayan hieroglyphic inscriptions include Jolja cave as well as in text and image scenes such as the Mundo Perdido vessel from Tikal.[1] In this scene, a ruler sits in his large *witz* (hill, mountain) throne and addresses a bestiary audience by proclaiming "my earth, my cave" (Stone and Zender 2011, 133). This declaration is a telling statement and may be expressing the ruler's dominion over the bush and wilderness along with the animals that inhabit it.

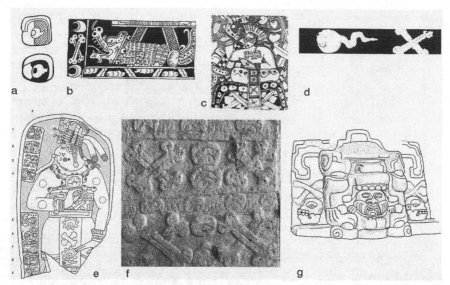

FIGURE 8.1. Ch'een *symbolism in Maya texts and art. (a) Disembodied eyeball expression of ch'een glyph denoting darkness (from Stone and Zender 2011, 52). (b) Cross-bone and disembodied eyeball set against black background, Vase of the Seven Gods. Courtesy, Karl Taube. (c) Late Classic vase with Jaguar God of the Underworld sitting on top of altar with the iconographic variant of ch'een. Detail of vase from the Boston Museum of Fine Arts. Artwork by John Pohl. (d) Black banding with cross-bones and eyeballs. Detail of interior rim of Late Classic Maya bowl. Drawing by Jeremy Coltman. (e) Ajasaaj Chan K'inich dressed as a ballplayer in the guise of Juun Ajaw, wearing a* yugo *and loincloth decorated with ch'een symbolism, Stela 47, Naranjo. Drawing by Alexandre Tokovinine (from Helmke, Yeager, and Eli 2018, 19). (f) Detail of Goddess O cross-bones and disembodied eyeballs skirt, Lower Temple of the Jaguars, Early Postclassic Chichen Itza. (g) Late Preclassic façade from Holmul, Guatemala, depicting* witz *mountain with skull and cross-bones flanking both sides. Courtesy, Alexandre Tokovinine.*

The iconographic variant of ch'een tends to follow the conventions of the glyph, with its most common variation an eyeball or bone set against a darkened cross-hatched background (Vogt and Stuart 2005, 157) (figure 8.1a). On the Vase of the Seven Gods, God L holds court during an important creation event. A stack of witz mountain heads indicates that this event is taking place in a cave, with further confirmation coming from the cross-bones and eyes motif set against a black background (2005, figure 7.5) (figure 8.1b). A similar example occurs on a Late Classic vase, now in the Boston Museum of Fine

Arts, showing the so-called Jaguar God of the Underworld (JGU) holding a sacrificial blade and sitting on a big cushioned throne decorated with cross-bones and eyes (figure 8.1c). Like the Vase of the Seven Gods, stacked witz heads appear, which once again indicates that this scene is taking place in a dark cave (Boston Museum of Fine Arts, accession number 2004.2201). A Late Classic bowl, also in the Museum of Fine Arts, depicts a solid black band in the interior rim decorated with disembodied eyeballs and cross-bones (figure 8.1d). This symbolism recalls the same motif from the Vase of the Seven Gods. It is therefore likely that the interior of this bowl represents a symbolic cave. Stela 47 from Naranjo depicts the local king Ajasaaj Chan K'inich dressed as a ballplayer in the guise of Juun Ajaw (Helmke, Yeager, and Eli 2018, 19) (figure 8.1e). He wears a *yugo* and loincloth that are decorated with cross-bones, eyes, and a spiral eye mirror. The ch'een symbolism is fitting for the ballgame context, since ball courts are equivalent to watery cave-like portals and are known to be ritually flooded, perhaps in reenactment of the primordial pool of emergence.

This motif of cross-bones and eyeballs adorns the skirt of Goddess O from the Classic to Late Postclassic periods (figure 8.1f). An aged midwife and curer, Goddess O was a probable antecedent to several Late Postclassic central Mexican female deities. Among the Late Postclassic Aztec, the earth deity, Tlaltecuhtli, appears with a bowl in her hip region that is decorated with skulls and cross-bones, the same motifs that decorate her skirt (Taube 2009, figure 6a–b; Coltman 2007) (figure 8.2a–b). As Karl Taube (2009, 92) has noted, in Aztec stone sculpture of *cuauhxicalli* (receptacles used to hold hearts), Tlaltecuhtli appears to give birth to the rising sun. Indeed, it is likely that this skull and cross-bone bowl-skirt represents a dark cave-like womb (Coltman 2018). Furthermore, Tlaltecuhtli frequently appears in the "hocker," or *mamazouhticac*, parturition position (Nicholson 1967).

Sometimes ch'een symbolism appears in more creative ways. The bowl depicting the interior rim as a solid black band decorated with cross-bones and eyeballs, mentioned above, indicates that the interior of the bowl is the cave itself. The scene unfolding on the outside of the bowl depicts a ruler sitting on his bone throne addressing a gopher and a bat who hold *ak'bal* jars. These animals are anything but ordinary. They are wahy entities with detached eyeballs extending far out of their sockets. Other wahy share this same feature. According to Nikolai Grube and Werner Nahm (1994, 692, figure 14), the Colonial *Ritual of the Bakabs* mentions the phrase "*colop u uich*" "torn out eyes," which is an epithet referring to creator deities. While most wahy are powerful and potent deities that have primordial origins, they are also the

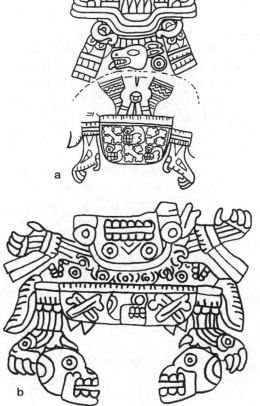

FIGURE 8.2. *The Aztec Earth Goddess, Tlaltecuhtli, with skull and cross-bone skirt. (a) Tlaltecuhtli on base of Bilimek pulque vessel. Note skull and cross-bone skirt as bowl (from Taube 2009). (b) Tlaltecuhtli on base of Stuttgart statuette. Note skull and cross-bone skirt as bowl. Drawing by Jeremy Coltman.*

personified diseases, curses, and nightmarish spooks that fuel the darker side of the ancient Maya imagination (Stuart 2005, 2021).

The earliest known example of ch'een symbolism occurs on a Preclassic façade on Structure B from Holmul, Guatemala (Estrada-Belli 2011, 93–95; Martin 2015, 202–204; Tokovinine 2013, 54–55) (figure 8.1g). This façade depicts an old toothless man emerging from a jaguar cave maw, which is part of the larger cleft mountain. Mountains and caves are often linked together naturally, and the very architecture of the Classic Maya temple is a fine example of this conceptualization. A notable feature of this mountain is its display of skull and cross-bone pairs flanking each side. The Old Man grasps a plumed serpent, which is exhaled from the open maw. Many essential ideas are expressed in this single image. As Alexandre Tokovinine (2013, 55) notes, "No other image combines in such a clear and powerful manner the idea of a mountain as a source of wind (and therefore, rain), of the place of caves, of the dead, and of the dwelling of ancestors." The Old Man probably represents an aged and powerful god of creation. Simon Martin (2015, 204) observes that because the first phase of this structure dates to 400 BCE, the beginning of the Late Preclassic period, this image of the Old Man is the earliest known. I would add that it is also the earliest pairing of the skull and cross-bones motif in ancient Mesoamerica, which became one of the most widely known symbols in the Late Postclassic International Style. As previously mentioned, in Late Postclassic Aztec iconography, the motif appears most frequently on stone altars and on the skirt of the Earth Goddess, Tlaltecuhtli (see Klein, this volume). Simply put, the skull and cross-bones motif, so widely known for the Aztec of Mexico-Tenochtitlan, had a precursor in ancient Maya ch'een symbolism (Coltman 2018). While the motif underwent a slight change over the centuries, it still retained its most basic meaning as a symbol of primordial darkness associated with dark spaces like caves and of specific actions associated with ritual drinking, curing, and childbirth.

Ch'een iconography appears in another context marking the textile garments of powerful deities, such as the aged midwife Goddess O who wears a distinctive skirt decorated with cross-bones and eyeballs (Coltman 2018; Miller 2005; Taube 1992).[2] The Birth Vase depicts several variations of this goddess in her role as midwife (Taube 1994). In another scene, the old goddess holds out her hand as a feline-looking figure vomits into it (K6020), imagery likely referring to another role as curer. One form of sacred ritual behavior involves alcoholic inebriation. Noting the curative and healing properties attributed to *balché*, John Chuchiak (2003, 148) relates a relevant Colonial account that says the Maya believed ingesting large quantities of balché caused them to expel their illness through vomiting profusely. Balché thus caused them to "vomit from their mouths and from below in such a manner that there was no greater purgative in the world which is better suited for them and this purging proved helpful to them because once they were purged they remained clean and had good appetites."

Like dreams, inebriation conjures the realm of supernatural beings from the otherworld. As Karl Taube (2016, 302) notes, "Classic Maya vessel scenes indicate that along with dreaming, drinking and intoxication served as means of contacting the spirit world through the use of mirrors." Since drunkenness was equated with a dreamlike state, intoxication was the most logical way to conjure the spirit forces shown on many Late Classic Maya vessels. A variation of the deity Ahkan, Mok Chih (Pulque Sickness), embodied intoxication and its unpleasant aftereffects (Grube 2004). In one scene, Mok Chih appears vomiting while holding an enema syringe (figure 8.3a).[3] Furthermore, in this

FIGURE 8.3. *The Spiral Eye Mirror motif in ancient Maya art. (a) Ahkan vomiting while holding an enema syringe. Note cross-bones and eyeballs on cape and Spiral Eye Mirror motif on textile element extending from head. Drawing by Linda Schele. (b) God Zero with Spiral Eye Mirror motif affixed to headdress. Drawing by Jeremy Coltman. (c) Late Classic Museo Popol Vuh vase depicting Ahkan with cape decorated with cross-bones, eyeballs, and mirror motifs. (d) Late Classic Maya fan or parasol depicting Spiral Eye Mirror motif in center. Note cross-bones, hands, and feet (after Taube 2010, figure 6e).*

scene and on a vase in the Museo Popol Vuh, Mok Chih wears a cape decorated with cross-bones and eyeballs, which is the standard symbolism denoting ch'een (figure 8.3c). In the enema scene, a textile is bound to his headdress with the same articulation of ch'een symbolism found on his cape.

Another element frequently appears in tandem with the cross-bones and eyeballs. This motif depicts a swirl or spiral eye that is often associated with deities who embodied the night and darkness. The spiral shows similarity with aquatic emblems and likely symbolizes bodies of water (Houston and Taube 2000, 284–285). The curling element appears as the eye of the Jaguar God of the Underworld, a stark contrast to the eye of K'inich Ajaw, the diurnal Maya Sun God. The Spiral Eye Mirror motif is also a stylized mirror. The spiral eye mirror appears fixed to the headdress of God Zero, a poorly understood deity related to Ahkan (Coltman 2021) (figure 8.3b).[4] As noted by Houston and Taube (2000, 283–284), this central element on God Zero's forehead symbolizes a mirror denoting darkness. This motif also appears on the cape of Mok Chih along with the other standard ch'een symbolism (figure 8.3a). A Late Classic vase depicting the realm of the wahy depicts a fan or parasol showing body parts such as feet, hands, cross-bones, and eyeballs surrounding the Spiral Eye Mirror motif, which is placed in the center (figure 8.3d). The spiral eye mirror is different than the disembodied eyeball, and some representations of the spiral eye may be surrounded by splattering blood. For the Classic Maya, appearances of wahy beings painted on Maya pots implied the invocation of these beings by people drinking from vessels (Houston and Inomata 2010, 208). Furthermore, wahy beings belong to the wild environs where part of one's soul is constantly connected to the realm of night and dreaming (Pellizzi 1996, 11).

LEAFY ARBORS AND THE FOREST WILDS

It is productive to look at other aspects in which this iconographic variant of ch'een occurs. As noted, ch'een symbolism appears to mark dark and liminal terrestrial spaces as well as the garments of powerful deities engaged in ritual acts of drinking and curing. Another context where this motif appears with a certain degree of consistency is on leafy arbors or bowers that are portrayals of the ritual forest (Taube 2003). A Late Classic Maya vessel depicting a jaguar sitting within a leafy arbor is decorated with cross-bones and skulls (figure 8.4a). A black curtain or possible textile appears in the interior upper portion of the arbor and depicts the cross-bones and eyeball motif, the standard iconographic variant of ch'een. This motif in the leafy arbor is strikingly similar to the example on the Vase of the Seven Gods, which indicates that the scene is taking place in a dark cave. Given the cutaway shape of the arbors made from the leaves of the forest, they were also likely conceived of as cave-like structures. Another scene depicts a jaguar sitting within a leafy arbor decorated with probable ritual paper made to mimic the design of cross-bones (figure 8.4b). From this leafy arbor, the jaguar addresses other creatures of the forest and the night. A similar leafy arbor depicts a ruler in jaguar costume

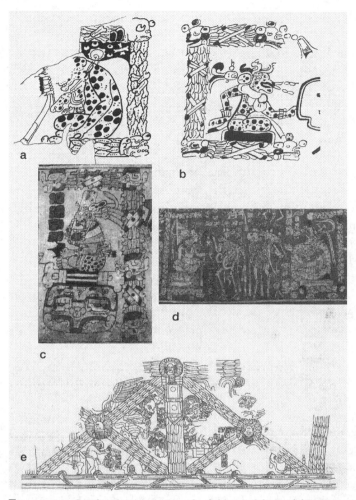

FIGURE 8.4. *Leafy arbors as portrayals of the ritual forest. (a) Jaguar* wahy *sitting in a leafy arbor. Note* ch'een *symbolism in upper interior portion decorated with cross-bones, eyeballs, and Spiral Eye Mirror motif (from Houston, Stuart, and Taube 2006, 6.18b). (b) Jaguar sitting in leafy arbor. Note heads affixed to arbor and symbolic cross-bones (K3038). Courtesy, Justin Kerr. (c) Jaguar impersonator sitting on bone throne atop* witz *head. Note heads and symbolic cross-bones on leafy arbor (K5847). Courtesy, Justin Kerr. (d) Late Classic vase depicting two facing leafy arbors decorated with decapitated heads (K3924). (e) Façade from Tonina depicting a leafy arbor decorated with heads. Note jaguar in scene. Drawing by Linda Schele. Courtesy, Los Angeles County Museum of Art.*

addressing an audience as he sits on a bone throne that rests on a large witz head (figure 8.4c). One vase is particularly telling in the type of supernatural environment with which these leafy arbors were thought to exist. Here, there are two leafy arbors facing each other amid a cast of ghastly and frightening skeletal and animal creatures of the Maya netherworld (figure 8.4d). A stucco façade from Tonina, Chiapas, depicts the so-called frieze of the dream lords, which displays a remarkable version of the leafy bower as skeletal individuals, known as "Turtle Foot Death," clutch decapitated heads in their hands (figure 8.4e). As Taube (2003, 478) notes, these beings "appear in and behind the structure, much like furtive beings seen briefly in the forest trees." What is common to all these leafy arbors is that they have human, animal, or other supernatural heads attached to them. These disembodied heads attached to arbors suggest the *tzompantli* skull racks, which found their most vivid expression among the Aztec and would have constituted a major visual expression for instilling fright and terror in those who laid eyes on them (Taube 2003, 2017). According to Stephen Houston and colleagues (2006, 72), Classic period decapitation can best be understood through the prism of personhood and its signifiers by the captor preserving the head and absorbing that person's identity.

The symbolism of leafy arbors and bowers indicates a ritual portrayal of the wilderness and forest wilds, a region that in many ways lacks internal order and spatial division. The lower half of Piedras Negras Stela 5 depicts a leafy band decorated with cross-bones and the Spiral Eye Mirror motif (Stuart and Graham 2003, 33–35). This band is placed between a witz and water symbolism, which attests to its terrestrial significance. Piedras Negras Stela 10 provides another example of a leafy arbor decorated with cross-bones (Taube 2003, figure 26.8c). A ruler sits in front of the arbor with a huge jaguar looming behind him. The domain of these ritual portrayals of the dark forest is temporally distant and enters deep into the mythological past, predating the creation of the world (Stone 1995, 15–16). In this respect, this wild domain, of which caves are also a crucial part, is closely related to the concept of chaos. In Greek, chaos indicates a chasm or "passage into the underworld darkness." In both Greek and English, "chaos" and "chasm" have a shared etymology, with chaos denoting a yawning space or gap (Bussanich 1983, 213; Stone 1995, 16). John Bussanich (1983, 214) notes that chaos "symbolizes the initial stage of pre-cosmic reality—a yawning chasm or abyss. Since it stands at the beginning of things, it cannot be envisioned according to the laws of perspective or dimension."[5]

The wilderness and bush are fraught with danger and inhabited by spooks, demons, and fierce beasts (Stone 1995; Taube 2003; Wisdom 1940, 426). In the Yucatan, the bush is a dangerous place where witches take animal form (Redfield and Villa Rojas 1934, 121). Robert Redfield (1941, 117) relates that "the bush teems with unseen inhabitants. Especially at night does the native hear a multitude of rustlings, murmurings, and whistlings that make known the presence of the many beings who people the bush. And each of these is disposed, well or ill, toward man, and of them man must take account."

The forest wilds are also naturally home to the various animals that are hunted. Hunting connects the world of the domestic inside with that of the outside, which is wild and unfamiliar (Helms 1993). As Yannis Hamilakis (2003, 240) has observed, "The landscape of hunting is not the domesticated landscape of settlements or agricultural land; it is the landscape of wilderness with its distinctive temporality." A number of rituals are carried out for hunting in contemporary Maya communities in Central Quintana Roo, Mexico, in which the Sip character, known from ancient times, is still invoked as the primary entity among the Lords of the Animals. One of the more significant ceremonies for hunters is the Loojil Ts'oon, whose purpose is to correctly perform the ritual and make sure rules are not broken that may anger the animals of the forest, particularly the Sip (Santos-Fita et al. 2015). While there are different names for the ceremonies, they all involve the renewing of divine permission to hunt. The old hunting god and lord of the forest wilds, Huk Sip, is often depicted with deer characteristics and is marked by the color black (Houston et al. 2009, 35; Stone and Zender 2011, 78). However, it is his alter ego, the deer, that is frequently draped with a textile depicting the cross-bones and eyeball motif. In at least one case, the deer appears wearing this textile and standing in front of a cave. Indeed, there is some evidence that deer rituals took place in caves, and I suspect that this cape draped over the deer marks it as an animal of the dark forest wilds as well as caves (Chinchilla Mazariegos 2011, figures 64–66, 68, 2017, 230–231; Pohl and Pohl 1983). The ch'een symbolism marking this textile appears on the Vase of the Seven Gods, where the ch'een symbolism sets the scene in a dark cave.

The forest was imbued with such supernatural power in part because it included significant landscape features that had to be visited (Stone 1995, 16). According to a highland Maya Tzotzil man, "In the cultivated fields there is neither shadow or darkness, it is open land and we are not afraid; in the forests it is dark and there are snakes, sink holes, caves . . . and we are afraid" (Guiteras-Holmes 1961, 287). The forest is a dark and untamed place well outside the realm of the cultivated landscape and is inhabited by destructive beings of chaos and darkness that seek to destroy man's life (Guiteras-Holmes 1961, 287; Redfield and Villa Rojas 1934, 112–114). Indeed, certain ritual objects such as leafy arbors and bowers would seem to invoke the ritual forest. It is therefore unsurprising that these arbors often appear with ch'een symbolism.

STONE ALTARS

While leafy arbors certainly relate to the dark and dangerous forest wilds, they are also versions of the tzompantli skull racks known for the later Aztec of Tenochtitlan (Taube 2017). In addition, they are symbolically related to stone altars and low-lying platforms. A number of Late Classic vases depict sacrificial scenes taking place on stone altars that lie directly in front of erected stela. One vase (K0718) depicts a sacrificial scene in front of what Andrea Stone (2005, 220) interprets as a speleothem idol taking the place of a stela (figure 8.5a). Stone (2005, 220) notes that this speleothem shaft is decorated with the "teardrop-shaped floating eyeballs" related to ch'een symbolism, providing evidence that the shaft is "cave-specific." The altar itself is just as telling. The victim lies prone on the altar that depicts stone markings and disembodied eyeballs, imagery consistent with ch'een symbolism.

In a study of early Maya stela, David Stuart (2010, 286) perceives that the Maya and perhaps other Mesoamericans "saw upright stones and associated altars, both carved and uncarved, as evoking the very natural substance of the earth and its interior." The scene with the speleothem stela spares little frightening detail, with a skeletal figure holding a decapitated head while another holds a deceased child. A full-figured skeleton decorates the robe of one of the participating individuals. A jaguar adorned with a red scarf lies on top of the upright motif. Stone (2005, 222) observes that the stela itself is outfitted with garments that may reflect the tying of stelae but may have also had something to do with human sacrifices taking place in front of stelae, which could have been uncovered and recovered time and again when overseeing gruesome sacrificial rites (Houston 2016; Stuart 1996, 2014). In another vase scene, a sacrificial victim breaks the fourth wall by looking helplessly at the viewer (figure 8.5b). Two supernatural beings holding a jaguar and a macaw float around while presiding over the ritual. A stela decorated with an arrangement of cloth or garments and intertwined human body parts is depicted directly behind the stone altar. Stelae like this one were likely covered and uncovered for such rites (Houston 2016). The peccary skull excavated from Tomb 1 at Copan (376 CE) is well-known for showing a stela wrapped in entwined ropes (Fash 1991: 52). The skull depicts numerous creatures of the forest including a were-monkey clown, jaguar, peccary, and deer surrounding human lords in a quatrefoil cave (Taube

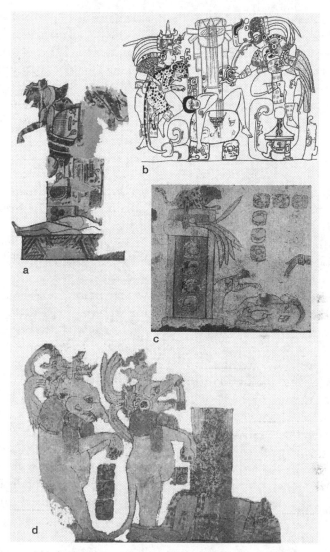

FIGURE 8.5. *Sacrificial stone altars in ancient Maya art. (a) Speleothem stelae in front of stone altar with sacrificial victim. Note* ch'een *symbolism on speleothem and altar and jaguar sitting atop speleothem (K0718). Courtesy, Justin Kerr. (b) Sacrificial victim on altar in front of stela with wrappings. Drawing by Alexandre Tokovinine. (c) Sacrificial victim on stone altar in front of stela. Note jaguar sitting on top of stela (K928). Courtesy, Justin Kerr. (d) Decapitated individual in front of stela. Note* wahy *beings with red scarves (K8719). Courtesy, Justin Kerr.*

2003, 483). The human lords within the quatrefoil are glyphically labeled as the *mako'm*, "the ones who keep the portal shut" (Helmke and Nielson 2009, 57). The creatures on the peccary skull recall the contemporary Chamula Carnival in which a time of "anti-structure" and a breaking of normative codes prevails: "The opposite of order is symbolized by the cold darkness in which the demons, Jews, and monkeys lived before the forced ascension of the sun in the sky" (Gossen 1974, 37). This "cold darkness" characterizes the specific contexts in which we see the iconography of ch'een symbolism.

Another vase (K928) depicts the sacrifice of an individual over a stone altar, once again in front of a stela (figure 8.5c). A small old woman seems to be dictating the gruesome event in front of three individuals, one of whom has a bulbous nose. A probable clown or buffoon, he is far from humorous, for he holds a decapitated head in his hands. Unsurprisingly, there is a jaguar sitting directly on top of the stela. It is significant that in most of the scenes discussed regarding these leafy arbors and stone altars, the jaguar is often present and is sitting within the leafy arbor or resting on top of the stelae placed in front of the sacrificial stone altar. Stuart (2014) notes that the sacrificial scene taking place in front of the stela on vessel K8719 has been not just overseen but carried out by the strange animal beings wearing red scarves, much like the jaguar lying on top of the speleothem stela (figure 8.5d). Perhaps as the preeminent king of the forest, the jaguar is overseer of these events. The forest wilds were under the domain of primeval night and were home to some of the most powerful and dangerous beings conjured up in the ancient Maya religious and philosophical imagination. As the undisputed king of the forest, the jaguar is also one of the wahy beings (Stone 2005, 222). Because the wilderness held its own cosmogonic function, which was characterized by the primeval night, Maya rulers would have also assumed part of their authority through a contract with this domain. It is little wonder then that Maya kings associated themselves with this powerful nocturnal creature that frequently appears as an overseer of rituals that incorporate symbolism associated with ch'een.

The sacrifice of individuals on altars placed in front of stelae that appear in Late Classic vase scenes likely took place on actual altars in plazas (Stuart 2014, figure 2). The northern lowlands depict some interesting examples of low-lying stone platform altars emblazoned with ch'een symbolism. Perhaps the best example is the Cementerio Platform group at Uxmal (figure 8.6a), where cross-bones are intertwined and interwoven in a pattern mimicking a textile and appear with the disembodied eyeballs and skulls. This depiction is significant: for the first time since Late Preclassic Holmul, cross-bones are

FIGURE 8.6. *Stone altars from the northern Maya Lowlands. (a) Stone altar depicting skulls, cross-bones, and disembodied eyeballs, Cementerio platform, Uxmal. Courtesy, David Stuart. (b) Stone altar with skulls and cross-bones, Glyphic Panel 3, Nohpat (from Mayer 2010, figure 20). (c) Stone altar depicting skull and cross-bones from Structure 99, Dzibilchaltun (from Andrews 1962, 175, figure 12b).*

juxtaposed with the skull (Stone and Zender 2011, 55). An almost identical altar is found at the site of Nohpat, which was originally seen long ago by John Lloyd Stephens in 1842 and sketched by Frederick Catherwood (Mayer 2010, figures 20, 22, 23; Stephens 1963, 1: 223) (figure 8.6b).[6] Karl Mayer (2010, 12) comments that Nohpat Monument 1, Panel 3 belonged to a destroyed platform consisting of bas-relief panels bearing cross-bones, skulls, and round elements that look strikingly similar to the Spiral Eye Mirror motif. The platform blocks seen by Stephens and illustrated by Mayer have been removed by looters (2010, 12). Nohpat Altar 9 depicts several skulls and other elements that clearly link them to the other sculpted blocks that once formed a now destroyed platform located to the south of the Nohpat ball court. At this time, the eyeballs were also very much still a part of the assemblage, but by the Late Postclassic period, the eyeballs were dropped, as seen on Structure 99 at Postclassic Dzibilchaltun (Andrews 1962, 175, figure 12b) (figure 8.6c). The altars from the northern lowlands probably had a similar function to the altars shown on Late Classic vases where sacrificial rites took place. These altars from the northern lowlands are likely precursors to the skull and cross-bone platforms known for the Late Postclassic Aztec of Mexico-Tenochtitlan (Coltman 2018) (figure 8.7a). However, I suspect that they would have functioned differently than the leafy forest arbors and tzompantli, which were both used specifically for the display of severed heads. Michael Smith (2003, 185) mentions that the sculpted stone platforms or stone effigy skull racks at Chichen Itza and Tenochtitlan have repeating images of skulls but lack the juxtaposition with cross-bones that other altars at Tenochtitlan have, which may signify a difference in function. Cecelia Klein (2000) argued convincingly that the skull and cross-bone altars from Tenochtitlan were dedicated to the Tzitzimime and Cihuateteo, frightening female spirit beings who could cause harm as well as cure. It is possible that sacrificial rites also took place on the skull and cross-bone altars. In the Codex Magliabechiano 88r, a frightening Tzitzimitl with arms raised in a menacing fashion stands on a skull and cross-bone altar and is covered with blood (figure 8.7b). Tlaltecuhtli could certainly be counted among the Tzitzimime; and in Late Postclassic Central Mexico, this is the goddess who most frequently wears a skull and cross-bone skirt. It is little wonder that she is the dark and devouring earth itself. In fact, the skull and cross-bones motif may allude to both the destructive forces and the more generative ones like childbirth. As Aztec scholar Henry B. Nicholson (1971, 422) remarked, "The earth is at one and the same time, the great womb and tomb of all life."

FIGURE 8.7. *Aztec skull and cross-bone altars and platforms. (a) Stone altar platform from Tenochtitlan. Note skull and cross-bones design and textile edging (from Batres 1902, 45). (b) Tzitzimitl standing on a skull and cross-bone altar. Codex Magliabechiano, 88r (Boone 1983).*

CONCLUSIONS

What is certain is that with its own spatiotemporal domains, the night is an unavoidable part of the human religious and philosophical imagination (Schnepel and Ben-Ari 2005; Galinier et al. 2010). As such, the night, and darkness that characterizes it, was conveyed in fascinating ways in ancient Maya art and belief. Depictions of leafy arbors and bowers denoting the ritual forest and sacrificial stone altars in ancient Maya art tend to be frequently emblazoned with iconographic variants of ch'een symbolism. Both objects allude to the wild, untamed, and chaotic environment and those that dwell in it, such as the many powerful and potentially dangerous animal and skeletal beings known as *wahy*. As discussed in this chapter, however, the ch'een glyph and the more flexible iconography, though closely related, are not necessarily equivalent. The origins of ch'een symbolism may lie in the Late Preclassic Maya region of Holmul, Guatemala, where it is manifested as a skull and cross-bone pair flanking each side of a witz from which an old ancestral deity emerges (Tokovinine 2013, 54–55). This scene may convey concepts of both death and birth, qualities held by the Aztec Earth Goddess, Tlaltecuhtli, in her skull and cross-bones skirt. While there is a clear pairing of skulls and cross-bones at Holmul, this exact articulation of motifs was relatively absent during the Classic period, where cross-bones were paired instead with disembodied eyes—a logical choice for indicating dark and terrestrial environments. In the Late Classic, leafy forest arbors began to integrate ch'een symbolism with skulls, and by the Terminal Classic in the northern lowlands, skulls once again made a strong appearance on stone altars as part of the new package of ch'een symbolism. In many ways, the Cementerio Platform at Uxmal provides the perfect example of ch'een iconography with its skull, interwoven cross-bones, and disembodied eye-balls. It also provides an interesting bridge between ch'een symbolism in the Classic period and its transition into the Late Postclassic. In a sense, this altar invokes a "dark space" like that of a cave but also recalls the skirt of Goddess O and anticipates the skirt of Tlaltecuhtli and other Tziztimime and the skull and cross-bone altars rendered as textiles in later Aztec art. By the time this motif is expressed in the capital of the Aztec Empire, the eyes are dropped altogether, and the standard skull and cross-bones motif continues to adorn altars and skirts, much as the ancestral version of the motif did centuries earlier for the Classic Maya. While it has been argued that the skull and cross-bone platforms known in the Maya area were an adoption of central Mexican traits in southern Mesoamerica in a process known as "Mexicanization" (Navarette 1976; Smith 2003), the Late Preclassic façade from Holmul, Guatemala, remains the earliest image of the skull paired with cross-bones in Mesoamerica.

The precise meaning of ch'een symbolism appearing in different contexts, particularly on stela and sacrificial stone altars, may allude to Stuart's (2010, 286) statement that these objects were somehow linked to the natural substance of the earth. This pattern is consistent and appears with temporal and spatial variation as we follow examples from what I argue is one of the earliest articulations at Late Preclassic Holmul, through the Late and Terminal Classic periods, to its final form in Late Postclassic Central Mexico. Ultimately associated with the dark interior spaces of caves, ch'een symbolism extends to the textile garments of powerful deities related to birth and curing and to stone altars and leafy arbors meant for sacrificial rites. As some of the most recognizable motifs in all of Mesoamerica, the iconographic variants of ch'een were a major contribution to the International Style by the ancient Maya and one that endured centuries of use, all the while being able to maintain these primary meanings.

ACKNOWLEDGMENTS

I would like to thank Nancy Gonlin and David Reed for the kind invitation to contribute to this volume. I would also like to thank the following for photo and drawing permissions: Justin Kerr, David Stuart, Karl Taube, Alexandre Tokovinine, and Marc Zender—all of whom offered the usual kindness and collegiality. Many of the ideas in this chapter were presented in the talk "The Cave and the Skirt: Classic Maya Origins of a Pervasive Mesoamerican Symbol in the Late Postclassic International Style," presented at the 2017 Maya Meetings, University of Austin, Texas.

NOTES

1. Tokovinine (2013, 22–23) notes several problems with this reading, including the lack of the T571/T598/T599 designations for caves occurring with other well-known cave signs in Mesoamerica, such as the quatrefoil. That is why I contend that ch'een iconography represents a particular kind of primordial darkness, perhaps associated with the dark zones of caves and the darkest interiors of temples.

2. Goddess O is a likely predecessor to Late Postclassic central Mexican deities, such as the Cihuateteo and the preeminent Earth Goddess, Tlaltecuhtli (Miller 2005).

3. There was widespread use of enemas among the Maya, and it is likely that the enema syringes sitting on top of vessels marked with the *chih* glyph reference the intoxicating substance held within (Henderson 2008, 60, figure 10 a–c). In other scenes, animals are seen holding enema syringes and vomiting (K5538; Henderson 2008, figure 16c). There are Maya scenes of drunken abandon, often shown with large pulque vessels and sometimes with enema syringes (K1381, K1092, and K1900).

4. Stela 16 from Tikal depicts the ruler Jasaw Chan Kawil gesturing like the God Zero. Although he lacks the hand over the mouth, his hands are in the same positioning that typically appears over the face, and he wears a kilt decorated with cross-bones and eyeballs (Stone and Zender 2011, 119).

5. In Hesiod's Theogony, chaos produces a cosmogonic function. It is the first level of cosmic articulation and therefore necessary for the generation of the cosmos and the gods (Bussanich 1983, 214).

6. Nicholas Dunning (1992, 143) notes that the platform at Nohpat supported four stone figures of jaguars or human figures emerging from the maw of full-form jaguars. This imagery is consistent with the jaguar resting on top of stelae and in leafy arbors.

REFERENCES

Andrews, E. Wyllys. 1962. "Excavaciones en Dzibilchaltun, Yucatan, 1956–1962." *Estudios de Cultura Maya* 2: 149–183.

Barerra Vásquez, Alfredo, Juan Ramón Bastarrachea Manzano, William Brito Sansores, Refugio Vermont Salas, David Dzul Góngora, and Domingo Dzul Poot. 1995. *Diccionario maya: Maya-español, español-maya*, 3rd ed. Mexico City: Editorial Porrúa.

Batres, Leopoldo. 1902. *Excavations in Escalerillas Street, City of Mexico—1900*. Mexico City: J. Aguilar Vera.

Boone, Elizabeth Hill. 1983. *The Codex Magliabechiano and the Lost Prototype of the Magliabechiano Group*. Berkeley: University of California Press.

Brady, James E. 1997. "Settlement Configuration and Cosmology: The Role of Caves at Dos Pilas." *American Anthropologist* 99 (3): 602–618.

Bussanich, John. 1983. "A Theoretical Interpretation of Hesiod's Chaos." *Classical Philology* 78 (3): 212–219.

Chinchilla Mazariegos, Oswaldo. 2011. *Imágenes de la mitología maya*. Guatemala City: Museo Popol Vuh, Universidad Francisco Marroquín.

Chinchilla Mazariegos, Oswaldo. 2017. *Art and Myth of the Ancient Maya*. New Haven, CT: Yale University Press.

Chuchiak, John F., IV. 2003. "'It Is Their Drinking That Hinders Them': Balché and the Use of Ritual Intoxicants among the Colonial Yucatec Maya, 1550–1780." *Estudios de cultura maya* 24: 137–171.

Coltman, Jeremy D. 2007. "The Aztec Stuttgart Statuette: An Iconographic Analysis." *Mexicon* 29: 70–77.

Coltman, Jeremy D. 2018. "Where Night Reigns Eternal: Darkness and Deep Time among the Ancient Maya." In *Archaeology of the Night: Life after Dark in the Ancient World*, ed. Nancy Gonlin and April Nowell, 201–222. Boulder: University Press of Colorado.

Coltman, Jeremy D. 2021. "Nahua Sorcery and the Classic Maya Antecedents of the Macuiltonaleque." In *Sorcery in Mesoamerica*, ed. Jeremy D. Coltman and John M.D. Pohl, 306–329. Louisville: University Press of Colorado.

Dunning, Nicholas P. 1992. *Lords of the Hills: Ancient Maya Settlement in the Puuc Region, Yucatan, Mexico*. Monographs in World Archaeology 15. Madison, WI: Prehistory Press.

Estrada-Belli, Francisco. 2011. *The First Maya Civilization: Ritual and Power before the Classic Period*. New York: Routledge.

Fash, William L. 1991. *Scribes, Warriors, and Kings: The City of Copan and the Ancient Maya*. London: Thames & Hudson.

Galinier, Jacques, Aurore Monod Becquelin, Guy Bordin, Laurent Fontaine, Francine Fourmaux, Juliette Roullet Ponce, Piero Salzarulo, Philippe Simonnot, Michèle Therrien, and Iole Zilli. 2010. "Anthropology of the Night: Cross-Disciplinary Investigations." *Current Anthropology* 51 (6): 819–847.

Gossen, Gary H. 1974. *Chamulas in the World of the Sun*. Austin: University of Texas Press.

Grube, Nikolai. 2004. "Akan: The God of Drinking, Disease, and Death." In *Continuity and Change: Maya Religious Practices in Temporal Perspective*, ed. Daniel Graña Behrens, Nikolai Grube, Christian M. Prager, Frauke Sachse, Stefanie Teufel, and Elizabeth Wagner, 59–76. München: Verlag Anton Sauerwein, Markt Schwaben.

Grube, Nikolai, and Werner Nahm. 1994. "A Census of Xibalba: A Complete Inventory of Way Characters on Maya Ceramics." In *The Maya Vase Book*, vol. 4, ed. Justin Kerr, 686–715. New York: Kerr Associates.

Guiteras-Holmes, Calixta. 1961. *Perils of the Soul: The Worldview of a Tzotzil Indian*. New York: Free Press.

Hamilakis, Yannis. 2003. "The Sacred Geography of Hunting: Wild Animals, Social Power, and Gender in Early Farming Societies." *British School at Athens Studies* 9: 239–247.

Helmke, Christophe, and Jesper Nielsen. 2009. "Hidden Identity and Power in Ancient Mesoamerica: Supernatural Alter Egos as Personified Diseases." *Acta Americana* 17 (2): 49–98.

Helmke, Christophe, Jason Yeager, and Mark Eli. 2018. "A Figurative *Hacha* from Buenavista del Cayo, Belize." *PARI Journal* 18 (3): 7–26.

Helms, Mary W. 1993. *Craft and the Kingly Ideal: Art, Trade, and Power*. Austin: University of Texas Press.

Henderson, Lucia. 2008. "Blood, Water, Vomit, and Wine: Pulque in Maya and Aztec Belief." *Mesoamerican Voices* 3: 53–76.

Houston, Stephen. 2016. "Maya Stelae and Multi-Media." In *Maya Decipherment: Ideas on Ancient Maya Writing and Iconography*. https://decipherment.wordpress.com/2016/07/22/maya-stelae-and-multi-media/.

Houston, Stephen, Claudia Brittenham, Cassandra Mesick, Alexandre Tokovinine, and Christina Warinner. 2009. *Veiled Brightness: A History of Ancient Maya Color*. Austin: University of Texas Press.

Houston, Stephen D., and Takeshi Inomata. 2010. *The Classic Maya.* Cambridge: Cambridge University Press.

Houston, Stephen, David Stuart, and Karl Taube. 2006. *The Memory of Bones: Body, Being, and Experience among the Classic Maya.* Austin: University of Texas Press.

Houston, Stephen, and Karl Taube. 2000. "An Archaeology of the Senses: Perception and Cultural Expression in Ancient Mesoamerica." *Cambridge Archaeological Journal* 10 (2): 261–294.

Klein, Cecelia. 2000. "The Devil and the Skirt: An Iconographic Inquiry into the Pre-Hispanic Nature of the Tzitzimime." *Ancient Mesoamerica* 11 (1): 1–26.

Laughlin, Robert M. 1975. *The Great Tzotzil Dictionary of San Lorenzo Zinacantán.* Smithsonian Contributions to Anthropology. Washington, DC: Smithsonian Institution Press.

Laughlin, Robert M., and John Beard Haviland. 1988. *The Great Tzotzil Dictionary of Santo Domingo Zinacantán* Washington, DC: Smithsonian Institution Press.

Martin, Simon. 2015. "The Old Man of the Maya Universe: A Unitary Dimension to Ancient Maya Religion." In *Maya Archaeology*, vol. 3, ed. Charles Golden, Stephen Houston, and Joel Skidmore, 186–227. San Francisco: Precolumbia, Mesoweb Press.

Mayer, Karl Herbert. 2010. "Maya Hieroglyphic Inscriptions from Nohpat, Yucatan, Mexico." *Mexicon* 32: 9–13.

Miller, Mary E. 2005. "Rethinking Jaina: Goddesses, Skirts, and the Jolly Roger." *Record of the Art Museum, Princeton University* 64: 63–70.

Navarrete, Carlos. 1976. "Algunas influencias mexicanas en el área maya meridional durante el postclásico tardío." *Estudios de cultura nahuatl* 12: 345–382.

Nicholson, Henry B. 1967. "A Fragment of an Aztec Relief Carving of the Earth Monster." *Journal de la Société des Américanistes*, new series, 56: 81–94.

Nicholson, Henry B. 1971. "Religion in Pre-Hispanic Central Mexico." In *Handbook of Middle American Indians*, vol. 10: *Archaeology of Northern Mesoamerica*, ed. Gordon F. Ekholm and Ignacio Bernal, 395–445, Robert Wauchope, general ed. Austin: University of Texas Press.

Pellizzi, Francesco. 1996. "Editorial: The Pre-Columbian." *RES: Anthropology and Aesthetics* 29–30: 5–15.

Pohl, Mary E.D., and John M.D. Pohl. 1983. "Ancient Maya Cave Ritual." *Archaeology* 3: 28–51.

Redfield, Robert. 1941. *The Folk Culture of Yucatan.* Chicago: University of Chicago Press.

Redfield, Robert, and Alfonso Villa Rojas. 1934. *Chan Kom, a Maya Village.* Publication 448. Washington, DC: Carnegie Institution of Washington.

Santos-Fita, Dídac, Eduardo J. Naranjo, Erin I.J. Estrada, Ramón Mariaca, and Eduardo Bello. 2015. "Symbolism and Ritual Practices Related to Hunting in Maya Communities from Central Quintana Roo, Mexico." *Journal of Ethnobiology and Ethnomedicine* 11: 1–13.

Schnepel, Burkhard, and Eyal Ben-Ari. 2005. "Introduction, 'When Darkness Comes . . .': Steps toward an Anthropology of the Night." *Paidemua: Mitteilungen zur Kulturkunde* 51: 153–163.

Smith, Michael E. 2003. "Information Networks in Postclassic Mesoamerica." In *The Postclassic Mesoamerican World*, ed. Michael E. Smith and Frances F. Berdan, 181–185. Salt Lake City: University of Utah Press.

Stephens, John Lloyd. 1963. *Incidents of Travel in Yucatán*, vol. 1. New York: Dover.

Stone, Andrea. 1995. *Images from the Underworld: Naj Tunich and the Tradition of Maya Cave Painting*. Austin: University of Texas Press.

Stone, Andrea. 2005. "Divine Stalagmites: Modified Speleothems in Maya Caves and Aesthetic Variation in Classic Maya Art." In *Aesthetics and Rock Art*, ed. Thomas Heyd and John Clegg, 215–233. London: Ashgate.

Stone, Andrea, and Marc Zender. 2011. *Reading Maya Art: A Hieroglyphic Guide to Ancient Maya Painting and Sculpture*. London: Thames and Hudson.

Stuart, David. 1996. "Kings of Stone: A Consideration of Stelae in Ancient Maya Ritual and Representation." *RES: Anthropology and Aesthetics* 29–30: 148–171.

Stuart, David. 2005. "Way Beings." In *Sourcebook for the 29th Maya Hieroglyphic Forum (N.A.)*, by David Stuart, 160–165. Austin: University of Texas Press.

Stuart, David. 2010. "Shining Stones: Observations on the Ritual Meaning of Early Maya Stelae." In *The Place of Stone Monuments: Context, Use, and Meaning in Mesoamerica's Preclassic Transition*, ed. Julia Guernsey, John Clark, and Barbara Arroyo, 283–298. Washington, DC: Dumbarton Oaks.

Stuart, David. 2014. "Notes on a Sacrifice Scene." *Maya Decipherment: Ideas on Ancient Maya Writing and Iconography*. https://decipherment.wordpress.com/2014/10/31/notes-on-a-sacrifice-scene/.

Stuart, David. 2021. "The *Wahys* of Witchcraft: Sorcery and Political Power among the Classic Maya." In *Sorcery in Mesoamerica*, ed. Jeremy D. Coltman and John M.D. Pohl, 179–205. Louisville: University Press of Colorado.

Stuart, David, and Ian Graham. 2003. *Piedras Negras*, vol. 9.1. Corpus of Maya Hieroglyphic Inscriptions, Peabody Museum of Ethnology and Archaeology. Cambridge, MA: Harvard University.

Taube, Karl A. 1992. *The Major Gods of Ancient Yucatan*. Studies in Pre-Columbian Art and Archaeology 32. Washington, DC: Dumbarton Oaks.

Taube, Karl A. 1994. "The Birth Vase: Natal Imagery in Ancient Maya Myth and Ritual." In *The Maya Vase Book*, vol. 4, ed. Justin Kerr, 650–685. New York: Kerr Associates.

Taube, Karl A. 2003. "Ancient and Contemporary Maya Conceptions about the Field and Forest." In *The Lowland Maya Area: Three Millennia at the Human-Wildland Interface*, ed. Arturo Gomez-Pompa, Michael Allen, Scott L. Fedick, and Juan Jimenez-Osornio, 461–492. New York: Haworth.

Taube, Karl A. 2009. "The Womb of the World: The *Cuauhxicalli* and Other Offering Bowls in Ancient and Contemporary Mesoamerica." In *Maya Archaeology 1*, ed. Charles Golden, Stephen Houston, and Joel Skidmore, 86–106. San Francisco: Precolumbia Mesoweb Press.

Taube, Karl A. 2010. "At Dawn's Edge: Tulum, Santa Rita, and Floral Symbolism of Late Postclassic Yucatan." In *Astronomers, Scribes, and Priests: Intellectual Interchange between the Northern Maya Lowlands and Highland Mexico in the Late Postclassic Period*, ed. Gabrielle Vail and Christine Hernandez, 145–191. Washington, DC: Dumbarton Oaks.

Taube, Karl A. 2016. "Through a Glass, Brightly: Recent Investigations Concerning Mirrors and Scrying in Ancient and Contemporary Mesoamerica." In *Manufactured Light: Mirrors in the Mesoamerican Realm*, ed. Emiliano Gallaga and Marc G. Blainey, 285–314. Boulder: University Press of Colorado.

Taube, Karl A. 2017. "Los 'Andamios de Cráneos' entre los Antiguos Mayas." *Arqueología Mexicana* 25 (148): 28–33.

Tokovinine, Alexandre. 2013. *Place and Identity in Classic Maya Narratives*. Studies in Pre-Columbian Art and Archaeology 37. Washington, DC: Dumbarton Oaks.

Vogt, Evon Z., and David Stuart. 2005. "Some Notes on Ritual Caves among the Ancient and Modern Maya." In *The Maw of the Earth Monster: Mesoamerican Ritual Cave Use*, ed. James E. Brady and Keith M. Prufer, 155–185. Austin: University of Texas Press.

Wilkinson, John Gardner. 1878. *The Manners and Customs of the Ancient Egyptians*, vol. 2. London: John Murray.

Wisdom, Charles. 1940. *The Chorti Indians of Guatemala*. Chicago: University of Chicago Press.

9

Night and the Underworld in the Classic Period Ulúa Valley, Honduras

Jeanne Lopiparo

As the sun set and the light dimmed in the Ulúa Valley, Honduras, the ancient inhabitants were surrounded by a dark nighttime sky and the soundscape of nocturnal animals. The transition between day and night was marked by the shifting sensory experience of the nightscape and the passage of the sun through the underworld, as the realm of death and the ancestors came alive. The night was inhabited and animated by liminal animals and ancestors that moved between the worlds of the living and the dead. Representations of animals that are nocturnal or crepuscular, especially of animals, supernaturals, and zooanthropomorphic hybrids associated with the underworld, are prevalent in the corpus of figural artifacts recovered from fine-grained horizontal excavations at four Late to Terminal Classic sites (ca. 600–1000 AD) in the central alluvium of the Ulúa Valley (figure 0.1 and table 0.1). At both monumental and household sites, representations of nocturnal and underworld imagery in structured deposition associated with life-cycle rituals suggest that the nighttime was crucial to everyday life, death, and renewal. The animal and zooanthropomorphic bodies of these figural artifacts were frequently whistles, which would have animated a soundscape that accompanied transition-marking events. Solar and life-cycle rituals on the monumental scale featured large figural censers that heralded the passage among life, death, and afterlife—which at night became journeys that transcended the boundaries between the earthly world and the underworld.

DOI: 10.5876/9781646421879.c009

As I have described elsewhere, both the treatment of the dead and the associated ritual practices through which they were commemorated entailed the intentional dissolution of materiality that demarcated shared social identities, followed by the interment of what remained in the renovation of sites over hundreds of years (Hendon, Joyce, and Lopiparo 2014; Lopiparo 2003, 2007, 2008, n.d.; Lopiparo and Hendon 2009). In this chapter, I turn to an explicit consideration of the role of the night and the nocturnal in these rituals and the beliefs they expressed. Structured deposition associated with the burial of houses and their inhabitants indicates that an elaborate and shared set of practices marked the transition between life and death and the ongoing relationships between the living in the earthly world above and the dead in the dark underworld below, a boundary that was permeable and subject to traversal and interchange (Hendon, Joyce, and Lopiparo 2014; Lopiparo 2007, n.d.; compare Chase and Chase 2011; Fitzsimmons 2009; Gillespie 2000a, 2000b, 2001, 2002; Joyce 2008, 2011; Lucero 2008; compare McAnany 1995; Mock 1998; Navarro-Farr and Arroyave Prera 2014).

SUPERNATURALS, NOCTURNAL ANIMALS, AND CO-ESSENCES THAT GO BUMP IN THE NIGHT

Imagery from both Lowland Maya and Ulúa Polychrome vessels depicts an underworld that was inhabited by a host of supernatural, zoomorphic, and hybrid beings—many of whom could transcend the boundaries between worlds (Chase and Chase 2011; Halperin 2014; Joyce 2017; Meskell and Joyce 2003). Another widespread set of beliefs surrounding zoomorphic and hybrid beings involves the concept of co-essences—a broad supernatural category that appears in ethnographic, ethnohistoric, iconographic, and epigraphic sources from the region (Chapman 1982, 1985, 1986; Coltman 2018; Fitzsimmons 2009; Grube and Nahm 1994; Halperin 2014; Houston and Stuart 1989; Houston, Stuart, and Taube 2006; Monaghan 1995; Scherer 2015; Stuart 1998). Common characteristics attributed to co-essences are that they are often zoomorphic, nocturnal, and dangerous—and sometimes they wander about at night wreaking havoc (compare Coltman 2018; Fitzsimmons 2009). Two of the most abundant categories of figural artifacts recovered from structured deposition in the lower Ulúa Valley are supernatural beings and a wide range of animals, some of which are anthropomorphized and many of which are part of single- or multi-chamber whistles (Hendon, Joyce, and Lopiparo 2014; Lopiparo 2003; Lopiparo and Hendon 2009).

To identify patterns in zoomorphic, supernatural, and zooanthropomorphic hybrid representations, I carried out an iconographic analysis of all figural

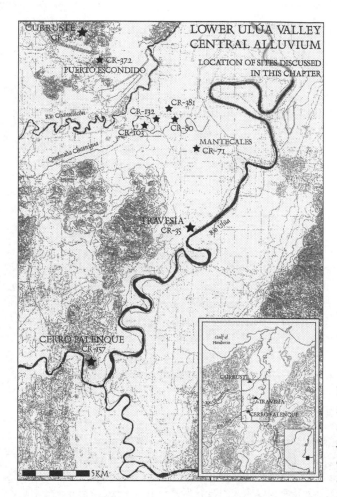

FIGURE 9.1. *Map of the central alluvium of the lower Ulúa Valley showing the location of the sites discussed in this chapter.*

ceramic artifacts from three household sites in the central alluvium of the Ulúa Valley (CR-80, CR-103, and CR-381). Extensive, fine-grained excavations at these household sites and at Currusté (CR-32), one of several Late to Terminal Classic centers in the central Ulúa Valley (figure 9.1), revealed structured deposition resulting from activities associated with multigenerational site renovations and intergenerational commemoration of the dead (Hendon, Joyce, and Lopiparo 2014; Lopiparo 2003, 2007, 2008). The household sites all featured multiple large earthen mounds, each serving as the foundation for a patio group that was built up through successive renovations over hundreds of years. In one of the more dramatic examples of this phenomenon, meters-deep excavations at Puerto Escondido (CR-372), a nearby loma site, revealed a history of occupation, burial, and renovation that spanned over two millennia (Joyce 2008, 2011). Currusté featured a site core with two large central plazas surrounded by tall earthen and cobble mounds, the largest of which is approximately 6 m tall (figure 9.2). Surrounding the main plazas were a number of formal and informal mound groups, including a large formal patio group adjacent to the main plaza to the south and several less formally organized groups adjoining the plazas. A previous survey of the site documented over 200 mounds extending into the surrounding valley and hillsides (Hasemann, Veliz, and Van Gerpen 1978). The earthen and cobble mound groups at Currusté show similar sequences of construction, destruction and burial, and renovation as those seen in the smaller sites.

Excavations at the household sites yielded a large corpus of mold-made ceramic artifacts with zoomorphic, anthropomorphic, and supernatural imagery—including figurines, figural whistles, stamps, pendants and beads, and mold-impressed miniature vessels with panels that contained representations of profile human and animal heads (Lopiparo 2003). The total assemblage from the three household sites included over 2,800 figural artifact fragments. To get an idea of the relative density of figural artifacts to ceramic sherds, approximately 200,000 sherds were recovered from these excavations, so the ratio of figural artifacts to sherds equals roughly 1.4:100. Iconographic analysis was carried out using a systematic 100 percent inventory of figural artifacts from the three sites.

Of the artifact fragments that were complete enough to be diagnostic, I identified 236 zoomorphic representations; a total of 206 were identifiable by zoomorphic category. Most zoomorphic images depicted in the corpus of ceramic figural artifacts have one or more of the following characteristics: (1) they are nocturnal or crepuscular, (2) they are associated with underworld imagery or death in Classic Maya iconography, (3) they are associated with communication with the ancestors or movement between earthly and supernatural realms, and (4) they represent animal-human or animal-supernatural hybrids. The corpus of diagnostic zoomorphic artifacts includes 62 nocturnal and crepuscular animals (or 30.1% of the total), representing (in order of frequency): deer (21), owls (13), caimans (9), felines (8), bats (5), armadillos (3), and frogs (3) (figure 9.3a–g). In addition to nocturnal animals, other zoomorphic categories had strong associations with underworld and death imagery, with ancestors, or with movement between earthly and supernatural realms (see, for example, Benson 1996; Emery 2004; Freidel 2017; Freidel, Schele, and Parker 1993; Grube and Nahm 1994; Izquierdo y de la Cueva and Vega Villalobos 2016; Quirarte 1979; Stuart 2005). A total of 117 artifacts, or 56.8 percent of

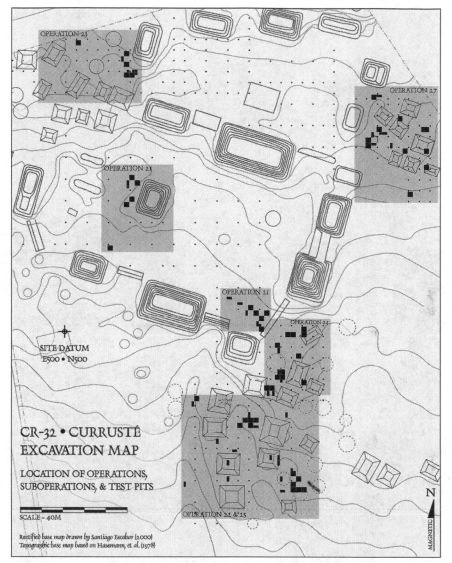

FIGURE 9.2. *Plan map of the site core of Currusté (CR-32), Ulúa Valley, Honduras.*

the corpus of diagnostic zoomorphic artifacts, fall into one of these categories, including (in order of frequency): monkeys (51), serpents (25), vultures (15), water birds, including herons, ducks, and pelicans (9), macaws (9), ocellated turkeys (4), turtles (3), and dogs (1) (figure 9.4a–h).

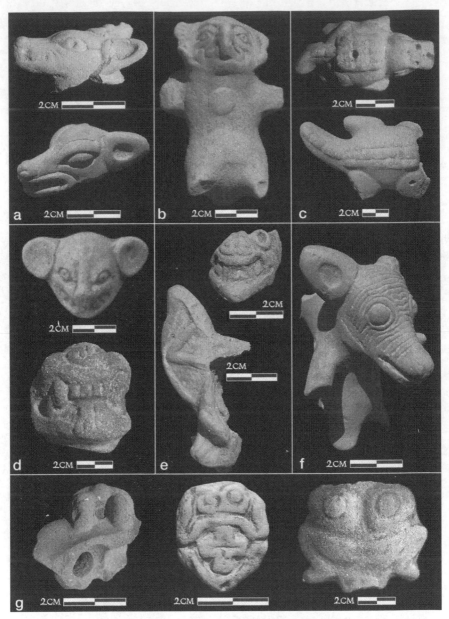

FIGURE 9.3. *Zoomorphic and zooanthropomorphic figural artifacts depicting nocturnal and crepuscular animals, including: (a) deer, (b) owls, (c) caimans, (d) felines, (e) bats, (f) armadillos, and (g) frogs.*

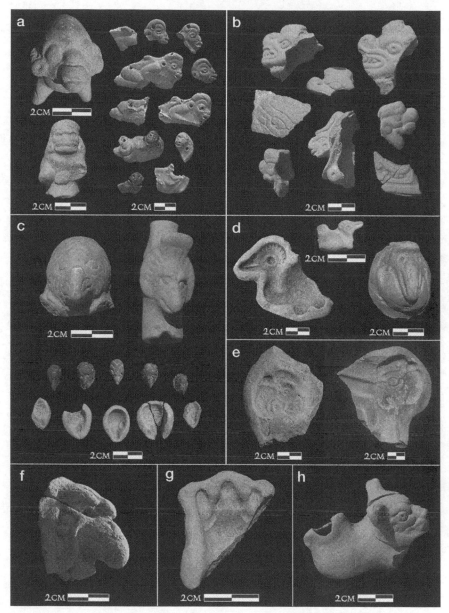

FIGURE 9.4. *Zoomorphic figural artifacts depicting animals associated with supernatural realms, including: (a) monkeys, (b) serpents, (c) vultures, (d) water birds, (e) macaws, (f) ocellated turkeys, (g) turtles, and (h) dogs.*

Interestingly, other than monkeys, which are sometimes in human-like poses, it is primarily the nocturnal animals that are represented with anthropomorphized, hybrid bodies—including owls, bats, armadillos, and frogs (see, for example, figure 9.3b, 9.3e, 9.3f, and 9.3g). I would also note that howler monkeys, while considered primarily diurnal, are characterized by particularly active crepuscular vocalizations (Carpenter 1934; Cornick and Markowitz 2002), often creating a cacophony during the transitions between night and day. Anthropomorphic figurines with zoomorphic headdresses feature a range of animals, including serpents, several varieties of birds, deer, felines, monkeys, and possibly bats. An Ulúa polychrome presented by Rosemary Joyce (2017, 68, figure 34a, 34b) from the collection of the National Museum of the American Indian (catalog number 24/4275) illustrates some possible ways these zoomorphic headdresses might have been worn. This vessel depicts anthropomorphic figures in ritual procession with zoomorphic figures wrapped into elaborate headdresses with netted scarfs—a motif that is similarly depicted in a polychrome vessel attributed to the region in the collection of the Denver Art Museum (object ID number 1991.57, published in the museum's Online Collections; see also rollout photograph by Justin Kerr of vessel number K6621 in the MayaVase Database).

Joyce (2017) has studied zoomorphic iconography in late Ulúa Polychromes and argues that differential patterns in the popularity of particular animal representations across sites might be related to local claims promoting versions of origin myths whereby certain mythological animals play a prominent role. She posits that powerful groups associated themselves with certain animals and made claims to knowledge and gifts bestowed by the animals at the beginning of time—creating a kind of mythical genealogy that is analogous to totemic crests in the Pacific Northwest of North America. While it appears that aspects of zoomorphic symbolism in the corpus of figural artifacts were shared across the sites, we need to consider the possibility that some site-specific variation was the product of representations of local identities (a pattern I have previously documented for figural headdress styles in the Ulúa Valley; see Hendon, Joyce, and Lopiparo 2014; Lopiparo 2003). Finer-grained distributional patterns of the zoomorphic figurines are difficult to discern because, in addition to the fragmentation of the materials, there is enormous variability in the corpus, so the number of diagnostic examples of any particular category can be small. Despite the elaboration of an enormous variety of figural representations, the corpus of zoomorphic and hybrid artifacts demonstrates a widespread emphasis on animals associated with nocturnal and underworld realms.

Given the presence of nocturnal and crepuscular faunal remains at sites in the Ulúa Valley (Henderson and Joyce 2004) and the representation of nocturnal animal skins on polychrome vessels (Joyce 2017), it is likely that one activity that happened at night was nocturnal hunting. Animal offerings have been recovered from structured deposition at numerous sites in the valley, including, for example, animal burials (discussed below) and a deposit of whole metapodials and phalanges from medium-sized mammals found in association with large fragments from a smashed figural incensario at CR-103 (Lopiparo 2003; Stone 1941; compare Henderson and Joyce 2004 for discussion of probable nonsubsistence use of animals, including the presence of deer lower-limb bones in public spaces at Cerro Palenque, a Late to Terminal Classic center). These offerings suggest parallels with Linda Brown's (2005) ethnohistoric and ethnographic research on hunting in the Highlands of Guatemala. In particular, her argument that the ritual of "planting the bones" associated bones, seed, and regeneration has several parallels with my interpretation that ongoing interactions between the living and the dead, especially the "planting" or interment of human bone bundles, represented the transmission of vital substances essential to intergenerational continuity (Lopiparo n.d.). Interactions with the ancestors in the supernatural realm, including transubstantiation of bodily essences through time, represented a kind of partible personhood (after Strathern 1988), analogous to animal co-essences, whereby the sharing of substances between people and supernatural beings through time is vital to survival and prosperity (compare Geller 2012, 2014; Gillespie 2001, 2002).

An emphasis on animal-human hybridity in figurines and polychrome vessels from the valley parallels some of the commonalities between ethnographic accounts of mythologies from the region (Hendon, Joyce, and Lopiparo 2014; Joyce 2017; Meskell and Joyce 2003). The central role of anthropomorphic animals in the mythologies of the Lenca and the Tolupan are particularly noteworthy, where this emphasis can be seen in Anne Chapman's (1982, 1985, 1986) ethnographic work northeast, and south and west, of the Ulúa Valley. Chapman (1985, 211–214) documents complex sets of relationships among humans, animals, and their supernatural *dueños* (owners) and describes a belief in *nagualismo*, in which animals become "individual totems" of people—usually shortly after their birth—by sharing co-essences that bind them for life.

John Monaghan's (1995) discussion of the significance of animal co-essences to Mixtec personhood provides an apt analogy for how, through this kind of permeability, humans and animals animate each other with a vital essence that links them together from birth, sharing characteristics that humans embody throughout their lives. Monaghan (1995) also describes the Mixtec belief that living things are defined and differentiated from each other through the sounds they make. Given that many of the animal figural artifacts in the Ulúa Valley are also whistles, it seems plausible that these animal co-essences were similarly animated when humans breathed life into them to produce sound (compare Houston, Stuart, and Taube 2006). Animal whistles are a common item found in structured deposition at sites throughout the region, sometimes with their heads or entire bodies intact amid a deposit that has been otherwise burned or broken. I have also recovered deposits of bones from nocturnal animals (including a possible feline burial discussed below) that were found in association with household renovations at sites in the central alluvium of the valley (Lopiparo 2003). The animal burial is similar to one reported by Doris Stone (1941, 75) at Travesía, where a feline was interred in association with burned material within a series of deposits that represented several episodes of dissolution, burning, and burial. James Fitzsimmons (2009) has described Classic Maya representations of animal "avatars" as messengers between humans and the underworld, and the abundant presence of animal and supernatural depictions in structured deposition in the Ulúa Valley lends support to an analogous interpretation (Lopiparo 2003).

At sites across the valley, the sets of fantastical figurines in ritual deposits are frequently found broken in half or with heads separate from bodies. In referring to these types of figurines found at Altar de Sacrificios as "grotesques," Gordon Willey (1972) argues that they represent supernatural beings, an interpretation supported by the depiction of "monstrous" figures on Classic Maya polychrome pots representing the supernatural inhabitants of the underworld (Fitzsimmons 2009; Halperin 2014; Reents-Budet 1986, 1994; Schele and Miller 1986). In addition to aged and skeletal figures, Maya polychromes with scenes from the underworld depict anthropomorphic and zoomorphic hybrids (Fitzsimmons 2009; Grube and Nahm 1994; Schele and Miller 1986). For Late Classic Ulúa Polychromes, animals—often anthropomorphized or depicting animal-human hybrids (or possibly humans in animal costumes)—predominate the imagery, and they frequently carry ritual paraphernalia (Hendon, Joyce, and Lopiparo 2014; Joyce 2017; Meskell and Joyce 2003). The "grotesque" figurines recovered from structured deposition in the Ulúa Valley share similar stylistic conventions (figure 9.5a–e), and given that several designs appear to be unusual, if not unique, in the known figural corpus of the valley, it is possible that some represent supernaturals that are tied to the households themselves (Lopiparo 2003, 2006).

In the depictions of lavish events that are often featured in Classic Maya art and architecture, characters are sometimes shown wearing headdresses and

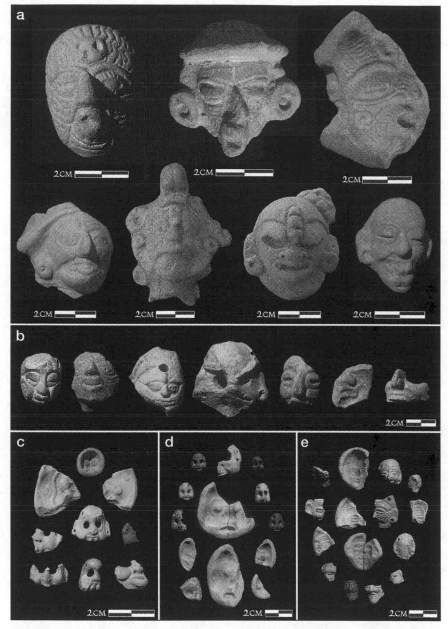

FIGURE 9.5. *"Grotesque" supernatural artifacts depicting aged, skeletal, and monstrous figures.*

masks through which they embody supernatural figures in processions and dances (Looper 2009). One unusual set of artifacts from a small household site in the central valley (CR-381) depicts a set of miniature masks (figure 9.5b–e) that feature the kinds of iconographic elements commonly interpreted as supernaturals associated with the underworld, including aged, skeletal, and monstrous figures (Lopiparo 2003, 2006; compare Fitzsimmons 2009; Halperin 2014; Schele and Miller 1986; Willey 1972). Representations of masks with this iconography provide evidence for the practice of rituals, akin to those seen in polychrome vessels and murals, in which household members would have embodied supernaturals in dances and processions. Caching of these figural artifacts in structured deposition indicates that the supernaturals depicted played a key role in cycles of time and the life cycles of the living and the dead. The kinds of masked underworld processions depicted on polychrome vessels suggest that these rituals were part of the process of communicating or even transcending the boundary between the earthly world and the dark underworld below and between the living and the dead.

NIGHT AND NECROSOCIALITY: INTERACTIONS BETWEEN THE LIVING AND THE DEAD

Figural representations of women throughout the Ulúa Valley indicate that they held a central role in creating a nexus between the living and the dead, acting as both literal and metaphoric vessels for the transgenerational transmission of vital substances that were essential to ensuring the persistence of the group through time (Lopiparo 2006, 2007, n.d.). At Currusté, evidence for large-scale life-cycle events at the site included material culture that tied the procreation of the living to the creation and care of ancestors through the curation and interment of human bone bundles (Hendon, Joyce, and Lopiparo 2014; Lopiparo 2008, n.d.). An elaborate deposit at the western entrance of the north plaza featured at least six anthropomorphic and zoomorphic ceramic incensarios that had been used and smashed in place. Among them was an almost life-sized figure of a pregnant woman carrying a container tied to her back through which the smoke from the incense would have emerged (figure 9.6a, 9.6b).

The container itself appears to represent some kind of house, shrine, or structure. Because the reconstruction is incomplete, it is unclear whether the container had an opening, but a small lip near the base suggests that this might have been an effigy house with a door, analogous to the miniature stone houses recovered from Copan (Andrews and Fash 1992; Gillespie 2000b; Gonlin 2007; Stuart 1998). Susan Gillespie (2000b) describes the Copan effigies as

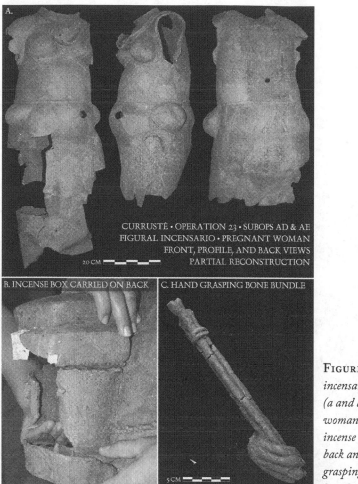

FIGURE 9.6. *Figural incensarios depicting (a and b) a pregnant woman carrying an incense box on her back and (c) a hand grasping a bundle of long bones.*

ancestral altars or "sleeping houses" of spirits. A similar interpretation for this object is supported by the nearby recovery of another incensario fragment representing an anthropomorphic hand grasping a bundle of human long bones (figure 9.6c). And beneath the smashed and buried remains of the elaborate figural incensarios, we recovered several deposits of actual human long-bone bundles and two human skulls (figure 9.7). This evidence indicates the performance of an elaborate set of practices through which the living interacted with the dead: from their reentry into primary burials, to the secondary assemblage and processing of human remains, to the bundling, curation, and transport of

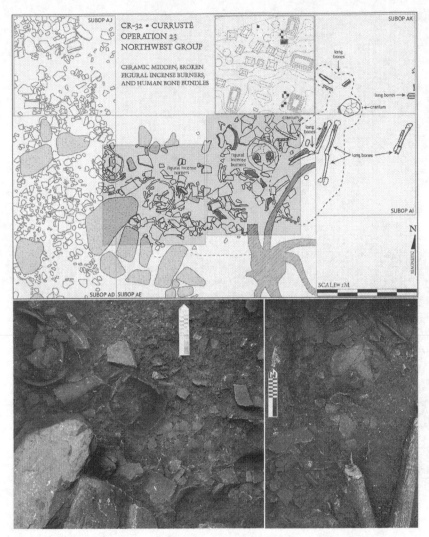

FIGURE 9.7. *Human skulls and long-bone bundles buried beneath a deposit of six smashed figural incensarios.*

the more "permanent" substances of household membership, to their transformation through censing, and finally to their return to the underworld through re-interment.

Miguel Ángel Astor-Aguilera's (2010, 147–180) description of contemporary bone-bundling practices among Maya communities in Quintana Roo (along with his synthesis of ethnohistoric and archaeological evidence for similar practices) presents a vivid analog for how we might understand the processes by which the dead became ancestors and interacted with the living. As he notes, "Dying, in terms of Maya cosmology, does not automatically make one an ancestor" (2010, 147). The deposits at Currusté provide a window into what might be interpreted as the "afterlife cycles" of the ancestors, or the processes of exhumation, preparation, bundling, sheltering, care, and feeding that were acts of propitiation and veneration essential to the reciprocal relationships between the living and the dead (Ashmore and Geller 2005; Chase and Chase 1994, 1996, 2011; Fitzsimmons 2009; Fitzsimmons and Shimada 2011; Geller 2012, 2014; Gillespie 2001, 2002; McAnany 1995, 1998; Navarro-Farr and Arroyave Prera 2014). While burying the dead underneath and around their houses indicates the intimacy of these relationships in everyday life, the relationships did not end with interment; rather, the inhabitants of the Classic period Ulúa Valley engaged in an ongoing, active exchange with the dead, a kind of "necrosociality" in which interactions between the worlds above and below were essential to social reproduction.

It also appears that these interactions were not just private matters on the intimate scale of the household but were also a vital part of social relations at many scales. The Currusté deposits were adjacent to a massive and dense ceramic midden containing the remains of repeated episodes of feasting, which indicates that the use, destruction, and interment of these incensarios, along with elaborate interactions with the remains of the ancestors, were public events with large audiences. The fact that one of the figural incensarios is represented as being pregnant provides a powerful metaphor for the intergenerational continuity of social houses, as vital perishable substances were consumed and permanent substances were interred to guarantee renewal by transcending the boundaries among the living, the dead, and the soon-to-be-born.

Beyond the celestial and subterranean spectacle of incense smoke going skyward and bone bundles going belowground, David Freidel (2017, 182) reminds us about the possibilities of large, open plazas for observations of astronomical phenomena, noting that "in a canopied world cleared space is by definition sky-watching space." While we have not identified any E Group types of architectural arrangements for solar observations in the Ulúa Valley, the frequent replication of solstitial alignments discussed below could indicate a widespread knowledge of observational astronomy. The documentation of sophisticated understandings of lunar, planetary, and sidereal movements in sixteenth-century Maya codices and Classic Maya monumental art and architecture (Aveni 2001; Milbrath 1999) provides indirect evidence that analogous practices of observational astronomy might have been a nocturnal activity in the Ulúa Valley. The ubiquity of representations of nocturnal and crepuscular animals in figural artifacts indicates a detailed knowledge of the local "night-life" that is suggestive of participation in nighttime activities.

Cycles linking the living and the dead paralleled the path of the sun into the underworld at night (Milbrath 1999; Stone 1995)—and in the Maya area, the association between death and travel to the underworld has been mapped back to the Classic period from the Popol Vuh, the sixteenth-century creation story of the Quiché Maya, based on parallels between ethnohistoric documents and representations on polychrome pottery and monumental art and architecture (Chase and Chase 1994; Freidel, Schele, and Parker 1993; Schele and Miller 1986; Weiss-Krejci 2011). Iconography representing ritual interactions between the living in the earthly world and ancestors and supernaturals in other realms was highlighted in depictions ranging from monumental art at Classic Maya centers such as Yaxchilan to underworld and ritual scenes portrayed in Late Classic Maya and Ulúa Polychrome vessels (Joyce 2017; Meskell and Joyce 2003; Schele and Miller 1986). Joyce (2017, 75) has identified iconographic elements on late Ulúa Polychromes from the valley that she argues are demarcating specific "cosmographic" spaces where ritually significant events are given meaning; late Ulúa Polychromes, with their ubiquitous black background, place the events they depict in "darkness, night, or the time before the sun rose."

SUBTERRANEAN TO CELESTIAL: NECROMANTIC, GEOMANTIC, AND ASTRONOMIC ENTANGLEMENTS

Interaction between the world of the living and the world below, literally and figuratively, was an essential component of household renewal. Several examples serve to illustrate how repeated practices of destruction, interment, and reentry demarcated particular places—both aboveground and belowground—over time, indicating that social memory associated with these locations was maintained even when the features belowground were hidden from view (Lopiparo 2008, n.d.; compare Joyce 2008, 2011). In the case of a double burial excavated at CR-80, we recovered the remains of several episodes of sub-floor activities and interment, including the burial of a jar neck and two obsidian blades associated with the burning of organic material, the smashing and interment of a figural incensario (presumably after its use) and a figural whistle, and two burials that appear to have been interred at different times but where the second was placed directly adjacent to the first in the same position and orientation (figure 9.8a, 9.8b).

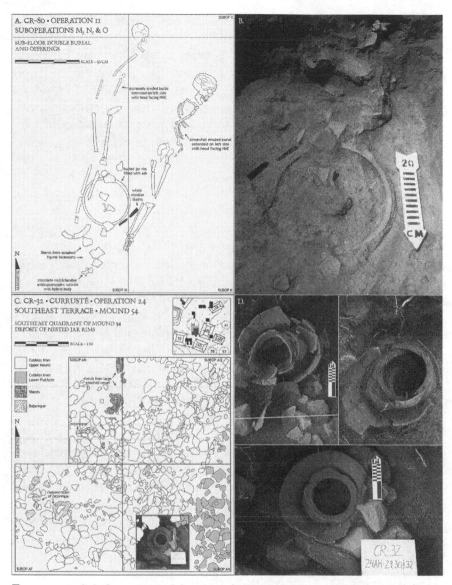

FIGURE 9.8. *Sub-floor structured deposition featuring multiple reentries: (a and b) double burial and sub-floor offerings from CR-80; and (c and d) series of nested jar necks deposited beneath the corner of a mound at Currusté (CR-32).*

In a second example, excavated at the site of Currusté (CR-32), a series of seven nested jar necks was deposited beneath the corner of a cobble and earthen mound (figure 9.8c, 9.8d). This deposit also appears to have been interred in at least three episodes and then covered during the final construction of the mound. While not as elaborate as the structured deposition described by Joyce at the nearby site of Mantecales (CR-71), those deposits featured an analogous sequence of seven stacked jar necks placed in different episodes that were associated with a tightly seriated sequence of ceramics and that allowed Joyce and colleagues to demonstrate repeated deposition over more than two centuries (Joyce and Pollard 2010; Joyce et al. 2002).

A third example from CR-103 included the burning of a wattle and daub structure associated with an adjacent sub-adult burial, which preceded a fill episode and the construction of another structure on the next occupation surface—a structure that itself was later burned before the following construction episode. Adjacent to the earlier structure was a small beehive oven, which had also been burned and collapsed. Four figural ceramic artifacts were then placed in the remains of its superstructure, including a stylized human figurine head in a netted headdress, an anthropomorphic, supernatural mask with an elaborate curvilinear design, a small, complete caiman whistle, and an upward-looking standing monkey with a zooanthropomorphic body (figure 9.9a, 9.9b). The destruction and burial of the oven was adjacent to a deposit that featured a layer of smashed and burned jar sherds, one quarter of a footed basalt metate, and half of a basalt mano. An animal burial (possibly feline) was placed, unburned, directly on top of this layer of burned sherds, along with a complete, miniature figural mask of the style classified as "grotesque" by Gordon Willey (1972). The mask features an old man with wrinkles, a protruding tongue, and a protruding chin. Above this deposit was another layer of burned sherds, a burned figurine head with a net headdress, and a burned figurine featuring a seated body with its head broken off (figure 9.9c, 9.9d).

Although the specific contents of structured deposition varied, they represent shared, complex patterns of destruction and renewal across the sites; and in many cases, they were closely associated with human burials. The burials themselves revealed a narrow range of shared orientations across all of the sites (figure 9.10a). Of the eight adult and sub-adult burials from the residential sites that were well enough preserved to identify burial position, three were oriented at approximately 24° (extended, with heads toward the north, on their sides facing east) and five were oriented perpendicularly between 113° and 120° (extended, four with heads toward the east, one with the head toward the west, all on their sides facing north). An infant burial at CR-103 shared the latter

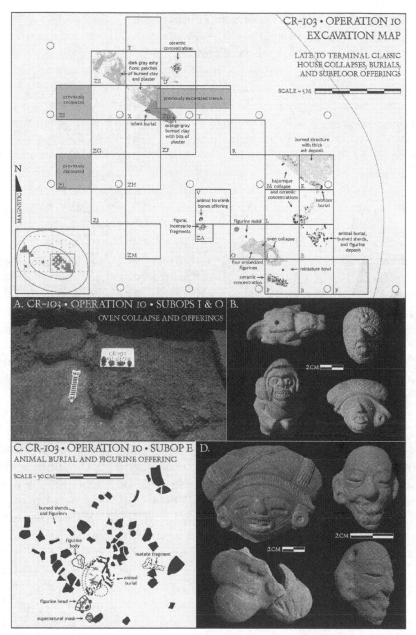

FIGURE 9.9. *Sub-floor structured deposition from CR-103 featuring (a and b) a collapsed oven with unburned figurine offerings and (c and d) an animal burial with burned sherds and figurines and a mano and metate fragment.*

orientation and was slightly flexed, with the head toward the west facing south. Another poorly preserved burial at CR-80 was too badly eroded to precisely identify the orientation, but the angle appears to be roughly aligned with the burials that are oriented east of north with the head to the north facing east. The two burials uncovered at Currusté were also extremely eroded and too poorly preserved to get a precise orientation, although both were oriented slightly east of north (roughly 10°–20°) with their heads toward the north.

As I have discussed elsewhere (Lopiparo 2007), in addition to the remarkable consistency in burial practices across sites in the central alluvium, these orientations were also shared by those buried in the main plaza groups at monumental centers such as Currusté, Travesía, and Cerro Palenque but with slight variations among them. Mapping this diversity among the centers and the burials at the household sites revealed that their east-northeast/south-southwest axes would have closely aligned them with the Montaña de Santa Bárbara, the tallest mountain at the southern end of the valley (figure 9.10b) (compare Inomata 2017). The burials oriented toward the east-southeast would have been aligned with the sunrise on the eastern horizon during the winter solstice and the sunset on the western horizon during the summer solstice (compare Reese-Taylor 2017). At Travesía, one of the largest Classic period centers in the central valley, the orientation of the main plaza group also aligned it with the largest mountain peaks to the east and west of the valley—which, with an east-west axis at 118°, would also have been closely aligned with the solar horizon extremes on the solstices (figure 9.10c), the two moments in the annual cycle when darkness and light hang in the balance (compare Gillespie 1991).

The association of night and darkness with the underworld is supported by ethnohistoric and iconographic sources from the Maya world indicating that the sun was believed to journey to the underworld at night (Fitzsimmons 2009; Freidel, Schele, and Parker 1993; Gillespie 1991)—a journey that has been further associated with a daily death and rebirth in ethnographic and epigraphic sources (Meskell and Joyce 2003; Milbrath 1999). As the days shortened and the winter solstice approached, the sun's increasing time in the underworld presented a critical juncture that threatened its rebirth and necessitated ritual intervention focused on renewal (compare Gillespie 1991). There is abundant evidence that solstice events and alignments were demarcated in Classic Maya landscapes (Aveni 2001; Aveni and Hartung 1989; Dowd 2015; Freidel et al. 2017; Milbrath 1999) and that the moment when the sun emerged on the winter solstice symbolized its "rebirth" in Maya cosmology (Cohodas 1975; Stuart 2009). The reemergence of the sun after its nocturnal and seasonal

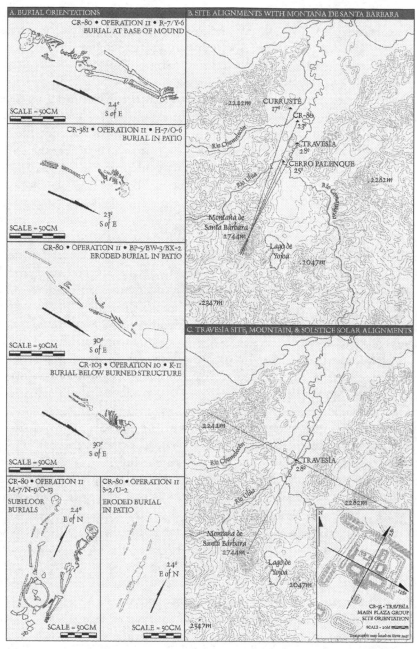

FIGURE 9.10. *Orientations of burials from household sites and alignments of main plaza groups at Late to Terminal Classic centers.*

journeys through the underworld mirrored the cycles of life, death, interment, and renewal that tied daily, solar, and astronomical cycles to human life cycles (compare Gillespie 1991; these associations are further reinforced by evidence for ancestor veneration recovered from E Group complexes in the Maya Lowlands; Brown 2017; Robin 2017; Robin et al. 2012).

The movement between the earthly world and the underworld has been associated with celestial events in the night sky in both ethnohistoric and Classic period representations of Maya cosmology. In the introduction to his translation of the Popol Vuh, Dennis Tedlock (1996, 34) describes the movement of the Hero Twins between the earthly world and the underworld as representing the origins of movements of celestial bodies: "The aboveground episodes might alternate with those below, with the heroes descending into the underworld, emerging on the earth again, and so forth. These sowing and dawning movements of the heroes, along with those of their supporting cast, prefigure the present-day movements of the sun, moon, planets, and stars." David Freidel, Linda Schele, and Joy Parker (1993) have argued that the emergence of the night sky represented the revolution of the underworld overhead, describing both the conveyance of the sun through the underworld along the east-west path of the Milky Way and the significance of constellations and planets in creation symbolism in Classic Maya monumental art. They describe representations of supernatural portals between worlds, which appeared on the backs of celestial caimans and turtles and were manifested in sacred landscape features in the earthly world that were made permeable through acts of sacrifice, including the consumption of vital essences through burning (1993; compare Fitzsimmons 2009; Freidel 2017; Stuart 1998, 2005).

Ethnographic examples from the Maya region of the associations among mountains, ancestors, origins, and renewal—especially of ritualized practices that sacralize natural landmarks and facilitate interaction with their supernatural inhabitants—provide possible analogies for understanding the relationship among the living, the dead, and sacred landscape features in the Ulúa Valley (see, for example, Brown 2004; Christenson 2008, 2016; Palka 2014; Vogt 1969). In several of these examples, ritualized practices at mountain shrines, caves, clefts, or holes demarcate portals that become permeable boundaries between the world of the living and the supernatural realm within (Christenson 2008; Palka 2014). In his ethnographic work in Santiago Atitlán, Allen Christenson describes how ritualized practices demarcating sacred landscape features facilitate the interpenetration of the world of the living with the world below, linking participants not just with agricultural and solar cycles but with creation and the renewal of the world itself:

In traditional Maya worldview, the creation of the world is not a singular event set in the far-distant past. Like the agricultural cycle of maize and the movement of the sun, the cosmos goes through orderly phases of birth, maturity, death, and rebirth. For the traditionalist Maya of Santiago Atitlan, ceremonies are conducted in mountain shrines as well as "otherworld" cofradía houses decorated in such a way that they represent the abodes of sacred ancestors and gods. These are not just symbolic representations of sacred mountains. They are, in a sense, the first mountain where creation first took place. Each of the ten cofradía houses in Santiago Atitlán is the center of the world, the underground place where sacred beings live and carry out their work to keep the world perpetually in a state of rebirth and renewal. It is a focal point for regenerative power, charged with the same animative presence that caves possess as divine houses.

Ceremonies conducted in either cofradía houses or mountain shrines have the same power to regenerate the world because they are conceptually the same, both giving access to the other world beyond the earth's surface. Each is a place of origin in the sense that ritual activity conducted there opens a portal not only into sacred space, but also into sacred time. Participants in these ceremonies consider themselves to be present at the moment of first beginnings when their gods and ancestors set the pattern for the world's existence. Such regeneration allows the Maya to periodically re-birth their world, making it pristine, uncorrupted, and conducive to life as it was meant to be lived in harmony with divinely sanctioned order. Such ceremonies are considered essential to the very existence of the world. (Christenson 2008, 119)

In conversation with ethnohistoric and ethnographic researchers from the Maya Highlands, several interpretations of Classic Maya monumental architecture focus on the iconography surrounding temples at the top of pyramids, placing rulers atop symbolic mountains entering portals that connect them with supernatural beings and powerful ancestors. It was through interaction with this supernatural realm—including the performance of appropriate rituals, the interment of the dead, and the consumption and burial of vital substances—that abundance and renewal were secured by rulers, who placed themselves in divine genealogies and promoted their essential role in the renewal of the world and significant cycles of time (Fitzsimmons 2009; Freidel, Schele, and Parker 1993; Schele and Freidel 1990; Stuart 1997, 1998).

In the Classic period Ulúa Valley, the alignment of plazas and burials with the Montaña de Santa Bárbara and the path of the sun through the underworld—and the recapitulation of this cosmogram in everyday life both aboveground and belowground—demarcated sacred landscape features that linked the life cycles of humans and the built environment to cosmological cycles of day and night and of creation, death, and renewal. As manifested in the sun's death and journey through the underworld every night, rebirth could be accomplished only by transcending the boundaries between the worlds of lightness and darkness. As I have argued elsewhere (Lopiparo n.d.), this transcendence was accomplished through the consumption via burning, dissembling, and burial of vital substances, where the remains of these ritual practices were buried below the sites of renewed construction and served to link the living to the dead through repeated interaction in space through time.

CONCLUSIONS

The association of interment with birth and renewal linked the cycles of the living and the dead and the worlds above and below with astronomical cycles that were inscribed in the local built environment and the broader natural landscape. Through their solstitial alignments, burials of the dead indexed the rebirth of cycles of night and day and also the agricultural renewal and cycles of time that annual solar cycles ensure. Ritual circuits associated with agricultural cycles and sacred landscape features have many analogs in the archaeological, ethnohistoric, and ethnographic documentation of Mesoamerican and Central American agricultural societies, frequently with the purpose of communication with and propitiation of supernaturals to ensure fertility (e.g., Broda and Báez-Jorge 2001; Broda and Good Eshelman 2004; Broda, Iwaniszewski, and Montero 2001; Chapman 1985, 1986; Christenson 2008, 2016; Gillespie 1991; Gossen 1974; Monaghan 1995; Palka 2014; Reese-Taylor 2002; Vogt 1969). The evidence presented here indicates that public gatherings in the Ulúa Valley were similarly organized around life-cycle events and significant moments in astronomical cycles, particularly the solstices—an interpretation that is further supported by previous research documenting the solstitial alignments of regional ball courts (Hendon, Joyce, and Lopiparo 2014; Joyce and Hendon 2000; Joyce, Hendon, and Lopiparo 2009; Lopiparo 2007). At the winter solstice, when the sun reached its nadir, ritual intervention would have ensured its return from the darkness of night and the underworld and thus the continuity of time—a cycle of death and rebirth that was recapitulated in everyday (and "everynight") life.

The constant work of renewal and regeneration—of human life cycles, ancestor afterlife cycles, agricultural cycles, and astronomical cycles—involved communication and movement between the earthly world and the underworld, between the lightness and the darkness, between the day and the night.

The evidence I have presented here from figural artifacts, polychrome vessels, and structured deposition associated with the renewal of sites and their inhabitants suggests that much of this work took place in the nightscape, as zoomorphic and anthropomorphic supernaturals who roamed at night moved between earthly and supernatural realms. In the Classic period Ulúa Valley, descent, death, and darkness were in constant interplay with rebirth, reemergence, and light; and nothing buried remained below for long. From the smoke and ashes emerged new life, just as the sun, reborn, reemerged from the underworld to end another night.

REFERENCES

Andrews, E. Wyllys, V, and Barbara W. Fash. 1992. "Continuity and Change in a Royal Maya Residential Complex at Copan." *Ancient Mesoamerica* 3 (1): 63–88.

Ashmore, Wendy, and Pamela L. Geller. 2005. "Social Dimensions of Mortuary Space." In *Interacting with the Dead: Perspectives on Mortuary Archaeology for the New Millennium*, ed. Gordon F.M. Rakita, Jane E. Buikstra, Lane A. Beck, and Sloan R. Williams, 81–92. Gainesville: University Press of Florida.

Astor-Aguilera, Miguel Ángel. 2010. *The Maya World of Communicating Objects: Quadripartite Crosses, Trees, and Stones*. Albuquerque: University of New Mexico Press.

Aveni, Anthony F. 2001. *Skywatchers: A Revised and Updated Version of Skywatchers of Ancient Mexico*. Austin: University of Texas Press.

Aveni, Anthony F., and Horst Hartung. 1989. "Uaxactún, Guatemala, Group E and Similar Assemblages: An Archaeoastronomical Reconsideration." In *World Archaeoastronomy*, ed. Anthony F. Aveni, 441–461. Cambridge: Cambridge University Press.

Benson, Elizabeth P. 1996. "The Vulture: The Sky and the Earth." In *Eight Palenque Round Table, 1993*, ed. Martha J. Macri and Jan McHargue, 309–320. San Francisco: Pre-Columbian Art Research Institute.

Broda, Johanna, and Félix Báez-Jorge, eds. 2001. *Cosmovisión, Ritual e Identidad de los Pueblos Indígenas de México*. Mexico City: Consejo Nacional para la Cultura y las Artes, Fondo Cultura Económica.

Broda, Johanna, and Catharine Good Eshelman, eds. 2004. *Historia y Vida Ritual en las Comunidades Mesoamericanas: Los Ritos Agrícola*. Mexico City: Instituto Nacional de Antropología e Historia, Universidad Nacional Autónoma de México.

Broda, Johanna, Stanislaw Iwaniszewski, and Arturo Montero, eds. 2001. *La Montaña en el Paisaje Ritual*. Mexico City: Instituto de Investigaciones Históricas, Escuela Nacional de Antropología e Historia.

Brown, Linda A. 2004. "Dangerous Places and Wild Spaces: Creating Meaning with Materials and Space at Contemporary Maya Shrines on El Duende Mountain." *Journal of Archaeological Method and Theory* 11 (1): 31–58.

Brown, Linda A. 2005. "Planting the Bones: Hunting Ceremonialism at Contemporary and Nineteenth-Century Shrines in the Guatemalan Highlands." *Latin American Antiquity* 16 (2): 131–146.

Brown, M. Kathryn. 2017. "E Groups and Ancestors: The Sunrise of Complexity at Xunantunich, Belize." In *Maya E Groups: Calendars, Astronomy, and Urbanism in the Early Lowlands*, ed. David A. Freidel, Arlen F. Chase, Anne S. Dowd, and Jerry Murdock, 387–411. Gainesville: University Press of Florida.

Carpenter, Charles R. 1934. *A Field Study of the Behavior and Social Relations of Howling Monkeys*. Comparative Psychology Monographs 10 (2). Baltimore: Johns Hopkins Press.

Chapman, Anne. 1982. *Los Hijos de la Muerte: El Universo Mítico de los Tolupan-Jicaques (Honduras)*. Mexico City: Instituto Nacional de Antropología e Historia.

Chapman, Anne. 1985. *Los Hijos del Copal y la Candela*, tomo 1: *Ritos Agrarios y Tradición Oral de los Lencas de Honduras*. Mexico City: Universidad Nacional Autónoma de México.

Chapman, Anne. 1986. *Los Hijos del Copal y la Candela*, tomo 2: *Tradición Católica de los Lencas de Honduras*. Mexico City: Universidad Nacional Autónoma de México.

Chase, Arlen F., and Diane Z. Chase. 1994. "Maya Veneration of the Dead at Caracol, Belize." In *Seventh Palenque Round Table, 1989*, ed. Merle Greene Robertson and Virginia M. Fields, 53–60. San Francisco: Pre-Columbian Art Research Institute.

Chase, Arlen F., and Diane Z. Chase. 1996. "Maya Multiples: Individuals, Entries, and Tombs in Structure A34 of Caracol, Belize." *Latin American Antiquity* 7: 61–79.

Chase, Diane Z., and Arlen F. Chase. 2011. "Ghosts amid the Ruins: Analyzing Relationships between the Living and the Dead among the Ancient Maya at Caracol, Belize." In *Living with the Dead: Mortuary Ritual in Mesoamerica*, ed. James L. Fitzsimmons and Izumi Shimada, 78–101. Tucson: University of Arizona Press.

Christenson, Allen. 2008. "Places of Emergence: Sacred Mountains and Cofradía Ceremonies." In *Pre-Columbian Landscapes of Creation and Origin*, ed. John Edward Staller, 95–121. New York: Springer.

Christenson, Allen. 2016. *The Burden of the Ancients: Maya Ceremonies of World Renewal from the Pre-Columbian Period to the Present*. Austin: University of Texas Press.

Cohodas, Marvin. 1975. "The Symbolism and Ritual Function of the Middle Classic Ball Game in Mesoamerica." *American Indian Quarterly* 2 (2): 99–130.

Coltman, Jeremy D. 2018. "Where Night Reigns Eternal: Darkness and Deep Time among the Ancient Maya." In *Archaeology of the Night: Life after Dark in the*

Ancient World, ed. Nancy Gonlin and April Nowell, 201–222. Boulder: University Press of Colorado.

Cornick, Leslie A., and Hal Markowitz. 2002. "Diurnal Vocal Patterns of the Black Howler Monkey (*Alouatta Pigra*) at Lamanai, Belize." *Journal of Mammalogy* 83 (1): 159–166.

Denver Art Museum Online Collections. "Tripod Vessel | Denver Art Museum." https://denverartmuseum.org/object/1991.57.

Dowd, Anne S. 2015. "Maya Architectural Hierophanies." In *Cosmology, Calendars, and Horizon-Based Astronomy in Ancient Mesoamerica*, ed. Anne S. Dowd and Susan Milbrath, 37–75. Boulder: University Press of Colorado.

Emery, Kitty F. 2004. "Animals from the Maya Underworld: Reconstructing Elite Maya Ritual at the Cueva de los Quetzales, Guatemala." In *Behavior Behind Bones: The Zooarchaeology of Ritual, Religion, Status, and Identity*, ed. Sharyn Jones O'Day, Wim Van Neer, and Anton Ervynck, 101–113. Oxford: Oxbow Books.

Fitzsimmons, James L. 2009. *Death and the Classic Maya Kings*. Austin: University of Texas Press.

Fitzsimmons, James L., and Izumi Shimada, eds. 2011. *Living with the Dead: Mortuary Ritual in Mesoamerica*. Tucson: University of Arizona Press.

Freidel, David A. 2017. "E Groups, Cosmology, and the Origins of Maya Rulership." In *Maya E Groups: Calendars, Astronomy, and Urbanism in the Early Lowlands*, ed. David A. Freidel, Arlen F. Chase, Anne S. Dowd, and Jerry Murdock, 177–211. Gainesville: University Press of Florida.

Freidel, David A., Arlen F. Chase, Anne S. Dowd, and Jerry Murdock, eds. 2017. *Maya E Groups: Calendars, Astronomy, and Urbanism in the Early Lowlands*. Gainesville: University Press of Florida.

Freidel, David, Linda Schele, and Joy Parker. 1993. *Maya Cosmos: Three Thousand Years on the Shaman's Path*. New York: Quill William Morrow.

Geller, Pamela L. 2012. "Parting (with) the Dead: Body Partibility as Evidence of Commoner Ancestor Veneration." *Ancient Mesoamerica* 23 (1): 115–130.

Geller, Pamela L. 2014. "Sedimenting Social Identity: The Practice of Pre-Columbian Maya Body Partibility." In *The Bioarchaeology of Space and Place: Ideology, Power, and Meaning in Maya Mortuary Contexts*, ed. Gabriel D. Wrobel, 15–38. New York: Springer.

Gillespie, Susan D. 1991. "Ballgames and Boundaries." In *The Mesoamerican Ballgame*, ed. Vernon L. Scarborough and David R. Wilcox, 317–345. Tucson: University of Arizona Press.

Gillespie, Susan D. 2000a. "Beyond Kinship: An Introduction." In *Beyond Kinship: Social and Material Reproduction in House Societies*, ed. Rosemary A. Joyce and Susan D. Gillespie, 135–160. Philadelphia: University of Pennsylvania Press.

Gillespie, Susan D. 2000b. "Maya 'Nested Houses': The Ritual Construction of Place." In *Beyond Kinship: Social and Material Reproduction in House Societies*, ed. Rosemary A. Joyce and Susan D. Gillespie, 1–21. Philadelphia: University of Pennsylvania Press.

Gillespie, Susan D. 2001. "Personhood, Agency, and Mortuary Ritual: A Case Study from the Ancient Maya." *Journal of Anthropological Archaeology* 20: 73–112.

Gillespie, Susan D. 2002. "Body and Soul among the Maya: Keeping the Spirits in Place." In *The Space and Place of Death*, ed. Helaine Silverman and David B. Small, 67–78. Archeological Papers 11 (1). Washington, DC: American Anthropological Association.

Gonlin, Nancy. 2007. "Ritual and Ideology among Classic Maya Commoners at Copan, Honduras." In *Commoner Ritual and Ideology in Ancient Mesoamerica*, ed. Nancy Gonlin and Jon C. Lohse, 83–121. Boulder: University Press of Colorado.

Gossen, Gary. 1974. *Chamulas in the World of the Sun: Time and Space in a Maya Oral Tradition*. Cambridge, MA: Harvard University Press.

Grube, Nikolai, and Werner Nahm. 1994. "A Census of Xibalba: A Complete Inventory of *Way* Characters on Maya Ceramics." In *The Maya Vase Book*, vol. 4, ed. Barbara Kerr and Justin Kerr, 686–715. New York: Kerr Associates.

Halperin, Christina. 2014. *Maya Figurines: Intersections between State and Household*. Austin: University of Texas Press.

Hasemann, George, Vito Veliz, and Lori Van Gerpen. 1978. "Informe Preliminar, Currusté: Fase I." Technical Report. Tegucigalpa, Honduras: Instituto Hondureño de Antropología e Historia.

Henderson, John S., and Rosemary A. Joyce. 2004. "Human Use of Animals in Prehispanic Honduras: A Preliminary Report from the Lower Ulúa Valley." In *Maya Zooarchaeology: New Directions in Method and Theory*, ed. Kitty F. Emery, 223–236. Los Angeles: Cotsen Institute of Archaeology, University of California.

Hendon, Julia A., Rosemary A. Joyce, and Jeanne Lopiparo. 2014. *Material Relations: The Marriage Figurines of Prehispanic Honduras*. Boulder: University Press of Colorado.

Houston, Stephen, and David Stuart. 1989. *The Way Glyph: Evidence for "Co-Essences" among the Classic Maya*. Research Reports on Ancient Maya Writing 30. Washington, DC: Center for Maya Research.

Houston, Stephen, David Stuart, and Karl Taube. 2006. *The Memory of Bones: Body, Being, and Experience among the Classic Maya*. Austin: University of Texas Press.

Inomata, Takeshi. 2017. "The Isthmian Origins of the E Group and Its Adoption in the Maya Lowlands." In *Maya E Groups: Calendars, Astronomy, and Urbanism in the Early Lowlands*, ed. David A. Freidel, Arlen F. Chase, Anne S. Dowd, and Jerry Murdock, 215–252. Gainesville: University Press of Florida.

Izquierdo y de la Cueva, Ana Luisa, and María Elena Vega Villalobos. 2016. "The Ocellated Turkey in Maya Thought." *PARI Journal* 16 (4): 15–23.

Joyce, Rosemary A. 2008. "Practice in and as Deposition." In *Memory Work: Archaeologies of Material Practices*, ed. Barbara J. Mills and William H. Walker, 25–40. Santa Fe, NM: School for Advanced Research Press.

Joyce, Rosemary A. 2011. "In the Beginning: The Experience of Residential Burial in Prehispanic Honduras." In *Residential Burial: A Multiregional Exploration*, ed. Ron L. Adams and Stacie M. King, 33–43. Archeological Papers 20 (1). Washington, DC: American Anthropological Association.

Joyce, Rosemary A. 2017. *Painted Pottery of Honduras: Object Lives and Itineraries*. Leiden: Brill.

Joyce, Rosemary A., and Julia A. Hendon. 2000. "Heterarchy, History, and Material Reality: 'Communities' in Late Classic Honduras." In *The Archaeology of Communities: A New World Perspective*, ed. Marcello A. Canuto and Jason Yaeger, 143–160. London: Routledge.

Joyce, Rosemary A., Julia A. Hendon, and Jeanne Lopiparo. 2009. "Being in Place: Intersections of Identity and Experience on the Honduran Landscape." In *The Archaeology of Meaningful Places*, ed. Brenda J. Bowser and María Nieves Zedeño, 53–72. Salt Lake City: University of Utah Press.

Joyce, Rosemary A., with Joshua Pollard. 2010. "Archaeological Assemblages and Practices of Deposition." In *Oxford Handbook of Material Culture Studies*, ed. Dan Hicks and Mary Beaudry, 291–309. Oxford: Oxford University Press.

Joyce, Rosemary A., with Robert W. Preucel, Jeanne Lopiparo, Carolyn Guyer, and Michael Joyce. 2002. *The Languages of Archaeology*. Oxford: Blackwell.

Looper, Matthew G. 2009. *To Be Like Gods: Dance in Ancient Maya Civilization*. Austin: University of Texas Press.

Lopiparo, Jeanne. 2003. "Household Ceramic Production and the Crafting of Society in the Terminal Classic Ulúa Valley Honduras." PhD dissertation, University of California, Berkeley.

Lopiparo, Jeanne. 2006. "Crafting Children: Materiality, Social Memory, and the Reproduction of Terminal Classic House Societies in the Ulúa Valley, Honduras." In *The Social Experience of Childhood in Ancient Mesoamerica*, ed. Traci Ardren and Scott R. Hutson, 133–168. Boulder: University Press of Colorado.

Lopiparo, Jeanne. 2007. "House Societies and Heterarchy in the Terminal Classic Ulúa Valley, Honduras." In *The Durable House: Architecture, Ancestors, and Origins*, ed. Robin A. Beck Jr., 73–96. Carbondale: Center for Archaeological Investigations, Southern Illinois University.

Lopiparo, Jeanne. 2008. "Proyecto Arqueológico Currusté 2007, Informe sobre la Primera Temporada: Technical Report." Tegucigalpa, Honduras: Instituto Hondureño de Antropología e Historia.

Lopiparo, Jeanne. n.d. "Destroying Objects, Constructing Subjects: Materiality, Social Relations, and Placemaking at Currusté, Honduras." In *Materiality of Gendered Practices: Archaeological Perspectives across Historical Landscapes*, ed. Kimberly Kasper and Susan Kus. Boulder: University Press of Colorado. Under review.

Lopiparo, Jeanne, and Julia A. Hendon. 2009. "Honduran Figurine-Whistles in Social Context: Production, Use, and Meaning in the Ulúa Valley." In *Mesoamerican Figurines: Small-Scale Indices of Large-Scale Social Phenomena*, ed. Christina Halperin, Katherine A. Faust, Rhonda Taube, and Aurore Giguet, 51–74. Gainesville: University Press of Florida.

Lucero, Lisa A. 2008. "Memorializing Place among Classic Maya Commoners." In *Memory Work: Archaeologies of Material Practices*, ed. Barbara J. Mills and William H. Walker, 187–205. Santa Fe, NM: School for Advanced Research Press.

MayaVase Database. "MayaVase Hi-Resolution for Vase K6621." http://research .mayavase.com/kerrmaya_hires.php?vase=6621.

McAnany, Patricia A. 1995. *Living with the Ancestors: Kinship and Kingship in Ancient Maya Society*. Austin: University of Texas Press.

McAnany, Patricia A. 1998. "Ancestors and the Classic Maya Built Environment." In *Function and Meaning in Classic Maya Architecture*, ed. Stephen D. Houston, 271–298. Washington, DC: Dumbarton Oaks Research Library and Collection.

Meskell, Lynn, and Rosemary A. Joyce. 2003. *Embodied Lives: Figuring Ancient Maya and Egyptian Experience*. New York: Routledge.

Milbrath, Susan. 1999. *Star Gods of the Maya: Astronomy in Art, Folklore, and Calendars*. Austin: University of Texas Press.

Mock, Shirley Boteler, ed. 1998. *The Sowing and the Dawning: Termination, Dedication, and Transformation in the Archaeological and Ethnographic Record of Mesoamerica*. Albuquerque: University of New Mexico Press.

Monaghan, John. 1995. *The Covenants with Earth and Rain: Exchange Sacrifice and Revelation in Mixtec Society*. Norman: University of Oklahoma Press.

Navarro-Farr, Olivia C., and Ana Lucía Arroyave Prera. 2014. "A Cumulative Palimpsest Effect: The Multilayered Meaning of Late-to-Terminal Classic Era, Above-Floor Deposits at Structure M13–1." In *Archaeology at El Perú-Waka': Ancient Maya Performances of Ritual, Memory, and Power*, ed. Olivia C. Navarro-Farr and Michelle Rich, 34–52. Tucson: University of Arizona Press.

Palka, Joel W. 2014. *Maya Pilgrimage to Ritual Landscapes: Insights from Archaeology, History, and Ethnography*. Albuquerque: University of New Mexico Press.

Quirarte, Jacinto. 1979. "The Representation of Underworld Procession in Maya Vase Painting: An Iconographic Study." In *Maya Archaeology and Ethnohistory*, ed. Norman Hammond and Gordon R. Willey, 116–148. Austin: University of Texas Press.

Reents-Budet, Dorie. 1986. "The 'Holmul Dancer' Theme in Maya Art." In *Sixth Palenque Round Table, 1986*, ed. Merle Greene Robertson and Virginia M. Fields, 217–222. Norman: University of Oklahoma Press.

Reents-Budet, Dorie. 1994. *Painting the Maya Universe: Royal Ceramics of the Classic Period*. Durham, NC: Duke University Press.

Reese-Taylor, Kathryn V. 2002. "Ritual Circuits as Key Elements in Maya Civic Center Designs." In *Heart of Creation: The Mesoamerican World and the Legacy of Linda Schele*, ed. Andrea J. Stone, 143–165. Tuscaloosa: University of Alabama Press.

Reese-Taylor, Kathryn V. 2017. "Founding Landscapes in the Central Karstic Uplands." In *Maya E Groups: Calendars, Astronomy, and Urbanism in the Early Lowlands*, ed. David A. Freidel, Arlen F. Chase, Anne S. Dowd, and Jerry Murdock, 480–513. Gainesville: University Press of Florida.

Robin, Cynthia. 2017. "Ordinary People and East-West Symbolism." In *Maya E Groups: Calendars, Astronomy, and Urbanism in the Early Lowlands*, ed. David A. Freidel, Arlen F. Chase, Anne S. Dowd, and Jerry Murdock, 365–381. Gainesville: University Press of Florida.

Robin, Cynthia, James Meierhoff, Caleb Kestle, Chelsea Blackmore, Laura J. Kosakowsky, and Anna C. Novotny. 2012. "Ritual in a Farming Community." In *Chan: An Ancient Maya Farming Community*, ed. Cynthia Robin, 113–132. Gainesville: University Press of Florida.

Schele, Linda, and David Freidel. 1990. *A Forest of Kings: The Untold Story of the Ancient Maya*. New York: William Morrow.

Schele, Linda, and Mary Ellen Miller. 1986. *The Blood of Kings: Dynasty and Ritual in Maya Art*. New York: George Braziller, Inc.

Scherer, Andrew K. 2015. *Mortuary Landscapes of the Classic Maya: Rituals of Body and Soul*. Austin: University of Texas Press.

Stone, Andrea J. 1995. *Images from the Underworld: Naj Tunich and the Tradition of Maya Cave Painting*. Austin: University of Texas Press.

Stone, Doris. 1941. *Archaeology of the North Coast of Honduras*. Memoirs of the Peabody Museum of Archaeology and Ethnology 9 (1). Cambridge, MA: Harvard University.

Strathern, Marilyn. 1988. *The Gender of the Gift*. Berkeley: University of California Press.

Stuart, David. 1997. "The Hills Are Alive: Sacred Mountains in the Maya Cosmos." *Symbols* Spring: 13–17.

Stuart, David. 1998. "'The Fire Enters His House': Architecture and Ritual in Classic Maya Texts." In *Function and Meaning in Classic Maya Architecture*, ed. Stephen D. Houston, 373–425. Washington, DC: Dumbarton Oaks Research Library and Collection.

Stuart, David. 2005. *The Inscriptions from Temple XIX at Palenque*. San Francisco: Pre-Columbian Art Research Institute.

Stuart, David. 2009. "The Symbolism of Zacpetén Altar 1." In *The Kowoj: Identity, Migration, and Geopolitics in Late Postclassic Petén, Guatemala*, ed. Prudence M. Rice and Don S. Rice, 317–326. Boulder: University Press of Colorado.

Tedlock, Dennis, trans. 1996. *Popol Vuh: The Definitive Edition of the Mayan Book of the Dawn of Life and the Glories of Gods and Kings*, revised and expanded ed. New York: Simon and Schuster.

Vogt, Evon Z. 1969. *Zinacantán: A Maya Community in the Highlands of Chiapas*. Cambridge, MA: Harvard University Press.

Weiss-Krejci, Estella. 2011. "The Role of Dead Bodies in Late Classic Maya Politics: Cross-Cultural Reflections on the Meaning of Tikal Altar 5." In *Living with the Dead: Mortuary Ritual in Mesoamerica*, ed. James L. Fitzsimmons and Izumi Shimada, 17–52. Tucson: University of Arizona Press.

Willey, Gordon R. 1972. *The Artifacts of Altar de Sacrificios*. Papers of the Peabody Museum of Archaeology and Ethnology 64 (1). Cambridge, MA: Harvard University.

10

Ancient Mesoamericans believed nighttime held earthly and supernatural dangers, a fact known from archaeological, iconographic, and ethnohistorical evidence. As visibility declined with the setting of the sun, nocturnal animals—including threatening predators—awoke and embarked on their nightly pursuits. Human depravity and supernatural threats also increased at nighttime. To this day, folktales among indigenous groups in Mexico and Central America recount the legendary tragedies that transpired under the cover of darkness (Friedlander 1990; Martín del Campo 2009; Preuss 2012; Signorini 1982). Other chapters in this volume have highlighted how the ancient inhabitants of Mexico and Central America conceptualized, utilized, and venerated darkness and nighttime. Given how acutely the all-consuming darkness of nighttime was experienced in times that pre-dated electricity, it is unsurprising that it was a subject of great interest to people living in the past.

Although nighttime was associated with a wide variety of natural and supernatural dangers, it was also the time of the day when most of cosmic bodies—the moon, the stars, and planets (especially Venus)—became visible. Thus the night was essential for divination and observations of the night sky. Numerous rituals were conducted during the night, especially those that necessitated conference with the cosmos, and many of these nocturnal rituals involved fire. Fire was a sacred substance for ancient Mesoamericans and was

The Light Burned Brightly

Postclassic New Fire Ceremonies of the Aztec and at Xaltocan in the Basin of Mexico

Kirby Farah

DOI: 10.5876/9781646421879.c010

symbolically associated with the cosmos, particularly the sun (Taube 2004). Like the sun and other cosmic bodies, fire was a vital source of warmth and light during the night, but unlike its cosmic counterparts, fire could be manipulated and controlled by people, making it a powerful and symbolically potent tool for Mesoamerican ritual practitioners.

The visual and sensual impacts of fire within the context of a night ritual added to the drama and mystery of ceremonial events. Against the backdrop of the expansive darkness of night, the bright light of fires burned brilliantly, and their intense heat juxtaposed the cooler temperatures of the night air. Although fire and burning were common aspects of many Mesoamerican rituals, especially those that took place at night, among the most illustrious of these rituals was the New Fire Ceremony.

The New Fire Ceremony is generally associated with the Aztecs of Central Mexico, but similar fire rituals were practiced in the Basin of Mexico long before the formation of the Aztec Triple Alliance (ca. 1427 CE) (figure 10.1). Although Early Colonial (1521–1700 CE) ethnohistorical documents have provided a great deal of information concerning the diverse motivations and the intricate activities involved with the Aztec New Fire Ceremony, relatively little is known about the specific practices or motivations associated with earlier iterations of the ritual. Given this relative lack of information about earlier versions, it has long been assumed that other Basin of Mexico polities practiced the New Fire Ceremony in much the same way as the Aztecs. However, recent archaeological evidence for a New Fire Ceremony at the northern Basin of Mexico site of Xaltocan (figure 0.1 and table 0.1) has provided significant new insights into the diverse activities that were associated with such performances across the Basin of Mexico, particularly in the centuries that pre-date the establishment of the Aztec Empire. These differences are especially noteworthy because the Aztec New Fire Ceremony was so intricately bound up with Aztec ideology and political strategy. Thus comparing the Aztec New Fire Ceremony with other Basin of Mexico New Fire rituals—especially those not tied directly to the Aztec Empire—has the potential to reveal significant differences in ideology and sociopolitical organization, especially those practices related to night and darkness.

STUDYING THE EARLY POSTCLASSIC BASIN OF MEXICO: PROBLEMS AND BIASES

In the shadow of the extensive corpus of ethnohistorical and archaeological information that has been produced over the centuries concerning the

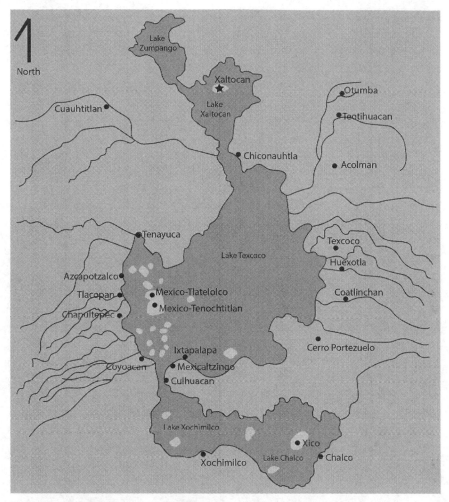

FIGURE 10.1. *Major towns and capitals in the Postclassic Basin of Mexico.*

celebrated Aztec Empire of Central Mexico, both archaeologists and historians are guilty of having largely overlooked the varied and distinctive Postclassic Basin of Mexico polities that immediately pre-dated it. Despite the fact that the economic, political, and religious systems—which structured (and were structured by) the everyday actions of the inhabitants of these Early Postclassic polities—were quite diverse, the materials recovered from these places have typically been interpreted through an "Aztec lens" (that is, using known Aztec practices and social structures to inform interpretations of earlier

Basin of Mexico polities). As a result, the social structures, ideologies, and identity-making practices of these polities have been over-generalized and presented as mere fledglings of the Aztec Empire or even erased (Farah 2017).

The relative lack of research focused on Early Postclassic Basin of Mexico polities is especially troubling considering that at least some of the success of the vast Aztec Empire is owed to Aztec rulers, who often allowed conquered polities to retain their existing political and economic structures (Berdan 1994, 2005; Berdan et al. 1996; Hassig 1995). This decision was strategic on the part of Aztec leaders, as it probably decreased resistance among newly conquered territories and simplified the political transition. An unintended consequence of this strategy, however, was that new territories were sometimes able to retain their distinctive cultural practices and ideologies—despite the great efforts on the part of Aztec leaders to erase and replace ideologies and histories that conflicted with their own (see Gillespie 1989; Sahagún 1950–1982, book 10). Thus Aztec provinces were unified under Aztec leadership but often retained local practices and ideologies that dated to long before the Mexicas rose to power.

Scholars often note the great diversity (especially pertaining to language and ethnicity) that characterized the Postclassic Basin of Mexico in the centuries leading up to the formation of the Aztec Empire, but specific differences in everyday practices, sociopolitical organization, and ideology remain poorly understood. Thus more intensive research, focused on the sociopolitical organization and identity-making practices of Early Postclassic polities, has the potential to facilitate a greater and more tangible understanding of the diversity that existed in the Basin of Mexico prior to the rise of the Aztec Empire. Although this chapter focuses primarily on ritual practices, those practices reflect broader social and political processes and contribute to our understanding of the ways Postclassic Basin polities differed from the Aztec Empire.

ARCHAEOLOGICAL EVIDENCE OF NEW FIRE CEREMONIES

Archaeological evidence for burning rituals that likely influenced the New Fire Ceremony has been recovered across Mesoamerica dating back to as early as the Preclassic (ca. 1000 BCE–200 CE). Fire has long been a central component of Mesoamerican ritual. Burning sacrificial materials helped purify them and transform them for consumption by the gods (McGee 1990, 44; Plunket 2002, 7; Rice 1999, 28). The burning of incense served to consecrate places and actions and was a common component of building dedication and termination rituals (Stockett 2007, 98), which continue to this day in some parts of Mesoamerica (McGee 1998). Thus ideology concerning the transformative power of fire originated much earlier than the Postclassic and was widespread throughout Mesoamerica.

Although ethnohistorical records have meticulous descriptions of how Aztec leaders conducted the ceremony during the fifteenth and sixteenth centuries, we now know that New Fire rituals were practiced elsewhere in Central Mexico, in some cases long before the formation of the Aztec Empire. George Vaillant (1937, 1938) was perhaps the first to interpret artifact dumps recovered from the sites of Chiconautla and Nonoalca as New Fire deposits. There was initially some skepticism surrounding Vaillant's interpretations because they were coupled with a problematic ceramic chronology and overly simplistic associations between material culture and ethnic groups (Elson and Smith 2001; Nicholson 1955, 1971). However, Christina Elson and Michael Smith (2001) revisited Vaillant's data and tested the accuracy of his interpretations using a set of credentials for what a New Fire deposit should entail. According to Elson and Smith (2001), New Fire deposits should contain a high proportion of reconstructable vessels and objects that are typical of household assemblages. Deposits should also be unstratified, consisting of only a single cluster of artifacts, and should be near a house or house group. Based on these criteria, Vaillant's interpretations do appear to have been accurate, and the artifact dumps he recovered likely were New Fire deposits. Elson and Smith (2001) also used the criteria outlined above to determine that the "rock pile" deposits that were excavated from the site of Cuexcomate in Morelos (Smith 1992) were also examples of New Fire dumps. More recently, an artifact dump excavated at a wealthy household in Xaltocan has been interpreted as a New Fire deposit (De Lucia 2011, 2014). The deposit dates to the Early Postclassic and contained reconstructable vessels and rare objects, including a temple model figurine and an effigy vessel of the underworld deity (De Lucia 2014, 386). Despite the sparse archaeological evidence for New Fire rituals outside the Aztec core, these discoveries provide evidence that versions of the New Fire Ceremony were practiced—probably in diverse ways—throughout Postclassic Central Mexico.

THE AZTEC NEW FIRE CEREMONY

While scholars have found substantial evidence that the New Fire Ceremony was practiced across the Basin of Mexico long before the formation of the Aztec Triple Alliance (De Lucia 2011, 2014; Elson and Smith 2001; Farah 2017), most of what we know about the ceremony has been gleaned from ethnohistorical sources written during the Early Colonial period (e.g., Alvarado

Tezozómoc 1975; Codex Borbonicus 1974; Sahagún 1950–1982). Even though these documents provide reference only to the Aztec version of the New Fire Ceremony, they do include descriptions of the activities of both leaders and commoners. The records also contain information regarding how the New Fire Ceremony was deeply ingrained in Aztec ideology and how the rituals were used tactically by Aztec rulers to reinforce their specific political agendas. The ceremony simultaneously signified the start of a new calendrical cycle, reiterated the authority of Aztec political leaders, and served to unite a diverse and expansive empire.

The New Fire (*xiuhtlalpilli*) Ceremony took place every fifty-two years, at a time when the solar calendar (*xiuhpohualli*) and ritual calendar (*tonalpohualli*) converged. Each successive New Fire Ceremony was probably a little different than the last. Over time and as preferences and cultural practices shifted, new practices and paraphernalia were likely incorporated into the New Fire ritual. Davíd Carrasco (1999) describes in detail a New Fire Ceremony that took place in the year 1507 CE, drawing mostly on book 7 of the Florentine Codex (Sahagún 1950–1982). The description that follows is based on the events and practices that have been documented as having occurred in association with that particular New Fire Ceremony.

Preparation began the morning before the ritual. A group of high-ranking priests and political leaders gathered in the city of Tenochtitlan before setting off on their journey to Huixachtlan (today, Cerro de la Estrella), where the rite would ultimately be performed. The priests and leaders were dressed in elaborate garb, impersonating gods, and they wore intricate masks and feather headdresses. A priest dressed as the god Quetzalcoatl led them in procession. Although the procession was composed almost entirely of high-ranking religious and political leaders, it also included a single war captive, one who was likely selected based on his bravery in combat. He would eventually meet his fate as the sacrificial victim at the center of the ceremony, but it is unclear whether the prisoner conceived of his sacrifice as an honor or a punishment.

As the priests began their journey to Huixachtlan, across the empire the rest of the populace began their own preparations for the ceremony. All fires were extinguished, including those burning in households and temples, leaving the kingdom in natural darkness as night approached. Houses and common buildings were cleaned, streets were swept, and old hearthstones were thrown away along with old cooking vessels and utensils. Objects that remained, including household idols, were thoroughly washed. Essentially everything considered old or used up was done away with, and everything that would carry over into the new cycle was cleaned.

As night fell and darkness blanketed the land, special precautions were taken to ensure that the dangers associated with this particularly potent night would not harm anyone. Pregnant women were locked in granaries, and their faces were painted blue to prevent them from becoming monsters during the night. Children likewise had their faces painted and were urged to stay awake during the night to protect them from being turned into mice. By nightfall, all work across the kingdom halted and the populace made their way to the roofs of their houses, heads craned toward Huixachtlan, to wait silently for the ceremony to commence and to learn their fate.

Meanwhile, the priests and leaders gathered on the summit of Huixachtlan after their long journey from Tenochtitlan. Standing on a platform that was visible to the villages below, the priests and the captive waited, watching the stars. At precisely midnight, when the Pleiades (Tianquiztli) reached their zenith, the captive was sacrificed. The highest-ranking priest, who probably wore a turquoise mask and dressed as the god of fire, Xiuhtecuhtli, used a large knife to cut the heart out of the captive's chest. A fire was then quickly kindled in the gaping chest of the sacrificial victim using the sacred drill (*tlelquauitl*). If the fire lit and burned brightly, which it always did, this action indicated that Xiuhtecuhtli would bless the people with another sun cycle. Although the populace never had the misfortune of experiencing a failed New Fire Ceremony, a legend tells that if the fire did not light, then the Tzitzimimeh (monster deities) would emerge and roam in the darkness, killing and eating all humanity.

After the lighting of the New Fire, the initial flame was transferred to a huge, highly visible pyre. Using large torches, the New Fire flames were then transported to Tenochtitlan, where they were used to light a fire at the Temple of Huitzilopochtli, which served as the source of fire for the entire kingdom. Runners were sent from across the Basin of Mexico to light their torches at the Fire Temple. They carried their flames back to their local shrines from whence the fire could be disseminated throughout the empire.

SOCIAL AND POLITICAL SIGNIFICANCE OF THE AZTEC NEW FIRE CEREMONY

In the most fundamental sense, the New Fire Ceremony was religious in nature, honoring the gods and particularly the god of the sun, Xiuhtecuhtli, but it also had significant political and social implications that reverberated across the kingdom. First and foremost, the political and religious leaders of the Aztec Empire were responsible for conducting the New Fire Ceremony, upon which the fate of the world ostensibly hinged. Thus the survival of the populace at large was theoretically dependent on a small group of leaders who perpetuated long-standing power structures. By controlling religious institutions and presiding over rites that were integral to central Mexican ideology, Aztec leaders positioned themselves as the primary arbiters between the human and godly realms wherein they alone were capable of persuading the gods to protect and sustain the wider populace. This is not to say that all denizens of the empire or even of the Basin of Mexico bought into the impervious status of Aztec leaders (e.g., Brumfiel 2000), and in addition to controlling important religious practices and institutions, Aztec leaders also used a variety of economic, political, and social tactics—most notably, taxation—to assert their authority over their sprawling and sometimes subversive empire.

The New Fire Ceremony stands out as one of the most potent rituals for several reasons. First, despite its prominence in the literature, this ceremony was an infrequent ritual. Because it occurred only once every fifty-two years, for most Postclassic central Mexicans, it was an event experienced just once in a lifetime. Moreover, the potential negative impact of the ritual was unparalleled. The end of a fifty-two-year cycle carried with it the possibility of perpetual night and the end of humankind at the claws of the Tzitzimimeh. This fate was an understandably terrifying premise, and the wider populace was relieved when a New Fire Ceremony succeeded. In addition, the success acted as an indication to inhabitants across the Aztec Empire that the current ruler was capable of earning good favor and protection from the gods. Thus a New Fire Ceremony was a prime opportunity for Aztec leaders to remind their constituents of how essential they were in maintaining the welfare and cosmic balance of the kingdom. It is unsurprising then, that following successful New Fire ceremonies and bolstered by what was perceived as a divine endorsement of their rule, Aztec leaders often embarked on state-building projects. For example, in the year 1455 CE, Motecuhzoma I substantially enlarged the Templo Mayor at Tenochtitlan following his successful New Fire Ceremony.

Aztec New Fire ceremonies were also critical to fostering a sense of solidarity across the ethnically diverse Basin of Mexico. Among the most crucial aspects of the ritual was the dissemination of the flames of the New Fire. Through what was reportedly a rapid distribution program, priests carried torches with the New Fire's flames to other Basin of Mexico capitals to re-light temples and houses. This process was of great symbolic significance because the fires that illuminated the highest temples in the Aztec capital city were all born from the same "mother" flame as the fires that warmed and lit commoner households in the kingdom's lowliest villages. Thus fires across the Basin of

Mexico were ignited by what was perceived to be a common flame and were reminders of the momentous night and the ritual capabilities of Aztec rulers.

Perhaps the great influence of the New Fire Ceremony is partially attributable to similar kinds of rituals that existed in the Basin of Mexico prior to the formation of the Aztec Empire. As discussed earlier in this chapter, this ceremony did not originate with the Aztecs; nor were its origins necessarily in Central Mexico. It may have been among the most successful rituals in the Aztec Empire because of its ubiquity throughout Central Mexico. The fundamental premise and message of the ceremony may have been so widespread that even as the Aztec leaders modified aspects of the ritual, the underlying message (and impact of the ritual) persisted, as did the implicit implication that fire and its ritual nature bring life and light to the world.

In the remainder of this chapter, I focus on evidence for a fire ritual recovered from the northern Basin of Mexico site of Xaltocan that pre-dated the formation of the Aztec Empire. Although this earlier New Fire ritual probably had many of the same functions as the later Aztec New Fire Ceremony, it also demonstrates several significant differences that may reflect other broad areas of diversity among the Aztecs and earlier Basin of Mexico polities.

INTRODUCTION TO XALTOCAN

Postclassic Xaltocan was a constructed island located in the brackish Lake Xaltocan in the northern Basin of Mexico. Xaltocan was first occupied sometime during the tenth century by Otomí speakers, and by the end of the twelfth century, it had risen to regional prominence as the capital of the Otomí city-state (Alva Ixtlilxóchitl 1975–1977 1; Anales de Tlatelolco 2004; Barlow 1949, 1999; Berdan 1992; Bierhorst 1992; Hicks 1994; Pérez-Rocha and Tena 2000; Rodríguez-Alegría 2010; see also Carrasco Pizana 1950). During the mid-thirteenth century, Xaltocan entered into conflict with Cuauhtitlan, a neighboring polity to the west. Intermittent skirmishes took place over a 150-year period, with Cuauhtitlan slowly chipping away at the frontiers of Xaltocan's domain. By the end of the fourteenth century, an alliance between the Tepanecs of Cuauhtitlan and the city-state of Azcapotzalco eventually defeated the people of Xaltocan (Anales de Cuauhtitlan 1992). Ethnohistorians indicate that after defeat, Xaltocan was largely abandoned (Alva Ixtlilxóchitl 1975–1977 1; Anales de Cuauhtitlan 1992), although recent archaeological research has proven that at least some commoners living near the perimeter of the island persisted (Overholtzer 2012, 2013). Xaltocan did not remain under Tepanec control for long; by around 1428 CE, Xaltocan was incorporated into the Aztec Empire and repopulated by Acolman, Colhua, Tenochca, and Otomí peoples (Anales de Cuauhtitlan 1992, 104; Hicks 1994).

It is noteworthy that Xaltocan underwent a substantial population shift. The original inhabitants of Xaltocan, who probably identified themselves as Otomí, enjoyed political independence and considerable economic prominence in the region, but the replacement population was ethnically diverse and subservient to the Aztec Empire. Xaltocan appears unique compared with the majority of other Basin of Mexico polities in this respect. Although the Late Postclassic marked major political shifts for many central Mexican communities, few experienced such dramatic and well-documented population shifts. This ethnic change is especially significant for archaeologists and others who study Xaltocan's past because it means that, generally, the people who inhabited the small island of Xaltocan between the eleventh and fourteenth centuries were fundamentally different (certainly politically at least) from those who inhabited the island on the eve of the Spanish conquest (Farah 2017, 87).

Initiated by Elizabeth Brumfiel and sustained by her students and colleagues, extensive archaeological research has been conducted at Xaltocan since around 1990. Recently, at a large mound named Cerrito Central, near the center of modern-day Xaltocan (figure 10.2), excavators uncovered successive structures associated with Xaltocan's Postclassic leaders (Farah 2017). Excavations at Cerrito Central were diachronic in their general thrust, and although this methodology revealed only fragments of structures, many culturally rich contexts were encountered. Such contexts contain evidence that have allowed us to reveal how Xaltocan's leaders adapted their daily practices over time and how their practices were different from or similar to those of the wider community of Xaltocan. Cerrito Central was occupied for nearly the entire Postclassic and well into the Colonial period, with three major occupation phases dating roughly to Xaltocan's Hai, Dehe, and Tlalli phases (table 10.1). The first occupation phase occurred between 1000 and 1200 CE (corresponding roughly to Xaltocan's Dehe phase), the second occupation phase dates between 1200 and 1400 CE (corresponding roughly to Xaltocan's Hai phase), and the final occupation phase spans 1430–1521 CE (corresponding roughly to Xaltocan's Tlalli phase).

Cerrito Central was probably first occupied by Xaltocan's leaders as early as the eleventh century and possibly even earlier. A radiocarbon date taken from the earliest building phase yielded a two-sigma calibrated date range of 1017 to 1155 CE (969 ± 30, AA106208, wood charcoal, $\delta^{13}C$ = -24.3). The kinds of architectural remains recovered from this early period indicate that the original structure was constructed of high-quality materials. Plaster floors and large clay foundations were found, along with a considerable amount of

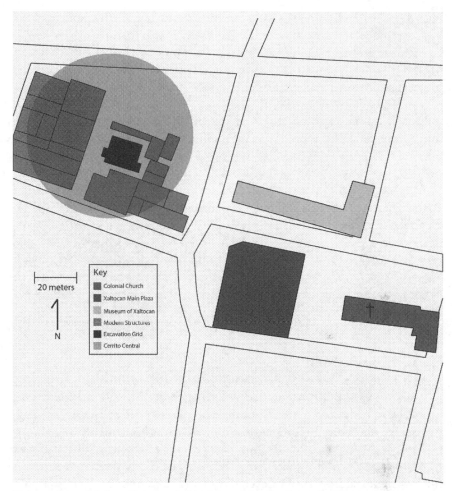

FIGURE 10.2. *Modern Xaltocan and location of Cerrito Central.*

TABLE 10.1. Ceramic chronology at Xaltocan

Phase Name	Time Period	Ceramic Type	Calendar Dates
Dehe (water in Otomí)	Early Postclassic	Aztec I	920–1240 CE
Hai (land in Otomí)	Middle Postclassic	Aztec II	1240–1350 CE
Tlalli (land in Nahuatl)	Late Postclassic	Aztec III	1350–1521 CE
Isla (island in Spanish)	Colonial	Aztec III and IV	1521–1680 CE

Reproduced from Overholtzer (2012, table 4.4)

stucco (red-painted and plain white) in the surrounding fill. Combined, these architectural features are indications that the original structure was built with greater care and that higher-quality materials were used than was typical of other Dehe phase structures at Xaltocan. It appears that Xaltocan's earliest leaders used monumental architecture to substantiate their role in the community and in so doing, marked Cerrito Central as a place of political significance.

Leadership was established at Xaltocan by the eleventh century, but it was during the thirteenth and fourteenth centuries that Xaltocan reached its political peak. As the autonomous capital of the Otomí city-state, its domain included forty-nine towns and twenty-four territories with tribute fields (Alva Ixtlilxóchitl 1975–1977 1:268, 283, 2:42, 79). At the beginning of the thirteenth century, Xaltocan's leaders initiated a major building program at Cerrito Central. All earlier architecture was razed, buried, and capped with a meter-deep level of fill and a large adobe platform, on top of which low-lying stone wall foundations were constructed that outlined a series of rooms. Although archaeologists revealed only portions of the Hai phase structure during excavations, substantial evidence for ritual activity was recovered, including evidence for a New Fire Ceremony.

RITUAL PRACTICES AT XALTOCAN

At Cerrito Central, excavators have revealed two main spaces dedicated to ritual practice. Both date to between the late twelfth and late fourteenth centuries, roughly corresponding to the Hai phase (table 10.1). One of these two spaces was a small room, measuring approximately 4 m × 2 m, retained by low-lying stone wall foundations with ceramic fragments lining their surfaces. The remains of five successive square-shaped features, referred to henceforth as "altar features," were recovered from inside the room, which measured approximately 50 cm × 50 cm. They were composed of numerous (between thirty and forty) ceramic fragments pressed flat into compacted dirt floors. In one instance, an altar feature was constructed on top of a plaster floor (figure 10.3). Altar features were embedded into floors and were therefore elevated only between 1 cm and 3 cm above floor surfaces. The altar features were not contemporaneous; nor were they located in the same horizontal place in the room. The reason appears to be that each square-shaped feature corresponded to a different floor. When an old floor was buried during renovations, the altar feature that sat atop it was buried as well, and when a new floor was constructed, a new altar feature was built on top of it but in a slightly different location in the room.

FIGURE 10.3. *Altar 4 located along the southern, interior edge of the altar room and built on top of a plaster floor.*

These features are interpreted as altars because there is ample evidence that they are associated with ritual burning practices. Fine ash, lacking pieces of wood charcoal, was recovered directly from the surface of three altar features, and more ash was recovered from the floor next to them. This ash might indicate that paper or incense was burned on top of them, possibly contained inside vessels because the surfaces of the altars do not appear burned. Fragments of censers and braziers, both common implements in central Mexican burning rituals, were recovered from associated contexts—that is, inside the room within the same stratigraphic layers as the altar features. There is little evidence that the room that contained the altar features was used for mundane activities such as cooking or other household production practices.

The room that contained the altar features was small and at any given time could probably accommodate only a small number of individuals. Although the wall foundations are all that remain from the surrounding room, making it difficult to determine if windows or an open roof allowed light to pour in, it is possible that the small room provided a dark space for ritual practices, not unlike a sweat bath (*temazcal*) (see chapters by Sheets and Thomason; and by Olson, this volume, for more insights about sweat baths in Mesoamerica) or a cloistered temple room. The restricted size is an indication that only a small group of individuals would have had the privilege of bearing witness to the activities that took place within, and they were probably high-ranking religious practitioners and political leaders. The purpose and frequency of the rituals that took place in this small room remain unclear; however, the consistency in the form and dimensions of the altar features is evidence that similar kinds of rituals took place in this room over the course of several decades, if not longer.

Although the ceremonies conducted in the small room were likely private, over time the leaders of Xaltocan opted to move their rituals to a slightly more public space—an open patio just to the north. Initially, another altar feature was constructed, identical to those built within the original room. Later, however, when the patio was resurfaced, the altar feature was covered. A large ceremonial hearth (*tlecuil*) was constructed on top of the new patio surface, partially overlapping the altar feature (figure 10.4). The hearth was made from a combination of adobe bricks and stones and included strips of ceramic fragments running along its northern and southern edges, reminiscent of those used to create the square-shaped altar features. A radiocarbon date taken from the hearth yielded a two-sigma calibrated date range of 1264–1388 CE (692 ± 31, AA106194, wood charcoal, $\delta^{13}C$ = -24.2)[1]. The hearth was also associated with Aztec II Black-on-Orange ceramics, which are characteristic of the Hai phase at Xaltocan (table 10.1). Combined, these data firmly place the hearth sometime between 1200 and 1350 CE, the period during which Xaltocan was still an autonomous city-state and long before the formation of the Aztec Triple Alliance.

There are aspects of this particular hearth that are suggestive of ritual purposes. First, the high-quality construction of the hearth is uncharacteristic of utilitarian cooking hearths found elsewhere at Xaltocan or throughout the Basin of Mexico. Central Mexican hearths dating to the Postclassic period are normally composed of a grouping of rocks (often three large stones; see chapter 4, this volume, for more on hearths), typically recovered in a context with considerable ash, scorched earth, or carbon. They are commonly also in spaces that otherwise may be associated with cooking activities or food preparation, which may include the remains of animal bone fragments or fish scales,

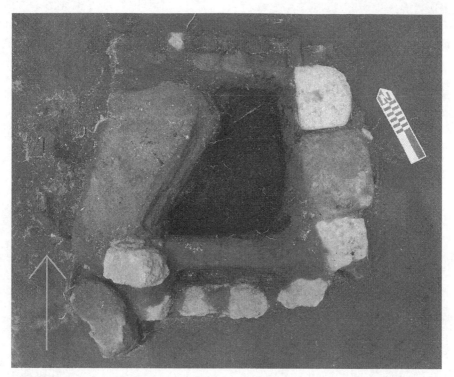

FIGURE 10.4. *Ceremonial hearth overlapping Altar 6 (see arrow) located in exterior patio north of the room containing the other five altars.*

charred corncobs or other plant remains, and chemical residues associated with cooking areas. Second, I suggest that there was a symbolic link among the placement of the hearth, the decoration with ceramic fragment strips running along the northern and southern edges, and the altar. Specifically, the placement of the hearth, which overlaps part of the altar, might be an indication that the hearth was constructed as a newer iteration of the altar. Perhaps more compelling, however, are the ceramic fragments. Archaeologists have not noted the use of ceramic fragments in the construction of hearths elsewhere in Xaltocan or in the Basin of Mexico. Discoveries made in the room to the south are indicative that Xaltocan's leaders used ceramic fragments to outline ritual spaces, and if this was the case with the ceramic fragments on the hearth, then that means the hearth was constructed for ritual purposes.

The hearth was also found in association with a large ritual deposit, further bolstering the interpretation that it was probably used for ritual purposes.

Traits of this deposit fit the criteria set forth by Elson and Smith (2001) for a New Fire deposit. The deposit was recovered about 1.5 m south of the hearth and just north of the enclosed room that contained the altar features. It contained of a number of ceramic vessels, including some that could be reconstructed, an indication that they may have been complete when they were originally placed and possibly broken while they were deposited (table 10.2). It also contained a bone rasp, a grinding stone with stucco on the surface, and a figurine fragment. While some of the objects recovered in the deposit were uncommon (a finely decorated ceramic goblet, for example), they were all household goods. The deposit also contained a high percentage of Black-on-Orange pottery, which both Brumfiel (2007, 2011) and Kristin De Lucia (2014) linked to solar cycles and the divinatory 260-day calendar (tonalpohualli), evidence that further supports the interpretation that this deposit was produced during a New Fire Ceremony. Near the surface of the deposit, large stones were mixed in, and they may have served to cap or mark it. Large stones were rare at Xaltocan because they did not exist naturally on the island and must have been imported from the mainland. The use of such costly resources to mark this deposit reinforces the interpretation that it did indeed pertain to a New Fire Ceremony.

DISCUSSION

Recent archaeological findings at Xaltocan contribute to the growing corpus of data confirming that iterations of the New Fire Ceremony already existed in the Basin of Mexico before the formation of the Aztec Triple Alliance. The discoveries at Xaltocan are especially notable because they reflect the aspects of the ceremony that were conducted and controlled by Xaltocan's leaders and thereby facilitate productive avenues for comparative analysis that have been previously unavailable. As noted above, ethnohistorical documents provide information concerning the role of Aztec leaders in conducting the New Fire Ceremony. The documents give information on how the leaders elaborated aspects of the ceremony to strategically emphasize their authority, religious capability, and political power to unite an ethnically diverse empire. Comparison of the material remains recovered at Xaltocan with the ethnohistorical records of the Aztec New Fire Ceremony demonstrates continuities and differences in the respective ceremonies, which may also speak to diversity in sociopolitical organization and the nature of leadership.

The remains recovered from Cerrito Central do not reflect all of the activities involved in what was likely a geographically expansive ceremony, probably

TABLE 10.2. Objects recovered from New Fire deposit at Cerrito Central.

Complete or Reconstructable Objects	Quantity
Aztec II Black-on-Orange *molcajete*	3
Aztec II Black-on-Orange plate	2
Black-and-White-on-Red bowl	1
Black-and-White-on-Red copa	1
Bone rasp	1
Figurine (partial)	1
Large olla (with doughnut handles at rim)	1
Mano (grinding stone) with plaster	1
Serpent-handled censer	1
Small olla	1
Other Objects	
Utilitarian ware (fragments)	237
Decorated ware (fragments)	29
Large stones (>20 cm diameter)	7
Obsidian blades (Pachuca green)	6

involving numerous locations in Xaltocan and throughout the surrounding landscape. They do, however, provide some insight into how the leaders of Xaltocan situated themselves within the context of the ritual. The hearth, which might have served as the principal vessel from which the flames of the Xaltocan New Fire were disseminated throughout the community, was in a partially enclosed patio. Although the patio space was much more open and accessible than the small enclosed room to the south, which apparently housed more private rituals in the decades leading up to the New Fire Ceremony at Xaltocan, it was still not open or completely visible to the public.

In this regard, the Xaltocan New Fire Ceremony was markedly different from the Aztec ceremony. Aztec leaders apparently took great care to ensure that the flames of the New Fire were as widely visible as possible. These efforts included moving the original fire from the chest cavity of the sacrificial victim (an understandably small receptacle) to a large pyre and then carrying the flames from Huixachtlan down to the Fire Temple and the Temple of Huitzilopochtli at Tenochtitlan, where they would have been widely visible to people living in the capital city. For the Aztecs, visibility of the New Fire was essential because it served as potent political propaganda, and wide viewership was necessary to the successful spread of such messages. In the case of Xaltocan, perhaps the New Fire Ceremony was not intended to meet the same political ends but may have held related messaging regarding light, darkness, and mythology. The location of the cloistered room to the south of the hearth is an indication that certainly some rituals conducted by Xaltocan's leaders were intentionally hidden from public view, and some of their symbol systems appear to have been esoteric (e.g., the use of ceramic fragments to outline ritual space). Thus it is possible that at Xaltocan, the lighting of the New Fire was not an event intended for wide viewership. Alternatively, it is also possible that Xaltocan's New Fire Ceremony took place in a more public location, perhaps one more akin to Huixachtlan, and that the hearth found at Cerrito Central represents the secondary receptacle for the fire (more similar to receptacles at the Fire Temple of the Temple of Huitzilopochtli at Tenochtitlan). In this case, the hearth might have housed the fire that would eventually be disseminated throughout the local community of Xaltocan. The patio space, while small, may have allowed heads of households to enter with torches and to carry New Fire flames back to their homes.

Regardless of whether the hearth served as the primary or secondary receptacle for the Xaltocan New Fire, clearly the fire was more sequestered than was the case for the Aztec New Fire. Perhaps this was in part because the smaller, more contained space was better shielded from the winds that swept across the Basin of Mexico, protecting the ritual flames from being quickly extinguished. It might also indicate that Xaltocan's leaders tightly controlled ritual practices to the extent of even hiding them. If this was the case, then perhaps Xaltocan's leaders did not rely on the New Fire Ceremony to emphasize or reinforce their political authority in the same fashion as the Aztecs, although it was possibly symbolic of renewal and tied to myths of the emergence of the world from darkness.

To date, there is no evidence that human sacrifice was a central component of the Xaltocan New Fire Ceremony. While a lack of evidence does not mean that human sacrifice was not involved, it may be the case that human sacrifice was far less prevalent at Xaltocan than it was at Tenochtitlan. The patron deity of Tenochtitlan, Huitzilopochtli, was the god of war and human sacrifice; among the Aztecs, human sacrifice was a central component of religious practice that was certainly used as another means of political propaganda. For Xaltocan, however, it is unclear if human sacrifice was ever an integral aspect of religious practice. Although some ethnohistorical sources cite instances when the Xaltocan army took war captives (Anales de Cuauhtitlan 1992, 60, 62), it is unclear whether they were sacrificed.

Furthermore, although Xaltocan was involved in conflicts with neighboring polities from time to time, little evidence has been found there for violent deaths, even those related to warfare. This lack of evidence may be partially attributed to the fact that many violent deaths linked to warfare occurred outside the central city and happened instead near the frontiers of Xaltocan's domain. It is also possible that although violent skirmishes may have been common during this period, the frequency with which they occurred resulted in a relatively low mortality rate. Whatever the reason, it certainly seems plausible that human sacrifice was simply not a central component of the Xaltocan New Fire Ceremony. Perhaps other Basin of Mexico polities also refrained from human sacrifice in their New Fire ceremonies. Even with the lack of evidence, it is certainly possible that the Aztecs incorporated human sacrifice into the ceremony when they adapted the ritual to fit their own political and religious narratives.

Although there are a number of apparent differences between the Aztec and Xaltocan versions of the New Fire Ceremony, considerable similarities existed as well. These similarities are noteworthy because they reveal those aspects of the ritual that were perhaps most essential and that endured over time, even as the ritual was co-opted by diverse ethnic groups and adapted to fit new political agendas. For example, a core component of the New Fire Ceremony, as it was practiced throughout Central Mexico, was the disposal of household goods. Ethnohistorians frequently mention that this practice took place among the Aztecs, especially the commoners. Archaeological evidence at Xaltocan (De Lucia 2011, 2014) and beyond (Elson and Smith 2001; Smith 1992; Vaillant 1937, 1938) proves that it was a characteristic component of the ritual long before the Aztec Empire rose to power. This process of disposing of domestic goods, which was almost certainly paired with the cleaning of homes and public spaces, indicates that at its core, the New Fire Ceremony has always been a rite of renewal.

Similarly, the notion of an origin fire, which was created, harnessed, and eventually dispersed by political leaders, appears to have been a significant component of both rituals. The Aztecs used a ritual hearth to house their New Fire at the Fire Temple in Tenochtitlan. An image from the Codex Borbonicus (1974) clearly illustrates how priests from surrounding villages descended on the Aztec New Fire with bundled twigs to carry the flames back to their home communities. The discovery of the ceremonial hearth at Xaltocan acts as evidence that Xaltocan's leaders were similarly the stewards of the New Fire and apparently controlled access to the sacred flames. From the continuity of the ritual, one can infer that the symbolical potency of the New Fire created a sense of unity, solidarity, and ostensibly loyalty that was a long-enduring and central aspect of the ritual.

CONCLUSIONS

The evidence presented in this chapter, particularly from recent excavations at Xaltocan, has expanded our knowledge of how New Fire ceremonies were performed in the Postclassic Basin of Mexico. When the Xaltocan and Aztec New Fire ceremonies are compared, differences and similarities emerge. Variations in how the ritual was displayed to the public and the emphasis on human sacrifice demonstrate how the ceremony was dissimilarly used and valued within the two polities while indirectly highlighting broader differences in worldviews and political ideologies. Based on these differences, I reiterate that diversity in ritual practices existed in the Basin of Mexico during the Postclassic, and this finding should encourage archaeologists to make more in-depth inquiries into the everyday practices, worldviews, and political strategies of the inhabitants of Postclassic Basin of Mexico polities, especially of those that pre-dated the ascension of the Aztec Empire.

Perhaps more important, comparisons of the Xaltocan and Aztec versions of the New Fire Ceremony highlight aspects of the ceremony that were similar and endured over time, over space, and across ethnic boundaries. The recognition of these more salient characteristics of the New Fire Ceremony facilitates a greater understanding of the ritual's most fundamental purpose: renewal. Moreover, although political strategies and social values surrounding the ritual likely shifted over time and were especially dependent on the political structures and ideologies of the practicing group, it seems that creating and sustaining solidarity and a sense of unity may have always been a core component of the ceremony.

Aztec and Xaltocan New Fire ceremonies both took place during the night, and there is little doubt that darkness was an essential element of these rituals. Darkness served to highlight the brilliance of the New Fire, and it was only in the darkness of night that ritual practitioners could create a flame that shone brightly enough to symbolically reignite the world. Darkness also served as a balancing force, contributing to a setting wherein night and the light of the new cycle could coexist. Thus studies of symbolically potent and politically strategic New Fire ceremonies provide significant insights into how Mesoamericans conceived of dark settings and how darkness was strategically used to enhance certain ritual events.

REFERENCES

Alva Ixtlilxóchitl, Fernando de. 1975–1977. *Obras históricas*, ed. Edmundo O'Gorman. Mexico City: Universidad Nacional Autónoma de México.

Alvarado Tezozómoc, Hernando. 1975. *Crónica Mexiáyotl.* Mexico City: Universidad Nacional Autónoma México.

Anales de Cuauhtitlan. 1992. *History and Mythology of the Aztecs: The Codex Chimalpopoca.* Trans. John Bierhorst. Tucson: University of Arizona Press.

Anales de Tlatelolco. 2004. *Anales de Tlatelolco.* Mexico City: CONACULTA.

Barlow, Robert H. 1949. "El códice Azcatítlan." *Journal de a Societe des Americanistas* 38: 101–135.

Barlow, Robert H. 1999. "Textos De Xaltocan." In *Escritos Diversos*, ed. Jesús Monjarás Ruiz and Elena Límon, 169–195. Mexico City: Instituto Nacional de Antropología e Historia.

Berdan, Frances F. 1992. *The Codex Mendoza.* Berkeley: University of California Press.

Berdan, Frances F. 1994. "Economic Alternatives under Imperial Rule: The Eastern Aztec Empire." In *Economies and Polities in the Aztec Realm*, ed. Mary G. Hodge and Michael E. Smith, 291–312. Albany, NY: Institute for Mesoamerican Studies.

Berdan, Frances F. 2005. *The Aztecs of Central Mexico: An Imperial Society.* Belmont, CA: Thomson Wadsworth.

Berdan, Frances F., Richard E. Blanton, Elizabeth Hill Boone, Mary G. Hodge, Michael E. Smith, and Emily Umberger, eds. 1996. *Aztec Imperial Strategies.* Washington, DC: Dumbarton Oaks.

Bierhorst, John. 1992. *History and Mythology of the Aztecs: The Codex Chimalpopoca.* Tucson: University of Arizona Press.

Brumfiel, Elizabeth M. 2000. "Making History in Xaltocan." In *Working Together: Native Americans and Archaeologists*, ed. Kurt Dongoske, Mark Aldenderfer, and Karen Doehner, 181–190. Washington, DC: Society for American Archaeology.

Brumfiel, Elizabeth M. 2007. "Solar Disks and Solar Cycles: Spindle Whorls and the Dawn of Solar Art in Postclassic Mexico." In *Interpreting Household Practices: Reflections on the Social and Cultural Roles of Maintenance Activities*, ed. Sandra Monton Subías, Paloma González Marcén, Marina Picazo, and Margarita Sánchez-Romero, 91–113. Treballs d'Arqueologia 13. Barcelona: Universidad Autónoma de Barcelona.

Brumfiel, Elizabeth M. 2011. "Technologies of Time: Calendrics and Commoners in Postclassic Mexico." *Ancient Mesoamerica* 22 (1): 53–70.

Carrasco, Davíd. 1999. *City of Sacrifice: The Aztec Empire and the Role of Violence in Civilization.* Boston: Beacon.

Carrasco Pizana, Pedro. 1950. *Los Otomíes: Cultura e historia prehispánicas de los pueblos mesoamericanos de habla Otomiana*. Mexico City: Instituto Nacional de Antropología e Historia.

Codex Borbonicus. 1974. *Codex Borbonicus, Codices Selecti, 44*. Graz, Austria: Akademische Druck- u. Verlagsanstalt.

De Lucia, Kristin. 2011. "Domestic Economies and Regional Transition: Household Production and Consumption in Early Postclassic Mexico." PhD dissertation, Northwestern University, Evanston, IL.

De Lucia, Kristin. 2014. "Everyday Practice and Ritual Space: The Organization of Domestic Ritual in Pre-Aztec Xaltocan, Mexico." *Cambridge Archaeological Journal* 24 (3): 379–403.

Elson, Christina M., and Michael E. Smith. 2001. "Archaeological Deposits from the Aztec New Fire Ceremony." *Ancient Mesoamerica* 12 (2): 157–174.

Farah, Kirby. 2017. "Leadership and Community Identity in Postclassic Xaltocan, Mexico." PhD dissertation, University of California, Riverside.

Friedlander, Judith. 1990. "Pacts with the Devil: Stories Told by an Indian Woman from Mexico." *New York Folklore* 16 (1–2): 25–42.

Gillespie, Susan D. 1989. *The Aztec Kings: The Construction of Rulership in Mexica History*. Tucson: University of Arizona Press.

Hassig, Ross. 1995. *Aztec Warfare: Imperial Expansion and Political Control*. Norman: University of Oklahoma Press.

Hicks, Fredrick. 1994. "Xaltocan under Mexica Domination, 1435–1520." In *Caciques and Their People: A Volume in Honor of Ronald Spores*, ed. Joyce Marcus and Judith F. Zeitlan, 67–85. Ann Arbor: Museum of Anthropology, University of Michigan Press.

Martín del Campo, Edgar. 2009. "The Global Making of a Mexican Vampire: Mesoamerican, European, African, and Twentieth-Century Media Influences on the Teyollohcuani." *History of Religions* 49 (2): 107–140.

McGee, R. Jon. 1990. *Life, Ritual, and Religion among the Lacandon Maya*. Belmont, CA: Wadsworth.

McGee, R. Jon. 1998. "The Lacandon Incense Burner Renewal Ceremony: Termination and Dedication Ritual among the Contemporary Maya." In *The Sowing and the Dawning: Termination, Dedication, and Transformation in the Archaeological and Ethnographic Record of Mesoamerica*, ed. Shirley Boteler Mock, 41–46. Albuquerque: University of New Mexico Press.

Nicholson, Henry B. 1955. "Native Historical Traditions of Nuclear America and the Problem of Their Archeological Correlation." *American Anthropologist* 57 (3): 594–613.

Nicholson, Henry B. 1971. "Pre-Hispanic Central Mexican Historiography." In *Investigaciones contemporáneas sobre la historia de México: memorias de la tecera reunion de historiadores Mexicanos y Norteamericanos (1969)*, 38–81. Mexico City: Universidad Nacional Autónoma de México.

Overholtzer, Lisa. 2012. "Empires and Everyday Material Practices: A Household Archaeology of Aztec and Spanish Imperialism at Xaltocan, Mexico." PhD dissertation, Northwestern University, Evanston, IL.

Overholtzer, Lisa. 2013. "Archaeological Interpretation and the Rewriting of History: Deimperializing and Decolonizing the Past at Xaltocan, Mexico." *American Anthropologist* 115 (3): 481–495.

Pérez-Rocha, Emma, and Rafael Tena. 2000. *La nobleza indígena del centro de México después de la conquista*. Mexico City: Instituto Nacional de Antropología e Historia.

Plunket, Patricia. 2002. *Domestic Ritual in Ancient Mesoamerica*. Los Angeles: Cotsen Institute of Archaeology.

Preuss, Mary H. 2012. "The Lights Dim but Don't Go Out on the Stars of Yucatec Maya Oral Literature." In *Parallel Worlds: Genre, Discourse, and Poetics in Contemporary, Colonial, and Classic Period Maya Literature*, ed. Kerry M. Hull and Michael D. Carrasco, 449–470. Boulder: University Press of Colorado.

Rice, Prudence M. 1999. "Rethinking Classic Lowland Maya Pottery Censers." *Ancient Mesoamerica* 10 (10): 25–50.

Rodríguez-Alegría, Enrique. 2010. "Incumbents and Challengers: Indigenous Politics and the Adoption of Spanish Material Culture in Colonial Xaltocan, Mexico." *Historical Archaeology* 44 (2): 51–71.

Sahagún, Bernardino de. 1950–1982. *General History of the Things of New Spain: Florentine Codex*. Trans. Arthur J.O. Anderson and Charles E. Dibble. Salt Lake City: University of Utah Press.

Signorini, Italo. 1982. "Patterns of Fright: Multiple Concepts of Susto in a Nahua-Ladino Community of the Sierra de Puebla (Mexico)." *Ethnology* 21 (4): 313–323.

Smith, Michael E. 1992. *Archaeological Research at Aztec-Period Rural Sites in Morelos, Mexico*, vol. 1: *Excavations and Architecture*. Mexico City and Pittsburgh: Instituto Nacional de Antropología e Historia and University of Pittsburgh Press.

Stockett, Miranda K. 2007. "Performing Power: Identity, Ritual, and Materiality in a Late Classic Southeast Mesoamerican Crafting Community." *Ancient Mesoamerica* 18 (1): 91–105.

Taube, Karl. 2004. "Structure 10L-16 and Its Early Classic Antecedents: Fire and the Evocation and Resurrection of the K'inich Yax K'uk' Mo'." In *Understanding Early Classic Copan*, ed. Ellen E. Bell, Marcello A. Canuto, and Robert J. Sharer,

265–295. Philadelphia: University of Pennsylvania Museum of Archaeology and Anthropology.

Vaillant, George C. 1937. "History and Stratigraphy in the Valley of Mexico." *Scientific Monthly* 44: 307–324.

Vaillant, George C. 1938. "A Correlation of Archaeological and Historical Sequences in the Valley of Mexico." *American Anthropologist* 40: 535–573.

11

She was looking right at him!
He froze. But then he realized that the lights were all on, and she
   probably couldn't see him. She probably couldn't see much
   at all,
   other than the glare of the lights on the glass.
   She would only see him if she turned out the dining room
   light
Funny how that was the case.
   That she'd have to put herself in darkness in order to see.
—RACHEL KUSHNER, *TELEX FROM CUBA*[1]

What is primordial and essential is the idea of regeneration,
—MIRCEA ELIADE, *COSMOS AND HISTORY*[2]

Close to six decades after the 1521 Spanish conquest,
the Spanish Franciscan Bernardino de Sahagún in
Mexico recorded, in the alphabetic script of his coun-
trymen, testimony of the Nahuatl-speaking natives
known today as the Aztecs (figure 0.1 and table 0.1).[3]
One of the many topics Sahagún addressed was the
Aztec practice of ritually confessing a misdeed in
hopes of reversing the misfortune believed to result
from it. The confession was prescribed by a soothsayer
(*tlapouqui*, pl. *tlapouque*), who, having consulted a divinatory manuscript, instructed the penitent to remove
his or her clothing at midnight on a particular date
and go forth to a crossroads to fast and make offerings
to Tloque Yohualli Ehecatl, "Our Lord the Night, the
Wind." Although the lord of the night and the wind
was himself invisible, his ability to see all is revealed

Under Cover of Darkness

*Blindfolds and the
Eternal Return in Late
Postclassic Mexican Art*

CECELIA F. KLEIN

DOI: 10.5876/9781646421879.c011

by a penitent's query to him: "Can these things [my secrets] be [kept] hidden, can they be darkened, when that which I have perpetrated is reflected, is clear in thy sight" (Sahagún 1950–1982, book 1, 27, book 2, 25).[4]

Neither Sahagún nor any other Colonial source says that the eyes of the soothsayer's client—or those of the soothsayer or the deity invoked for divine assistance—were covered at such times. Nonetheless, some pre-conquest and Early Colonial Aztec manuscript paintings include depictions of both human and divine figures wearing a blindfold. Beginning with Eduard Seler (e.g., 1902–1903, 144) at the turn of the twentieth century, previous writers have emphasized, largely on the basis of early Colonial texts, that the blindfolds on these figures are signs of—in their words—"guilt," "sin," "transgression," or "punishment."[5] The understanding is beyond question, for as these scholars have made clear, there is incontrovertible evidence that blindfolds in Aztec imagery identify their wearer, at one level, as having committed a grievous error.

As far back as 1976, however, Thelma Sullivan (1976, 259) warned that Early Colonial understandings of sin and transgression were substantially shaped by Christian theological tenets rather than pre-conquest Nahuatl beliefs, and Louise Burkhart (1989, 28, 177) later pointed out that the Nahuatl word *tlatlacolli*, which the Spaniards translated as "sin" (*pecado*), actually means "something damaged."[6] The damages were usually written on the body of the miscreant or on a loved one in the form of a specific sexual or reproductive disease or deformity cognitively linked to the infraction, but they often affected the eyes, either dimming the unfortunate's vision or causing blindness and a descent into total darkness (Graulich 1983, 577).[7] Burkhart points out, however, that because cleanliness and impurity were embedded in the same principle, it was possible to undo or reverse the damages they suffered. James Maffie (2014, 12–13, 137–140) labels this principle of "dual, mutually competitive, interdependent, and engendering polarities" as "agonistic inamic unity."

Accordingly, I propose that blindfolds did not only signify that a serious error had occurred. Rather, they simultaneously signaled a possibility of undoing the harm it had caused. To make this argument, I draw extensively on observations made by previous writers, to whom I am deeply indebted, but I do so to make a new point. Blindfolds could signal the erasure or reversal of misfortune, I suggest, because by virtue of being temporarily blinded, wearers were ritually returned to the darkness of the Creation. The Anales de Cuauhtitlan, the Leyenda de los soles, and the Historia de los Mexicanos por sus pinturas—all Early Colonial documents reflecting beliefs prominent in the Aztec capital, Tenochtitlan—state that the earth lay in near or total darkness for twenty-six years before the sun was born.[8] Similar beliefs recorded for other indigenous groups in Mexico and the Maya area suggest that the concept of a dark, "pre-sunrise" period was pan-Mesoamerican. For example, the Popol Vuh, an eighteenth-century Spanish transcription of a K'iche Maya text recording pre-conquest beliefs, contains a story of the very beginning of time that gives an account of the belief (?) that "all lies placid and silent in the darkness, in the night" (Christenson 2007, 68).[9]

Although the Aztecs often associated darkness with confusion, chaos, illness, and sorcery, they also perceived it as potentially generative.[10] It was, after all, in the darkness of the Creation that the primordial divine couple created not only the rest of the gods but also all of the world's plants, foods, beverages, medicines, and the first humans (Bierhorst 1992, 146–147; Boege 1988, 90–91). The belief was not confined to the Aztecs. Johannes Neurath (2000, 70) notes, for example, that the Huichols of West Mexico, who like the Aztecs speak a Uto-Aztecan language, still regard "the dark zone" not only as the place where the dead go but also as "the most fertile place in the universe."

No surviving Colonial written source specifically states that the Aztecs believed a blindfold returned one to the healing darkness of the Creation. Nonetheless, a picture, as the saying goes, is worth a thousand words. A good example is the scene at the top right of page 66 of the Codex Borgia, a pre-conquest manuscript painted by and for pre-conquest Nahuatl speakers living in Tlaxcala or Puebla, which gives its name to the so-called Borgia Group of divinatory manuscripts (figure 11.1).[11] The scene is one of a number of pre- and early post-conquest manuscript paintings in which one or more small, naked, and anonymous human figures appear in the company of a much larger, fully dressed deity.[12] Some of these little humans wear blindfolds, as do some of the deities who accompany them. Previous scholars have suggested that the smaller figures in these scenes accord well with Sahagún's description of the naked penitents who, in the darkness of night, sought the help of the Lord of the Night, the Wind.[13] As such they represent ordinary, "generic" persons who, as a result of having committed a major offense, have presumably incurred physical damages inflicted by the attending god or goddess, who they hope will reverse them.

Tezcatlipoca

The Lord of the Night, the Wind to whom the above-quoted petition was addressed was Tezcatlipoca, an important male deity whose personal name means "Mirror Smoking."[14] Tezcatlipoca was also sometimes addressed as Tloque Nahuaque, "Lord of the Near and the Nigh," according to Arthur

FIGURE 11.1. *Itzpapalotl and two penitents, detail of Codex Borgia 66 (from Díaz and Rodgers 1993, courtesy, Dover Publications)*

Anderson and Charles Dibble (in Sahagún 1950–1982 books 6–7, 12, 18, 24–25, 33, 41–43).[15] The personal name refers to a mirror (*tezcatl*) made of the dark volcanic glass we know as obsidian (*itztli*), which by reversing the real world was believed to offer a view into the darkness of the Creation, the underworld, and a person's fate (Olivier 2003, 252–259). In his most common pictorial guise, which does not include a blindfold, Tezcatlipoca typically wears a stylized smoking obsidian mirror attached to his temple, replacing his right foot, or both. The god also wears a diagnostic double-eagle-feather head ornament called an *axtexelli* and sports face paint in the form of broad horizontal bands or stripes. A large cut-shell ring called an *anahuatl* usually hangs down over the front of his torso (figure 11.2).

It was precisely because Tezcatlipoca himself had long ago committed a grievous offense that he was qualified to judge humans who made similar mistakes. His impropriety was, in other words, the divine prototype for those mistakes. The commentator of the Early Colonial Codex Telleriano-Remensis tells us on folio 18v that the god was a son of the creator couple who, along with his siblings, had fallen from heaven after "eating roses" in the primordial garden (Quiñones Keber 1995, 25).[16] Eating and picking roses were Nahua euphemisms for sexual wrongdoing. Exactly what kind of roses Tezcatlipoca picked is never stated, but one weeping Nahua penitent is said to have addressed him as "wretched sodomite" (Sahagún 1950–1982, book 3, 76, book 4, 35).[17] Tezcatlipoca is even blamed in several Aztec myths for introducing the Aztecs to what the Spaniards called the "nefarious sin"; in another source he

FIGURE 11.2. *Tezcatlipoca,*
detail of Codex Borgia 21
(from Díaz and Rodgers 1993,
courtesy, Dover Publications)

reportedly changed into a woman to seduce his enemy.[18] The implication is that Tezcatlipoca had a feminine side, which may explain why, as we see below, the only other Aztec deity to appear blindfolded in painted manuscripts—the goddess Tlazolteotl, "Divine Filth"—was also addressed as Tloque Nahuaque. All of the deities who ever wear a blindfold are aspects or variants of either Tezcatlipoca or Tlazolteotl.[19]

Tezcatlipoca's scandalous behavior in the darkness of the Creation explains why commoners blamed him for many of the physical "damages" they suffered. In particular, they charged him with causing illnesses affecting the anal and genital regions, such as hemorrhoids and what one Spanish writer slyly refers to as "the itch." A related problem was pustules, a common symptom of vene-real diseases (*tlapalanaltiliztli*) such as syphilis (*Treponema palladium*).[20] The illnesses occurred, we are told, because "someone had forsaken his promises, broken a fast," or "some man had lain with a woman, some woman had lain with a man" (Sahagún 1950–1982, book 3, 11–12). Presumably, they could also befall someone who slept with a member of the same sex.[21] In all cases, the Aztecs apparently thought Tezcatlipoca enjoyed their suffering, for Sahagún (1950–1982, book 6, 2), says he "taketh pleasure, delighteth in the castigation." Seler (1900–1901, 91) accordingly describes the god as "the emblem of aveng-ing justice."[22]

Because impurity and purity were embedded in the same principle, however, it was to Tezcatlipoca that these same unfortunates turned for a cure (Durán

1971, 97–99; Sahagún 1950–1982, book 3, 12). The cure was cast metaphorically as a return from darkness to the light and from death and to new life, with the confessor restored to the purity of a newborn human child, animal, or plant:

> Thou has come to appear; for thou hast descended into, thou hast beheld the land of the dead, the heavens. Now our lord hath caused the sun to shine, hath caused the dawn to break. Now thou causest the sun to appear, to come forth. Now once again thou art rejuvenated, thou emergest as a child. Once again thou becomest as a baby . . . Once again, newly, thou dost sprout, thou art hatched, thou art born on earth. (Sahagún 1950–1982, book 6, 32)[23]

In other words, the Lord of the Night, the Wind, by virtue of his/her own primordial peccadillos, was not only held responsible for those of humans but also had the power to undo the damages they caused.

It was at these times, I submit, that Tezcatlipoca was envisioned as blindfolded (ixquimilli). We see him wearing a blindfold on page 1 of the reverse side of the Codex Porfirio Díaz and on the upper right of page 15 of the Codex Borgia. The latter is one of a set of five "scenes" occupying the upper two registers of the page, each scene depicting a deity pulling a long, wrinkled yellow-brown tube from the abdomen of a much smaller, completely naked figure (figure 11.3). The set is essentially cognate to similar sets of scenes in the Codex Fejérváry-Mayer, pages 26–27, and the Codex Vaticanus B (Codex Vaticanus 3773), pages 38–40, which are likewise members of the Borgia Group of manuscripts.

Tezcatlipoca is easily recognized in the Codex Borgia 15 image by virtue of the obsidian mirror at his temple, his horizontal facial stripes, his *aztexelli* head ornament, and his anahuatl pectoral. The cognate scene on Fejérváry-Mayer 27 again features Tezcatlipoca, clearly identified by his facial stripes, aztexelli, and anahuatl. Here, however, the god's eyes are not literally covered; rather, they are missing altogether (figure 11.4). Missing eyes commonly served as an alternative to the blindfold in Aztec manuscripts. We see this, for example, in the figure of Tezcatlipoca on page 12 of yet another Borgia Group manuscript, the Codex Laud. Eyes that weep conveyed a similar message. A weeping woman named Ixnextli, "Eyes Blinded with Ashes," who appears on folio 11r of the Codex Telleriano-Remensis holding a bowl of excrement (*cuitlatl*), is described by a commentator as "always crying" because she "sinned by picking the roses" (Quiñones Keber 1995, 260). As becomes clear below, the excrement she holds represents her error.

I suggest that the blindfold covering Tezcatlipoca's eyes on Borgia 15, like his missing eyes on Codex Fejérváry-Mayer 27, not only reminds us that he

FIGURE 11.3.
*Tezcatlipoca
disemboweling penitent,
detail of Codex Borgia
15 (from Díaz and
Rodgers 1993, courtesy,
Dover Publications)*

FIGURE 11.4.
*Tezcatlipoca
disemboweling penitent,
detail of Codex
Fejérváry-Mayer 27.
National Museums
Liverpool (from Codex
Vaticanus 3773, page
39, detail from Seler
1901–1902)*

long ago committed a serious error but also tells us that, precisely for that reason, he has the power to undo the damage suffered by the smaller figure for having made a similar mistake. To explain why I think the blindfold represents a past error, we need to hone in on the action occurring in all three cognate sets, as well as the setting in which the act is carried out, the identities and meanings of the materials and other objects involved, and the context and probable use of the images themselves. To begin, it is important to note that the smaller figure in the Borgia 15 scene also wears a blindfold and that he sits partially in, partially out of, a dark rectangular field studded with round, half-lidded eyeballs. The eyeballs, a well-known Aztec pictorial convention for stars, function here to identify the dark area as the darkness of night. In the cognate scene on page 27 of the Codex Fejérváry-Mayer, the presence of a skull embedded in the dark field suggests that the dark zone further represents the underworld (figure 11.4). For the Aztecs, as for other Mesoamerican groups, including the Huichols, the darkness of night and the underworld was also synonymous with the darkness of the Creation, a time when, we are told, the gods were "still in their bones" (García Icazbalceta 1891, 229, 232). Because the smaller figures in these scenes are partly in and partly outside the dark rectangle, I take their positions to be a strong indication that they are either entering or emerging from the darkness as a result of the action taken by Tezcatlipoca.

ITZTLACOLIUHQUI

In the cognate scene in Codex Vaticanus B 39, the smaller naked figure lies on its back, but it is similarly represented as partly in and partly outside of the dark area (figure 11.5). This posture and its closed eyes, like the skull floating in the darkness on Codex Fejérváry-Mayer 27, appear to indicate that it is entering or emerging from a ritual death. The larger figure in this scene, which is blindfolded with vertical facial stripes, may at first glance look quite different from Tezcatlipoca, but it, too, wears the telltale aztexelli in its hair. Although it has no smoking mirrors, it is widely recognized as the variant, or aspect, of Tezcatlipoca called Itztlacoliuhqui, "Everything Has Become Curved [or Bent] by Means of Obsidian" (Andrews and Hassig 1984, 229; Olivier 2003, 117–118; Quiñones Keber 1995, 264, folio 16v; Seler 1902–1903, 261, 1963, 1:123).[24] J. Richard Andrews (2003, 600) explains that obsidian was "a metaphor . . . for coldness or . . . frost."[25] The Aztecs believed that extreme cold caused blindness, cataracts, and other eye ailments (Sahagún 1950–1982, book 10, 144).

Itztlacoliuhqui's curious moniker is "spelled out" in other images by his curved, vertically striped conical cap edged with obsidian blades, which Thelma

FIGURE 11.5. *Itztlacoliuhqui disemboweling penitent, detail of Codex Vaticanus B 39 (https://www.vatlib.it/home.php?pag=sezione_editoria&ling =eng; from Seler 1902–1903)*

Sullivan (1976, 253) thinks represents an obsidian knife.[26] In most cases, his eyes are again missing. Only his nose ornament in the form of the waxing or waning crescent moon (*yacametztli*, "nose moon") remains visible on his face to link him to the night and to darkness. In most depictions, the god also holds a broom consisting of a bunch of the wild, twisted grass known as *malinalli*; and one or two spindles, usually with cotton (*ichcatl*) balls attached, typically protrude from his hat. On Codex Borbonicus 12, he wears a full-body suit and headdress with earflaps of raw, unspun cotton (figure 11.6). This image is significant because malinalli and raw cotton, by virtue of their lack of structure, at one level connoted sexual chaos among the Aztecs (Burkhart 1989, 93; Sullivan 1976, 257, 1982, 14). This interpretation accords with the Spanish comment on Codex Telleriano-Remensis, folio 16v, that Itztlacoliuhqui's eyes are covered because he "sinned in paradise" (Quiñones Keber 1995, 264). Another commentator tells us that Itztlacoliuhqui ruled the twelfth 13-day period, or *trecena*, of the 260-day divinatory calendar (*tonalpohualli*), 1 Lizard

FIGURE 11.6. *Itztlacoliuhqui as patron of the twelfth* trecena, *1 Lizard, detail of Codex Borbonicus 12 (from Nowotny 1974, courtesy, Bibliothèque Nationale de France)*

(ce cuetzpalin), because "like the lizard he went about naked." The Aztecs associated lizards with sexual excess and gluttony.[27]

Itztlacoliuhqui's primordial error apparently involved adultery (*tetlaximaliz-tli*) because a third comment on Telleriano-Remensis 16v says that unrepentant adulterers were punished before his image. Two naked adulterers, who have been stoned to death, accordingly appear on the adjacent folio, 17r, just as two others lie on the ground in front of the god on Codex Borbonicus 12. Nahuatl speakers believed adultery could cause eye problems, including blindness, which they referred to as "filth disease of the eyes" (*ixtlazolcocoliztli*). Newborns were especially vulnerable (DiCesare 2009, 74).[28] The Nahuatl speakers studied by William Madsen (1960, 81, 191) in the 1950s still believed adultery could lead to blindness in a newborn. The belief was likely rooted in the real-life tendency for venereal diseases such as syphilis to eventually lead to blindness.

Itztlacoliuhqui's sins must also have included imbibing too much alcohol, for he appears blinded—that is, without eyes—on page 12 of the Tonalamatl Aubin, sitting in front of not only a naked and wounded adulteress but also a nearly naked man drinking pulque, the frothy fermented beverage made from the maguey plant.[29] Both miscreants in this scene have been stoned. The Aztecs understood very well that too much pulque could lead to licentious behavior. Sahagún (1950–1982, book 6, 68), for example, writes of the drunkard: "Behold: one [desireth] another's woman; one committeth adultery." In addition to becoming prone to cursing, shouting, stealing, bragging, disrespect, and gluttony, the drunkard might even sell his breechclout (1950–1982, book 4, 11).[30] The Aztecs believed people who drank to excess would be repaid not only with nausea, confusion, palsy, and mental illness but also with burning, aching, drooping, glazed, or inflamed eyes.[31] On the other hand, although we have no written record of an Aztec drunkard seeking relief from Itztlacoliuhqui, the god's willingness and ability to provide it are implicit in his images. The malinalli he holds, for example, represents the kind of broom actually used by Aztec women to remove dirt (Burkhart 1989, 117–124; Peterson 1983, 113–120). Even today, a Nahuatl-speaking curer in the Huasteca region of Veracruz uses brooms made of split palm leaves to cleanse his patients of disease (Sandstrom 1989, 360). In Itztlacoliuhqui's hand, the broom signifies his power to eradicate both physical and moral "filth."

Patecatl

Unsurprisingly, the most important Aztec pulque god Patecatl is likewise depicted on page 13 of the Tonalamatl Aubin and page 11 of the Codex Borbonicus with his eyes and other features missing; only a large, lunar crescent nose ornament appears on his face (figure 11.7).[32] Patecatl's name, which means "He from the Land of Medicines" according to Seler (1900–1901, 87, 190–198), comes from *patli*, "medicine or 'medicine herb.' The name alludes to the Aztec belief that it was Patecatl who discovered *oc-patli*, the stalks and roots of the maguey plant that are added to pulque to help it ferment." Like the other pulque gods, Patecatl appears in painted manuscripts wearing a necklace and sometimes a headband made of malinalli. Although the reasoning behind the association of malinalli with pulque is unclear, it was strong: Patecatl was the divine patron of the day sign Malinalli and the consort of Mayahuel, "Powerful Flow," the female personification of the maguey plant, who in turn ruled the thirteen-day period 1 Malinalli (*ce malinalli*). The Malinalli day sign is sometimes represented as a skeletal lower jaw combined

FIGURE 11.7. *Patecatl as patron of the eleventh* trecena, *1 Monkey, detail of Tonalamatl Aubin 13 (from Loubat 1900–1901, courtesy, Ancient Americas at the Los Angeles County Museum of Art)*

with a dangling, gouged-out eyeball.[33] Eyes that dangle from their socket seem to have had essentially the same meaning as eyes that are blindfolded, weeping, or simply absent.

In a number of painted manuscripts, including the Tonalamatl Aubin (page 13), Patecatl, like many of the other pulque gods depicted in the Codex Magliabechiano, holds a long object representing an axe.[34] An axe also appears in the enigmatic scenes described at the beginning of this chapter, one in the hand of the blindfolded Tezcatlipoca in Codex Fejérváry-Mayer 27 and another planted on a stand in front of Itztlacoliuhqui on Codex Vaticanus B 39. Seler (1900–1901, 90) was the first scholar to interpret the axe as an Aztec symbol of "punishment" and "justice." He based his opinion on the Nahuatl expression *tetl quauitl*, "stone and wood," a reference to the two primary materials used to make an axe. Telling, however, is the warning to an Aztec worker: "If thou dost not do . . . [a good job] . . . thou shalt become blind; thy knees, thy legs will become crippled." You will "looketh into stones [and] wood."

The warning concludes: "Take care not . . . to covet another's wife, another's daughter" (Sahagún 1950–1982, book 9, 57). The warning can be interpreted to mean that the axe specifically threatened the worker with blindness and deformed limbs. Like blindness, twisted and bent joints of the wrists, hands, legs, feet, and toes are commonly caused by venereal diseases such as syphilis (Klein 2001, 208–209; Mansilla et al. 2000, 2; McCafferty and McCafferty 1999, 120–121).

EXCREMENT

But what, exactly, are Tezcatlipoca and Itztlacoliuhqui doing to the smaller figures in the cognate scenes on Codices Borgia 15, Fejérváry-Mayer 26–27, and Vaticanus B 38–40? Most scholars, such as Elizabeth Boone (2007, 140–141), read the smaller figures in these scenes as infants and the wrinkled material being pulled from their abdomen as their umbilical cord. This is so because they appear next to a section showing goddesses nursing an infant. In an earlier article, however, I (Klein 1993, 24–25) argued—and I still believe—that the material being extracted is excrement and that the figures are unrelated to the nursing goddesses in the adjacent section. In the Codices Borgia and Vaticanus B, the material is the same color—and in the Codex Vaticanus B, where it is also stippled, the same "texture"—as excrement seen elsewhere in the same manuscript: yellow in the case of the substance issuing from the buttocks of a penitent on Codex Borgia, page 10, and a stippled yellow-brown on the right side of Codex Vaticanus B, page 29. Moreover, in the far right scene in the second register of Codex Vaticanus B 38, the smaller figure has been thrown backward over a sacrificial stone (*techcatl*). Blood spurts from its chest and pours down the front of the stone, an image I suggest of an adult person whose heart has been excised. In the cognate scene on Borgia 15, the smaller figure sits against, and drapes his arm over, a sacrificial stone. The implication is that the smaller figures in all three cognate sets are adults, as Seler (1963 [1904–1909], 1, 199–202) recognizes, rather than children. The Aztecs normally sacrificed children by strangulation or drowning, not by heart excision on a sacrificial stone.[35] The smaller figures here are therefore adult penitents.

While the frequency of depictions of excrement in these manuscripts may seem odd to us today, I (Klein 1990–1991, 81–86, 1993) have previously explained that the Aztecs believed their mistakes were, at least metaphorically, embedded in their excrement. Sahagún (1950–1982, book 4, 11, 1979, 1, folio 131), for example, describes the drunkard as having fallen into "ordure," an event depicted on folio 131 of the Florentine Codex. To reverse the damage a person's behavior had caused, the source of the filth had to be removed. In real life, as we saw above, this transformation was accomplished through a proscribed set of ritual actions dictated by a soothsayer, but in the visual images we have been studying, the artists make the same point by depicting the gods literally disemboweling their clients. The notion of disemboweling a miscreant would not have been unknown to the Aztecs, moreover, as they and other Mesoamericans apparently did, on occasion, disembowel people. Some of the victims were adulterers; others were men who played the passive role in homosexual encounters in the case of the Aztecs (Klein 1990–1991, 85–87). Among the Maya it was defeated enemies who were disemboweled (Schele and Miller 1984, 218, 228, 251, plate 94).

TLAZOLTEOTL

In the course of healing a patient, the deity, in effect, absorbed the errors embedded in its excrement. This action is implied on both page 12 of the Codex Borgia and page 91 of the Codex Vaticanus B, where a naked man not only vomits but also defecates on the blinded Tezcatlipoca. The Nahua goddess of illicit sex and drunkenness, Tlazolteotl, or "Filth Goddess," was said to "consume," or "eat," the errors—an act reflected in one of her alternate names, Tlaelquani, "Eater of Ordure." On page 28 of the Codex Fejérváry-Mayer, where she strangles a small naked figure, Tlazolteotl wears a curl of excrement at the tip of her nose. In the Codex Telleriano-Remensis, folio17v, where she appears as Ixcuina—"Divine Cotton" if the name originated among the Tenek (Huastecs) of Veracruz, "Mother of Twisted Face [or Eyes]" if it is Nahuatl—she holds a bowl containing human body parts and, like the weeping Ixnextli, a glob of excrement.[36] Elsewhere in the same manuscript (folio 12r), Tlazolteotl's disembodied head appears twice without eyes, whereas in the Codex Laud, page 42, she wears a blindfold while sitting on the back of a prone, apparently deceased or unconscious man and holding an axe (figure 11.8). Sahagún (1950–1982, book 1, 25) writes that the penitent who confessed to the goddess believed she perceived their "evil odor" and vices and describes the fast ordered by the soothsayer as starving the entrails.

Because the confessor's appeals for help were, like those to Tezcatlipoca, addressed to "Our Lord of the Near, the Nigh" as well as "the Night, the Wind," Tlazolteotl seems to represent the female aspect, or counterpart, of Tezcatlipoca. Like Itztlacoliuhqui and the pulque god Patecatl, moreover, she typically wears a lunar crescent nose ornament reflective of her role as the principal Aztec moon goddess (Thompson 1939).[37] Like them as well, she was

FIGURE 11.8. *Tlazolteotl sitting on penitent, detail of Codex Laud 42 (from Anders, Jansen, and Reyes García 1994, courtesy, the Bodleian Libraries, University of Oxford)*

associated with malinalli by virtue of her grass broom symbolizing the readiness to remove filth.[38] Tlazolteotl also typically wears a headband and, in some manuscript paintings, earflaps of raw, unspun cotton that further associate her with Itztlacoliuhqui, as do the one or two spindles she carries on her head. Katarzyna Mikulska (2001, 103) argues that because the word for cotton is closely related to that for maguey fiber, the raw cotton worn by all these deities reflects an association with the maguey plant.

According to a comment on Telleriano-Remensis 17v, Tlazolteotl had "caused everything evil and deceitful . . . before the flood," which tells us that, like Tezcatlipoca, she made a serious mistake back in the darkness of the Creation (Quiñones Keber 1995, 265).[39] Her mistake, like his, was apparently or primarily sexual, for glosses on the same folio describe her as a two-faced "shameless goddess" and "the goddess of evil women" who protected adulterers.[40] Sahagún (1950–1982, book 1, 23, 71, book 4, 74), in turn, identifies her as a "harlot" and a "mistress of lust and debauchery." Scholars often point to these charges as explanation for the numerous manuscript depictions of Tlazolteotl showing her either naked from the waist up, with her breasts exposed, or completely naked. In several manuscripts she is depicted sitting in a fully frontal (*en face*), or "displayed," view without any clothing and with her legs spread wide apart.[41] The exposure of her genitals in these scenes clearly testifies to her indecency, for in the Codex Borbonicus, page 13, where she is shown giving birth in a similarly displayed pose, her private parts are discreetly hidden by a large "bib" decorated with lunar crescents.

FIGURE 11.9. *Tlazolteotl as the first "sinner," Codex Borgia 31 (from Díaz and Rodgers 1993, courtesy, Dover Publications)*

BORGIA 31

I suggest that we see a stunning pictorial reference to Tlazolteotl's primordial debauchery and its potentially disastrous consequences on page 31 of the Codex Borgia (figure 11.9). The page is third in a series of eighteen pages (29–46), which are set apart from the rest of the manuscript by their 90-degree clockwise turn and large number of full-page compositions. Seler (1963 [1904–1909], 2, 9–61) dubbed them the "Venus pages" for reasons that have since been largely discredited. Exactly what they do present, however, is still controversial.[42] I agree with Boone (2006, 2007, 173–210) that most or all of them represent episodes in a now lost cosmogony that nonetheless correlate, in a number of respects, with Aztec creation myths recorded in the sixteenth century. In Boone's opinion, the first page of the series depicts an initial burst of primordial energy and power in the form of "dark winds" alluding to *yohualli ehecatl*, "the Night, the Wind," the common form of address for both Tezcatlipoca and Tlazolteotl. The second page of the series, according to Boone, presents the birth, or origin, of the 20-day count that, meshed with the numbers 1 through 13, made up the 260-day divinatory calendar.[43] Page 30 also shows the calendar being divided into quarters corresponding to the four world directions. The black, star-studded frames of these two pages make it clear that the events depicted on them occurred in darkness long before there was light and warmth in the world.

Boone (2007, 183) has little to say, however, about the third page in the series other than that it twice features Tlazolteotl giving birth.[44] The idea that the two fully frontal, naked, and displayed females, placed above the other in the center of the page, represent Tlazolteotl is evident from their diagnostic white, raw cotton headbands. Because their upturned profile heads face in opposite directions, however, the figures arguably illustrate two acts performed by the same goddess. Other than the orientation of the heads and the black limbs and hair of the figure in the upper compartment, which differ from the red limbs and hair of the figure below her, the two figures are almost identical. Both are clearly in trouble, for they have the skeletal lower jaw, tousled black hair, tiny hat with a protruding cone and tassel, and clawed hands and feet characteristic of death deities elsewhere in the manuscript. The same can be said of their offspring, one of whom seems to be emerging and two of whom are descending from the figure's heart in an upper compartment framed by a starry black band symbolizing darkness. In the lower compartment, which is framed by a starry red band, a single "baby" descends from a bleeding jewel (*chalchihuitl*) in her abdomen that symbolizes her womb. Although the eyes of all five newborns are wide open, their skin is solid black—the color of death and the underworld—and they, too, have skeletal jaws and clawed hands and feet.

Significantly, both of the displayed figures of Tlazolteotl on Borgia 31 wear a blindfold. Susan Milbrath (1999, 111, 2013, 45) relates their blindfolds to a lunar eclipse that was visible in Central Mexico on January 30, 1496, whereas Maarten Jansen and Gabina Pérez Jiménez (2017, 462–463), who interpret the page as a mystical "encounter," see them as allowing the goddess to focus "on the power of inner vision."[45] While either reading may have some validity, I think the first and foremost message sent by Tlazolteotl's blindfold is that she has made a serious, primordial sexual error, and we are seeing the disastrous consequences of her mistake in the form of offspring who are either dying or stillborn. The babies' unfortunate condition accords with that of the off-spring of a mortal adulterer, whose survival and good health, as noted above, was severely jeopardized by its parents' infidelity. In other words, Tlazolteotl's primordial error has resulted in a major reproductive catastrophe that will serve as the prototype of future damages potentially inflicted on all newborns, human and otherwise, because of a sexual impropriety.

Additional black-skinned babies to the right and left of Tlazolteotl send a similar message. In the left side of the upper compartment, as Seler (1963 [1904–1909], 2:14–15) was the first to recognize, we see two more blindfolded females, one a personification of the maguey plant and the other, below it, personifying malinalli. Both of the personified plants reach toward or hold a small black-skinned "baby" on their right that is almost identical to the infants issuing from Tlazolteotl. The babies on the left are distinguished from all the other babies only by their yellow tufted hair. Seler (1963 [1904–1909], 2:15, 219) suggests that the hair represents flames, although he identifies the similarly yellow curls of a bound and naked penitent on Codex Borbonicus 26 as excrement. I suggest instead that the little figures' curly yellow hair tells us that they are the dead or dying seeds, sprouts, or nubbins of the personified plants who reach out to them. Their hair closely resembles that of a tiny naked figure on Codex Borbonicus 13 who is depicted descending into the parturi-ent Tlazolteotl in a remarkable graphic reference to human conception and is commonly seen on the maize god Cinteotl (Centeotl), "Divine Maize," who, as we see below, represented the first seeds. Milbrath (2013, 81) associates it with youth. Thus although they sit beneath a stylized black coverlet that I suggest represents soil, the unfortunate seeds on Borgia 31 will never break through to grow to maturity.[46] A similar message is embedded in the left side of the lower compartment on Borgia 31, where the pose of two female personified maize plants, each reclining on (in) a large vessel in front of a skeletal clawed female dressed as a death goddess, tells us they are dead.[47] Throughout Mesoamerica, the reclining pose signaled death and sacrifice (Jordan 2013, 256–260, 262).

Seler (1963 [1904–1909], 2:14–15) suggests that the little black figures on the left side of Borgia 31 relate in some way to pulque and the maize beer chicha but does not pursue the point. On the right side of the page, however, brightly colored female figures, three of whom are skull-headed and one of whom is blindfolded, do pour black, nasty-looking liquids over three more black-skinned, partially skeletal "babies." I propose that these liquids are beverages or medicines, made almost certainly of pulque, for they are being poured out of two vessels shaped exactly like an Aztec pulque vessel (e.g., the pulque vase in front of Patecatl in the Tonalamatl Aubin 13). The fact that the pulque has spoiled is indicated by its dark color, for drinkable pulque is normally white. The stream of black liquid in the upper right compartment, in turn, probably represents another spoiled drink or medicine, possibly another beverage made from the maguey (e.g., agave syrup or mescal) or one of the drinks made from corn, such as the light-colored corn flour drink *atole* or the corn beer *tesgüino* (which may be the drink Seler mistakenly refers to as chicha).[48] Or it could refer to one of the liquids derived from the malinalli plant, which is also depicted on page 30, that were used to cure illnesses.[49] The message sent by page 31, if I am right, is that because Tlazolteotl made a very serious mistake at the beginning of time, the earth's vegetation—and, by implication, human babies as well—will always be in peril.[50]

In peril, but not inevitably doomed. Page 31 also carries a positive message. Personified maize, malinalli, and maguey plants reappear, healthy and brightly colored, on pages 33–34 and 41 of the same manuscript to show that the species did survive. This continuity means that mistakes like Tlazolteotl's could be reversed, that, at a second level, her blindfold implied the possibility of recovery and redress. This potential is symbolized by her lunar nose ornament, for as Mikulska (2001, 110) points out, although the moon disappears and "dies" for three nights in the course of its cycle, it always reappears as a virtually universal symbol of rebirth (see also Eliade 1959, 86–87). It was in her role of moon goddess that Tlazolteotl was tied to the periodic death and rebirth of vegetation and plant fertility, for the belief that both were in greatest danger when the moon disappears during the new moon phase or an eclipse was widespread in Mesoamerica (Klein 2001, 234; Mikulska 2001, 117; Milbrath 1999, 30).

The Aztecs applied the same logic to people. As a result, as we have seen, just as a parent's sexual indiscretion could result in misfortune for the pregnant woman, her husband, or their child, so could the offender, through the mediation of a midwife or a soothsayer, petition Tlazolteotl to remove it. This construal explains why Tlazolteotl's most important clients were pregnant and childbearing women, midwives, and female curers.[51] Under the name Toci, "Our Grandmother," for example, she "patronized those who brought about abortions" (Sahagún 1950–1982, book 1, 15, 70). As Tlalli iyollo, "Heart of the Earth," she could relieve miscarriages.[52] By the same logic, given the association of blindness with sexual excess, Tlazolteotl was also vital to physicians who cured eye ailments (1950–1982, book 1, 15, 70). In other words, like Tezcatlipoca, Tlazolteotl represented both the problem and its possible solution. Sahagún (1950–1982, book 1, 23–24) says that in addition to inspiring "evil and perverseness" in people, the goddess "forgave, set aside, removed [corruption]. She cleansed one; she washed one . . . And thus she pardoned, thus she set aside, she removed [corruption]."

THE CIHUATETEO

A similar ambivalence characterized Tlazolteotl's avatars, or close relatives, the female supernaturals known collectively as both the Cihuateteo, "Divine Women" (sing. Cihuateotl), and the Cihuapipiltin, "Princesses" (sing. Cihuapilli). Sahagún (1950–1982, book 2, 32) usually describes the goddesses as the angry, unhappy shades of women who, having died in childbirth, periodically descended to their crossroad shrines at midnight to inflict harm on pregnant women and small children.[53] We see five of them in the middle register of Codex Borgia 47–48 and in the bottom row of the cognate set in Codex Vaticanus B 77–78.[54] In the Codex Borgia only, they are preceded, on the far right of page 47, by a scene in which a small, naked, and blindfolded Cihuateotl wearing Tlazolteotl's white cotton headband and earflaps is being born from a large bowl set on an altar decorated with lunar crescents (figure 11.10).[55] The dark background of the scene tells us that the birth is occurring in the blackness of the Creation, and the newborn's blindfold tells us that she has committed a primordial transgression. The transgression was again surely adultery, for adulterers were told to confess their mistakes on a day when the Cihuateteo were expected to descend (Sahagún 1950–1982, book 1, 19, 26–27). In his Primeros Memoriales, Sahagún (1993, folio 271; Sahagún, Sullivan, and Nicholson 1997, 122) lists adultery as the sole attribute of the Cihuateteo.

Like that of Tlazolteotl on Codex Borgia 31, the Cihuateteo's physical appearance in both manuscripts connotes intense misery and anger. Not only is their upper torso naked, but their visible eye is hanging from its socket. The idea that they are dangerous is implied by the noxious items that spew from their mouths or breasts: an unidentifiable blackish liquid in one case; a centipede in another that, on Borgia 47, descends to a crossroad; a snake; and in two of the scenes, one or two streams of blood. In addition, all of the Cihuateteo in Vaticanus 77–78 wear a male loincloth (*maxtlatl*) under their skirt that symbolizes the failure to become a proper mother.[56] Particularly relevant here are the in-turned feet of the Cihuateotl on the far left of Vaticanus B 79 (figure 11.11). As Sharisse and Geoffrey McCafferty (1999, 120) point out, the feet probably signal damage to the joints of the legs and feet caused by venereal disease. Venereal disease would also account for a person becoming "cross-eyed or of weak vision," two additional health problems attributed to the Cihuateteo (Sahagún 1950–1982, book 2, 81).[57]

FIGURE 11.10. *Birth of the first Cihuateteo (bottom) and Macuiltonaleque (top), detail of Codex Borgia 47 (from Díaz and Rodgers 1993, courtesy, Dover Publications)*

We see the same kinds of damage on the small, black male figure on the far right of the topmost register in Borgia 47. In the pitch black of the Creation, the male figure is being born from a knife inside a cooking vessel. The figure's hands and feet are bent backward 180 degrees, and his visible eyeball hangs from its socket. As Seler (1963 [1904–1909], 2:79–81) notes, he represents the first of the male supernaturals known collectively as the Macuiltonaleque, "Five Souls" or "Five Days" (sing. Macuiltonalequi), who represented the male counterparts of the Cihuateteo. Aztec curers, John Pohl (1998, 197–198) points out, often ritually invoked the Macuiltonaleque along with the Cihuateteo and the Cihuapipiltin.[58] Sahagún's (1950–1982, book 1, 71–72) description of a person under the Cihuateteos' spell therefore applied just as aptly to someone damaged by the Macuiltonaleque. Such a person, he tells us, "was possessed, his mouth was twisted, his face contorted, he lacked use of a hand, his feet were misshapen, his feet were deadened, his hand trembled, he foamed at the mouth."[59] Like most of the other health problems listed here, deadening of the feet points to venereal disease, which can cause neuropathy (Hosein 2008).

In the Codices Borgia and Vaticanus, the blindfolds and disengaged eyeballs of the Cihuateteo and the Macuiltonaleque clearly speak to their destructive potential. Nonetheless, the Aztecs would have understood that they also had the power to avert danger. Pohl (1998, 197–198) points to Jacinto de la Serna's

FIGURE II.II. *Cihuateteo (bottom) and Macuiltonaleque (top), detail of Codex Vaticanus B 79 (from Loubat 1902–1903, courtesy, Ancient Americas at LACMA)*

(1987, 430) mid-seventeenth-century claim that the Cihuateteo, who descended on the day 1 Rain (ce quiahuitl), were conceived of as clouds that brought rain to recently sown crops. As corroboration, Pohl notes that Sahagún's (1979, book 4, fols. 27v, 62r) native Aztec artists portrayed the Cihuateteo as literally hovering in or descending from the clouds. The Aztecs understood that the Cihuateteo had what Pohl (1998, 202) calls a "dualistic disposition," which is why curers and midwives approached them for assistance. So necessary were the Cihuateteo to midwives that the latter reportedly made offerings to them in their own homes (Sahagún 1950–1982, book 2, 9). Included among illnesses caused by the Cihuateteo, most of which affected the sexual organs, were "clouded" eyes (Ruiz de Alarcón, in Andrews and Hassig 1984, 171).

This is why, on the nights when the Cihuateteo were expected to descend, penitents who had incurred damages left offerings at their crossroad shrines.[60] Those who confessed also left their undergarments there, which, according to a comment on folio 18v of the Codex Telleriano-Remensis, was "the sign that they had forsaken sin" (Quiñones Keber 1995, 265). Pictorial evidence that forgiveness and a cure were possible appears in the form of the malinalli brooms held by most of the Cihuateteo and the Macuiltonaleque on Codex Borgia 47–48 and Codex Vaticanus B 77–78. Their brooms, like those carried by Itztlacoloiuhqui and Tlazolteotl, signaled their ability to sweep away, or undo, the mistakes that had caused the problem.

MATERIALS AND OBJECTS

Like virtually all the materials and objects worn or held by blindfolded figures in the Borgia Group manuscripts, malinalli had intrinsic and literal curative properties.[61] Some of the properties pertained to childbirth: malinalli was, for example, used to prevent abortions (Peterson 1983, 121; Torquemada 1975, 3:433). According to Durán (1971, 401), those born on the day Malinalli were deemed likely to become seriously ill but were assured that if they did, they would recover—like "the wild grass, which dries up every year and then grows green again." Maffie (2014, 263), accordingly, describes malinalli as "transformative." When combined with "powdered ordure," it was applied to eyelids that had become "immobile," only one of the many instances in which excrement was employed to cure a problem with vision (Cruz, in Gates 2000 [1939], 18). Powdered human excrement was used, for example, to cure glaucoma, cataracts, ectropion, ulcers, white spots, opacity, and glazing of the eyes (Cruz, in Gates 2000 [1939], 16–17; López Austin 1988a, 1:179, 1988b, 63; Sahagún 1950–1982, book 1, 39). Similarly, lizard excrement mixed with lamp-black could remove films over the eyes, whereas when mixed with urine, it was a cure for epilepsy (López Austin 1988a, 1:31; Ortiz de Montellano 1990, 180; Sahagún 1993, folio 81r, 18v, 1950–1982, book 10, 144, book 11, 162; Sahagún, Sullivan, and Nicholson 1997, 290–294). So vital was human excrement to the Aztecs that they systematically collected it at way stations placed alongside their roads. They used the material not only for medicinal purposes but also, once it had decomposed and transformed into humus, as fertilizer in their fields (Harvey 1981).

A positive, transformative nature also characterized obsidian, the magical glass carried on the person of Tezcatlipoca in the form of the dark mirror that gives him his name and that was personified by Itztlacoliuhqui. The Aztecs believed, for example, that obsidian could protect infants still in the womb during an eclipse (Sahagún 1950–1982, book 7, 8–9; Saunders 2001, 224). Obsidian could also cure palsy and rheumatism and was said to counteract serious eye problems like cataracts (Hernández 1959, 407, 411; Ruiz de Alarcón, in Andrews and Hassig 1984, 176, 291).[62] The cotton plant, in turn, helped induce menstruation, uterine contractions, and lactation, as well as calm the bites of poisonous creatures such as scorpions and snakes (Hernández 1959, 426, 2000, 187; Sullivan 1982, 19, 24). Even sensations like coldness, the principal property of Itztlacoliuhqui, had curative properties. Cold water or some other cold substance, for example, was applied to the eyes in cases of discomforts like burning, disease, and blindness (Ruiz de Alarcón, in Andrews and Hassig 1984, 168).[63]

But it is the maguey plant that provides pulque and the dietary staple, maize, that give us the best insight into the dual meaning of the blindfold. Regarding the maguey and pulque, Guilhem Olivier (2000b) argues that although the Aztecs understood drunkenness as symptomatic of chaos and symbolic death, they also saw it as a promise of rebirth. The model, he suggests, was the drunkard himself, who seems to be dying but always recovers. The message of rebirth was encoded, Olivier notes, in the Aztec myth of the origin of the maguey plant. The Histoyre du Mechique (Jonghe 1905, 27–28) recounts how the creator god Ehecatl, "Wind," desirous of finding a drink that would make men happy, rescued the young virgin Mayahuel from her wicked grandmother in the night sky and brought her to earth, where the pair turned into a tree with two branches, one for him and one for her. The grandmother and her allies discovered the girl's absence and, sweeping down to earth, broke off Mayahuel's branch, tore it into pieces, and ate the pieces. The other branch, which was left untouched, however, subsequently transformed back into Ehecatl, who reunited the pieces of Mayahuel's branch and buried them. From the pieces grew the first maguey plant. We can assume that this myth explains why pulque—which made people drunk, disorderly, and licentious—was also useful in myriad cures, including as an antiseptic for open wounds and a means to induce menstruation and lactation, ease childbirth, fortify new mothers, and cure venereal disease.[64]

Maize, which was sometimes blamed for health problems such as impotence, likewise had medicinal properties. It was used, for example, as a cure for the very impotence it was believed to cause (Ruiz de Alarcón, in Andrews and Hassig 1984, 250; Sahagún 1950–1982, book 11, 142, 281). More important, like maguey, the story of its origin contained a message of regeneration. Several Aztec Creation myths tell that the youthful maize god Cinteotl was born in a cave to the creator goddess Xochiquetzal, "Precious Flower," whose name, as Michel Graulich (1983, 577, 1997, 56–57) points out, alludes to her penchant for "picking flowers." A comment on folio 3r of the Codex

Telleriano-Remensis, which is dedicated to both the month Ochpaniztli and "Sweeping the Way," which focused on Tlazolteotl, equates Tlazolteotl with Xochiquetzal (Quiñones Keber 1995, 254). The Histoyre du Mechique adds that following his parents' presumably illicit act, Cinteotl burrowed into the earth. Later, however,

> from his hair grew cotton and from one ear a very good seed that some love to eat, called *huazoltli* (or catateztli?), from the other [ear], another seed. From the nose, yet another called chia, which is good to drink in the summer; from the fingers came a fruit called camotli, which is like colewort, a very good fruit. From the other (fingers) . . . *came a very tall kind of maize, which is the grain they eat now*, and from the rest of the body came many other fruits, which men sow and harvest. And for this the god is loved by all the gods and they called him Tlazopilli, which means beloved lord. (Jonghe 1905, 31–32, my translation and emphasis)

In other words, Cinteotl's burial in the dark, cold earth due to his mother's impropriety ultimately led not only to the rebirth of maize but to the birth of the rest of the earth's vegetation as well. Cinteotl of the curly yellow hair was, as Sullivan (1976, 259) puts it, "the first seed."

The eternal promise of another maize crop was acted out ritually during Ochpaniztli, which included the scattering of what Sahagún (1950–1982, book 2, 124) refers to as "maize seeds" (presumably dried kernels, but see note 47).[65] According to Sahagún (1950–1982, book 2, 120–121), at that time a woman representing Tlazolteotl was sacrificed and then flayed, whereupon a priest donned her skin, placing a piece of skin removed from the woman's thigh, called the *mexxayacatl*, on [an impersonator of] Tlazolteotl's "son." Here, the "son," whose eyes or face are covered with a specific kind of blindfold, is identified as Cinteotl. Mother and offspring then moved to the foot of the temple (Templo Mayor) dedicated to the Aztec patron god Huitzilopochtli ("Hummingbird Left"), where the former, facing [a statue of?] the god, four times "raised her arms and placed herself in a cross" (Sahagún 1977, 1, 192, my translation).[66] As numerous scholars have pointed out, the description compares well with the naked goddess's displayed pose on page 13 of the Codex Borbonicus, where, as in Borgia 31, she is giving birth. What Sahagún says happened next strengthens the likelihood that the "cross" pose symbolized coitis and childbirth. The goddess impersonator, he writes, then "turned about; she placed herself by her son, Cinteotl."[67] Later, Cinteotl left the thigh skin mask at a mountaintop called Popotl temi, "Filled with Brooms," an act interpreted by Sullivan (1976, 258–259) as a "symbol of birth, purification, and the cutting of the umbilical cord." In Sullivan's opinion, the mask represented the sticky substance still clinging to an infant at birth, which the Aztecs perceived as "filth" that accrued from its parents' union.

The Ochpaniztli rite is further significant here because, in describing it, Sahagún equates Cinteotl with Itztlacoliuhqui, who, as we saw above, represents cold and the frost (Sahagún 1950–1982, book 2, 122, 1993, folio 282r; Sullivan 1976, 253). Sahagún (1993, folio 277r; Sahagún, Sullivan, and Nicholson 1997, 139–140) notes that at the time of the Spanish conquest, Ochpaniztli fell during late August or early September, when temperatures start to fall and there are occasional frosts. In the Primeros Memoriales, folio 78v, we see Itztlacoliuhqui in his distinctive hat, wearing Cinteotl's mexxayacatl in the form of a simple blindfold (Sahagún 1993). It appears that Cinteotl and Itztlacoliuhqui were so closely interrelated at these times that in peoples' minds they were essentially one and the same being.

The implication of this interrelationship is that, like Tezcatlipoca, Tlazolteotl, and the Cihuateteo, Itztlacoliuhqui's character had, in Sullivan's (1976, 255) words, "an inherent duality." That is, in addition to connoting the cold and darkness of the underworld, the sightless god carried the promise of warmth and light. The promise is confirmed not only by an Aztec hymn that relates Cinteotl to the moment of sunrise at dawn but also by a comment on folio 16v of the Codex Telleriano-Remensis, which says that Itztlacoliuhqui "is a star in the sky, which appears to go in reverse" (Quiñones Keber 1995, 264). The star is generally agreed to be to the planet Venus in its manifestation of Morning Star, which, when it rises from inferior conjunction in the East at dawn, is in retrograde motion. At this time, the Aztecs perceived Venus as leaving the cold, dark underworld as a welcome herald of the rising sun. In other words, as the Morning Star, Itztlacoliuhqui represented what Sullivan (1976, 259) refers to as "the first light."

This ascendancy explains why on Codex Telleriano-Remensis 16v, as on the Tonalamatl Aubin 12, much of Itztlacoliuhqui's exposed skin is covered with red-and-white vertical stripes. The personified god of the Morning Star, Tlahuizcalpantecuhtli—"Lord–at-the-Dawn," according to J. Richard Andrews and Ross Hassig (1984, 236)—is usually covered with vertical red-and-white stripes. On Codex Telleriano-Remensis 16v and Tonalamatl Aubin 12, as in most other depictions of Itztlacoliuhqui, a large arrow penetrating the god's hat refers to a Creation myth recounted by both Jerónimo de Mendieta (1971 [1770], 79–80) and the Leyenda de los soles (Bierhorst 1992, 148–149). In these accounts, the newly born but still stubbornly stationary sun retaliated against Tlahuizcalpantecuhtli's efforts to get it moving by shooting him with an arrow.[68] The mortally wounded Tlahuizcalpantecuhtli plummeted into the dark earth where, the Leyenda tells us, the nine layers [of the underworld] "covered up his face." This Tlahuizcalpantecuhtli, it adds, "is the frost." Because the Morning Star always eventually reappears from inferior conjunction, however, the Aztecs would have seen Itztlacoliuhqui-Cinteotl's blindfold not only as a reminder of his parents' primordial "sin" but also as a promise that, like it and that error, their own mistakes could be reversed.[69]

CONCLUSIONS

The message embedded in all of the images analyzed above is that the healing that darkness afforded by the blindfold enabled the reversal, or "undoing," of a grievous mistake and the damage it had caused. Because a blindfolded deity had itself committed a "sin" in the darkness of the Creation, it was able to "undo" its client's error and subsequent damages as well. The blindfolds donned, usually at midnight, by its naked client in turn signaled that the client was seeking god's help in reversing the error and damages. This predicament is why all pre-conquest blindfolded figures appear in divinatory manuscripts consulted by soothsayers who, by predicting the future, could advise their clients of ways to avoid any dire prognoses and atone for any errors. There was no need for stone sculptors to depict either a deity or a person wearing a blindfold because their creations were of no use to a soothsayer.

The idea that, for the Aztecs, blindfolds were much more than symbols of transgression and punishment resonates with what we know about their meaning elsewhere in Mesoamerica and in many other cultures. For example, blindfolded Huichol peyote pilgrims ritually return, over a period of weeks, to what Johannes Neurath (2000, 74) calls "the night of mythic time."[70] During the pilgrimage they confess their sexual transgressions, which their leader records as knots on a long cord. The mistakes are symbolically untied when the cord is ritually burned. Peter Furst (1972, 151, 154–157, 168), who witnessed one of these rituals, reports that the leader of a pilgrimage he attended told his followers that the fire "has removed it all from you." The pilgrims make the trip because they hope to return to their origins and connect there with their ancestors, with some hoping to be cured of an ailment in the process. As they progress along their path, they are believed to regress in age "from man to child," finally arriving at what Furst describes as a prenatal state of total darkness. Afterward, they are said to be reborn "new," like a baby. Everything, as Barbara Meyerhoff (1974, 147–148) puts it, has been "reversed."

Alfredo López Austin (1993a, 51) notes that the Nahuatl word for festival, *ilhuitl*, contains the syllable *il-*, "return," and points out that today the Mocho' Maya always introduce a myth by taking their listeners back in time. Mazatec curers in Oaxaca, when under the influence of hallucinogenic mushrooms, explain that they are trying "to go back to the beginning and forward to the future" (Boege 1988, 90). According to María del Carmen Anzures y Bolaños (1983), the Mazatec curer at these times returns to the Creation, where he is transformed into the appropriate deity and the original generative act can be re-created. All of these acts, which are usually undertaken in the darkness of night, exemplify what the historian of religions Mircea Eliade (1959) calls "the myth of the eternal return." Eliade (1964, 148) states that the Samoyed healer in Siberia blindfolds himself with a kerchief "so that he can enter the spirit world by his own inner light." The Magyar of Nepal and some Buddhists in Tibet have a similar custom (Kohn 2001, 152). In these cases, blindfolds are used to return an ill, imperfect, and "damaged" client to the fecund, healing darkness of the Creation. The Aztecs, I submit, were no exception.

NOTES

*Earlier versions of this argument were read at the Pre-Columbian Society of Washington, DC, 2010 symposium The Meaning of Night in Ancient Mesoamerica; the USC/EMSI 2011 seminar Visual and Material Culture in Pre- and Post-Conquest Mexico and Peru: Case Studies and Methodological Approaches; and the 2017 Society for American Archaeology symposium Night and Darkness in Pre-Columbian Mexico and Central America in Vancouver, BC, March 30, 2017, organized by Nancy Gonlin. I am very grateful for the counsel of many people along the way, especially that of Elizabeth Boone, Linda Brown, Eulogio Guzman, Nicholas Hopkins, James Maffie, Susan Milbrath, and John Pohl, and for the invaluable assistance of my intrepid research assistant at the time, Erin Vaden.

1. Kushner (2008, 253).

2. Eliade (1959, 64).

3. I use the modern term *Aztecs* in its broadest sense to refer to Nahuatl speakers whose culture was closely related to that of people living in the Aztec capital. Because this situation was not the case for all Nahuatl speakers, I avoid using the more generic terms *Nahua* and *Nahuas*.

4. For a detailed discussion of Yohualli Ehecatl as a form of address, see Olivier (2003, 16–25, 175). Confessions were made only once in a person's lifetime, usually late in life (Sahagún 1950–1982, book 6, 9).

5. See also Carrasco (1999, 18); Graulich (1981a, 1983, 1997, 52–59); López Austin (1993a, 65–66); Olivier (2000a, 2003, 113–121, 154–155, 257). Olivier (2003, 121) acknowledges that under some circumstances, blindness signaled special powers.

6. The word tlatlacolli derives from the verb *tlacoa*, "to damage [something], to deteriorate a thing, to do harm, to violate" (Siméon 1977 [1885], 638, my translation). Just as there was no comparable Nahuatl word for sin, there was none for guilt; to the extent that the concept of guilt existed, it was subsumed by tlatlacolli. For examples of the Spanish equation of sin (*pecado*) with tlatlacolli, see Molina (1970 [1571], part 1, 93v, part 2, 132r, 137r).

7. For more on the relationship of sexual misbehaviors to reproductive problems, see Burkhart (1989, 51); López Austin (1988a, 1:235, 262); Sahagún (1950–1982, book 6, 102–103).

8. For the Anales de Cuauhtitlan and the Leyenda de los soles, see Bierhorst (1992, 26, 145). For the Historia de los Mexicanos por sus pinturas, see García Icazbalceta (1891, 229, 231). The Historia claims that early on, the gods made a half sun, which shed only a little light on the world. It was only later that they created a whole sun, thereby ending the period of darkness. Other Aztec sources say only that the earth lay in darkness for a long period before the sun was born (e.g., Durán 1967, 2:16).

9. See also Christenson (2007, 70, 91, 205, 218, 222–228). For Mixtec beliefs regarding the "pre-sunrise" period, see García (1981 [1607], 327); for a general discussion, López Austin (1993a, 38–39).

10. Linguistic evidence that darkness was equated with illness and confusion appears in the numerous Nahuatl words and phrases for illness, dizziness, confusion, and deception that are based on the root word *yohualli* (*youalli*), "night" (Campbell 1985, 263, 437; Siméon 1977, 590). Both the false wise man and the ignorant physician were described as "a lover of darkness" (Sahagún 1950–1982, book 10, 30).

11. In addition to the Codex Borgia, the Borgia Group manuscripts include the Codices Cospi, Fejéváry-Mayer, Laud, Porfirio Díaz, Vaticanus B, and Aubin no. 20. All are screenfolds—that is, they are painted on a single sheet, which, with one exception, is made of animal skin that has been folded "accordion-style." For discussions of the individual manuscript, see Boone (2007, 240–252).

12. Small, unnamed, and blindfolded "penitents" not discussed further in this chapter appear in the Tonalamatl Aubin 15 and Codex Borgia 32.

13. Seler (1963 [1904–1908], 2:219) was the first major scholar to describe a little blindfolded figure, in this case the one on Borgia 66, as a "sinner" (*pecador*).

14. For a full discussion of the etymology of Tezcatlipoca's name, see Andrews and Hassig (1984, 235–236); Olivier (2003, 11–44).

15. Tloque Nahuaque is translated as the "Lord of the Close Vicinity" and the "Lord of the Everywhere" by Burkhart (1988, 68) and as the "Possessor of the Near,

Possessor of the Surrounding" by León-Portilla (1963, 63, 91–94). Tezcatlipoca is accordingly described in the Historia de los Mexicanos por sus pinturas as one "who knew all thoughts and was in all places and read all hearts" (García Icazbalceta 1891, 229). See Olivier (2003, 310–311n28) for additional references.

16. The Codex Telleriano-Remensis is to a large extent cognate to the slightly later Codex Vaticanus A (Codex Vaticanus 3738, Codex Ríos), which was based on it. The latter was made for the Dominican Pedro de los Ríos and bears annotations in Italian. In this chapter I do not refer to the Codex Vaticanus A unless an image, comment, or gloss differs significantly from its cognate in the Codex Telleriano-Remensis.

17. See Klein (2001, 220–221) for further discussion of the evidence that Tezcatlipoca was associated with same-sex relations.

18. Evidence that Tezcatlipoca was held responsible for the introduction of sodomy appears in Alva Ixtlilxochitl (1974–1977, 1:277); Casas (1909, 627); Sahagún (1950–1982, book 4, 35); Torquemada (1975, 1:34–35, 2:393). For a reference to his change into a woman, see Bierhorst (1992, 38).

19. Many Aztec deities had multiple aspects, or personas, each with a different name.

20. On health problems attributed to Tezcatlipoca, see Durán (1971, 97, 99); Klein (1993, 23, 2001, 225–226); Sahagún (1950–1982, book 1, 31, book 3, 11–12). Although it is still unclear whether syphilis was known before the conquest in Central Mexico, skeletal remains show that many people suffered from the closely related venereal disease known today as yaws (*Treponema perenue*) (Mansilla and Pijoan 2005; Mansilla et al. 2000).

21. According to Ortiz de Montellano (1990, 125), citing Viesca Treviño, hemorrhoids would have been common in Aztec times due to the prevalent diet.

22. For more on Tezcatlipoca's love of vengeance, see Seler (1900–1901, 91, 1901–1902, 104, 1902–1903, 262–263).

23. González Torres (1993, 17) was the first to emphasize a confessed Aztec miscreant's return to the pure state of an infant.

24. For further discussion of the identification of Itztlacoliuhqui as a variant of Tezcatlipoca, which is primarily based on iconographic comparisons, see Olivier (2003, 118, 123); Milbrath (2013, 65).

25. On Itztlacoliuhqui's association with cold and frost, see also Sahagún (1950–1982, book 7, 19, 1993, folio 282v); Sahagún, Sullivan, and Nicholson (1997, 157); Sullivan (1976, 253).

26. For other depictions of Itztlacoliuhqui, see Codex Borbonicus 12, Codex Borgia 69 Codex Cospi 12, Codex Telleriano-Remensis 16v, Tonalamatl Aubin 12, Codex Vaticanus A 24v, Codex Vaticanus B 60, and Sahagún's Primeros Memoriales, folio 251v.

27. On the lizard's association with sexuality and gluttony, see Anders, Jansen, and Reyes García (1996, 247); López Austin (1988a, 1:31); Sahagún (1993, folios 81r,

81v, 1950–1982, book 10, 144); Sahagún, Sullivan, and Nicholson (1997, 290–294); Seler (1900–1901, 90). The Nahuatl word *cuetzpal* means glutton (Molina 1970 [1571], part 1, 66r, part 2, 66v, 26v). In the Codices Borgia and Vaticanus A (Vaticanus 3738, Codex Ríos), which present, *en face*, a male figure with the twenty-day signs distributed over his body, the lizard is attached to the penis.

28. On adultery and its relation to blindness, see also López Austin (1988a, 1:235, 262); Ortiz de Montellano (1990, 151–152); Sahagún (1950–1982, book 6, 102–103).

29. On the Aztec deities and rites associated with pulque, see Goncalves de Lima (1956); Nicholson (1991).

30. Graulich (1997, 194) suggests that people may also have believed that drunkenness could lead to incest.

31. For references to the ailments caused by excessive drinking, see Sahagún (1950–1982, book 1, 48–49, book 2, 13, 171, book 4, 11, 13, book 6, 68–72).

32. Patecatl also wears a *yacametztli* in Codex Telleriano-Remensis 15v, Codex Magliabechiano 56, Codex Borgia 13, and Codex Borbonicus 11.

33. Among the Maya, eyes that have been torn out of their socket symbolized defeat; see Christenson (2007, 100) and Roys (1967 [1933], 92), who notes a warning in the Chilam Balam of Chumayel that the eyes of captured chiefs "shall be torn out" (cf. Seler 1901–1902, 167–168, who thinks the gouging of eyes symbolized self-sacrifice).

34. Patecatl also appears with an axe in Codex Borbonicus 11 and Codex Telleriano-Remensis 15v. Pulque gods who carry an axe in the Codex Magliabechiano are depicted on pages 49–52, 54, and 56–57.

35. Skeletal evidence of a notable exception to the general rule that Aztecs did not excise the heart of children was found in Offering 111 at the Aztecs' main temple (Templo Mayor) in their capital. The child had been dressed as the Aztec patron god Huitzilopochtli and surrounded by precious artifacts, which suggests that he and his death were very special (López Luján et al. 2010). Seler (1963 [1904–1909], 1, 199–202) refers to the long tubes as "strips" (*tiras*).

36. Johansson (2006, 194) provides the Nahuatl translation of Ixcuina's name. Most scholars follow Sullivan (1982) in thinking that Tlazolteotl's cult originated in the Huasteca region of Veracruz.

37. The Aztecs in the capital seem to have conceived of the moon as male, but outside the capital it was typically personified as female.

38. Tlazolteotl holds a malinalli broom, for example, on Codices Borbonicus 30 and Telleriano-Remensis 3r.

39. The reference here to a flood may seem to suggest the influence of Christianity, but the notion of a primordial deluge is evident in some pre-conquest sources as well; see, for example, Velásquez García (2006) regarding the Maya.

40. Codex Vaticanus A 17v; Quiñones Keber (1995, 265). Adulterers were reportedly killed before Tlazolteotl's image.

41. Tlazolteotl appears naked, legs apart, in Codices Vaticanus B 74 and Borgia 74.

42. For later, post-Selerian analyses of the Codex Borgia's "Venus pages," see especially Anders, Jansen, and Reyes García (1993, 191–245); Batalla Rosado (2008); Brotherston (1999); Byland (1993, xxiii–xxvi); Jansen and Pérez Jiménez (2017); Milbrath (1989, 1999, 2013); Nowotny (1976, 26–30, 2005, 264–279).

43. The 260-day divinatory calendar meshed with the solar year to create a larger cycle of 52 years.

44. Milbrath (1999, 111, 2013 45, 78–79) bolsters Boone's opinion that the Borgia 31 figures represent Tlazolteotl. Seler (1963 [1904–1909], 2:14–15) identifies them simply as death goddesses. Anders and colleagues (1993, 197–199) opine instead that the two displayed females in Borgia 31 represent the creator goddess Cihuacoatl (Woman Snake) (see also Jansen 2002, 307). Cihuacoatl does appear in Aztec sculpture with a skeletal jaw and clawed hands and feet, but she never wears a cotton headband. I (Klein 2021) have argued that the demonic Cihuacoatl we see in stone sculptures from the Aztec capital was of little interest to diviners and soothsayers outside Tenochtitlan, who instead seem to have focused on her positive attributes.

45. In support of her argument that the Borgia 31 figures' blindfolds refer to the eclipse, Milbrath notes that among the Maya, removal of the eyes served as a metaphor for an eclipse.

46. Similar coverings, which appear with clearly healthy figures on Borgia 33, 34, and 38, are brightly colored. Boone (2007, 189–190, 193) interprets them as capes or cloaks.

47. Although the maize plant can reproduce from seed, it more readily reproduces from pollen shed by its tassel onto its silks. For more about the reproduction of maize, see Ellis (2015).

48. Chicha is found only in the lower Central and Southern Americas. For more on Mexican beverages made from plants, including those from maize, see Bruman (2000); Ellis (2015); Smalley and Blake (2003).

49. I do not include the possibility that a spoiled chocolate beverage is referenced here because the cacao plant, unlike the maguey, malinalli, and maize plants, is not illustrated on page 30. Nor, for that matter, does the plant appear anywhere in Codex Borgia, although several pages do include a cup of foaming chocolate. Cacao, moreover, because it thrives in warm climates, was not grown in the cool highlands of Central Mexico; instead, it had to be imported as tribute, where use of the beverage made from it seems to have been the sole prerogative of Aztec elites. True to form, however, although the Aztecs worried about excessive imbibing of chocolate, which they said could make a person drunk, confused, or crazy, they made ample use of it and the pod

itself for a variety of medicinal purposes (Coe and Coe 2019, 79–105; Dillinger et al. 2000, 2060).

50. Boone (2007, 179) suggests that all of the little black-skinned and clawed figures in this section of the codex are "essences, personifications, and anonymous agents of action, rather than . . . specific supernaturals or persons." The birth of the first human figures from a personified knife representing Tezcatlipoca-Itztlacoliuhqui is depicted on the following page (32). One of the tiny, naked newborns on that page is blindfolded.

51. Durán (1971, 232); Gómez de Orozco (1945, 55); Sahagún (1950–1982, book 1, 15, 70, book 5, 191); Serna (1987, 408). So closely was Tlazolteotl associated with crossroads that she appears on or next to one in the Codex Borgia, pages 14, 72, 76; the Codex Vaticanus B, page 22; the Codex Fejérváry-Mayer, pages 1, 4, 17; and the Codex Laud, page 10.

52. Ruiz de Alarcón (in Andrews and Hassig 1984, 31); Sahagún (1950–1982, book 1, 15, 70).

53. On page 107 the friar says the "goddesses," whom he sometimes says were happy, were honored "on the roads and at street crossings and crossroads." This honoring occurred "at midnight, just at the dividing of the night." The nights when the Cihuateteo were said to descend were 1 Monkey (*ce ozomatli*), 1 Deer (*ce mazatl*), 1 Rain (*ce quiahuitl*), 1 House (*ce calli*), and 1 Eagle (*ce cuauhtli*).

54. For identification of these figures as Cihuateteo/Cihuapipiltin, see Anders, Jansen, and Reyes García (1993, 247); Boone (2007, 120); Milbrath (2013, 54–58); Nowotny (2005); Seler (1963 [1904–1909], 2:74); Sullivan (1982, 18–19).

55. The Cihuateteo on Codex Vaticanus B 47–48 are preceded by a large and enigmatic deer, its closed eyes signifying death, which seems to be lying on the ground. Another fallen deer, its body penetrated by an arrow, appears directly above it.

56. On the significance of the maxtlatl, see Hunt (1977, 102, 105); Klein (2001, 206).

57. For additional references to eye problems attributed to the Cihuateteo, see Sahagún (1950–1982, book 1, 19, book 2, 38, 41, book 4, 81).

58. Although the five adult Macuiltonaleque on Borgia 47–48 and Vaticanus B 77–78 lack deformed eyes and extremities, those seen elsewhere in the Codex Borgia—for example, on page 10—have them. For more on the Macuiltonaleque, who were also known as the Ahuiateteo, "Pleasure Gods," see Seler (1963 [1904–1909], 2:63–83). The Macuiltonaleque were expected on the days 5 Lizard (*macuil cuetzpalin*), 5 Vulture (*macuil cozcaquauhtli*), 5 Rabbit (*macuil tochtli*), and 5 Grass (*macuil malinalli*). In the Aubin Manuscript no. 20 (Fonds Mexicain 20), none of the five Cihuateteo paired with the five Macuiltonaleque display any evidence of blindness or other physical problems (Pohl 2007).

59. Deformation and "twisting" of the facial features, like trembling hands, can also be a symptom of palsy—another condition that, like epilepsy, was often blamed on the

Cihuateteo; see Sahagún (1950–1982, book 1, 19, book 2, 38, book 4, 81); Ortiz de Montellano (1990, 132, 157, 159).

60. Sahagún (1950–1982, book 1, 19, 71–77, book 2, 37, 41–44, 81, 107–109, book 4, 41).

61. The literature on the medical benefits of Aztec plants, plant products, and other materials is vast. For overviews, see López Austin (1971, 1993b).

62. The present-day Tz'utujil Maya believe "pre-sunrise" beings use obsidian to cure certain illnesses. They say the same of stone celts, which are used as axe blades (Brown 2015, 62–66). The latter raises the possibility that the axe had a similarly dual meaning among the Aztecs.

63. Cruz (in Gates 2000 [1939], 15), writing in the mid-sixteenth century, says, in contrast, that people with eye problems were supposed to abstain from heat and hot foods.

64. For more on medicinal uses of the maguey plant, including pulque, see Davidson and Ortiz de Montellano (1983); Dolley (1911); Hernández (1959, 350); López Austin (1993b, 49); Martinéz (1944, 29); Ruiz de Alarcón (in Andrews and Hassig 1984, 250); Sahagún (1993, folio 60v); Sahagún, Sullivan, and Nicholson (1997, 284); Sullivan (1982, 24).

65. Many scholars have examined Ochpaniztli, for example, Margáin Araujo (1945), with most interpreting it as a harvest festival. Graulich (1981b), in contrast, thinks Ochpaniztli was originally held in the spring and celebrated the onset of the planting season. For a more recent and different reading of the festival, see DiCesare (2009).

66. In his Florentine Codex, Sahagún (1950–1982, book 2, 121) makes no mention of Tlazolteotl assuming the "cross" pose; rather, he says only that "she raised her arms, she spread her arms."

67. For a discussion of the symbolism of Tlazolteotl's ritual pose, see, for example, Sullivan (1976, 1982).

68. Mendieta does not specify Tlahuizcalpantecuhtli's involvement, simply referring to the defeated aggressor as Citli, or "Star." The Morning Star, however, is referred to as Citlalpul, "Great Star," by Sahagún (1993, folio 282r; Sahagún, Sullivan, and Nicholson 1997, 155).

69. On Itztlacoliuhqui's relationship to Tlahuizcalpantecuhtli, see López Austin (1993a, 239); Milbrath (2013, 133n103); Olivier (2000b, 46, 118, 2000a, 345–346); Quiñones Keber (1995, 262–264); Seler (1901–1902, 104, 174, 1963 [1904–1909], 2:204–205); Sullivan (1976, 259). Taube (1992, 108–111) identifies the blindfolded god known as God Q in the Maya Codex Madrid, page 60, as the Maya equivalent of Itztlacoliuhqui. A similar comparison has been made regarding the blindfolded figure on the Maya Codex Dresden, page 50 (Thompson 1960, 222; Vail 1996, 139–141).

70. The Uto-Aztecan language family is commonly believed to have originated in the western United States; see, for example, Fowler (1983).

REFERENCES

Aguilera, Carmen. 1981. *El Tonalamatl de Aubin*. Tlaxcala: Códices y manuscritos 1. Mexico City: Rosette y Associados Artes Gráficas.

Alva Ixtlilxochitl, Fernando de. 1975–1985. *Obras históricas: Incluyen el texto completo de las llamadas Relaciones e Historia de la nación chichimeca en una nueva versión establecida con el cotejo de los manuscritos más antiguos que se conocen / Fernando de Alva Ixtlilxóchitl; ed., estudio introductorio y un apéndice documental por Edmundo O'Gorman*, 4th ed. 2 vols. Mexico City: Universidad Nacional Autónoma de México, Instituto de Investigaciones Históricas. (Compiled ca. 1600–1640.)

Anales de Cuauhtitlan. See Bierhorst 1992.

Anders, Ferdinand, ed. 1967. *Codex Tro-Cortesianus (Codex Madrid)*. Madrid: Museo de América, Madrid. Einleitung und summary: M. Anders. Facsimile. Graz, Austria: Akademische Druck- u. Verlagsanstalt.

Anders, Ferdinand, ed. 1970. *Codex Magliabechiano, CL. XIII 3 (B.R. 232): Biblioteca nazionale centrale di Firenze*. Facsimile. Graz, Austria: Akademische Druck- u. Verlagsanstalt.

Anders, Ferdinand, ed. 1972. *Codex Vaticanus 3773 (Codex Vaticanus B) Biblioteca Apostolica Vaticanus/Einleitung, Summary und Resumen, Ferdinand Anders*. Facsimile. Graz, Austria: Akademische Druck- u. Verlagsanstalt.

Anders, Ferdinand, Helmet Deckert, and Rolf Krusche, eds. 1975. *Codex Dresdensis, Sächsische Landesbibliothek Dresden (Mscr. Dresd. R 310)*. Facsimile. Graz, Austria: Akademische Druck- u. Verlagsanstalt.

Anders, Ferdinand, Maarten Jansen, and Luis Reyes García, eds. 1993. *Los templos del cielo y la oscuridad: Oráculos y liturgia: Libro explicativo del llamado Códice Borgia*. Facsimile. Madrid: Society Estatal Quinto Centenario [u.a.] / Graz, Austria: Akademische Druck- u. Verlagsanstalt / Mexico City: Fondo de Cultura Económica.

Anders, Ferdinand, Maarten Jansen, and Luis Reyes García, eds. 1994. *La pintura de la muerte y de los destinos: Libro explicativo del llamado Códice Laud*. Facsimile. Graz, Austria: Akademische Druck- u. Verlagsanstalt / Mexico City: Fondo de Cultura Económica.

Anders, Ferdinand, Maarten Jansen, and Luis Reyes García, eds. 1996. *Religión, costumbres e historia de los antiguos mexicanos: libro explicativo del llamado Códice Vaticano A, Codex Vatic. Lat. 3738 de la Biblioteca Apostólica Vaticana*. Facsimile. Graz, Austria: Akademische Druck- u. Verlagsanstalt / Mexico City: Fondo de Cultura Económica.

Andrews, J. Richard. 2003. *Introduction to Classical Nahuatl*. Rev. ed. Norman: University of Oklahoma Press.

Andrews, J. Richard, and Ross Hassig, trans. and eds. 1984. *Treatise on the Heathen Superstitions That Today Live among the Indians Native to This New Spain, 1629/by Hernando Ruíz de Alarcón*. Norman: University of Oklahoma Press. (Originally compiled 1629.)

Anzures y Bolaños, María del Carmen. 1983. "Tiempo mitico y curacion." *Revista Mexicana de Estudios Antropologicos* 29 (1): 67–70.

Aubin Tonalamatl. See Tonalamatl Aubin.

Batalla Rosado, Juan José. 2008. *Codex Borgia*. Facsimile. Madrid: Testimonio Companía Editorial.

Berdan, Frances, and Patricia Rieff Anawalt. 1992. *The Codex Mendoza*. 4 vols. Berkeley: University of California Press.

Bierhorst, John. 1992. *History and Mythology of the Aztecs: Codex Chimalpopoca*. Tucson: University of Arizona Press.

Boege, Eckart. 1988. *Los Mazatecos ante la nación: Contradicciones de la identidad étnica en el México actual*. Mexico City: Siglo Veintiuno Editores.

Boone, Elizabeth Hill. 2006. "The Birth of the Day Count in the Codex Borgia." In *Arqueología e historia del centro de México: Homenaje a Eduardo Matos Moctezuma*, ed. Leonardo López Luján, Davíd Carrasco, and Lourdes Cué, 599–612. Mexico City: Instituto Nacional de Antropología e Historia.

Boone, Elizabeth Hill. 2007. *Cycles of Time and Meaning in the Mexican Books of Fate*. Austin: University of Texas Press.

Brotherston, Gordon. 1999. "The Yearly Seasons and Skies in the Borgia and Related Codices." *ARARA* 2. University of Essex electronic journal. Manchester eScholar Services ID #1b7241.

Brown, Linda A. 2015. "When Pre-Sunrise Beings Inhabit a Post-Sunrise World: Time, Animate Objects, and Contemporary Tz'utujil Maya Ritual Practitioners." In *The Measure and Meaning of Time in Mesoamerica and the Andes*, ed. Anthony F. Aveni, 53–77. Washington, DC: Dumbarton Oaks Research Library and Collection.

Bruman, Henry J. 2000. *Alcohol in Ancient Mexico*. Salt Lake City: University of Utah Press.

Burkhart, Louise M. 1988. "Doctrinal Aspects of Sahagún's Colloquios." In *The Work of Bernardino de Sahagún, Pioneer Ethnographer of Sixteenth-Century Aztec Mexico*, ed. J. Jorge Klor de Alva, H. B. Nicholson, and Eloise Quiñones Keber, 65–82. Albany: Institute for Mesoamerican Studies, University at Albany, State University of New York.

Burkhart, Louise M. 1989. *The Slippery Earth: Nahua-Christian Moral Dialogue in Sixteenth-Century Mexico*. Tucson: University of Arizona Press.

Burland, C(ottie) A. 1971. *Codex Fejérváry-Mayer 12014 M City of Liverpool Museums.* Facsimile. Graz, Austria: Akademische Druck- u. Verlagsanstalt.

Byland, Bruce E. 1993. "Introduction and Commentary." In *The Codex Borgia: A Full-Color Restoration of the Ancient Mexican Manuscript,* ed. Gisele Díaz and Alan Rodgers, xiii–xxxii. New York: Dover.

Campbell, R. Joe. 1985. *A Morphological Dictionary of Classical Nahuatl: A Morpheme Index to the Vocabulario en lengua mexicana y castellana of Fray Alonso de Molina.* Madison, WI: Hispanic Seminary of Medieval Studies, Ltd.

Carrasco, Davíd. 1999. "Uttered from the Heart." *History of Religions* 39 (1) (August): 1–31.

Casas, Bartolomé de las. 1909. *Apologética historia de las Indias.* Nueva Biblioteca de Autores Españoles 13. Historiadores de Indias 1. Madrid: Bailly, Baillere e hijos. (Written 1551–1554.)

Chilam Balam of Chumayel. See Roys 1967 [1933].

Christenson, Allen J. 2007. *Popol Vuh: The Sacred Book of the Maya: The Great Classic of Central American Spirituality, Translated from the Original Maya Text.* Norman: University of Oklahoma Press.

Codex Borbonicus. See Nowotny 1974.

Codex Borgia. See Nowotny 1976.

Codex Cospi. See Nowotny 1968.

Codex Dresden. See Anders, Deckert, and Krusche 1975.

Codex Fejérváry-Mayer. See Burland 1971; Seler/Loubat 1901–1902.

Codex Laud. See Anders, Jansen, and Reyes García 1994.

Codex Madrid (Codex Tro-Cortesianus). See Anders 1967.

Codex Porfirio Díaz. See Doesburg 2001.

Codex Telleriano-Remensis. See Quiñones Keber 1995.

Codex Vaticanus A (Codex Vaticanus 3738, also known as Codex Ríos). See Anders, Jansen, and Reyes García 1996.

Codex Vaticanus B (Codex Vaticanus 3773). See Anders 1972; Seler/Loubat 1902–1903.

Coe, Sophie D., and Michael D. Coe. 2019. *The True History of Chocolate,* 3rd ed. London: Thames and Hudson.

Cruz, Martín de la. (Written 1552.) See Gates 2000 [1939].

Davidson, Judith R., and Bernard R. Ortiz de Montellano. 1983. "The Antibacterial Properties of an Aztec Wound Remedy." *Journal of Ethnopharmacology* 8: 149–161.

Díaz, Gisele, and Alan Rodgers. 1993. *The Codex Borgia: A Full-Color Restoration of the Ancient Mexican Manuscript,* with an introduction and commentary by Bruce E. Byland. Facsimile. New York: Dover.

DiCesare, Catherine R. 2009. *Sweeping the Way: Divine Transformation in the Aztec Festival of Ochpaniztli*. Boulder: University Press of Colorado.

Dillinger, Teresa L., Patricia Barriga, Sylvia Escáraga, Martha Jimenez, Diana Salazar Lowe, and Louis E. Grivetti. 2000. "Food for the Gods: Cure for Humanity? A Cultural History of the Medicinal and Ritual Use of Chocolate." *Journal of Nutrition* 130 (8), Supplement: 2057S–2072S.

Doesburg, Sebastián von. 2001. *Códices cuicatecos Porfirio Díaz y Fernando Leal*. Facsimile ed. 2 vols. Mexico City: Porrúa and Gobierno de Oaxaca.

Dolley, Charles S. 1911. "Notes on Maguey Sap and Aguamiel, a Therapeutic Agent of High Values." *Therapeutic Gazette* 35 (3) (March 15): 163–168.

Durán, Diego. 1967. *Historia de las Indias de Nueva España e Islas de la Tierra Firme*. Ed. Angel Ma. Garibay K. 2 vols. Mexico City: Porrúa. (Written 1581.)

Durán, Diego. 1971. *Book of the Gods and Rites and the Ancient Calendar*. Trans. Fernando Horcasitas and Doris Heyden. Norman: University of Oklahoma Press. (Written 1574–1576, 1579.)

Eliade, Mircea. 1959. *Cosmos and History: The Eternal Return*. Trans. Willard R. Trask. New York: Harper and Row.

Eliade, Mircea. 1964. *Shamanism: Archaic Techniques of Ecstasy*. Trans. Willard R. Trask. New York: Bollingen Foundation and Pantheon.

Ellis, Helen. 2015. "Maize, Quetzalcoatl, and Grass Imagery: Science in the Central Mexican Codex Borgia." PhD dissertation University of California, Los Angeles.

Florentine Codex. See Sahagún 1950–1982.

Fowler, Catherine. 1983. "Some Lexical Clues to Uto-Aztecan Prehistory." *International Journal of American Linguistics* 49 (3): 224–257. Papers presented at a Symposium on Uto-Aztecan Historical Linguistics (July 1983).

Furst, Peter T. 1972. "To Find Our Life: Peyote among the Huichol Indians of Mexico." In *Flesh of the Gods: The Ritual Use of Hallucinogens*, ed. Peter T. Furst, 136–184. New York: Praeger.

García, Gregorio. 1981. *Origen de los indios del Nuevo Mundo*. Mexico City: Fondo de Cultura Económica. (First published 1607.)

García Icazbalceta, Joaquin, ed. 1891. "Historia de los Mexicanos por sus pinturas." In *Nueva colección de documentos para la historia de México*, 3:228–263. Mexico City: Francisco Díaz de León. (Written 1531–1534.)

Gates, William, trans. and commentator. 2000 [1939]. *An Aztec Herbal: The Classic Codex of 1552*. Mineola, NY: Dover. (Study of Martín de la Cruz's *Libellus de Medicinalibus Indorum Herbis*, also known as the Badianus Manuscript after its translator, Juan Badiano, written 1552.)

Gómez de Orozco, Federico. 1945. "Costumbres, fiestas, enterramientos y diversas formas de proceder de los Indios de Nueva España." *Tlalocan* 2 (1): 37–63. (Written 1553.)

Goncalves de Lima, Oswaldo. 1956. *El maguey y el pulque en los códices mexicanas*, 2nd ed. Mexico City: Fondo de Cultura Económica.

González Torres, Yolotl. 1993. "Confesión y enfermedad." In *III Coloquio de Historia de la Religión en Mesoamerica y Areas Afines*, ed. Barbro Dahlgren Jordan, 13–21. Mexico City: Universidad Nacional Autónoma de México.

Graulich, Michel. 1981a. "The Metaphor of the Day in Ancient Mexican Myth and Ritual" [with Comments and Reply]. *Current Anthropology* 22 (1): 45–60.

Graulich, Michel. 1981b. "Ochpaniztli, la féte des demailles des anciens mexicains." *Anales de Antropología* 18 (2): 59–100.

Graulich, Michel. 1983. "Myths of Paradise Lost in Pre-Hispanic Central Mexico." *Current Anthropology* 24 (5): 575–588.

Graulich, Michel. 1997. *Myths of Ancient Mexico*. Trans. Bernard R. Ortiz de Montellano and Thelma Ortiz de Montellano. Norman: University of Oklahoma Press.

Harvey, Herbert R. 1981. "Public Health in Aztec Society." *Bulletin of the New York Academy of Medicine* 57 (2): 157–165.

Hernández, Francisco. 1959. *Obras completas*, vol. 1. Mexico City: Universidad Nacional de México. (Compiled 1570s.)

Hernández, Francisco. 2000. *The Mexican Treasury: The Writings of Dr. Francisco Hernández*. Ed. Simon Varey, trans. Rafael Chabrán, Cynthia L. Chamberlin, and Simon Varey. Stanford, CA: Stanford University Press.

Historia de los Mexicanos por sus pinturas. See García Icazbalceta 1891.

Histoyre du Mechique. See Jonghe 1905.

Hosein, Sean R. 2008. "Syphilia—a Dreadful Disease on the Move." In *The Body: The Complete HIV/AIDS Resource*. December. http://www.thebody.com/content /art50147.html.

Hunt, Eva. 1977. *The Transformation of the Hummingbird: Cultural Roots of a Zinacantecan Mythical Poem*. Ithaca, NY: Cornell University Press.

Jansen, Maarten. 2002. "Una Mirada al interior del Templo de Cihuacoatl: Aspectos de la function religiosa de la escritura pictórica." In *Libros y escritura de tradición indígena: Ensayos sobre los codices prehispánicos y colonials de México*, ed. Carmen Arellano, Peer Schmidt, and Xavier Noguez, 279–326. Facsimile. Mexico City: El Colegio Mexiquense–Katholische Universität Eichstätt.

Jansen, Maarten, and Gabina Pérez Jiménez. 2017. *Time and the Ancestors: Aztec and Mixtec Ritual Art*. Leiden: Brill.

Johansson, Patrick. 2006. "*Mocihuaquetzqueh*. ¿Mujeres divinas o mujeres siniestras?" *Estudios de Cultura Nahuatl* 37: 193–230.

Jonghe, M. Edward de. 1905. "Histoyre du Mechique: manuscrit français inedit du XVIe siècle, translated by André Thevet." *Journal de la Societé des Américanistes*, n.s. 2: 1–41. (Written 1543.)

Jordan, Keith. 2013. "Serpents, Skeletons, and Ancestors: The Tula Coatepantli Revisited." *Ancient Mesoamerica* 24: 243–274.

Klein, Cecelia F. 1990–1991. "Snares and Entrails: Mesoamerican Symbols of Sin and Punishment." *RES: Anthropology and Aesthetics* 19–20: 81–103.

Klein, Cecelia F. 1993. "Teocuitlatl, Divine Excrement: The Symbolism of 'Holy Shit' in Ancient Mexico." *Art Journal* 52 (3): 20–27. Special issue, *Merde*, guest ed. Gabriel P. Weisberg.

Klein, Cecelia F. 2001. "None of the Above: Gender Ambiguity in Nahua Ideology." In *Gender in Pre-Hispanic America*, ed. Cecelia F. Klein, 183–253. Washington, DC: Dumbarton Oaks Research Library and Collection.

Klein, Cecelia F. 2021. "From Clay to Stone: The Demonization of the Aztec Goddess Cihuacoatl." In *Sorcery in Mesoamerica*, ed. Jeremy Coltman and John M.D. Pohl, 330–380. Louisville: University Press of Colorado.

Kohn, Richard J. 2001. *Lord of the Dance: The Mani Rimdu Festival in Tibet and Nepal*. Albany: State University of New York Press.

Kushner, Rachel. 2008. *Telex from Cuba: A Novel*. New York: Scribner.

León-Portilla, Miguel. 1963. *Aztec Thought and Culture: A Study of the Ancient Nahuatl Mind*. Trans. Jack Emory Davis. Norman: University of Oklahoma Press.

Leyenda de los soles. See Bierhorst 1992.

López Austin, Alfredo. 1971. "De las plantas medicinales y de otras cosas medicinales." *Estudios de Cultural Nahuatl* 9: 125–230.

López Austin, Alfredo. 1988a. *The Human Body and Ideology: Concepts of the Ancient Nahuas*. 2 vols. Trans. Bernard Ortiz de Montellano and Thelma Ortiz de Montellano. Salt Lake City: University of Utah Press.

López Austin, Alfredo. 1988b. *Una vieja historia de la mierda*. Mexico City: Ediciones Toledo.

López Austin, Alfredo. 1993a. *The Myths of the Opossum: Pathways of Mesoamerican Mythology*. Trans. Bernard R. Ortiz de Montellano and Thelma Ortiz de Montellano. Albuquerque: University of New Mexico Press.

López Austin, Alfredo. 1993b. *Textos de medicina Nahuatl*. Mexico City: Universidad Nacional Autónoma de México.

López Luján, Leonardo, Ximena Chávez Balderas, Norma Valentín, and Aurora Montúfar. 2010. "Huitzilopochtli y el sacrificio de niños en el Templo Mayor de Tenochtitlan." In *El sacrificio humano en la tradición religiosa mesoamericana*, ed. Leonardo López Luján and Guilhem Olivier, 367–394. Mexico City: Instituto Nacional de Arqueología e Historia and Universidad Nacional Autónoma de México.

Loubat, J. F. (Joseph Florimond). 1900–1901. *The Tonalamatl of the Aubin Collection, an Old Mexican Picture Manuscript in the Paris National Library (Manuscrits no. 18–19): Published at the Expense of His Excellency the Duke of Loubat, with Introduction and Explanatory Text by Dr. Eduard Seler*. English ed. by A. H. Keane. Facsimile. Berlin: Hazell, Waters and Viney.

Loubat, J. F. (Joseph Florimond). 1901–1902. *Codex Fejérváry-Mayer, an Old Mexican Picture Manuscript in the Liverpool Free Public Museums (12014/M): Published at the Expense of His Excellency the Duke of Loubat, Elucidated by Dr. Eduard Seler*. English ed. by A. H. Keane. Facsimile. Berlin: T. and A. Constable.

Loubat, J. F. (Joseph Florimond). 1902–1903. *Codex Vaticanus no. 3773 (Codex Vaticanus B), an Old Mexican Pictorial Manuscript in the Vatican Library: Published at the Expense of His Excellency the Duke of Loubat, Elucidated by Dr. Eduard Seler*. English ed. by A. H. Keane. Facsimile. Berlin: T. and A. Constable.

Madsen, William. 1960. *The Virgin's Children: Life in an Aztec Village Today*. Austin: University of Texas Press.

Maffie, James. 2014. *Aztec Philosophy: Understanding a World in Motion*. Boulder: University Press of Colorado.

Mansilla, Josefina, and Carmen Pijoan. 2005. "Treponematosis in Ancient Mexico." In *The Myth of Syphilis: The Natural History of Treponematosis in North America*, ed. Mary Lucas Powell and Della Collins Cook, 368–385. Gainesville: University Press of Florida.

Mansilla, Josefina, Bruce M. Rothschild, Carmen Pijoan, and Christine Rothschild. 2000. "Transitions among Treponematoses in Ancient Mexico." *Chungará* (Arica) 32 (2) (Julio): 167–174.

Margáin Araujo, Carlos. 1945. "La fiesta Azteca de la cosecha Ochpaniztli." *Anales del Instituto Nacional de Arqueología e Historia* 6 (1): 157–175.

Martínez, Maximo. 1944. *Las plantas medicinales de México*. Mexico City: Ediciones Botas.

McCafferty, Sharisse D., and Geoffrey G. McCafferty. 1999. "The Metamorphosis of Xochiquetzal: A Window on Womanhood in Pre- and Post-Conquest Mexico." In *Manifesting Power: Gender and the Interpretation of Power in Archaeology*, ed. Tracy Sweely, 103–125. London: Routledge.

Mendieta, Jerónimo de. 1971 [1770]. *Historia eclesiástica indiana: obra escrita a fines del siglo XVI*, 2nd ed. Mexico City: Porrúa. (Written 1596.)

Meyerhoff, Barbara G. 1974. *Peyote Hunt: The Sacred Journey of the Huichol Indians.* Ithaca, NY: Cornell University Press.

Mikulska, Katarzina (Katarzyna). 2001. "Tlazolteotl, una diosa del maguey." *Anales de Antropología* 35: 91–123.

Milbrath, Susan. 1989. "A Seasonal Calendar with Venus Periods in Borgia 29–46." In *The Imagination of Matter: Religion and Ecology in Mesoamerican Traditions,* ed. Davíd Carrasco, 103–127. BAR International Series 515. Oxford, UK: British Archaeological Review.

Milbrath, Susan. 1999. *Star Gods of the Maya: Astronomy in Art, Folklore, and Calendars.* Austin: University of Texas Press.

Milbrath, Susan. 2013. *Heaven and Earth in Ancient Mexico: Astronomy and Seasonal Cycles in the Codex Borgia.* Austin: University of Texas Press.

Molina, Alonso de. 1970 [1571]. *Vocabulario en lengua castellana y mexicana y mexicana y castellana.* 2 parts. Mexico City: Porrúa.

Neurath, Johannes. 2000. "El don de ver: El proceso de iniciación y sus implicaciones para la osmovisión huichola." *Desacatos: Revista de Antropología Social* 5: 57–77.

Nicholson, H. B. 1991. "The Octli Cult in Late Pre-Hispanic Central Mexico." In *To Change Place: Aztec Ceremonial Landscapes,* ed. Davíd Carrasco, 158–187. Niwot: University Press of Colorado.

Nowotny, Karl Anton, ed. 1968. *Codex Cospi: Calendario Messicano 4093, Biblioteca Universitaria Bologna.* Facsimile. Graz, Austria: Akademische Druck- u. Verlagsanstalt.

Nowotny, Karl Anton, ed. 1974. *Codex Borbonicus: Bibliothèque de l'Assemblée Nationale, Paris (Y120).* Facsimile. Graz, Austria: Akademische Druck- u. Verlagsanstalt.

Nowotny, Karl Anton, ed. 1976. *Codex Borgia: Biblioteca Apostolica Vaticana (Cod. Borg. Messicano 1): vollst. Faks.-Ausg. des Codex im Original Format.* Facsimile. Graz, Austria: Akademische Druck- u. Verlagsanstalt.

Nowotny, Karl Anton. 2005. *Tlacuilolli: Style and Contents of the Mexican Pictorial Manuscripts with a Catalog of the Borgia Group.* Trans. and ed. George A. Everett Jr. and Edward B. Sisson. Norman: University of Oklahoma Press.

Olivier, Guilhem. 2000a. "¿Dios del maíz o dios del hielo? ¿Señor del pecado o señor de la justicia? Esbozo sobre la identidad de Itztlacoliuhqui." In *Códices y documentos sobre México: Tercer Simposio Internacional,* ed. Constanza Vega Sosa, 335–353. Mexico City: Instituto Nacional de Antropología e Historia.

Olivier, Guilhem. 2000b. "Entre transgresión y renacimiento, el papel de la ebriedad en los mitos de México antiguo." In *El héroe entre el mito y la historia,* ed. Federico Navarrete and Guilhem Oliver, 101–121. Mexico City: Universidad Nacional Autónoma de México.

Olivier, Guilhem. 2003. *Mockeries and Metamorphoses of an Aztec God: Tezcatlipoca, "Lord of the Smoking Mirror."* Trans. Michel Besson. Boulder: University Press of Colorado.

Ortiz de Montellano, Bernard R. 1990. *Aztec Medicine, Health, and Nutrition.* New Brunswick, NJ: Rutgers University Press.

Peterson, Jeanette F. 1983. "Sacrificial Earth: The Iconography and Function of Malinalli Grass in Aztec Culture." In *Flora and Fauna Imagery in Precolumbian Cultures: Iconography and Function,* ed. Jeanette F. Peterson, 113–148. BAR International Series 171. Oxford, UK: British Archaeological Review.

Pohl, John M.D. 1998. "Themes of Drunkenness, Violence, and Factionalism in Tlaxcalan Altar Paintings." *RES: Anthropology and Aesthetics* 33: 184–207.

Pohl, John M. D. 2007. *Sorcerers of the Fifth Heaven: Nahua Art and Ritual of Ancient Southern Mexico.* Princeton, NJ: Princeton University Program in Latin American Studies.

Popol Vuh. See Christenson 2007.

Primeros Memoriales. See Sahagún 1993.

Quiñones Keber, Eloise. 1995. *Codex Telleriano-Remensis: Ritual, Divination, and History in a Pictorial Aztec Manuscript.* Austin: University of Texas Press.

Roys, Ralph L., trans. and ed. 1967 [1933]. *The Book of Chilam Balam of Chumayel.* Norman: University of Oklahoma Press. (Compiled sixteenth–eighteenth centuries.)

Ruiz de Alarcón, Hernando. (Written ca. 1629.) See Andrews and Hassig 1984.

Sahagún, Bernardino de. 1950–1982. *Florentine Codex: General History of the Things of New Spain.* Trans. Arthur J.O. Anderson and Charles E. Dibble. 13 vols. Monographs of the School of American Research 14. Santa Fe, NM: School of American Research and University of Utah. (Originally compiled ca. 1569.)

Sahagún, Bernardino de. 1977. *Historia general de las cosas de Nueva Espana.* 3rd ed. 4 vols. Mexico City: Editorial Porrua.

Sahagún, Bernardino de. 1979. *Códice florentino, manuscrito 218–220 de la Colección Palatina de la Biblioteca Medicca Laurenziana.* 3 vols. Facsimile. Mexico City: Secretaria de Gobernación and Archivo General de la Nación. (Originally compiled ca. 1569.)

Sahagún, Bernardino de. 1993. *Primeros Memoriales by Fray Bernardino de Sahagún: Facsimile Edition.* Photographed by Ferdinand Anders. Norman: University of Oklahoma Press, in cooperation with the Patrimonio Nacional and the Real Academia de la Historia, Madrid. (Originally compiled ca. 1550.)

Sahagún, Bernardino de, Thelma Sullivan, and H. B. Nicholson. 1997. *Primeros Memoriales: Paleography of Nahuatl Text and English Translation by Thelma D.*

Sullivan, Completed and Revised, with Additions, by H. B. Nicholson, Arthur J.O.
Anderson, Charles E. Dibble, Eloise Quiñones Keber, and Wayne Ruwet. Norman:
University of Oklahoma Press.

Sandstrom, Alan R. 1989. "The Face of the Devil: Concepts of Disease and Pollution
among Nahua Indians of the Southern Huasteca." In *Enquêtes sur L'Amérique
Moyenne: Mélanges offerts à Guy Stresser-Péan*, ed. Dominique Michelet, 357–372.
Mexico City: Instituto Nacional de Antropología e Historia, Consejo Nacional
para la Cultura y las Artes, and Centre D'Études Mexicaines et Centreaméric-
aines México.

Saunders, Nicholas J. 2001. "A Dark Light: Reflections on Obsidian in Mesoamerica."
World Archaeology 33 (2): 220–236.

Schele, Linda, and Mary Ellen Miller. 1984. *The Blood of Kings: Dynasty and Ritual in
Maya Art*. Fort Worth, TX: Kimbell Art Museum.

Seler, Eduard. 1900–1901. *The Tonalamatl of the Aubin Collection, an Old Mexican Picture
Manuscript in the Paris National Library (Manuscrits Mexicains no. 18–19): Published
at the Expense of His Excellency the Duke of Loubat, with Introduction and Explanatory
Text by Dr. Eduard Seler*. Facsimile. London: Hazell, Watson, and Viney.

Seler, Eduard. 1901–1902. *Codex Fejérváry-Mayer, an Old Mexican Picture Manuscript
in the Liverpool Free Public Museums (1204/M): Published at the Expense of His
Excellency the Duke of Loubat, Elucidated by Dr. Eduard Seler*. English ed. A. H.
Keane. Facsimile. Berlin: T. and A. Constable.

Seler, Eduard. 1902–1903. *Codex Vaticanus no. 3773 (Codex Vaticanus B), an Old Mexican Pictorial Manuscript in the Vatican Library: Published at the Expense of His Excellency the Duke of Loubat, Elucidated by Dr. Eduard Seler*. English ed. A. H. Keane.
Facsimile. Berlin: T. and A. Constable.

Seler, Eduard. 1963 [1904–1909]. *Códice Borgia*. Trans. Mariana Frenk. 3 vols. Facsimile. Mexico City: Fondo de Cultura Económica.

Serna, Jacinto de la. 1987. "Manual de Ministros de Indios." In *El Alma Encantada
Anales del Museo Nacional de Mexico*, ed. Fernando Benítez, 263–475. Mexico City:
Instituto Nacional Indigenista and Fondo de Cultural Económica. (Written
1630.)

Siméon, Réné. 1977 [1885]. *Diccionario de la lengua nahuatl o mexicano*. Trans. Josefina
Oliva de Coll. Mexico City: Siglo Veintiuno.

Smalley, John, and Michael Blake. 2003. "Sweet Beginnings: Stalk Sugar and the
Domestication of Maize" [with Comments and Reply]. *Current Anthropology* 44
(5) (December): 675–703.

Sullivan, Thelma. 1966. "Pregnancy, Childbirth, and the Deification of the Women
Who Died in Childbirth." *Estudios de Cultura Nahuatl* 6: 63–75.

Sullivan, Thelma. 1976. "The Mask of Itztlacoliuhqui." *Actas del XLI Congreso Internacional de Americanistas, Mexico, 2 a 17 de septiembre de 1974*, 2: 252–262. Mexico City: Instituto Nacional de Antropología e Historia.

Sullivan, Thelma. 1982. "Tlazolteotl-Ixcuina: The Great Spinner and Weaver." In *The Art and Iconography of Late Post-Classic Central Mexico*, ed. Elizabeth Hill Boone, 7–35. Washington, DC: Dumbarton Oaks Research Library and Collection.

Taube, Karl. 1992. *The Major Gods of Ancient Yucatan*. Studies in Pre-Columbian Art and Archaeology 32. Washington, DC: Dumbarton Oaks Research Library and Collection.

Thompson, J. Eric. S. 1939. *The Moon Goddess in Middle America*. Contributions to American Archaeology, Carnegie Institution of Washington 5. Washington, DC: Carnegie Institution.

Thompson, J. Eric. S. 1960. *Maya Hieroglyphic Writing: An Introduction*, 2nd ed. Norman: University of Oklahoma Press.

Tonalamatl Aubin. See Aguilera 1981; Seler/Loubat 1900–1901.

Torquemada, Juan de. 1975. *Monarquía Indiana*, 5th ed. 3 vols. Mexico City: Porrúa. (Written 1592–1613.)

Vail, Gabrielle. 1996. "The Gods in the Madrid Codex: An Iconographic and Glyphic Analysis." PhD dissertation, Tulane University, New Orleans, LA.

Velásquez García, Erik. 2006. "The Maya Flood Myth and the Decapitation of the Cosmic Caiman." *PARI Journal* 7 (1) (Summer): 1–10.

12

Nighttime and Darkness

*Activities, Practices,
Customs, and Beliefs*

Julia A. Hendon

Night follows day, day follows night. This regular alternation is a central part of the world in which people live and always has been. It is universal and natural, but the way humans understand and experience it is profoundly cultural. Darkness is now becoming a presence in archaeological investigations of ancient lives (Dowd and Hensey 2016; Gonlin and Nowell 2018a). The authors in this volume consider how darkness and the night were understood by the ancient people of Mexico and Central America, how it was taken advantage of for both positive and negative reasons, and how nocturnal resources and activities played a central role in these societies. However, the authors also draw on other kinds of phenomena and experiences that turn day into night, such as volcanic eruptions or the obscuring of natural light inside buildings. This willingness to include many different ways the world turns dark represents one strength of the volume. Another strength is how the authors explore the effects of more or less light on Mesoamerican societies from many different perspectives. The twelve chapters expand our understanding of the connection of darkness to lived experiences, practical applications, natural disasters, and religious beliefs.

Why has the night not been more of a presence in archaeological research on how people lived in the past? I would propose two interconnected reasons for this neglect of nighttime. The first reason is that we should not underestimate the effect of living in the

DOI: 10.5876/9781646421879.c012

kind of heavily lighted environment that currently exists. Historians of artificial lighting and its usage in private and public spaces have demonstrated
that these developments are part and parcel of the ways urbanization and
industrialization changed economy and society on a global scale (Jakle 2001;
Schivelbusch 1988; Sharman and Sharman 2008). Technological innovations
accelerated in the nineteenth and twentieth centuries with developments in
electricity (Schiffer 2008); but efforts to extend the workday, increase public safety, and expand opportunities for entertainment have a long history in
Western Europe and North America (Schivelbusch 1988). The spread of artificial lighting into the hours of darkness has had profound consequences for
all living things. The fact that the lights are always on affects "biological systems from the molecule to the ecosystem" as natural light cycles are disrupted
(Gaston et al. 2014, 917).

The second reason for this neglect can be explained by the way light carries
such positive associations in Western history and culture, going back no doubt
to the framing provided by fundamental religious texts. Darkness as dangerous, as fearful, as treacherous—these ideas are deeply ingrained in Western
thought (Verdon 2002). Such beliefs are, of course, connected to the reality
that crime, accidents, and animal attacks often occur under cover of darkness,
but they transcend such pragmatic concerns. Believing that light is beneficial,
helpful, and necessary makes it difficult to "see" darkness. These beliefs make
darkness an enemy. Even in a more secular age, ideologies of progress, the
prioritization of economic development, and support for state's responsibility
for public safety underpin the view that darkness is something to be countered
through technological innovation. John Jakle (2001, 56–57) writes, "Electric
lighting became a new symbol of the emergent modern world . . . As metaphor, things electrical were associated with intelligence and drive. Above all,
electric light meant progress."

All this light obscures our view of non-industrial societies. When we look
back on societies that had less nighttime illumination than we are used to, the
tendency is to assume that not much happened. This regular period of darkness was nothing more than "a backdrop to daily existence or a natural hiatus"
(Ekirch 2005, xxv). This impact is intellectual, philosophical, and ideological.
As Jakle notes, the metaphors are pervasive. Archaeologists "shed light on,"
they "illuminate," they "bring to light," they "dig through darkness," and they
define "Dark Ages." These metaphors are fundamental to scholarly writing in
English and I suspect in other languages as well (Hensey 2016).

Darkness and light loom large in the beliefs of many cultures. In Mesoamerica,
darkness signals the passage of time but also those moments when "people can

meet and talk with their dead ancestors and with the gods" (Tedlock 1986, 128). Darkness before "the dawning" is a crucial mythic time during which the world is created and the relationships between humans and sacred beings are established (Tedlock 1996). Everyone experiences periods of darkness over the course of their life as beings who live in the world. In Mesoamerica, located in the tropics, the seasonal variation between the length of day and night is much less extreme than further north or south. Mesoamerican people were used to a regular and more even alternation of day and night. They never experienced the long summer days or winter nights of Arctic dwellers such as the Inuit (Dawson et al. 2007).

Indigenous Mesoamerican societies are well-known for their systems of charting the passage of time over the course of the day (and night), the year, and beyond, even back to the creation of the world. These time-telling systems were integral to religion, politics, warfare, agriculture, and daily life (Aveni 1989; Hendon 2010; Tedlock 1992). By defining a "day" as covering some identifiable period of time that included both the hours of light and those of darkness, Mesoamerican societies moved beyond simple observation. They created a culturally defined and socially supported idea of daytime and nighttime. Jean Verdon (2002) notes that in Medieval European cities, the night was cosmic—that is, the period bounded by the setting and rising of the sun—but also legal and social. It was inaugurated by a set of proscribed activities—the ringing of bells, the banking of hearth fires, the blocking of streets, and the closing of city gates. Religious observances imposed another set of temporal divisions and associated activities. Verdon's notion of the night as defined as much by social custom as by the movement of the sun applies to Mesoamerica as much as to Medieval Europe. In the introduction to this volume, David Reed and Nancy Gonlin use the concepts of "nightscape" and "nightways" as framing concepts for the exploration of beliefs and practices associated with darkness. Their coinage of the term *nightways* provides a way to refer to the study of "the role of the night in society." Thus it is not surprising that the chapters in this volume demonstrate how the meanings associated with darkness were complex and wide-ranging—connecting to ecology, religion, daily life, politics, and specialized knowledge.

David Reed, Scott Zeleznik, and Nancy Gonlin use their chapter to hone in on the production and use of food and drink, central elements in events related to ritual, healing, and politics. Communicating with the dead required feeding them. Shared commensality lubricates social relations. Fermented drinks and highly valued dishes and their ingredients help reinforce or undermine social prestige and political hierarchies. Feasts become a focus of resources, a way to display material goods and provide opportunities for the performance of social identities and relations. Feeding family, guests, political rivals, or the honored dead requires the expenditure of much time and effort by men and women, children and adults, beginning before the event itself. For example, starting the steps to provide food—kindling the fire, drawing water, grinding maize, cooking tortillas—is one of those socially proscribed activities that signals the start of a new day even before daybreak (Eber and "Antonia" 2011, 52; Hendon 2010; Vogt 1969, 58).

More evidence of nighttime activities comes from the chapter by Venicia Slotten. Slotten reviews the ways the Maya use of plants is related to the night, suggesting that the importance of night-blooming plants made it necessary for people to be out and about after dark, moving through the countryside to collect plants and carry out rituals. Names for plants reflect these nighttime associations. Plants also connect to sleep and insomnia. Night-blooming plants play a vital role in Maya medicine. Their importance gives insight into the wide range of specialized knowledge Maya *curanderos* possess. Night-blooming plants are not incidental to Maya medicine and ritual practice. Their use provides an excellent example of Reed and Gonlin's concept of nightways.

The chapter by Rachel Egan moves beyond expectable and controllable periods of darkness such as nighttime to consider one kind of natural event: volcanic eruptions. Volcanic activity is widespread in Mesoamerica, and explosive eruptions have been very destructive. The archaeologically well-documented case of the Cerén village, discussed by Payson Sheets and Michael Thomason in chapter 6, provides a stark picture of the consequences of living in a volcanically active region. Egan concentrates on explosive eruptions, which, among other things, send large amounts of materials into the air, creating ash clouds. These clouds have long-term and widespread consequences. The ash clouds spread and take months or years to disperse.

Volcanic eruptions thus create a different form of night—an artificial one that disrupts diurnal and seasonal patterns of light and darkness. During these times, day does not follow night. Extended darkness—with the associated changes in temperature, rainfall, and other natural phenomena—imposes hardships on people for a long time. Egan notes, however, that Maya written and visual sources for the period before the Spanish conquest are silent on the topic of volcanoes. Thus we have little direct information on how people incorporated these events into their understanding of darkness or the night. Egan considers eclipses, which are well-documented in ancient Maya records (Aveni 1980, 67–82). These events evoked dread and required a ritualized response from individuals and society to ward off permanent consequences

(Aveni 2018). Her inference that volcanic eruptions and the darkness they caused were the subject of similar reactions and practices is a reasonable one, although eclipses were of much shorter duration and more predictable.

As noted at the beginning of my remarks, the brilliance of electricity blinds us to the importance of other forms of lighting. More broadly, the emphasis on sight threatens to crowd out other ways of sensing and experiencing. As David Howes (2003, 45) has noted, appreciating the "multisensory modes of constructing and experiencing the world" expands anthropology's understanding of cultural reasoning. Howes goes on to argue that anthropology has been limited by its adherence to a Western notion that privileges vision or the gaze over other senses. Perhaps here again we have another reason why darkness has been overlooked by most archaeologists.

Two chapters address the question of light directly. Nancy Gonlin and Christine Dixon explore how people in Mesoamerica lit their public and private spaces. Their catalog of different kinds of light sources and associated material culture demonstrates the importance of flame as a light source but also suggests that mirrors, censers, and candles supplemented torches and hearths. They note that we should not discount the moon and stars as contributing to the nocturnal lightscape. Perhaps their most intriguing suggestion is that Mesoamerican peoples may have taken advantage of naturally occurring bioluminescence. Insects such as fireflies might have been collected. Although direct evidence of this practice is lacking, fireflies appear in the Popol Vuh. The Hero Twins persuade insects to sit on the end of their cigars, thus fooling the Lords of Xibalba into thinking the cigars are still burning (Tedlock 1996). Randolph Widmer engages with a sensory archaeology in his review of nighttime activities at the city of Teotihuacan. He considers sources of lighting as well as the aromas and sounds residents experienced after dark as they engaged in various activities—some socially acceptable, some not. Through his discussion of sources of light, especially wood and beeswax, Widmer helps us understand what kinds of lighting were available and how they would have affected the look and feel of the city.

While these two chapters make it clear that nighttime was not completely dark and that sources of light existed, they do not claim that Mesoamerican cities and villages were as brightly lit as their twenty-first-century counterparts. The fact that ancient lighting does not meet contemporary expectations hinders the ability of archaeologists to understand these places. In an interesting effort at experimental archaeology, Peter Dawson and coauthors simulated the amount of light shed by Thule Inuit oil lamps. These lamps served as the principal light source inside winter dwellings in the Canadian

Arctic. Although the amount of light provided by these lamps is far below what modern standards recommend for task lighting, Thule Inuit carried out such delicate crafts as sewing. Dawson and his coauthors (2007), following Howes, argue that other senses, such as touch, were important to the Inuit crafters. Working in dim settings has been attested in Mesoamerican houses such as those at Copan (Hendon 2010; Widmer 2009).

Chapters 6 and 7 draw our attention to a type of construction—the sweat bath—that creates a dark setting for ritual and healing. The dark interior of the sweat bath is part of the experience. Starting from this premise, Payson Sheets and Michael Thomason describe their experimental work inside a modern reproduction of a sweat bath at the village of Cerén in El Salvador. Their work demonstrates that being in darkness is an active experience in which other sensory phenomena are magnified. Speaking inside the replica sweat bath, for example, resulted in echoes and resonances, heightening the experience of the space as a sound chamber. Hearing over seeing becomes central to what it means to be in a sweat bath.

Jan Marie Olson's discussion of the importance of the sweat bath in Aztec medical practices continues the exploration of the relationship between darkness and ritual. Olson's chapter describes how this specialized building was used for healing, parturition, and bathing in domestic and more public urban settings. Sweat baths were dark, perhaps because, as Cecelia Klein discusses in chapter 11, darkness was itself an active component in healing.

Chapters 8 through 10 explore rituals and beliefs associated with darkness by considering these practices in varying locations and differing social scales. Jeremy Coltman distinguishes between evening and primeval night. The latter concept has strong associations with caves or other dark interior places in wild locations. Coltman explores the many meanings of the *ch'een* sign, related iconography, and associated rituals for the Maya. Dark places associated with the earth are chaotic, dangerous, and home to powerful beings. And yet people need to engage with these places and the dark times of day. They need to hunt and they need to move through a sacred landscape. As Slotten demonstrates, they need to gather night-blooming plants. Thus nighttime and the primeval darkness cannot be ignored.

Jeanne Lopiparo's excavations in villages and towns in north-central Honduras have revealed evidence of ritual practices that placed both the living residents and their dead relatives in a sacred landscape defined by natural features such as mountains, human-built places such as ball courts, and astronomical phenomena such as the sun. Clay figurines are important elements of the rituals. They often depict animals or hybrid beings with some animal features. Many of these animals are active at night or during the in-between times of dawn and dusk. Examples include owls, bats, armadillos, and frogs. Lopiparo's model emphasizes the importance of cycles, including the regular shift from daytime to nighttime. Darkness may indeed be a time of chaos, but it is through chaos that life, society, and the world are renewed through communication with ancestors.

Kirby Farah brings light into the picture through a discussion of central Mexican New Fire Ceremonies, another cyclical event, although on a grander scale than those discussed by Lopiparo. Best known from visual and documentary sources describing Aztec rituals, there is nevertheless archaeological evidence that the ceremonies predate the Mexica Empire in the region. New Fire ceremonies used the rekindling of light as the central practice and metaphor for regeneration of society and reestablishment of an ordered relationship between humans and the sacred world. Coltman draws attention to the ways ritual practices provide opportunities for political control. This intersection of ritual and political emerges in Farah's discussion of the New Fire Ceremony as well.

Klein dives deeply into the generative aspect of darkness through a study of the Aztec. Drawing on the rich visual and written record of Aztec ritual and belief, Klein shows us how darkness's negative associations made it a source of change, creation, and healing. The generative and recuperative aspects of darkness do not exist in spite of it being a source of chaos but because of its undisciplined and unstructured nature. Klein uses this mix of apparently contradictory meanings to interpret the use of blindfolds in certain rituals. Those practices that require the penitent to be blindfolded become a way to immerse individuals in this chaotic but generative state.

The authors in this book debunk the assumption that nothing much happens at night in societies without modern pervasive lighting. Furthermore, they help us develop an understanding of nighttime's "distinct culture, with many of its own customs and rituals" (Ekirch 2005, xxv). To put it another way, people in Mesoamerica recognized practices, activities, and behaviors that they considered normal to do at night, regardless of whether those practices, activities, or behaviors were considered proper or improper. Gathering plants, hunting, star watching, communing with one's ancestors, moving through a sacred landscape, preparing food and drink, feasting, and healing are some of the positively viewed customary actions. Stealing, conducting rituals with evil intentions, and committing adultery are just a few of the negatively viewed actions that formed part of a nighttime culture, or the nightways, of Mesoamerica.

Night and Darkness in Ancient Mesoamerica provides many new ideas that should change or expand our understanding of the societies in this region. The authors' ideas have important implications for several areas of research. One is household archaeology (Gonlin and Nowell 2018b, 11). We need to think more about what practices were accepted parts of the nighttime customs of households at different levels of society. More attention to lighting and nighttime experiences will enrich our understanding of crafting, feasting, and the design of the built environment, especially in urban settings. A second area of research affected is the study of political power and how it was created, affirmed, contested, and disrupted by beliefs about darkness. The consequences of natural disasters must also be factored into this research. A third area of inquiry that gains from greater attention to nighttime and darkness is the study of the connection among religious beliefs, ritual practices, and the social construction of relationships. By shedding light on darkness, the contributors to this volume have indeed helped bring scholarly attention to an important aspect of the human experience.

REFERENCES

Aveni, Anthony F. 1980. *Skywatchers of Ancient Mexico*. Austin: University of Texas Press.

Aveni, Anthony F. 1989. *Empires of Time: Calendars, Clocks, and Cultures*. New York: Basic Books.

Aveni, Anthony F. 2018. "Night in Day: Contrasting Ancient and Contemporary Maya and Hindu Responses to Total Solar Eclipses." In *Archaeology of the Night: Life after Dark in the Ancient World*, ed. Nancy Gonlin and April Nowell, 139–154. Boulder: University Press of Colorado.

Dawson, Peter, Richard Levy, Don Gardner, and Matthew Walls. 2007. "Simulating the Behaviour of Light Inside Arctic Dwellings: Implications for Assessing the Role of Vision in Task Performances." *World Archaeology* 39: 17–35.

Dowd, Marion, and Robert Hensey, eds. 2016. *The Archaeology of Darkness*. Oxford: Oxbow Books.

Eber, Christine, and "Antonia." 2011. *The Journey of a Tzotzil-Maya Woman of Chiapas, Mexico*. Austin: University of Texas Press.

Ekirch, A. Roger. 2005. *At Day's Close: Night in Times Past*. New York: Norton.

Gaston, Kevin J., James P. Duffy, Sian Gaston, Jonathan Bennie, and Thomas W. Davies. 2014. "Human Alternation of Natural Light Cycles: Causes and Ecological Consequences." *Oecologia* 176: 917–931.

Gonlin, Nancy, and April Nowell, eds. 2018a. *Archaeology of the Night: Life after Dark in the Ancient World*. Boulder: University Press of Colorado.

Gonlin, Nancy, and April Nowell. 2018b. "Introduction to the Archaeology of the Night." In *Archaeology of the Night: Life after Dark in the Ancient World*, ed. Nancy Gonlin and April Nowell, 5–24. Boulder: University Press of Colorado.

Hendon, Julia A. 2010. *Houses in a Landscape: Memory and Everyday Life in Mesoamerica*. Durham, NC: Duke University Press.

Hensey, Robert. 2016. "Past Dark: A Short Introduction to the Human Relationship with Darkness over Time." In *The Archaeology of Darkness*, ed. Marion Down and Robert Hensey, 1–10. Oxford: Oxbow Books.

Howes, David. 2003. *Sensual Relations: Engaging the Senses in Culture and Social Theory*. Ann Arbor: University of Michigan Press.

Jakle, John A. 2001. *City Lights: Illuminating the American Night*. Baltimore: Johns Hopkins University Press.

Schiffer, Michael B. 2008. *Power Struggles: Scientific Authority and the Creation of Practical Electricity before Einstein*. Cambridge, MA: MIT Press.

Schivelbusch, Wolfgang. 1988. *Disenchanted Light: The Industrialization of Light in the Nineteenth Century*. Trans. Angela Davies. Berkeley: University of California Press.

Sharman, Russell Leigh, and Cheryl Harris Sharman. 2008. *Nightshift NYC*. Berkeley: University of California Press.

Tedlock, Barbara. 1986. "On a Mountain Road in the Dark: Encounters with the Quiché Maya Culture Hero." In *Symbol and Meaning beyond the Closed Community: Essays in Mesoamerican Ideas*, ed. Gary H. Gossen, 125–138. Albany: Institute for Mesoamerican Studies, University of Albany, State University of New York.

Tedlock, Barbara. 1992. *Time and the Highland Maya*. Rev. ed. Albuquerque: University of New Mexico Press.

Tedlock, Dennis. 1996. *Popol Vuh: The Mayan Book of the Dawn of Life*. Revised ed. New York: Simon and Schuster.

Verdon, Jean. 2002. *Night in the Middle Ages*. Trans. George Holoch. Notre Dame, IN: University of Notre Dame Press.

Vogt, Evon Z. 1969. *Zinacantan: A Maya Community in the Highlands of Chiapas*. Cambridge, MA: Belknap Press, Harvard University Press.

Widmer, Randolph J. 2009. "Elite Household Multicrafting Specialization at 9N-8, Patio H, Copán." In *Housework: Craft Production and Domestic Economy in Ancient Mesoamerica*, ed. Kenneth G. Hirth, 174–204. Archaeological Papers of the American Anthropological Association 19. Hoboken, NJ: Wiley.

political economy, 50
politics, 27, 39, 40, 104, 105, 175, 328
pollen, 60, 147, 312n47
pollinator, 14, 60
pollution, light, 60, 108, 122
Pompeii, 97
Popocatépetl, 153
Popocatzin, 88
popol na, 122
Popol Vuh, 3, 15, 70, 89, 120, 121, 240, 246, 283, 330
Popotl temi, 305
portal, 5, 10, 182, 204, 214, 246, 247
postpartum cleansings, 184
pottery; Black-on-Orange, 270, 272; production, 40; use, 40
power (political), 4, 16, 23, 27, 28, 39–43, 66, 95, 104, 109, 264, 272, 286, 333
pozole, 149
Pozzolanic, 127
practices, 27, 41, 51, 79, 237, 240, 258, 259, 260, 266, 269, 270, 276, 332, 333, 326; daily, 51, 59, 266; quotidian, 7, 11, 39
practice theory, 4, 23
pre-sunrise, 283, 309n9, 314n62
Preclassic, *8*, 15, 16, 26, 110, 129n2, 189, 205, 206, 216, 218, 260
predator, 13, 15, 257
pregnancy, 183, 184; pregnant, 89, 183, 236, *237*, 239, 263, 299, 300
prestige, 41, 328
prestige goods, 50
priest, 27, 95, 148, 149, 150, 151, 153, 155, 177, 178, 183, 190, 192, 194n1, 262–264, 275, 305
Primeros Memoriales, 300, 306, 310n26
procession, 16, *17*, 149, 232, 236, 262
promiscuity, 178
propaganda, 41, 273, 274
prostitution, 151, 154
psychopomp, 16
Puerto Escondido, Honduras, 228
Pulltrouser Swamp, Belize, 64, 67
pulque, 47, 48, 51, 161, 194n1, *205*, 206, 219n3, 291, 298, 299, 304, 311n29, 314n64; god, 206, 291, 292, 294, 311n34. *See also* beverages
puma, 12, 51
pumice, 80
punishment, 152, 262, 282, 290, 292, 307
Pyramid of the Sun, Teotihuacan, 192

pyre, 263, 273
pyrite, 119
pyroclastic flows, 83, 97

Q

Quetzalcoatl, 19, 150, 153, 262
quimichin, 13
quincunx, 67
Quintana Roo, Mexico, 211, 238

R

rabbits, 12
rain, 19, 109, 206, 302; rainwater, 126; rainy season, 107
rasps, 150, 272, *273*
Ratinlinxul vase, 16
rebirth, 172, 179, 191, 244, 247, 248, 249, 299, 304, 305
residences, 10, 64, 74, 117, 119, 122, 124, 149, 190
residue analysis, 117, 118, 119, 130n6, 146, 148, 271
resin, 64, 116, 145, 151
resonances, 25, 165, 166–170, 331
rheumatism, 180, 303
rituals, 23, 26, 155, 172, 226, 258, 269–271, 273–276, 288, 294, 307, 331, 332; daily, 91, 96. *See also* ceremonies
Rome, Italy, 88
royalty, 15, 42, 48, 119
rubber, 61
ruler, 15, 19, 21, 39, 45, 47, *48*, 48, 94–96, 154, 175, 190, 202, 204, 208, 210, 214, 219n4, 247, 260, 262, 264, 265. *See also individual rulers by name*
rulership, 15, 66, 109
rural, 108, 111, 116, 124, 125, 178, 188, 191, 192, 193; -urban continuum, 104; semi-, 189, 190, 191, 192, 193

S

sacbe, 126, 127; *sacbeob* (plural), 122, 127, 128
sacrifice, 14, 15, 16, 19, 20, 21, 95, 150, 153, 154, 176, 202, 204, 212, *213*, 214, 216–219, 246, 260, 262, 263, 273–275, 276, 293, 298, 305, 311n33
Sahagún, Bernardino de, 114, 142, 144, 145, 146, 147, 151, 153, 154, 178, 181, 185, 194n1, 281, 282, 283, 285, 288, 291, 293, 294, 295, 299, 300, 301, 302, 303, 304, 305, 306
sak pojp, 66

Xibalba, 16, 121; Lords of, 330
xicocuitlatl, 129n3
Xilonen, 150
Xiuhtecuhtli, 152, 263
Xochicalco, Mexico, 123, 190
Xochiquetzal, 180, 193, 304, 305
xōlōitzcuīntli, 17. *See also* dogs
Xolotl, 17

Y

yacametztli, 289, 311n32
yaws (*Treponema perenue*), 310
Yaxchilan, Mexico, 15, 47, 109, 112, 240
Yaxha, Guatemala, 189
Yaxnohcah, Yucatan, 110, 129n2
Yax Pasaj Chan Yopaat, 15
Yoaltícitl, 180, 181
yohualli, 309n10

Yohualli Ehecatl, 21, 281, 297, 308n4
Yucatan, *8*, 17, 62, 83, 110, 127, 147, 211
Yucatec Maya, 44, 60, 61, 65, 66, 67, 68. *See also* Maya
yugo, *203*, 204

Z

Zanthoxylum, 67, *74*
Zapotecs, 46, 61
Zapotitán Valley, El Salvador, *9*, 159
Zea mays. *See* maize
zenith, 68, 91, 263
Zinacantán, Mexico, 44
zooanthropomorphic, 225, 226, 230, 242
zoomorphic, 226, 228–232, 234, 236, 249
zotz, 13. *See also* bats; tzotz
Zumpango, Mexico, 144

Jeremy D. Coltman received his Ph.D. from the University of California, Riverside. His most recent research has focused on the Early Postclassic site of Chchen Itza, Yucatan, Mexico, and the ideological and artistic influence of the ancient Maya on the Late Postclassic Nahua and Aztec civilizations. Coltman has conducted fieldwork in Belize and Mexico. He is co-editor (with John M.D. Pohl) of *Sorcery in Mesoamerica*, recently published by the University Press of Colorado.

Christine C. Dixon-Hundredmark is a tenured faculty member in anthropology at Green River College, WA. She has conducted fieldwork in Mexico, Honduras, Belize, El Salvador, and Costa Rica, as well as Hawaii. Her research focuses on sociopolitical economy, especially as it relates to farmer autonomy.

Rachel Egan is a registered professional archaeologist (18163) who specializes in the archaeology of Mesoamerica and Colorado, as well as hazard and disaster studies. She works for Colorado Parks and Wildlife-Resource Stewardship as a Cultural Research Technician and teaches at Front Range Community College.

Kirby Farah is an anthropological archaeologist and assistant professor in the Department of Anthropology at Gettysburg College, PA. Her research and teaching interests intersect archaeology, ethnohistory, and critical cultural heritage, with particular emphasis on community identity and social cohesion in the Postclassic Basin of Mexico.

Nancy Gonlin is Registered Professional Archaeologist 16354 who investigates Classic Maya commoners, household archaeology, and archaeology of the night. She is editor-in-chief of the journal *Ancient Mesoamerica*. Her co-edited volumes and contributions are *Commoner Ritual and Ideology in Ancient Mesoamerica*, *Ancient Households of the Americas*, *Human Adaptation in Ancient Mesoamerica*, and *Archaeology of the Night*. She has coauthored a case study *Copán: The Rise and Fall of an Ancient Maya Kingdom* and a textbook titled *The Archaeology of Native North America*. Gonlin is a professor of anthropology at Bellevue College, WA.

Julia A. Hendon is professor emerita of anthropology at Gettysburg College and co-editor of *Latin American Antiquity*. Her research interests include household archaeology, crafting and its relationship to social identity including gender and social class, and the connections between social memory and landscape in the Maya area and Honduras. She is the author of *Houses in a Landscape: Memory and Everyday Life in Mesoamerica* (awarded the 2015 Linda S. Cordell Book Award in Archaeology) and coauthor of *Material Relations: The Marriage Figurines of Prehispanic Honduras*. She is co-editor of *Mesoamerican Archaeology: Theory and Practice* and *Relational Identities and Other-than-Human Agency in Archaeology*.

Cecelia F. Klein is professor emerita at the University of California, Los Angeles, where she taught Pre-Columbian and Early Colonial art history for thirty-five years. Her research has focused largely on the complex interrelationships among Aztec religion, politics, gender, and art but in recent years has shifted to the Maya site Chichen Itza and its Aztec legacy. She is author of *The Face of the Earth: Frontality in Postclassic Mexico* and editor of and contributor to *Gender in Pre-Columbian America*; she has also written numerous book chapters and articles.

Jeanne Lopiparo is an associate professor of anthropology at Rhodes College. She is a Mesoamerican archaeologist specializing in household and social archaeology in northwest Honduras and southern Mexico and is coauthor of *Material Relations: The Marriage Figurines of Prehispanic Honduras*.

Jan Marie Olson is a retired professor from the University of Alberta and MacEwan University who has specialized in Mesoamerican and Ecuadorian archaeology. Her research has focused on socioeconomic relationships between commoner and elite households among Postclassic Aztec and Manteño cultures. She is an invited presenter of Aztec archaeology and culture to middle school children in Alberta.

David M. Reed is an anthropological archaeologist by training with extensive experience in stable isotope biogeochemistry, mortuary analyses, archaeology of the Maya, human genetics, and quantitative analysis. Following his doctoral work on ancient Copan Maya paleodiets at The Pennsylvania State University, he did pioneering research on ancient mitochondrial DNA of the Copan Maya. David held a post-doc at the Uni-